Lincoln County Tennessee

WILL BOOK

1827–1850

WPA RECORDS

Heritage Books
2024

HERITAGE BOOKS

AN IMPRINT OF HERITAGE BOOKS, INC.

Books, CDs, and more—Worldwide

For our listing of thousands of titles see our website
at
www.HeritageBooks.com

A Facsimile Reprint
Published 2024 by
HERITAGE BOOKS, INC.
Publishing Division
5810 Ruatan Street
Berwyn Heights, MD 20740

Originally published 1936

International Standard Book Number
Paperbound: 978-0-7884-8700-2

C

Cathey, George		226
Chambers, Moses		136
Chaetham, James	Last will	19
Chapman, Thomas		259
Childress, Thomas		190
Cole, John-	Will	235
Cole, Stephen		184
Coleman, Samuel		309
Collier, Charles		87
Collins, William		206
Cona wa y, Frederick		123
Cowley, William		51
Crawford, John		328,330
Culbertson, Heriam m		139
Cunningham, Abra ham		169
Cunningham, Nancy		199
Cunningham, Robert		242

D

Da nce, Thoma s	Copy will	371
Da rnel, Cornelius		120
Davis, Amos		105
Davis, John		247
Da vis, Morga n	La st will	64,65
Davis, William A.		109
Dean, James M.	Last will	174
Dickey, Ephraim		173
Dismeekes, E.E.		383
Dobbins, Samuel		185
Duff, James Colonel		276

E

Ea stland, Davis	Will	133
Ellis, James		349,350
English, James B.		161,162
Evans, Hannah	Will	289,290
Ewing, Joshua		326

F

Farrar, John	Will	51,52
Foster, Abednego		75
Fox, Philip		182
Fros t, James		340

G

Ga ttis , Isaac		195
Gee, George	Las t will	385
Gibson, John		231
Gibson, Joshua		254
Gleghorn, Andrew	Last will	391
Gragg, John Sen.		211
Grant, James		179
Grant, Thomas	Will	360
Gray, John		143,144
Gray, Rachel	Will	375
Greer, Joseph	Last will	60,61,62
Gregory, Fenton	Will	375
Griffis, John O.		218
Griffis, William	Last will	342
Gunter, Joshua		254
Gunter, William		168
Guyder, John		45

H

Ha gue, James	Will	305
Hairston, Robert		204
Halcomb, Kinchin	Last will	37
Hall, William S.		149
Hardin, Moses	Will	370
Harris, Edward		163
Harrison, John	Last will	39
Heath, Ab C.		149
Hea th, George	" "	18
Hea ralds on, Vincent	Will	277
Henderson, John	"	304,305
Hester, Joseph	"	214
Hill, Thomas W.		105
Hobbs, William		141
Hodges, Milton	"	293
Holbert, Daniel	"	271
Holma n, Daniel		153
Howard, William	La st will	117
Hughey, Alex ander	Will	224
Hughey, Elizabeth		84,85
Hunter, Reuben	"	96,97

I

Ingle, William	Last will	63,64

J

Ja mes , William		101
Jenkins, Samuel		70,71
Johnson, Joel		97,98
Jones, Thomas N.		301
Jordan, Hogekiah		166

M

Moores, William	Last will	8,9
Morgan, Lewis	" "	11,12,13
Mullen, Anthony		129
Murdock, John		128

N

Nees, Jesse	Last will	332
Ness,,James K.	" "	226
Newman, Wiley C.	" "	210
Norris, Ezekial's	" "	33

P

Pamplin, Armstead	Last will	100
Parkes, Thos. H.D.	" "	351,352
Parr, Mary	" "	62
Patterson, William	" "	114
Phaga n, Philip	^	372
Price, Mathews	" "	226
Pruett, Jacob	" "	31
Pryor, John Sr.	" "	198
Pulley, Thomas	" "	24
Purton, Purlina	" "	223
Pybss, James	" "	221,222

R

Ranall,James	Last will	18
Reeds, David	" "	72,73
Reese, Jordan	" "	47
Rees e,Soloman	" "	108
Rhea, John	" "	137
Rhea , Sally	" "	322
Robertson, Henry	" "	236
Ros son, John	" "	65,66,67
Roundtree, Thomas	" "	29-
Rowell, William	" "	250
Russell, James	" "	212
Rutledge, Isaac	" "	126
Rutledge, John	" "	95
Rya h, Noah	" "	121

S

Saihebroa d, Henry	" "	172
Scott, James		137,138
Scott, William	Will	306
Sebastian, Jno. W.	"	303
Sharp, Allice	Last will	401
Sharp, Walter B.		115

S

Shaw, Sarah Dec.		333
Shelton, William B.D.		307
Sherrell, A. A.		337
Shull, A. B.	Will	317
Simmons, James A.		311
Simmons, James	Last will	25
Sivily, John		76,77,78
Smith, Henry B.		168
Smith, John N.		353
Smith, Ralph's	Will	262
Smith, William		43,44,45
Snow, Henry Sr.		358,359
Soloman, William	Will	272
Stephens, Robert		137,138
Stewart, Robert		167
Stewart, Sarah	Last will	68
Stiles, Jesse	Will	365
Stone, Micajah	Last will	345
Stone, Moses		327
Strong, John		345
Sullivan, Cornelius	Will	302
Summers, Abraham		152
Summers, John	"	264

T

Tate, Samuel		344
Taylor, Henry		317
Taylor, Woody		298
Thoop, Charles		191
Thurston, Benjamen		390
Thwing, David	Last will	6,7,8
Thwing, Martha's	" "	187
Timmons, Ambrose		319
Todd, John	" "	53,54,55
Toole, Jas. R.		388
Tuley, Charles		90,91

V

Vance, Sarah	Last will	56
Vaugn, Peter	" "	69
Vickers,, John	" "	221

W

Waggoner, Daniel		98,99,100
Waggoner, George	Will	255
Walker, Andrew W.	"	396
Walker, James S.		34
Wall, Jashua		85
Warren, Henry		280-4
Warren, Wm. R.		122

W

LINCOLN COUNTY

WILL BOOK 1827-1850

    In the name of God Amen, I, JAMES W. BARNES of the County
of Lincoln & State of Tennessee being perfect in Soundness of mind
& Memory thanks unto God calling to mind the mortality of my body
a nd that it is appointed once for all men to die, Do make ordain & constitute this my last will and testament viz, Principally & first of all I give & recommend my Soul to God who gave
it, & my body to the earth nC. And as to my worldly estate which
it has pleased God to bless me with, I give demise & dispose of
in the following manner viz, first I will that all my lawful debts
be paid, next I will that all the negroes, goods and Chattle I die
possessed with, be left to the proper use and behoof of my beloved
wife Charlotte Barnes during her life, and should she inter-marry,
the property is still to remain in possession of her & her husband, provided he shall keep it for the use of my children that
shall hereafter be described & provided he should not take that c
care of said property that may be thought necessary, and for the
use purpose, as above described, She, the said Charlotte Barnes s
shall have Power to assert the same from his hands & convert it
to the proper use of the family, Item, I give my son Samuel a
horse worth fifty dollars, saddle & blanket, which cost thirty
to hold as his own individual property and he is to,have no more
of my estate during the life of his mother, my sons John W. Wilson
and William, are to be educated until they can cypher as far as the
double rule of three, they are there to receive after having ar-
rived to the age of eighteen a horse, saddle & so, to the same
amount of Samuel's, provided their mother may find it convenient
to give it to them, I have loaned unto my oldest daughter Leady G.
Elone one bed & stead & furniture for the same & some kitchen
furniture for her benefit during life, then to the lawful heirs
of her body, unless her mother may see proper to deprive her of
the same. My daughters Betty W. Rhoda H. and Susanna Barnes are
to receive at a proper age, or when married the same amount of
property that my oldest daughter has in her possession, provided
my wife sees best to confer it on them, provided my wife lives to
raise my little or three ypungest children; Then at her decease
all the property I wish sold and an equal division made amongst
them all, but in case my wife should die before the said youngest
arrive to mature age, then I bequeth one hundred dollars more to
each of them than to the other children. In witness whereof I
have hereunto set my hand and seal this 30th Sept. eighteen hundred & twenty seven.

Test
H. H. Hopkins   James W. Barnes
Coleman Smith   (Seal)

(2)   State of Tennessee- Oct. Term 1827, Lincoln County Court.
The last will and Testament of JAMES W. BARNES, dec'd, was exhibited in open Court for probate whereupon came H.H.Hopkins and
Coleman Smith the subscribing witness'thereto and proved the due
execution thereof, and proved further that the said JAMES W. BARNES
dec'd was at the time of signing, sealing, publishing and declaring the same of sound mind and memory, which was by the court ordered to be so certified. In Testuary whereof I have hereunto
set my hand and affixed the Seal of Court at office in Fayetteville
this 17th day of October 1827.

1 copy of this given   Brice M. Gardner, Clerk.
to the widow Dec. 18th, 1829.

(3)   State of Tennessee- Lincoln County. In the name of God Amen,
I, MICAJAH STONE of the County and State aforesaid being weak in
body but of sound mind and disposing memory, make this my last
will and Testament (as follows): First,of all I commend my soul to
God who gave it; I next request and desire all debts to be paid,
out of the debts that is due and owing to me. Item 1st, I give
a nd bequest unto my dearly beloved wife Sally all my Estate, both
real and personal during her natural life or widowhood for the
use or purpose of raising and educating my Children, and her comfort, and convenience, but should she enter into a second marriage
then and in that case she is to have her third only,and the balance
to be equally divided between the Legatees, save my son Joel, who
I desire to have one third of a childs part more than the others
in consequence of his helpless situation. 2nd, I give and bequeth unto my son William when he arrives at lawful age, three
hundred dollars, cow and calf, bed and furniture. 3rd, I give and
bequeth unto my son Joel one hundred and fifty dollars extra, to
be advanced as he may need it for the purpose of his education
with the additional sum of Three hundred dallars, cow and calf,
bed and furniture, when he arrives at lawful age. 4th, I give and
bequeth to my son Washington, three hundred dollars, one cow and
calf, bed and furniture when he arrives at lawful age. 5th, I
give and bequeth unto my son James, Three hundred dollars, a horse,
saddle and bridle, one cow and calf, bed and furniture, when he
arrives at lawful age. 6th, I give and bequeth unto my daughter
(4) Mary, Three hundred dollars, one horse, saddle and bridle, one
cow and calf, a bed and furniture when she is of lawful age. 7th,
Igive and bequeth unto my son Hopkins, Three hundred dollars, one
horse and saddle and bridle, one cow and calf, a bed and furniture,
when he arrives at lawful age. 8th, I give unto my daughter
Martha, Three hundred, one saddle and bridle, one cow and calf,
a bed and furniture& one horse, when she arrives at lawful age.
9th, I give and bequeth unto my son Jefferson, Three hundred dollars, one horse, saddle and bridle, one cow and calf, a bed &
furniture, when he arrives at lawful age. 10th, My beloved wife
Sally being at this time pregnant, should her Issue live to be
born whether male or female, I give and bequeth unto it one Equal
Share with my other children. 11th, I have already gave my son L
Littleberry Stone $300.00, one horse and saddle & bridle, 1 cow
and calf. 12th,I gave my daughter Frances $300.00, 1 horse,sad-
dle & bridle, 1 cow& calf, bed and furniture. 13th, I have gave
already my daughter Eglantine $300.00, 1 horse, saddle & bridle,
1 cow and calf, bed and furniture.

1)   14th, I gave my son Wm. 1 horse, saddle & bridle. 15th, Joel I have given 1 horse, saddle & bridle. 16th, Washington I have given 1 horse, saddle & bridle. It is my will and request that my

5) son Berry, my daughter Frances, & my daughter Eglantine receive no more of my estate until my other children receives an equal amount with them, and should there be a balance left after they do receive an equal amount, that balance I desire to be equally divided among the whole of my children, save Joel who is to have one third of a part more than an equal share. And lastly I do hereby constitute and appoint my friends, John H. Leftwich and Abner Stud, Executors of this my last will and Testament, hereby making all other wills or Testaments by me heretofore made. In witness whereof I have hereunto set my hand and seal this 2nd. day of October, in the yea r of our Lord, 1827. Sighned, Sea led, and Published, and declared to be MICAJAH STONE. Seal.

    The last will and Testament of the above named MICAJAH STONE, in presence, br ds who atohis request and in his presence have hereunto subscribed our names as witnesses to the same.
Abel Landis.
John Landess.

    State of Tennessee, October Term, 1827, Lincoln County Court. The last will and testament of MICAJAH STONE, dec'd, was produced in open Court for probate, whereupon came Abel Landis & John Looney the subscribing witnesses thereto and being sworn proved the due execution thereof, and on motion of Jack H. Leftwich and Abner Stud the executors named in said will and took upon themselves the execution thereof and extend into bond with security as the law requiring and the oath required by law, therefore let letters Testamentary Issue to them accordingly.

(6) In testimony whereof I have hereunto set my hand and affixed the seal of said Court at office in Fayetteville this 15th, day of October, 1827.
                    Brice M. Garner. Clerk.

    State of Tennessee- Lincoln County. In the name of God Amen, I DAVID THWING of the County and State aforesaid Ship Joiner being in an infirm State of health, but of Sound intellect and disposing mind, memory and understanding, do make public and declare this my last will and testament, in manner and form, following (viz) 'Im Primus', I will and direct that all my just debts and funeral expenses be paid as soon after my decease as may be convenient by my Executrix hereafter named. Item, I give and bequeath to my adopted son David Thwing Brice, one roan colt, two or three years old, one cow, one saddle & bridle, to be worth twenty five dollars, and one new suit of clothes to be worth thirty dol-

(7) lars, Item, I give and bequeath to my step-son-in-law, John Wheeler, thirty acres of land off the South east corner of the tract wher in I now reside to be run off in such a manner it will be most suitable to him to include the house where he now lives, and the adjacent improvement made by him. Item, at the death of my wife Martha Thwing, I desire that my negro man Peter shall be set free, & that he shall have given to him a horse to be worth not less than fifty dollars, one cow and calf, and one sow and pigs, a nd twenty dollars in cash to be laid out in farming tools, and other necessary implements for house-hold uses; all of which shall be given him at the time of his emancipation.

(7)   Item- The balance of my property both real and personal, I leave and bequeath to my dear wife, Martha Thwing for and during her life,and at her death, that she may dispose of it, both real and personal in such a manner as she may think proper. And lastly, I do hereby constitute, nominate and appoint the said Martha Thwing my Sole Executrix of this my last will and testament,earnestly requesting my son-in-law, John Wheeler to give her every assistance after my death in the management of her affairs, and to act the part of a son by her. I do hereby revoke and annull all other wills heretofore made by me, satisfying and confirming this and no other, as my only and last will and testament. Witness whereof I, the said DAVID THWING have hereunto set my hand, affixed my seal, this 11th day of June in the year of our Lord, one thousand,eight hundred and twenty seven.

    Signed & Sealed in the presence of us whose names are hereunto signed and acknowledged to be his last will or testament by the said DAVID THWING.

Wm. B. Benge.

Champian Smith.

    State of Tennessee- July Term, 1827, Lincoln County Court. The last will and Testament of DAVID THWING dec'd. was exhibited in open Court for probate, where upon came William B. Benge and

(8)   Champian Smith, the Subscribing witnesses thereto, and proved the due execution thereof, and proved he was at the time of signing the same of Sound mind and memory. Whereupon came Martha Thwing the Executrix therein named and took the oath prescribed, and entered into bond and security.

    In Testimony whereof I have hereunto set my hand and affixed the seal of said Court at office in Fayetteville, this 21st day of July A.D. 1827.

    Brice M. Garner, Clerk;

    I, WILLIAM MOORES of the County of Lincoln & State of Tennessee, do hereby make my last will and testament in the manner a and form following: that is, first I desire that all of my perishable property be immediately sold after my decease, and out of all the money arising therefrom all my just debts & funeral expenses be paid. 2ndly, after all my just debts & funeral expenses is paid, I give to my son Daniel R. all my lands, rights, titles and heriditaments thereunto, belonging,but for & in consideration of said lands and tenement he, the said D.R. is to give the estate two hundred & fifty dollars. 3rdly, My desire is that my c children, namely, Henry, Isaac, Josiah, Samuel, William, Joshua, Arthur, Elizabeth & Daniel R. receive an equal share to have and to hold, them & their heirs forever. 4thly, My desire is that my children namely, Pheba, Jane & Rachel receive one half as much as my first named children, to have & to hold; Them & their heirs forever. My son Arthur has received one hundred & twenty five dollars which sum is to be taken out of his part of the estate,

(9)   & lastly I do hereby constitute & appoint my sons Josiah & Daniel R. Executors of this my last will & testament hereby revoking all other or former wills or testament by me heretofore made, In witness whereof I have hereunto set my hand and seal, This 6th of June in the year of our Lord, one thousand, eight hundred & twenty six. WILLIAM MOORES. Seal. Signed, Sealed? Published and declared to be the last will & testament of the above named WILLIAM MOORES in the presence of us, who at his request & in his

(9)   presence have hereunto subscribed our names as witness to the
same,
                James Wilson
                William Owens
                Joshua Owens

        The last will & testament of WILLIAM MOORES was exhibited
in open Court to probate & James Wilson & William Owens, two of
the subscribing witnesses thereto appeared in open Court &
proved the due execution thereof, and proved that he was at the
time of signing, publishing & declaring the same of sound mind
& memory. whereupon came Josiah Moores & Daniel R. Moores, the
Executors therein named and took the necessary oaths & entered
into bond as the law directs, July 16th, 1827. In witness
whereof I have hereunto set my hand & affixed the seal of said
court at office in Fayetteville, this 16th, July 1827.
                                Brice M. Garner, Clerk.
1 copy of this given to D.R.Moores, 24th Dec. 1827.

        DAVID P. MONROE'S last will. In the name of God Amen. I,
DAVID P. MONROE of the county of Lincoln and State of Tennessee,
being of sound mind & memory and being mindful of my mortality,
do this day of, in the year of our Lord 1828, make and publish
this, my last will and testament in manner and form following:
I desire to be decently buried; and my worldly estate I desire a
a   as follows: First, I desire that all of my Just debts due me to
(10) be collected and my just debts to be paid. I desire that my estate, consisting of the land whereon I now live, my negroes, to
wit; Patty, Edmond, Neldon, Hartwell, Brown and Sophy Stills& C.
Horses, Cattle, Hogs, House-hold & Kitchen furniture, farming
tools and crops of every description to be sold on a credit of
twelve months and the proceeds thereof to be equally divided a-
mong my seven children, to wit, William Monroe, Louisa V. Nolen,
Polly W. G. Armstrong, Sarah G. W. Wardlaw, Susan M. G. Blair,
Martha F. Harris and Amanda M. Monroe. I desire that the portion
which I have bequeathed to my daughter Louisa V. Nolen be placed
in the hand of my son William Monroe as trustee for her use during her life time, and at her death that the same descend to the
heirs of her body. I desire that in the event I should die before my daughter Amanda M. Monroe should marry that she has
choice of one of my horses and as much property of other kind
as I have given to each off my daughters that is married. I
hereby appoint my son William Monroe and my son-in-law William
Armstrong, Hugh Wardlaw and Abner Blair Executors of this my
last will and testament, hereby revoking all former wills by
me made. In testamony whereof I have hereunto set my hand &
seal, the day and year above written. DAVID P. MONROE.
Signed, Sealed, Published and Declared by the above named DAVID
P. MONROE to be his last will and testament, in the presence
of us who have hereunto subscribed our names as witnesses in
the presence of the testator.
Constant Scales
I. G. Wright
Enos Rust
William Johnson
(11)   State of Tennessee, Lincoln County Court, January Term,
1828. I, Brice M. Garner clerk of the Court of Pleas & Quar-

(11) ter Sessions for the county aforesaid do hereby certify that the due execution of the foregoing, the last will and testament of DAVID P. MONROE was this 26th day of January 1828, duly proven in open Court by the oath of Constant Scales, I. G. Wright, and William Johnson who swear that they saw DAVID P. MONROE sign the same to be his last will and testament, and that he was at the time, of sound mind & memory in their belief. Given under my hand this 26th day of January 1828.
Recorded this 5th   Brice M. Garner, Clerk.
day of March, 1828.   By his deputy, B.W.D.Carter.

LEWIS MORGAN'S last will. The last will and testament of LEWIS MORGAN, of the State of Tennessee, Lincoln County. I LEWIS MORGAN, considering the uncertainty of this mortal life and being of sound mind and memory (Blessed be the Almighty God for the same) do make and publish this my last will and testament in manner and form following, (that is to say): First, My wish and desire is that all my Just debts shall be first be paid out of my perishable property. 2nd, I give and bequeath to my son Henry Morgan the tract of land on which he now lives, bounded by the same lines by which it has heretofore been laid off to him; I also give him one third of the twen twenty-five entry lying east of where I now live. 3rd, I have given my son Smith Morgan one sorrel horse and one sorrel colt. also one cow. 4th I give to my daughter Polly one bed and furniture, One bureau and one cow.

(12) 5th, I give and bequeath to my beloved wife the balance of my land during her natural life, also all of my household & kitchen furniture, plantation utensils together with all of my perishable property to have the use of the same during her natural life and at her death to be divided as follows: 6th, I give to my son Joab Morgan at my wife's death one half of the land of my wife's dower which dividing line will run North and South equally dividing the same according to quality and quantity. 7th I give my son Smith Morgan the other half of my wife's dower of land being divided as above named. 8th, I give at my wife's death to the Ayers of my son-in-law Robert Clarke five dollars. 9th, I give at my wife's death to the Ayers of my son Edward Morgan five dollars. 10th I give at the death of my wife to my son-in-law Andy Greer five dollars. 11th, I give at the death of my wife to my son-in-law Joseph Calvert five dollars. 12th, I give at the death of my wife to my son-in-law Pleasant Flemmen five dollars. 13th, I give at the death of my wife to my daughter Nancy Merrill five dollars. 14th, I give at the death of my wife to my son-in-law Redden Reddick five dollars. 15th, I give at the death of my wife to my son-in-law Gideon Austin five dollars. 16th I have given to my grandson Andrew Flemmen one Bay Mare & Colt.

I do hereby nominate and appoint my friends Benjamin Reeves and Zachariah Harrison executors of this my last will
(13) and testament, revoking all other will or wills made by me heretofore in witness whereof I have hereunto set my hand and seal this 26th day of November in the year of our Lord one thousand, eight hundred a nd twenty seven. LEWIS MORGAN. Seal. Signed, sealed, published and declared by the above named LEWIS MORGAN to be his last will and testament in the presence of us who at his request and in his presence have sub-

(13)   subscribed our names as witnesses thereunto.

                                        I. H. Leftwick
                                        Amos Morris
                                        John S. Johnson.

     State of Tennessee, Lincoln County Court, January term 1828.
I, Brice M. Gardner, Clerk of the Court of Pleas and Quarter
Sessions of said County hereby certify that the foregoing last
will and testament of LEWIS MORGAN was exhibited for probate
whereupon came Jack H. Leftwick and Amos Morris two of the subscribing witnesses thereto and proved the due execution thereof,
and proved that the said LEWIS MORGAN was at the time of signing
of, sealing and publishing the same, of sound mind and memory, and
that the same was so exhibited & proven the 21st day of January
1828. Given under my hand this 5th day of March 1828.
                                        Brice M. Garner, Clerk
                    By his deputy--   B.W.D.Carter.
Recorded & compared 6th March 1828.

     JOHN BLAKE'S last will. In the name of God Amen. Being
infirm and far advanced of age and of sound mind and memory,
but knowing that it is once appointed for all men to die. I now
make this my last will & testament in writing revoking all former
wills and testaments by me heretofore made. First I will and
(14)   bequeath my soul into the hands of God who gave it, and Secondly
my worldly estate which it hath pleased God to bless me with in
the following manner (to wit) 2d, I allow all my funeral expenses
to be paid together with my other just debts of other description
by a sale, and out of the proceeds of the money arising from the
sale of my stock and other household and kitchen furniture,
which is to take place as soon as possible after my decease, and
the money arising from the proceeds of the sale of said stock &
furniture, after paying my funeral expenses and other just debts,
I allow to be equally divided amongst the whole of my children,
(viz) Hugh M. Blake, John W. Blake, William D. Blake, Sally Marr,
& Lone Blake & Peggy Scales. Third, I will and bequeath to my
dearly beloved wife Elizabeth Blake one negro girl, Hannah & her
three children (viz) Aggy, Mary & Lidda and their increase forever, with her bed and furniture and one horse, her choice of
my stock & two cows & calves, her choice before any sale takes
place, to be disposed of as she may think proper at her death.
I also will and bequeath to my son Wm.D. Blake one hundred acres
of land in Lincoln County and State of Tennessee, whereon I now
live, and one negro boy Tom as his own right and to be disposed
of as he ma y think fit after my death (but not before).
Furthermore, I give and bequeath to my daughter Ione Blake one
bed and furniture, her choice; and lastly I appoint my dearly
beloved wife Elizabeth Executrix & my son W. D. Blake executor
to this my last will and testament advising them to put this my
last will and testament into execution and further they are not
to be required to give any security to execute said will & testament & agreeable to the true intent & meaning of said will as
I have all confidence they will carry this my last will into effect. In testimony whereof I have hereunto Set my hand and seal
this 28th day of September, 1824.
Test   John Blake, Seal.
Brice M. Garner
John C. Garner
Recorded 26th June 1828.

(15)   SAMUEL BUTLER'S last Will. In the name of God Amen. I,
SAMUEL BUTLER of the State of Tennessee and Lincoln County being sick & weak of body but of sound mind and disposing memory
for which I thank God and calling to mind the uncertainty of
human life and being desirous to dispose of all such worldly
substance as it hath pleased God to bless me with: I give and
bequeath to my dear beloved wife Elizabeth a part of the plantation that I now live on. Beginning at my barn. thence running
with the lane towards the mill within six poles of said mill
thence north west to Jas. M. Clusky's line, thence east with
said line to John Yeargers line, thence South so as to include
the Peach orchard, thence west to the road, thence North with
said road to the barn, to hold during her natural life or widowhood and provided she should marry that she pay half rent for
the land; and likewise one work creature worth fifty dollars, &
two cows & calves, & two Beds and furniture, one pot and one
oven with one hundred and twenty dollars; And the balance of my
perishable property to be sold and the money arising therefrom
I give and bequeath that my son Constant shall have one hundred
dollars. And my son Thomas shall have one hundred dollars.
And my daughter Teressee Camele shall have a negro boy by the
name of Linsey & twenty dollars. And my daughter Nancy Caroline
I give a negro boy named Jerry and one hundred dollars when it
(16)   can be got by the rent of my land or the hire of my negroes.
And my sons William and Samuel H. and John and Edmond and Lewis,
and my daughter Mary Ann the balance of the Money arising from
my perishable property with my mill and mill yard and all the
land lying on the west side of the creek to be sold, and the hire
of my negroes and the rent of my land, also one Lot in Hazle-
green to be sold and equally divided among the six last named
children; and when my youngest child comes of age my negroes and
the balance of my land to be sold and equally divided, the money
arising from that sale amongst all my children. And I do appoint
Joseph Dean & John Pinkerton to be my Executors of this my last
will & testament. In witness whereof I have hereunto set my
hand and seal this 18th day of October in the year of our Lord,
One thousand, eight hundred and twenty-six (signed)
                                        Samuel Butler, Seal.
Signed, sealed, published and declared to be the last will and
testament of the above named SAMUEL BUTLER in presence of us who
at his request and in his presence hath hereunto subscribed our
names as witness to the same.
Test.
William Cox
Sealia Cox.
Recorded 26th June 1828.

     MALCOM McCOWAN'S last will. I, MALCOM MC?COWAN of the
County of Lincoln being sick and weak in body, but of sound
mind and memory as touching such worldly estate as hathpleased
God to blesss me with in this life. I hereby desire and bequeath in the manner & form following: But first of all I order
a ll my legal debts to be paid. 1st, I leave and bequeath to
my wife Mary the one third of all my real and personal estate
during her natural life, and after her decease to be divided
Among my children. 2nd, I leave and bequeath to my children,
named as follows; John, Emaline, Lewis, Carrol,Moleena,William,
Farlaw and James Fletcher the remainder of all my real and

(17) personal estate, and to be divided equally amongst them as
they come of age, and in case of the death of any of the above
named children before they come of age, then, and in that case
the part or share thereof pertaining to be equally divided
among the remainder. 3rd, I have and bequeath to my daughter
Lavina Blair (otherwise, McKeown) so much as shall be of value
sufficient to make up the said Lavina part or share so as to
amount to the same of any of the other above named after the
deduction of one hundred and fifty dollars as taken out of the
same and making it on hers an equal to any of the rest, and
and said amount that is coming to said Lavina's part to be paid
so soon as all or the whole of the money may be collected of
said estate or so soon as there is sufficient funds collected
to discharge the same. And lastly, I nominate and appoint my
friends William Barrow and George McKeown executor, of this my
last will and testament, hereby revoking all others or former
wills or testaments by heretofore made. In witness whereof I
have hereunto set my hand and seal this 13th day of Feby, 1827.
Malcom McKeown, Seal.

Signed, sealed, published and declared to be the last will
and testament of the above named MALCOM McKEOWN in presence of
us who at his request and in his presence have hereunto subscribed our names as witness's to the same.
David Jones
John W. Street
Isaac McCown.

Recorded 26th June 1828.

(18) JAMES RANDALL'S WILL. I, JAMES RANDALL being sound in
mind and conscious of my approaching end, being weak in body,
having first committed my soul to God, do thus make and constitute this my last will and testament. First, It is my will
that after my business has been properly settled and wound up
by the persons and in the manner hereafter appointed, The property that may then be remaining in the hands of my Executors
be given to my Mother, Catharine Randall of Down Patrick, Down-
shire Ireland, and that she be my heir; and heir the whole of
my property exclusively. Second, It is my will that Robert
Dickson and John P. McConnell of the town of Fayetteville,
County of Lincoln & state of Tennessee be my executors to this
my last will and testament, to effect a settlement with my
partner in business, James Mudd, and be clothed with full power
and authority to settle and wind up my estate.
Witness my hand & seal at Fayetteville, August 26th, 1826.
James Randall, Seal.
John Morgan
W, H. Martin
Jno. Coleman   Recorded 26th June 1828.

George Heath's Will. Memorandum: That I, GEORGE HEATH of
the State of Tennessee and Lincoln County, being in my perfect
senses and right mind, and contemplating that it is appointed
for all men once to die, I do make this my last will & testament in the words following: N.B. First of all being impressed of the rights of man being entitled to freedom, I do
as an act of Justice & humanity emancipate & set free from
slaving my negro women, namely, Sary at my decease and at my

(19) wife's decease and do hereby emancipate the said Sary from my
heirs, executors, administrators or assigns from all slavery forever. Item. I give and bequeath to my wife the place that I now
live on; and all the property that is left her lifetime, and
after her decease I want what property will be left equally divided among my children. And do appoint my two sons Nathaniel
P. Heath and Abner C. Heath, executors of this my last will and
testament, revoking and dis-annulling all other wills, testaments
or covenants desiring this and only this to be my last will and
testament and no other. In witness whereof I have hereunto set
my hand and seal this 19th of May A.D. 1826.
Signed, sealed and delivered   George Heath, Seal.
in presence of us Witnesses
Attest
James Frame
William Lea   Recorded 26th June 1828.

        JAMES CHEATHAM'S last Will. In the name of God Amen. I,
JAMES CHEATHAM of the County of Lincoln & State of Tennessee, being of sound mind & memory calling to mind the mortality of my
body and knowing that it is appointed for all men once to die, do
make, ordain, publish & declare the following to be my last will
and testament in writing to wit: 1st, I recommend my soul to
God who gave it, and my body to the earth to be decently buried.
2nd, I will and desire that all my just debts be paid, and that
all seems due me be collected for that purpose. 3rd, I give and
bequeath to my dear and well beloved wife Rebecca Cheatham for
and during the term of her natural life, or during the term of
(20) her widowhood and no longer, the whole of the land & plantation
on which I now live, and also the whole of my household & kitchen
furniture; and also two work horses & farming tools accordingly;
and also such parts of my stock of cattle and hogs as she may
need for the support of our surviving family, and also the following slaves, to wit: George and his wife Rose and their children, John & Lydia. 4th, It is my will and desire that my negro
man slave Anthony be sold, and also all such parts of my personal
estate as can be spared by my family, which may be determined
by my widow,& Executors, having due regard to the interest of my
heirs. 5th, I give and bequeath to my four children Elmer,Cheat-
ham, Betsy R. Cheatham and Albert W. Cheatham the whole of my
estate as well as real or personal of every description to be
equally divided among them, share & share alike, agreeably to the
provisions of law, and I do further give and bequeath to my son
Elmer Cheatham, my young mare Phoenia, & to my son Soloman Cheatham my young horse colt Dolphin, both of which to be accounted
for at their value on a final settlement, and also I give and
bequeath to each of my aforesaid four children a feather bed and
furniture to be as near of equal value as convenient, And it is
further my will & desire that each of my aforesaid children on
his or her arriving or coming of age shall be paid his or her
distribution share of whatever amount may be in the hands of my
Executor, arising from sales and the collection of debts. 6th,
It is my will and desire that my family all be kept together,
and that each of my above named children may receive a Suitable
(21) education. 7th, I hereby constitute and appoint William Shipp
and Joel Pinson executors to this my last will & testament, and

(21) hereby charge them with the faithful execution of the same.
In testamony whereof I have hereunto set my hand and seal this
12th day of December 1826.

               James   Cheatham, Seal.

Signed, sealed, published & declared in presence of,
Obadiah Pinson
Lewis Shipp
John Robinson   Recorded 26th June 1828.

     MARTHA McMILLEN'S last Will. In the name of God Amen. I,
MARTHA McMILLEN of the County of Lincoln and State of Tennessee,
being weak in body but of sound and perfect mind and memory,
blessed be Almighty God for the same, do make and publish this
my last will & testament in manner and form, following,(that is
to say) First, I give and bequeath unto my son James McMillen one
dollar. I also give and bequeath unto my son John McMillen one
dollar. I, also give and bequeath unto my son Joseph McMillen,
one dollar. I give and bequeath unto my son Thomas McMillen, one
dollar. I also give and bequeath unto the heirs of my son Andrew
McMillen one dollar. After the above named sums of money are
paid out of my estate to my above named sons, I wish my tract of
land containing six acres lying & being in the County of Lincoln
to be sold and the money arising from the sale thereof, together
with other monies, debts,dues or claims or property, wholly,
whatsoever kind it may be after my decease, to be equally divided

(22) between my five daughters (namely): Nancy,Wright, Sarah Chitwood,
June Gross, Martha Marshall & Polly Pinkston. I hereby appoint Jacob Wright Sears my sole Executor of this my last will
and testament, hereby revoking all former will by me made.
In witness whereof I have hereunto set my hand and seal the 27th
day of February, in the year of our Lord 1826.

                      her
             Martha   X McMillen.
                     mark

Signed, sealed, published and declared by the above named
MARTHA McMILLEN to be her last will and testament in the pres-
ence of us who have hereunto subscribed our names as witnesses
in the presence of the Testatrix.
David Crook
Jacob Wright,Junr. Recorded 26 June 1828.

(23)   AGNES ALDRIDGE'S last Will. In the name of God, Amen.
I, AGNESS ALDRIDGE of the County of Lincoln & State of Tennessee,
being in health of body and composed in mind, yet uncertain of
the time of my decease, do think proper to make my last will
& testament. I resign my soul to God in hope of eternal life
through the merits of Christ: and my body I consign th the grave
until the resurrection. And what Worldly goods God has blessed
me with I dispose of in the following manner(viz). First, I
give unto my beloved daughter Martha Harrison's children five
dollars to be equally divided among them all to have & to hold
forever. Secondly, I give unto my beloved daughter Elizabeth
Simmons' children five dollars to equally divided among them all
to have & to hold forever. Thirdly, I give unto my beloved
daughter Polly' Davis's Children five dollars to be equally divided among them all to have and hold forever. Fourthly, I
give unto my beloveddaughter Tabitha Hightower five dollars

(23) to her & her heirs forever. Fifthly, I give unto my beloved
grand daughter Agnes B. Hightower, a small yellow girl named Mary
to and her heirs forever. The balance of my estate consisting
of seven negroes (viz) Fanny, Tom, Kiziah, Moria, Natila, Jack &
Willa with their increase, two beds, bed clothing, a gun, a
brass Kettle & C. I wish appraised and equally divided among
my beloved Children (viz) Sally, Hutheson, Frances McGowan,
Richard, William and James Baugh to them & their heirs forever.

I constitute my sons William & James Baugh as Executors to
this my last will & testament. In confirmation of the whole I
(24) have hereunto set my hand and affixed my seal this twenty second of April One thousand, eight hundred and twenty four.

Agnes Aldridge, Seal.

Signed & sealed in presence of,
Willis S. McLaurine
Ellen Stevenson
Joseph McCrackin
Asa T. Stone   Recorded 27 June 1828.

Thomas Pully's last Will. State of Tennessee, Lincoln
County. In the name of God Amen. I, THOMAS PULLY of the
County & State aforesaid, taking into view the frailty of man
and uncertainty of life, do make, ordain & constitute this my
last will & testament to the exclusion of all others (that is to
say) 1st, I give and bequeath unto my beloved wife Lydia Pully,
the plantation whereon I reside during her natural life, also
my negro girl Maria & her child Rose for the same period, one
good bed & furniture, 1 chest and Bureau and all such household furniture as she may think proper to keep. Also one mare,
saddle and bridle, the mare's colt Fanny, two cows & calves,
two work steers & cart, two sows & pigs & two sheep. At her
death the above property to be equally divided among the following named heirs; Gideon N. Pully, Benjamin C. Pully, Thomas
W. Pully, Letha Thompson & Rhoda Noles; and to my son David
Pulley one hundred dollars. To my daughter Elizabeth Warren I
give & bequeath the sum of two dollars, and to my heirs Gideon
N. Pulley, Benjamin C. Pully, Thomas W, Pully, and Rhoda Noles
I give and bequeath an equal of the over-plus of property at
my death. And I do hereby constitute & appoint my sons Gideon
N. Pully and Benjamin C. Pully my sole executors to carry this
(25) my last will & testament into effect. And I do hereby revoke
and deny all others. In testimony whereof I have hereunto set
my hand and seal this 3rd day of January in the year of our
Lord, one thousand eight hundred and twenty eight.

Thos. Pully, Seal.
Signed, sealed & acknowledged in presence of us.
Arch I. Baxter
Jno. Dusenberry
State of Tennesseee, Lincoln County Court, April 21st, 1828.
I, Brice M. Garner, Clerk of said Court hereby certify that this
last will and testament of THOMAS PULLY was presented for probate whereupon came Archibald Baxter & John Dusenberry the
subscribing witnesses thereto and being sworn, state that they
saw THOMAS PULLY sign the same and heard him acknowledge it to
be his last will & testament and at the time of signing& acknow-
ledging the same, they believe him to be of sound mind & memory.
Given under my hand this 26 June 1828.

Brice M. Garner, Clerk.

25) Recorded 27 june 1828, By his deputy B.W.D. Carter.

James Simmons's last Will. In the name of God Amen. I, JAMES SIMMONS of the County of Lincoln & State of Tennessee, considering the uncertainty of this mortal life, and being of sound & perfect mind & memory, blessed be Almighty God for the same, do make and publish this my last will & testament in the manner and form following, that is to say: First I do give and bequeath unto my grand son Tryan Nichols, one sorrel filly two years old, one saddle and bridle worth twenty five dollars, one cow & calf of the Second rate, one feather Bed.

(26) I do give and bequeath unto my beloved wife Katharine Simmons all my land and one negro girl called Charlotte, and all other property belonging to me of what kind soever, it may be during her natural life. I will and ordain that there should be a sale and sell all such stock as she the sd. Katharine Simmons thinks proper, and the money arising from said Sale be at her will and disposal in anyway she sees cause during life. I will and ordain that after the death of my beloved Wife Katharine Simmons, all stock, all tools that are then & there found shall be sold, and all household & Kitchen furniture shall also be sold and the money arising from said sales be divided amongst my children, that is to say my daughter Polly Erwin, my daughter Agness Burden, my daughter Sally Davis, my daughter Katharine Barham, my daughter Elizabeth Simmons, so that each one of these, my daughters shall have an equal portion, and after the death of my beloved wife Kathrine Simmons, I do give and bequeath unto my son Thomas Simmons all my land lying on the north side of the creek, being the place whereon he now lives. And I do give and bequeath at the same time all my lands lying on the South side of the creek that being the place whereon I now live to my son James A. Simmons, him and his heirs forever and I will and ordain that after the death of my beloved wife Katharine Simmons, that my negro girl called Charlotte and increase should there be any be valued and that my son James A. Simmons take them and pay the valuation of them and I will and ordain that the money rising from said girl be equally divided amongst all my children, that is to say, my daughter Polly Erwin, my daughter Lucy Erwin, my daughter Agness Burden, my daughter Sally Davis, my daughter Katharine

(27) Barham, my daughter Elizabeth Simmons, my son Thomas Simmons, my son James A. Simmons, so that each on e shall have an equal portion, that is if my son James A. Simmons is living at the decease of my beloved wife, and if he is dead before my beloved wife, I will and ordain that she be sold amongst my children, and the money divided as above named, and as there is, as I suppose something coming to of fathering law estate, if that should be got, it is my will that after paying my executon for his trouble for collecting, that it should be for my beloved wife Katharine Simmons during her natural life, and as this money owing to me that I have notes for, I do hereby give and bequeath unto my beloved wife Katharine Simmons all money that is coming to me in any way whatever during her natural life, and all money that are then & there found at her death, I will and ordain that it be divided amongst my daughters, that is to say, Polly Erwin, Lucy Erwin, Agness Burden, Sally Davis, Katharine Barham, Elizabeth Simmons, so that each one of these, my daughters shall have an equal portion, and I do hereby

(27)   appoint my son James A. Simmons & Thomas Simmons my so
executors this witness whereof I have hereunto set my hand
and seal this the seventh of March, eighteen hundred and
twenty eight.   his
                James X Simmons, Seal.
Signed, sealed,   mark
published and declared by the above named JAMES SIMMONS to
be his will and testament in the presence of us.
James Cooper (seal)
Thomas Simmons (seal)
Abner Freeman (seal)
James A. Simmons (seal)

(28)   Codicil to the foregoing will, I, JAMES SIMMONS of the
County of Lincoln & State of Tennessee do this eighth of
March 1828 do make and publish this Codicil to my last will
& testament in the manner following: that is to say, whereas
in and by last will and testament bearing date, have given
to my daughter Sally Davis a portion and as I cannot tell
what the amount will be, I do hereby declare that my will is
that only one half of the legacy be paid unto her in full
of the sd. legacy. I have as aforesaid given her and that
the remainder part of the said legacy be given and paid to
my grand daughter Katharine Cooper and my grand son Tryon Nichols, equally divided betwixt them. And I have also in my
last will & testament left a portion to my daughter Agness
Burden, I do hereby order and declare that my will is that
only one half be paid unto her in full of the said legacy I
have as aforesaid given her, and that the remaining part of
the said legacy be given and paid unto James Nichols, Amy
Spradly, Tabithy Armstrong, Polly Nichols, Wm. Nichols,
Catherine Nichols, Mahaly Nichols equally divided amongst
them, these are the sons and daughters of Henry Nichols. And
I have also in my last will & testament given a portion to
my daughter Elizabeth Simmons, I do hereby order & declare
that my will is that only one half of the legacy be paid unto her in full of sd. legacy. I have as aforesaid given her,
and the remaining part of said legacy be given and paid unto
my grand son John Simmons and Sinai Simmons, son and daughter
of sd. Elizabeth Simmons. And lastly, it is my desire that
this my present Codicil be annexed and made a part pf my
last will and testament to all intents & purposes. In witness
whereof I have hereunto set my hand and seal. his
                    James x Simmons, Seal.
(29)   Signed, sealed, published and   mark
declared by the above named JAMES SIMMONS as a Codicil to be
annexed to his last will & testament in the presence of us.
                James Cooper (seal)
                Abner Freeman (seal)
                Thomas Simmons (seal)
                James A. Simmons (seal)

      THOMAS ROUNDTREE last WILL. In the name of God Amen.
I, THOMAS ROUNDTREE of the County of Lincoln and State of
Tennessee being weak in body, but perfectly sound in mind and
memory do make and publish this my last will & testament in
manner and form following: that it is to say, First, I give

(29) and bequeath unto my beloved wife Sarah Roundtree the tract of land whereon I now live, during her natural lifetime as widowhood with all the profits arising therefrom during said time and no longer. I also give and bequeath unto her, her

(30) heirs and assign forever one negro woman, her choice, One horse, all my farming tools, One bed and furniture, one cupboard and one Table with one set of ware for each. Secondly, I give and bequeath unto my son Jas. L, Roundtree my entire interest (being one half) of a tract of land owned jointly by myself and Wm. S. Smith containing about   acres with all its appurtenances and provided that I have heretoforemade or procured to be made to him the said James L. a deed of Conveyance to a tract of land whereon he now lives, he shall have his choice either relinquish to my estate all his right and title to the said land or to pay within twelve months after my decease to my said estate five hundred dollars, that being the Amount which I paid for the said land. Thirdly, I give and bequeath unto my son Wm. Roundtree the tract of land whereon I now live to have possession of the same at his mothers death or marriage. And lastly as to all the rest residue and remainder of my estate both real and personal goods & Chattle, land tenements, negroes and all other articles belonging to me of what kind and nature Sever . I will and order to be sold to the highest bidder on twelve months credit, and wherever the money arising from such sale is collected, I give and bequeath unto my wife Sarah and my children (viz) Katharine Shaw, James L. Rountree, William Roundtree, Elizabeth Landess and Nancy Smith, Mary Roundtree & Ann Roundtree to be equally divided amongst them all, share and share alike. And I do hereby appoint Thos. H. Shaw, Wm. S. Smith and W. F. Long Executors to this my last will & testament hereby revoking all wills by me heretofore made. In witness

(31) whereof I have hereunto set my hand and affixed my seal this ninth day of April A. D. one thousand eight hundred and twenty eight.

   Thomas Roundtree (seal)

Signed, sealed, published and declared by the above named, THOS. ROUNTREE to be his last will and testament in the presence of us who have hereunto subscribed our names as witnesses in the presence of the Testator.
James Curry
Thomas S. Stovall
W. F. Long

  State of Tennessee, Lincoln County Court, July Term 1828. I, Brice M. Garner, Clerk of said Court do certify that the foregoing last will & testament of THOMAS ROUNTREE deceased was exhibited in open Court for probate the 21st day of July, 1828, whereupon came James Curry and Thomas S. Stovall two of the subscribing witnesses & being Sworn under the direction of the Court, State that they saw THOMAS ROUNTREE sign, seal, publish & declare said will or heard him acknowledge the same about the time it bears date and that they believed him to be at the time of sound mind and memory. Given under my hand.
       Brice M. Garner
     By his deputy B.W.D. Carter

Recorded 15 Sept. 1828.

(31)   Jacob Pruitt's last will. I JACOB PRUITT knowing that
to I have to die sooner or later being very low in bodily
health but sound in mind and memory, wishing to leave my
worldly goods and chattles as follows: I leave to my lawful and loving wife Nancy the plantation on which I now live
on, containing four hundred acres of land, I also leave to
her five negroes, Nelly and her son Henry, and a young negro
man by the name of Tom, a girl by the name of Selvy, a boy

(32)   by the name of Sam. I also leave to her all my household
and Kitchen furniture, and stock of all kind, that is to say,
horses, cattle, sheep. hogs, her natural life, and then she
all to be sold and the money to be equally divided among her
children, except she should marry, then all to be sold as is
named above. I also leave to my son James the plantation on
which he now lives five year, and the to be sold and the money
equally divided mong said children. I also leave my negro
women suck and her five children to be sold and the money to
be equally divided among my first wife's Children, Reuben &
Lewis to be sold and the money to be equally divided among
my last wife's Children. And this being my last will and
testament, I also leave my wife Nancy and my son James A.
Pruitt as executors of said estate this fourth day of April
one thousand eight hundred twenty eight.   his

                                          Jacob x Pruitt

Thos Spencer   mark
John Pruett
Isham Burnett

(33)   Ezekiel Norris's last Will. In the name of God Amen.
I, EZEKIEL NORRIS of the County of Lincoln & State of Tennessee
being of Sound mind & Memory do make and ordain this my
last will & testament in manner following (viz) First,
after my decease I require my executors to pay all my just
debts out of money owing or that may be on hand. Second, I
give unto my son John M. Norris all that part of the tract
of land whereon I now live lying west of Norris's Creek and
South & West of the town of Fayetteville supposed to contain
one hundred & twenty acres. Also one negro boy named Daniel,
also my farming utensials, horse, bridle & saddle, and one
cow & calf, likewise bed & furniture. Third, I give unto my
son Henry Norris all that part of my land lying on the east of
Norris's Creek supposed to contain ninety five acres to be
placed in the hands of a suitable guardian for his use, to be
given up to him when thought capable of taking care of the
same. Also Bed & furniture. Fourth, I give unto my daughter
Cynthia Norris, forty & one half acres of land lying in the
North west corner of the tract I now live on, binding on the
north boundry line. Also one negro girl named Sophia, Bed
and furniture and bureau. Fifth I give unto my daughter Minerva forty and one half acres of land lying south of the
land that I have in this will given to my daughter Cynthia to
be placed in the hands of my sons William & John M. Norris
for her use to be kept in their possession until they may
think proper to give her the managament of the same. Sixth,
I give unto my daughter Emily, one negro girl named Mariah,

(34)   also one thousand dollars to be paid out of money owing me
by my son William Norris, Bed & furniture & Escretowe.

(34) Seventh & last, all that part of my estate not disposed of in this my will to be equally divided between my children. That part falling to my daughter Minerva to be placed in the hands of my sons William & J. M. Norris for her use & benefit to be surrendered to her when they may think proper. And I do hereby nominate & appoint my friends Francis Porterfield Esqr. & Thomas Clarke Esqr. Executors of this my last will & testament.

Given under my hand and seal this 17th day of January A.D. 1827.

Test.   Ezekiel Norris, (seal)
Wm. Neeld
John McMillen   (Recorded 14 January 1829).

(35) James Walker(s last Will. Know all men by these presents, that I, JAMES WALKER? Sr. of the State of Tennessee & County of Lincoln do make and ordain this to be my last will and testament in manner & forever, following to wit: First, I leave in the possession of my wife Nancy the whole of my estate consisting of negroes, horses, cattle, & household furniture, during her natural life or widowhood, and at her death or second marriage, the whole of the property to be taken & sold by my Executors and the money thence arising put to interest and my son Carter to have the interest of said money during his natural life, and at his death to be divided in the following forever, to wit; Polly Givens my daughter to have one Sixth part, My son Andrew Walker One sixth part, My Grandson Franklin Walker, one sixth part, my Grand children Alleline Butler & Franklin Butler one sixth part, my son James Walker one sixth part, And that my daughter Milly's legal heirs have one sixth part. And my will & desire is that the heirs she has by Drury McConnally may be made equal to her heirs by James Pearson, taking in what their Father left them. And that my Grand daughter Presly Kirkpatrick have one dollar, these two grand children having had their share of my estate previous to this time. And lastly, I constitute and appoint my son James Walker & my friend Abner Steed my Executor to see this my last will & testament executed Nov. 28, 1828.

James Walker, (seal)

Signed, sealed, published & pronounced to be the last will & testament of JAMES WALKER Sr. in presence of us.
James Scott
William C. Scott. Recorded 16 March 1829.

(36) Joel Bruce's last Will. In the name of God Amen. I, JOEL BRUCE of Lincoln County, Tennessee, revoking all others, appoint this to be my last will and testament. I give my lands, negroes and all my other property to my wife Sally so long as she lives. After her death I leave my land to my two youngest sons Arnold & Joel to be equally divided between them both. Item, my negroes and all my personal property I leave to be equally divided among my three other children, Normely, Letty & Sally after the death of my wife Sally. I appoint Stephen Hightower to be executor of this my last will and testament. Witness my hand and seal this 2d of January, eighteen hundred and twenty nine.

Test   Joel Bruce (seal)
William M. Rose
John x Harrison
his mark) James Macgown. Recorded March 20 1829.

(37)   Kinchin Holcomb(s last Will. In the name of God Amen.
I, KINCHIN HOLCOMB of the County of Lincoln & State of Tennessee being sick and weak of body but of sound mind and disposing memory for which I thank God, and calling to mind the
uncertainty of human life, being desirous to dispose of all
such worldly property as it hath pleased God to bless me with.
1st, I desire that all my preishable property be immediately
sold after my decease, and out of the money arising therefrom,
a ll my just debts and funeral expence be paid. 2d, After the
payment of my debts and funeral expence, I give to my wife
Nancy Holcomb, one black cow and also all the other property
she brought with her here. 3d, I desire that my land be equally
divided into three equal parts, and that my son Alfred Holcomb have first choice running so as to include the houses and
spring; and that my other two sons Hardy H. Holcomb & Robert
N. Holcomb have the other two lots. 4th, I give and bequeath
unto my son John Holcomb one negro woman named Fanny.
55h, I give and bequeath to son Hardy H. Holcomb one negro girl
named Kitty. 6th, I give and bequeath unto my son Alfred Holcomb one negro boy named Ephraim, also one feather Bed and
furniture & also the thrashing machine. 7th, I give and bequeath
unto my son Robert N. Holcomb one negro boy named Dick. 8th,
I give and bequeath to my daughter Sarah J. Holcomb one negro
girl named Sally, also one feather bed and furniture. 9th, I
(38)   give and bequeath unto my grand son Richard K. Hightower one
hundred dollars to be paid out of the money arising out of
the proceeds of the sale of the perishable property. And lastly, I hereby constitute and appoint my two sons Alfred Holcomb & Robert N. Holcomb Executors of this my last will and
testament. In witness whereof I have hereunto set my hand and
affixed my seal this the fifteenth of November 1828.(his)

                            Kinchin Holcomb x
Signed,sealed and delivered in the presence of us   (mark)
who have hereunto subscribed our names as witness to the same.
Jas. McCracken
Daniel Lee.
    We, Joseph McCracken and Daniel Lee do certify the above
is a true copy of the original will and testament of KINCHIN
HOLCOMB deceased.
Jas. M.cCracken
Daniel Lee.
State of Tennessee, Lincoln County Court, April 20th, 1829.
I, Brice M. Garner Clerk of said Court do certify that it appearing to the satisfaction of said Court that KINCHIN HOL-
comb late of this County had departed this life first having
made his last will & testament in writing. And it also appearing to the satisfaction of the Court from the testimony of
Joseph McCracken one of the subscribing witness thereto that
said will was deposited by said HOLCOMB with said McCracken for
safe keeping and also that said will is lost, stolen or destroyed,
so that the same cannot now be produced to this Court for probate. And it further appearing to the satisfaction of the Court
from the testimony of said McCracken and Daniel Lee that they
were subscribing witnesses to said will, who state that they
read or heard said will read, that they remember its contents
& State that this paper writing now by them here produced in
(39)

(39) Court is a true copy and tener of said Original will, and
that the said KINCHIN HOLCOMB signed, sealed, published &
declared the same to be his last will and testament and that
they subscribed their names therto as witnesses at his request and in his presence, and that they believed him to be at
the time of signing, sealing, published, and declaring the
same to be of sound mind and memory. It was therefore ordered
by the Court that this copy or tener together with this probate be recorded.

                    Brice M. Garner.
        By his deputy B. W. D. Carter.
Recorded 14 July, 1829.

        John Harrison's last Will. In the name of God Amen. I,
JOHN HARRISON do appoint this to be my last will & testament.
First, I give to my beloved wife all my estate of every kind.
At her death, I wish an equal division among my children,
taking into consideration what I paid them(viz) I have paid
Thomas Fifty dollars, and Meddleton One hundred and thirty.
A note on William Mosely of fifty dollars I wish given up to
him. I wish Ludy Couthun to be my Executor to this my last
will and testament. In witness I hereunto set my hand & seal
this ninth of April 1829.   his
                    John x Harrison (seal)
Signed, sealed and deliv-   mark
ered in presence of us.
Test
Ritter Brown
Robert R. Allsup
Morgan Holbert x his mark.
        State of Tennessee, Lincoln County Court, April 20th,
1829. I, Brice M. Garner Clerk of said Court do certify
(40) that this last will and testament of JOHN HARRISON deceased,
was produced in open Court for probate, whereupon came
Robert R. Allsup and Morgan Holbert the subscribing witnesses
thereto and being duly sworn state that they saw and heard
the said JOHN HARRISON sign, seal, publish and declare the
same to be his last will and testament, and that they believed
him to be at the time of sound mind and memory; whereupon
it was ordered by the Court that this will together with this
probate be recorded.
                    Brice M. Garner
Recorded 14 July 1829, By his deputy, B. M. D. Carter.

        James Brown last Will. April the tenth day 1829. In
the name of God Almighty & Almerciful, I do make this my
last will & testament for the disposition of my own affairs,
and the appropriation of my own estate. I want my wife
Mary Brown to have and to live on my tract of land whereon
I now live, to raise my nine youngest children and to educate them as well as she can, and at her death ordaining
her widow hood, then to be equally divided between my three
youngest sons my tract of land which consist of one hundred
and fifty acres between Alexander Brown, James Brown, William
Brown. I want my negroes to belong to my beloved wife Mary
during her widowhood or death, and then to be sold and the

(40) amount of such sale to be equally divided amongst my six youngest daughters Martha Brown, Harriet Brown, Clarrisa Brown, Ann Brown, Polly Brown, Elizabeth Brown, my land and claims that lies in the western District I want to be sold to pay all my just debts and the balance of except two hundred dollars I give unto my daughter Ione Waggoner, if any more after that I want to be divided with my three sons before mentioned. Any child being dissatisfied with this my last will is not to have more than five pound for its full portion. I do nominate, constitute and appoint William Husband of the State of Tennessee Executor to this my last will & testament and do publish the same as an act of my own. Signed, sealed, acknowledged in the presence of the undersigned.

Test   Jas. Brown (seal)
John Brown
Levingston J.Brown.

State of Tennessee, Lincoln County Court, July term,1829. I, Brice M. Garner Clerk of said Court do certify that the foregoing last will & testament of JAMES BROWN deceased was presented in open Court for probate & that John & Livingston J. Brown the subscribing witnesses thereto being duly sworn. stated that they saw said JAMES BROWN sign, seal and heard him publish & declare the same to be his last will & testament, & that the same was executed at the time it bears date and that they believed said JAMES BROWN at the time of executing said will to be of sound mind & memory, and subscribed their names thereto as witnesses in his presence and at his request.

                                        Brice M. Garner.
By his deputy B.M.D.Carter. Recorded 17 October 1829.

(42)   William Bledsoe's last will. In the name of God Amen. I, WILLIAM BLEDSOE of the County of Lincoln & State of Tennessee being sick & weak of body, but of sound mind & disposing memory for which I thank God, and calling to mind the uncertainty of human life, and being desirous do dispose of all such worldly substance as it hath pleased God to bless me with; I give & bequeath the same in the manner following, that is to say: I desire that all my just debts & funeral expenses be paid out of the personal property of my estate. 2d, I give and bequeath unto my son John Bledsoe all my tract of land whereon I now live Containing fifty acres during his life time, then after his decease to go to my son Lewis Bledsoe to be enjoyed by him & his heirs forever. But I further will & desire that my wife Mary Bledsoe do live with my son John Bledsoe during her lifetime and that my son John Bledsoe do take good care of her, and that she have a liberal support out of the proceeds of the said farm which I have given to my son John Bledsoe during lifetime. Thirdly, All the rest & residue of my personal estate (except one feather Bed & furniture which I give to my son John Bledsoe) I will, desire that it remain with my wife Mary and my son John for their support, but not to be other wise appropriated. And lastly, I do hereby constitute & appoint my son Lewis Bledsoe Executor of this my last will & testament, hereby revoking all other former will or testament by me heretofore made. In witness whereof I have hereunto set my hand and seal this 13th

(42) day of October in the year of our Lord 1825.

William Bledsoe,(seal)

(43) Signed, sealed, published, & declared to be the last will & testament of the above named WILLIAM BLEDSOE in presence of us who at his request and in his presence have hereunto subscribed our names as witnesses to the same.

A. Isaacs

Thos. Bottom.

State of Tennessee, Lincoln County Court, July term 1829, I, Brice M. Garner Clerk of said Court do certify that the foregoing last will & testament of WILLIAM BLEDSOE deceased was produced in open Court the 20 July 1829 for probate and Abraham Isaacs and Thomas Bottom the subscribing witness thereto being duly sworn state that they saw said testators sign & seal said will and heard him publish & declare the same to be his last will & testament, and that they believe him to be at the time of signing, sealing, publishing and declaring the same to be of sound mind and memory. Brice M. Garner.

By his deputy, B.M.D.Carter. Recorded 17th October 1829.

William Smiths last will. In the name of God Amen. I, WILLIAM SMITH of Lincoln County and State of Tennessee, being of sound mind and perfect memory do make and ordain this my last will and testament in manner & form following, viz, my desire is that all my just debts should be paid, After that the remainder of my property remaining to be sold, excepting the land and the money arising from the sale of the property sold, to be divided amongst such of my children as I shall hereafter name, with a deduction from those that I have already given more than the rest,(viz) I have give unto my son Jas. C. Smith one woman slave named Clary valued with other property worth one thousand dollars which is also I give him (Item) I give & bequeath unto my daughter Mary Murphy one girl slave named Rebecca & a small tract of land worth fourteen hundred dollars.

(44) (Item) I have given unto my daughter Franky Espridge, one woman slave named Crener, and a boy slave named Washington, valued with other property worth one thousand dollars.(Item) I have given unto my son John T. Smith one boy slave named John & a girl slave named Delpha, valued with other property worth one thousand dollars.(Item) I have given unto my daughter Ione Day, property worth two hundred & twenty dollars, which is all I shall give her. But lend her one girl slave named Lucy & a boy slave named Archer during her life, & at her death to be divided amongst her children, Also my desire is that my son Wm. S. Smith should be a trustee of the said property for her as it may be wasted & let her have a support from it during her life. (Item) I have given unto to my daughter Elizabeth L. Parks one girl slave named Rose & one boy slave named Samuel valued with other property worth eleven hundred dollars. (Item) I have given to my son Wm. Starke Smith 1 black boy named Harry & one girl slave named Nancy, valued with other prpperty worth one thousand dollars. Item, I have given unto my daughter Joanna Austin one woman slave named Eliza and one girl slave named Milly valued with other property worth one thousand dollars. Item, I have given unto my daughter Susanna B. Parks, one black slave named Mose and one black slave named Violet valued with other property

(44) worth twelve hundred dollars. (Item) I give and bequeath unto my son Wm. S. Smith my land that I possess with already improvements, also my family Bibb& no money, the property that I dissossed with my desire is for it to be sold, and the money to be equally divided amongst such of my children as I shall name.(viz) Fanny,Espridge and equal part,viz,Jane Days children an equal part, to lef in the case of Wm. Smith to let them have, when they shall come of age or marries,(viz) John T. Smith, I give an equal part, Joanna Hustor & children an equal part to be left in the hands of Wm. Smith. Eliza L. Parkson equal part, Susannah B. Parks an equal part. I appoint my son John T. Smith & Wm. S. Smith as my executors to this my last will & Testament In witness whereof I have set my hand and affixed my seal this 9th day of July 1829.
John Brown   Wm. Smith (seal)
I. Cooper.

State of Tennessee,Lincoln County Court,January Term,1830. I, Brice M. Garner Clerk of said Court do certify that the foregoing last will & testament of WILLIAM SMITH deceased was pro-
(45) duced in open Court the 2 of January 1830 for probate, and John Brown & I. Cooper, the subscribing witnesses thereto,being duly sworn, state that they saw the said tentator sign,& seal said will & heard him publish and declare the same to be his last will & testament and they believed him to be at the time of signing, sealing, publishing & declaring the same to be of sound mind & memory.
Recorded March 5th, 1830.   Brice M. Garner, Clerk.

John Guyders Last Will. In the name of God Amen. I, JOHN GUYDER of the State of Tennessee and County of Lincoln, being sick of body but of perfect memory, thanks be to God, calling into mind the mortality of my body and knowing that it is appointed for all men to die, do make ordain this my last will and testament, that is to say,principally and first of all, I give and recommend my soul into the hands of God, that gave it, and my body to the earth to beburied in a decent Christian manner, at the discretion of my friends,nothing doubting, but at the General resurrection I shall receive the same again by the Almighty Power of God, and as touching my worldly estate, wherewith it has blessed God to bless me with in this life, in the first place I wish my debts to be paid out of my property & the second is, I give unto Elizabeth Sharp, One negro girl named Mary, after the death of my wife, in the third place I give unto my mother, Nancy Weathers, if she is alive at this date ten dollars, in the fourth place,I leave all the balance of my property unto my wife Nancy to dispose of as she thinks proper, except my negro man named Frank, which at her death I allow him his Freedom, provided he is obedient servant, if not she may dispose of him as she thinks proper. Signed, Acknowledged in the presence of the subscribers this 13th day of December 1829.
W. McKinney   John Guyder x his mark.
Francis Patton

(45)   State of Tennessee, Lincoln County Court. I, Brice M. Garner clerk of said Court certify that the foregoing last will & testament of JOHN GUYDERS, dec'd was produced in open Court this day of Janry, 1830 for probate & W. McKinney & Francis Patton the subscribing witnesses thereto, being duly sworn, State that they saw the said testator sign & seal said will, heard him publish & declare the same to be his last will & testament that they believe him to be at the time of signing, sealing, publishing & declaring the same to be of sound mind & memory.
Recorded March 5th, 1830.   Brice M. Garner, Clerk.

(46)   Benjamin Merrill Will in 1829.
State of Tennessee, Lincoln County, June 1st, in the year of our Lord 1829. In the name of God Amen, I, BENJAMIN MERRILL of the State and County aforesaid, being now of perfect mind and memory, thanks be unto God, calling to mind, knowing it is appointed for all men once to die, do make and ordain this my last will and testament, that is to say principally and first of all, I give and recommend my soul into the hands of God that gave it, and my body I've commend to the earth, to be buried in a decent Christian burial at the discretion of my executors, nothing doubting at the general resurrection, I shall receive the same again by the mighty power of God and touching such worthy estate wherewith it has pleased God to bless me with in this life, I give and dismiss and dispose the same in the following manner & form, first, I give and bequeath to my beloved wife, Susan Merrell the house and plantation on which I now live to maintain her and her children during her widowhood, and she keeps the children together, and if she marries and scatter the children, then the land and plantation to be sold and equally divided with Polly Calvert, Margaret Merrell, Nancy Merrell, Benjamin & Iseline, and if Susan dont marry till the youngest child comes of age, then the land to be sold & let Susan have a share with the above named, likewise I will to have one bed & furniture and one cow and calf, and bacon & corn sufficient to maintain them for twelve months. Likewisw I will my daughter Margaret Merrell her bed & furniture & her horse & cow & calf, as they are now called, likewise I will Nancy Merrell and her children Andrew Merrell the sum of ten dollars for the benefit of them, also I will to my daughter Nancy one bed & furniture, and I will to my son Benj. my youngest filly & saddle, and I will to my daughter Iseline, the little Brindle heifer, & I do appoint my son John Merrell to Administer on the balance of my estate, and sell all the balance of my property, and also sell my negro man Mat, and when the money is collected make an equal divide with all of my children & wife, that is a living at that time after debts & charges are Satisfied & I further appoint my son John Merrell, sole executor of this my last will and testament, hereby revoking all other wills by me made, in witness whereof have unto set my hand & seal, this day & date, above written. Benjamin Merrell.
Signed, sealed and delivered by the above named BENJAMIN MERRELL to be his last will & testament, in the presence of us who have hereunto subscribed our names as witnesses in the
(47) presence of the testator. Witnesses, Wm. Jones, Andrew Merrill, & Garrett.

(47)   State of Tennessee, Lincoln County Court, January Term
1830. I, Brice M. Garner, Clerk of said Court do certify that
the foregoing last will & testament of BENJAMIN MERRELL dec'd,
was produced in open Court on the day 0ß January, 1830, for
probate & that William Jones, Abner Merrell, & Garrett Merrell,
the subscribing witnesses thereto, being duly sworn, State that
they saw said testator sign, & seal, said will & heard him publish and declare the same to be his last will and testament &
that they believe him to be at the time of signing, sealing,
publishing & declaring the same to be of sound mind and memory.
Recorded 5th, March 1830.

                    Brice M. Garner, Clerk.

        Jordan Reese's Will. In the name of God Amen, that I,
JORDAN REESE being weak in body but of sound & perfect mind
and memoryp or you may say this considering the uncertainty of
this mortal life & being of sound mind & perfect memory, blessed
be Almighty God for the same, do make and publish this my last
will & testament in manner and form following, that is to say,
First, I give and bequeath to my beloved wife Polly Reese, I
will & bequeath the tract of land on which I now live to my wife
Polly Reese during her life, containing two hundred and sixty
one acres. Also the following negroes,slaves, Peter, Simon,
Tinah, Betsy, my sorrel horse, gray mare, Pheby & riding gig,
my waggon and all my stock, consisting of cattle,hogs & sheep,
and all my farming tools. Also all my household & kitchen furniture, the side board at her death I give to my son Joel Reese,
and one bed,bedstead & furniture when may need it, also one bed,
bedstead & furniture to my Grand son Jordan R. Moore, when he
becomes of lawful age. I do give & bequeath to my daughter
Fanny H. Moore's three children, William H. Moore, Polly L. Moore
and Jordan R. Moore the North part of a certain tract or parcel
of land on the waters of Cane Creek to be divided as follows;
commencing in the west boundary of said survey on the top of a
(48) ridge at a corner made by William Boone, running with the various
meanders of a ridge, South east direction with the line made by
said Boone originally to a corner on side ridge lately made by
Patton Anderson containing east with the line run by said Anderson to the east boundary of said survey, the south part of said
survey will hereafter be disposed of. Also two negroes, slaves,
Tabby and her child Charity and their increase to said children,
which said land and negroes & their increase being considered
the legacy of my daughter Fanny H. Moore dec'd, I further bequeath to Jordan R. Moore a horse & saddle & bridle to be worth
one hundred dollars to be given him when he becomes of lawful
age, and a silver watch which is now in the possession of Littleberry Reese. Also I bequeath to my daughter, Finnetta W.
Boone in addition to what I have already given her by deed of
Conveyance a certain entry of land containing sixty eight acres
of land adjoining the South east part of the land originally
given, also a negro woman named Caroline & her child Isaac, and
a boy named Squire. Also I will and bequeath to my son Littleberry L. Reese the South division of the land on Cane Creek, on
which he now lives running as above stated in my deed of gift to
my grand children, also my negroes woman Celey with her increase
and my negro boy Winchester, one bay mare which he has now in

(48) possession, also my silver watch. Also, I will & bequeath to
my son Joel L. Reese the tract of land on which I now live, at
the death of my wife Polly Reese, and if he should marry before he becomes of lawful age to have all on the east side
of the creek for his own use and at his becoming of lawful age
to have all on the South side of the creek for his own benefit,
also my negro man Joe and a negro boy George, the hire of said
negroes to be for benefit during minority, also a negro girl
Betsy and her increase to go to him at the death of my wife,
Polly Reese, also my ball faced sorrel colt to be his at my
death. My negro girl Kitty to be sold at public sale and equally divided between my legal heirs, my daughter Fanny H. Moore's
dec'd, children to draw one share and the same to be equally divided between them, namely, William H. Moore, Polly L. Moore &
Jordan R. Moore. It is furthermore my will that all the negroes,
horses & oxen remain on the farm until the present crop is made
and gathered, and at the expiration of the year, my bay horse
(49) to be sold with the remaining part of my crop after setting a-
part what will be considered a sufficiency for the maintenance
of my wife Polly Reese & her family the ensuing year and the
proceeds to be equally divided between my legal heirs. After
all my debts, bond & open amounts are collected, or so many of
them as can be collected, in like manner to be equally divided
between my legal heirs after the payment of all my just debts.
Also a small thirty acre tract of land sold by the Sheriff as
the property of Thomas Hale and purchased by myself wishes to
be sold and in like manner, equally divided between my legal heirs.
It is furthermore my will that at the death of my wife Polly
Reese that all the property then remaining on the premises to
be sold and equally divided between my legal heirs. It is
furthermore my will & bequest that she educate my son Joel L.
Reese out of the proceeds of the plantation equal to the education of my other children. And lastly, I hereby appoint
my wife Polly Reese my executrix & Littleberry L. Reese &
James Fulton executors of this my last will and Testament, hereby revoking all former wills by me made. In witness whereof
I have hereunto set my hand & seal, this the sixteenth day of
our Lord One thousand eight hundred & thirty. Signed, sealed,
published & declared by the above named JORDAN REESE, to be his
last will and testament, who at his   (Jordan Reese, x his mark)
request, and at his presence have hereunto subscribed our names
as witnesses to the same.
Charles McKinney.
James D. Cole.
John P. Cole.

     I, JORDAN REESE of Lincoln County, Tennessee, not hereby
intending to revoke my last will & testament by me executed
on the 16th day of February 1830, but hereby ratifying and confirming the same, do make and publish this paper in addition,
and by way of codicil thereto which is to be deemed held &
taken as part and parcel of my said last will & testament.
And I give & bequeath to my son Joel L. Reese in addition to
what I have already given him, one yoke of young steers, one
cow & calf, one sow & pigs & six head of stock sheep which
he is to have whenever he may need them, and whenever I am

(50)   the owner of the mority of a small carry all wagon, which was heretofore purchased in the Town of Fayetteville the other half of which is owned by Ruben H. Boone, I do give and bequeath all my interest in said carry all wagon to my daughter Finnetta D. Boone. And whereas my said will to which this is a codicil I have divided that if my son Joel should marry or come of age before the death of my wife that he should have all the tract of land on which I now live lying on the east side of the Creek for his own benefit. It is my will that said devise shall be attend so far only as is herein after mentioned, that is to say, should my son marry or arrive at full age before the death of my wife, it is my will that my wife shall have and enjoy during her life the one half of the meadow, lying on the east side of the Creek. In witness whereof I have hereunto set my hand & seal this 19th day of February 1830.
Charles McKinney   Jordan Reese,x his mark.(seal)
Kenneth McKinzey.   Recorded 17th May 1830.

(51)   William Cowley's Will. In the name of God Amen. I, WILLIAM COWLEY of the County of Lincoln & state of Tennessee, being low in body but of sound mind & memory & knowing that it is appointed for all men once to die & being desirous to dispose of my Earthly goods & effect to the best interest of my little family, do make this my last will & testament,(viz) Item, 1st, I give & bequeath to Gincey, my beloved wife all my household & kitchen furniture, also my sorrel mare, saddle & bridle, one milk cow & calf, one feather bed & furniture & then for her also to have an equal share of the balance of my estate with my other children the natural heirs of my body, this is, my son Charles, Drury, George & my daughter Susann after all my just debts are paid, the balance of my property not herein above mentioned, I will &nbequeath that it be sold on a credit of twelve months (except the bonds & notes due to me) out of which I will that all my just debts be paid and then an equal division of my effects to take place as above, between my wife & children. Item,2nd, I do hereby nominate & appoint my wife Gincey Cowley my executrix of this my last will & testament, revoking all others given under my hand & seal this 9th day of February in the year of our Lord eighteen hundred & thirty, in presence of us.
Samuel Ramsey.   William Cowley x his mark.
I. Watkins.   Recorded 17 May 1830.

        John Farrar's last will. In the name of God Amen. I, JOHN FARRAR of the County of Lincoln and State of Tennessee, having attained a very advanced age and considering the uncertainty of the mortal life and being at this time through divine mercy, of sound mind & memory, do make, publish, and declare this my last will & testament to wit: 1st, It is my will & desire that all my just debts be paid. 2nd, I give & bequeath the sum of one dollar each to my ten oldest children, of the following names, viz, William, Robert, Miles, John, James,

(52) Mary, Sarah, Ann, Moses? Aaron & Franklin, making in the whole ten dollars to be equally divided among them, my reason for this not giving them more is because I have already given them more than what I will be able to give to the rest of my children, which they have already heretofore had and received.

(52) 3rd, I give and bequeath to my nine youngest children of the following names, to wit, Francis, Lucy, Nathaniel, Joseph, Nancy, Daniel, Betsy & Jane in equal propotions the whole of my worldly estate as well real & personal to be equally divided among them after paying the aforesaid sum of ten dollars to my ten oldest children as heretofore provided for. My estate hereby given and intended to be given unto my nine youngest children consist of the tract of land whereon I now live containing one hundred and sixty eight acres, one negro girl slave named Esther, now about seven years of age, together with the whole of my stock of horses, Cattle & hogs, farming tools, household & kitchen furniture and all other rights & credits, reserving unto my well beloved wife, Elizabeth Farrar the free use & possession of the whole of the aforesaid land & other property for and during the term of her natural life, for the purpose of enabling her to raise and educate our infant family, the distribution aforesaid not to take place until after her death, provided that she shall always in widowhood after my decease. 4th, If after my death my said wife Elizabeth Farrar should contract matrimony it is my will & desire, and I do hereby give and bequeath unto her an equal part with each of my children, aforesaid nine youngest children, equal to one tenth part of my aforesaid estate, hereby given to them, which said tenth part she is to have and retain for her own proper use & benefit and remain at her own disposal forever, and the whole balance of property rights & credits to pass into the hands of my other executors herein after named to be by them distributed agreeably to the provision aforesaid to my nine youngest children according to law.
5th, I do hereby nominate & appoint my well beloved wife Elizabeth Farrar and my trusty friends William Shipp & Joel

(53) Pinson, Executrix and executors of this my last will and testament, and I do hereby revoke and declare null and void all former wills and I do further declare that any changes that may hereafter take place in my property my life time shall not effect the validity of this my will & Testament. In testimony whereof I have hereunto set my hand & seal this 19th day of February, 1826.

Test.   John Farrar, (seal)
David Cowan
Lewis Shipp
Charles Williams
Eli Cole.
        State of Tennessee, Lincoln County Court, July Term, 1830. I, Brice M. Garner, Clerk of said Court do hereby certify that the foregoing last will & testament of JOHN FARRAR was presented in open Court for probate, whereupon came Lewis Shipp & Elizabeth, two of the subscribing witnesses thereto and being duly sworn, state that they saw JOHN FARRAR sign the same and heard declare it to be his last will & testament at which time they believe he was of sound mind and memory. Given under my hand this 19th day of July, A.D. 1830.
                          Brice M. Garner, Clerk.
Recorded 8th October 1830.   By C. Broyaes, D.C.

(53)   John Todd's Will. I, JOHN TODD of the County of Lincoln
& State of Tenness being of sound mind but under the affecting
hand of providence, and well knowing the uncertainty of life,
do make this my last will and testament as follows, that is to
say, whereas on or about the year 1816 I agreed to furnish my
son Samuel Todd with money for the purpose of purchasing land
for me and whereas in pursuance of such agreement I have at
various times heretofore furnished and advanced to my said son
for the purpose aforesaid the sum of two thousand, eight hundred dollars in money & other property, and whereas my said
son Samuel Todd die in the year 1818, lay out and invest the said
(54)   sum of money in a tract of land situated, lying & being in the
County of Lincoln, it being the same tract of land whereon the
said Samuel now lives, which said tract was purchased by my
said son in his own name and conveyances, therefore was executed
to him in his own name, and for his own proper use, and without expressing that it was to be held in trust for me or was
purchased for my use, Although the purchasd money or the principal part thereof, to wit, the said sum of two thousand, eight
hundred dollars was admanced by me as aforesaid, and by reason t
that the aforesaid sum of money was advanced with a View of
purchasing land for myself. I have neglected and failed to
take from my son Samuel, a receipt note, bond or other writing
evidencing the advancement thereof by me as aforesaid, and I
have no written evidence showing the advancement of the said
Sum of two thousand, eight hundred doalars to my son Samuel or
any portion thereof, except one note or bond now in the hand of
my relation EbenizerMcEwin, which note was executed to me by
my son Samuel for the sum of four hundred dollars for and in
consideration of so much money by me advanced to my son Samuel,
and constitute part of the said sum of two thousand, eight hundred dollars, which I advanced for the purchase of land as
aforesaid. Now therefore I do give, devise & bequeath to my
son Samuel Todd all & singular the tract of land & premises,
situate lying & being in the County of Lincoln and now in the
possession and occupation of the said Samuel or so much thereof,
as was purchased by the said Samuel with the said sum of $2,800
advanced by me as aforesaid, to have & to hold all & singular
the said tract of land unto & to the use of the said Samuel
Todd and his heirs forever. Item, I give and bequeath to my
daughter Elyiva Todd the sum of five hundred dollars in Cash to
be paid to her within ten days after my death, by my son
Samuel Todd out of the sum of two thousand eight hundred dollars so advanced by me to him as aforesaid. Item, I will and
direct that my son Samuel Todd out of the issue and profit of
the land so devised to him as aforesaid shall well amply &
sufficiently support and maintain my wife Margaret Todd and
my son Eli Milton Todd respectively, during their natural life
and in the event that my wife should desire to live separate
(55)   and apart from my son or should she be dissatisfied with the
support and maintenance aforesaid, her and my said son Eli
Milton Todd then & in that case my will is that upon applica-
tion for that purpose being made by my wife to my executor
herein after named, he shall and he is hereby requested & directed from time to time and each and every year set apart,
allow & apportion what sum of money in his direction not exceed-
ing the sum of one hundred and thirty eight dollars per annum,

(55) shall be annually paid by my said son Samuel for the support
and maintenance of my wife and my son Eli Milton Todd and my
will is & I do hereby declare that upon such allotment & ap-
portionment being made by my executor as aforesaid my son
Samuel shall forth with and without delay pay to my wife the
amount of money so alloted and set apart for her maintenance
and maintenance of my son Eli Milton Todd. Item, I desire
and request my son Levi Todd to pay unto my daughter Betsy
Todd the sum 6f two hundred and fifty dollars out of the proceeds of the property he received from me for and in consideration of the maintenance and support he has afforded to myself
and family. Also all the rest & residence of my goods & chattles,
and estate whatever and wheresoever and of whatever nature or
kind or quality soever.I give & bequeath the same and every
part thereof to my said son Samuel Todd, except one bed which I
hereby bequeath to my wife Margaret, and I do hereby make my
relation Robert H. McEwin sole executor of this my last will and
testament, in witness whereof I have hereunto set my hand and
affixed my seal this 4th day of September 1822.

John Todd,(seal)

Signed, sealed, published and declared by the above named JOHN
TODD ad & for his last will & testament in the present of us
who have hereto subscribed our names as witnesses therto in the
presence of the said testator & in the presence of each other.
Proven in open Court July 19th, 1830.   James Fulton
Recorded 9th October 1830.   Hiriam S. Morgan
                                             R. H. McCowen

(56)   Sarah Vance's Will. In the name of God Amen. I, SARAH
VANCE of the state of Tennessee and County of Lincoln, being
sick and weak of body, of sound mind and disposing memory,
(for which I thank God) and calling to mind the uncertainty of
human life and being desirous to dispose of all such worldly
substance as it hath pleased God to bless me with. I give and
bequeath the same in manner following, that is to say; After
all my just debts and funeral expenses is paid, I give & bequeath
to my three grand daughters, Lucinda, Sarah & Polly Vance,
daughters of Nancy Lemley, all my household furniture and
wearing apparel, and my side saddle & trunk to my grand daughter
Lucinda, whenever they shall arrive at proper age,to be by
them passed, enjoyed and disposed of as they see fit. And to
my grand son James Vance son of William Vance, I give my bay
mare to be by him possessed, enjoyed & disposed of as he sees
fit & convenient, and all the rest & residence of my estate,
both real & personal to be sold after my decease, and the proceeds of the same to be equally divided among my two sons,
William Vance & John Vance, and my four grand children, Wiley
H. Lemley, Lucinda, Sarah & Polly Vance the aforesaid afore-
named grand grand children to have an equal part with my own
(that is) their mothers'part, and wherever I have heretofore
advanced to my son James Vance at different times, about two
hundred dollars principally in cash, now in case he will pay
over the aforesaid sum of $200.00, then for him to have an
equal part with the rest and if he should fail to pay over the
aforesaid sum, for him not to have any more of my estate, as I

(56) consider the aforesaid sum fully, if not over & above his
equal part of my estate. And lastly, I do hereby constitute
& appoint my son John Vance executor of this my last will &
testament hereby revoking all other or forever wills or testaments heretofore by me made, in witness whereof I have hereunto set my hand & seal this 18th day of August in the year
of our Lord 1829. her
       Sarah x Vance, (seal)
       mark
Signed, sealed, published & declared to be the last will &
testament of the above named SARAH VANCE who at her request in
her presence have subscribed our names as witnesses to the same.
Nathan Briley x his mark.
A. Isaacs. Proved by A. Isaacs. Recorded 9 October 1830.

(57) Thomas Linthecum Will. This my last will & Testament. In
the name of God Amen. I, THOMAS LINTHECUM senior of the state
of Tennessee, Lincoln County, being weak in body but of sound
memory (Blessed be God) do this day the 24th of August 1830 do
make and publish this my last will & testament. In manner
following, that is to say; first, I give my daughter Elizabeth
Norwood one hundred & fifty acres of land, it being the tract
as parcel of land on which I now live, lying & being in State
& County above mentioned to hold to her during her natural life,
she making no waste or destruction thereupon and from & after
her decease I give & devise the same to my said grand sons,
Thomas & William Owen, it to be equally divided between them
for the term of their natural life. I also give & bequeath to Js
Jane Norwood my grand daughter, my feather bed, stead & furniture to have & to hold during her natural life. Also I give
& bequeath to my son William, fifty acres of land it being lying in the state & County aforesaid, joining the tract of land
whereon I now live, being & joining the north end of the tract
of land whereon I now live to have & to hold during his natural
life, and from & after the decease of my said son William Linthecum, then to remain to the first son or daughter of my son
William, lawfully issuing, and for default of such issue then
to the use & behoof of the aforesaid grand sons equally, Thomas
& William Owen during their natural life. I, THOMAS LINTHECUM,
as my last will & testament is that all my personal property
shall be sold to the highest bidder or to the best advantage,
on a credit of twelve months and all my just debts paid & the
remainder I give & bequeath to my daughter Elizabeth Norwood,
to have & to hold during her natural life. I, THOMAS LINTHECUM,
of the State & County aforesaid as my last will and testament
(58) is, I make and ordain John Norwood my said & sole Executor of
this my last will in Trust for the intents & purposes in this
my will contained & make these my loving friends, John Norwood
& James McDavid overseers of this my will to take care & see the
same performed according to my true intent & meaning & for their
pains & trouble I desire that each of them shall be liberally
paid & c. In witness whereof I the said THOMAS LINTHECUM have
to this my last will & testament set my hand & seal the day
above written, Signed, sealed & delivered by the said THOMAS
LINTHECUM, have to this my last will & testament set my hand
& seal the day above written. Signed, sealed & delivered by

(58) the said THOMAS LINTHECUM, as & for his last will & testament
      in the presence of us who were present at the signing & seal-
      ing thereof.
      Test.   Thomas Linthecum (Seal).
      Gideon Barnet.
      George Koonce.
      Duly proven at October Court 1830. Recorded 3d, June 1831.

          "Ann H. McCurdy's last will." In the name of God, Amen. I,
      ANNE H. MCCURDY of the State of Tennessee & County of Lincoln
      being sick & weak of body but of sound mind & disposing memory,
      for which I thank God & calling to mind the uncertainty of hu-
      man life and being desirous to dispose of all such worldly sub-
      stance as it hath pleased God to bless me with, I give & be-
      queath to my oldest daughter Mary A,H. Davis & the heirs of
      her body one negro woman called Rose and her children, that is
      in said Davis's possession. And I give & bequeath to my daughter
      Elizabeth L. McKinleys three youngest children, one negro
      woman named Mariah & her Offspring from this date, and to son
      Joseph McKinley I give eighteen or nineteen dollars, it being
      the balance of the price of my land that is in his hands.
      And I give & bequeath to my four grand children, the heirs of
      my son John H. McCurdy all my rights to the plantation I now
      live on, Containing one hundred & thirty acres as I paid son
(59) John for said land & never obtained a title from him, and his
      oldest daughter Loney A. McCurdy I give bed & one sheet, and
      to my son Nathaniel W. McCurdy I give & bequeath one negro girl
      named Jinny, and to my son Elijah McCurdy I give & bequeath one
      negro boy named Ben. And I give & bequeath to my daughter
      Rebecah H. Williamson the hire of three negroes for three years,
      to wit, one negro woman named Cinda, one girl named Sarah, &
      one boy named James Lewis and at the expiration of that time,
      I give and bequeath them to said daughter Rebecah and I give
      and bequeath to my daughter Sarather H.C. Williamson ten dollars.
      And my negro man named Joseph & all my perishable property to
      be sold and all my just debts & funeral expenses paid and the
      balance of the money arising from that sale & notes in hand I
      will that son Nathaniel W. McCurdy shall have one hundred dol-
      lars, and son Elijah shall have fifty dollars, son-in-law Wm.
      Davis $30.00, and the remainder of the money, if there should
      be any, to be equally divided between Mary Davis, Elizabeth
      McKinley, Rebeccah Williamson & John H. McCurdys heirs, Nath-
      aniel W. McCurdy & Elijah McCurdy, and I will that my negro
      woman named Sally to my daughter Mary Davis & two negro boys
      one married,Josiah & the other Ben, goes alone with her to lend
      on her as long as she lives & at the death of said negro woman
      I will that Josiah belong to my daughter Elizabeth McKinley's
      three youngest children & Ben to my daughter Rebecah, and I do
      appoint my son-in-law Wm. Davis, John L, Jackson, Nathaniel W.
      McCurdy or Elijah McCurdy or any of them to be my Executor of
      this my last will & testament, in witness whereof I have set
      my hand and affixed my seal this 31st day of December in the
      year of our Lord one thousand eight hundred & thirty.
                                         Anne H. McCurdy, (seal).
(60) Signed, sealed, published and acknowledged to be the last will

(60)   and testament of the above named ANNE H. McCURDY in the presence of us who at her request in her presence hath hereto subscribed our names as witnesses to the same.
J. Pinkerton.
Joseph Dean.

State of Tennessee, Lincoln County Court, January Term, 1831. I, Brice M. Garner, Clerk of said Court do certify that the due execution of the foregoing will of ANNE H. McCURDY was proven in open Court by the oaths of J. Pinkerton & Joseph Dean the subscribing witnesses thereto and that the said ANNE H. McCURDY was of sound mind at the time of executing the same, whereupon the Court order the same to be recorded & certified. Brice M. Garner, Clerk.
Recorded 27th June 1831, By C. Boyles, D. C.

Joseph Greer last will & C. In the name of God, Amen. I, JOSEPH GREER being weak in body, but of sound mind & disposing memory, first of all I commit my soul to God who gave it. 1st, my will is that after all my debts are paid, my remaining property shall be disposed of in the following manner; 2nd, all the land which I hold in Lincoln County shall be divided equally between my beloved wife Mary Ann, and my childred, giving her choice of situation for her residence, except the place whereas John H. Moore now lives, which is hereby reserved to him, and to which I wish my heirs to make him title agreeably to the following lines to wit: Beginning at William Olds', south west corner, running thence to the fork of the creek, below where the said John now lives, thence in a course to correspond with said line to the top of the ridge or the South of the creek, thence along the top of the ridge, eastwardly until it intersects the line of a three hundred and eighteen acre tract entered in the name of Thomas Talbott, thence North along said line, until it intersedts said Olds' line, thence west with said line to the beginning. 3rd, My negroes I wish to be divided equally between my beloved wife Mary Ann and my children. 4th, All the land & property I bought at Thomas Talbots sale I wish to be sold and after retaining the
(61)   money I paid out for said land & property with lawful interest from the state of said sale, the balance I wish to be disposed of in the following manner (to wit), to Eliza Talbott three thousand dollars, to Joseph A. Talbott two thousand dollars, & to Thomas Talbott two thousand; To Eli Talbott--to Polly Hogg--to Sarah Fletcher--To Caroline Talbott -- 5th, I hold two hundred acres of land in the Western district, which I have authorized John L. Harmon to sell for my benefit when such sale is effected my will is that the money arising from such sale shall be divided equally between my beloved wife & children. 6th, My land in Roane County, East Tennessee lying on Emery River, I also wish to be sold and the proceeds thereof divided as above. 7th, The land in Kentucky, belonging to the heirs of Joab Harmon deceased, my beloved wife being one of the heirs, and I being authorized as agent to dispose of the same for the benefit of all the heirs, I wish this land to be sold & such as have conveyed to me without consideration to have an equal proportion of the money arising from said sale, and the Balance divided amongst all my heirs. 8th, It is my

(61)
will that on the payment by my brother John, of the money
I paid for his part of the mills below town on Elk River, at
the Marshall sale, with legal interest from the date of said
sale to my heirs, together with the money I paid out & the
interest thereas for thirty acres of land, which land formerly
belonged to Brother John, then & in that Case, I wish my heirs
to convey back to him his part of said mills, together with
the thirty acres of land aforesaid. 9th, I hold a Mortgage
on my brother Johns' negroes, and my will is that he pay my
brother Thomas five hundred & two dollars, which I assured to p
pay him on my Brother Johns acct. and which expressly require
shall be paid on said mortgage, then & in that case my will
is that the said negroes be released from said mortgage with
the Plantation on which my brother John now lives, I purchased
at Marshalls' sale, which plantation I wish my heirs to (recov-
er) to on his paying the money I paid for it, with lawful interest from the date of said sale, which money I wish to be
divided as heretofore expressed. 11th, It is probable there
is at this time may be or shortly will be a quantity of Iron
at dittoes landing of mine, the rents of or every lands which
I think advisable to sell then afa sale can be effected, with-

(62)
out too much loss & the money applied. 12th, The estate of
Elizabeth Williamson deceased, I bought at Sheriffs sale,
which estate I wish conveyed to her only child Sarah Jane, on
payin to my heirs the money I gave for it, which shall be disposed of as other money of my estate & so _-. I appoint as my
executors to have this my last will & testament carried into
effect, to wit, my beloved Mary Ann, my son Joseph, my brother
Thomas, and John H. Moore, done this 23rd February 1831, in
the presence of us.
Elliott Hickman.   Joseph Greer, (seal)
Greenfield Buchanan,

        (Mary Parr's last will & Testament.) I, MARY PARR con-
sidering the uncertainty of this mortal life & being of
sound mind and memory, blessed be Almighty God for the same,
first, that all my just debts be paid, I will & bequeath unto
my daughter Jane Collier, my cupboard & its contents & one
chest & its contents, I will & bequeath unto my son Isham
Parr & James Collier & Fanny Read my property to be equally
divided between them, then & I appoint Isham Parr my executor,
witness my hand & seal this 7th January 1831.
                                        Mary Parr x her mark.
Signed, sealed & delivered in presence of,   (seal)
James R. Brown & Benjamin Rives.

(63)
        (William Ingles last will.) In the name of God, Amen, I,
WILLIAM INGLE of the State of Tennessee & County of Lincoln,
being weak of body, But of sound mind & disposing memory, do
make my last will & Testament in manner following, to wit;
First, my will & desire is that my just debts that I am now
owing, be paid out of money on hand or debts that is owing to
me & if there should not be a Sufficiency, my desire is that
any of my estate be sold on a credie of 12 months to supply
the deficiency. 2d My desire is that all the residence of my
Estate both real & personal, be left in the hand of my wife,
Sarah Ingle, in order to support her & enable her to raise,

(63) and educate my children during her natural life, except as hereafter named. 3rd, And at my wife's death all my property (except my land) to be sold & the money arising therefrom to be equally divided between my five following children, viz, Leonard W. Ingle, Polly Ingle, Permelia A. Ingle, Jacob Ingle & Benjamin B. Ingle, & my land to be also equally divided between my above five named children, except as hereinafter named. 4th, My desire is if a debt comes against me from E. Tennessee, as legatee of Nicholas Carriges, deceased, in order to meet it, that my part of the land I inherited from my father be sold, and if there should not be a sufficiency to meet said demand, then any property that can be best Spared be sold & the money thence arising go to settle said demand. 5th, And if my wife should alter her way of living by a second marriage, then & in that case my desire is that all my property, except my land, be sold & the money arising thence, be divided equally between my wife & my five above named children, & that my wife have in her possession the 56 acres of land that I purchased of Christian Carriges, including the building whereas I now live, during her life & at her death said land to be divided as above named in the 3rd Item. 6th, And if any of my children should arrive of lawful age while my wife has all my land in her possession, my will & desire is that they by using industry may have any part of to work, not tho, to interfere with the said 56 acres whereon I now live & that my interest in the land whereon Katharine Carriges now lives be sold if the above named debt from East Tennessee comes against my estate, But if not to remain with

(64) my estate to be divided as above, & 7th, I hereby appoint, authorize & empower my two friends, Howell Johnston, & Samuel Boone executors of this my last will & Testament, Believing that they will have it duly executed agreeable to the tenor thereof to the best of their abilities. Sept. 28th 1830. Signed, sealed, published & declared to be the last will & Testament of Wm. INGLE, revoking all others in presence as,

Abner Steed   Paul Ingle
Howell Johnston   Orpot Johnston x his mark.

State of Tennessee, Lincoln County Court, April Term, 1831. I, Brice M. Garner Clerk of said Court do Certify that the due executors of the foregoing will of WILLIAM INGLE was proven in open Court by the oaths of Abner Steed & Paul Ingle, two of the subscribing witnesses thereto, and that the said, Wm. INGLE was of sound mind at the time of executing the same, whereupon the Court ordered the same to be recorded & Certified (Sept. 2nd 1831 Recorded.)

                                        Brice M. Garner, Clk.

Morgan Davis last will & Testament, In the name of God, Amen. I, MORGAN DAVIS of the County of Lincoln & State of Tennessee, Being weak in body, But of perfect mind & memory, thanks be to the Almighty God, calling unto mind the immortality of my body & knowing it is appointed for all men once to die, do make & ordain this my last will & Testament, that is to say, principally & first of all I give & recommend my soul into the hands of God that gave it & my body recommended to the earth to be buried in a decent Christian Burial at the

64)

discretion of my executors which I shall appoint, nothing
doubting. But at the general resurrection I shall receive
the same again by the mighty power of God, and as touching
such worldly estate as wherewith it has pleased God to bless
me with in this life, I give & dismiss of the same in the
manner & form following, First it is my will that my four

(65)

daughters, to wit, Elizabeth Smith, Sally Clayton, Ann Williams & Hannah Halbert have fifty dollars each to be paid out
of my money that is owing to me,& my household furniture to
be equally divided amongst my said four daughters and it is
my will that my beloved Daughter Mary Clayton have thirty
dollars paid out of my money that is owing to me, It is also
my will that beloved son Johnathan have thirty dollars to be
equally divided amongst them, to be paid out of my money that
is owing to me. It is also my will that my beloved son Amos
have my negro girl Malinda and all her increase if ever she
has any, it is also that at my decease that my beloved sons
Jesse & John have all the balance of my estate equally divided
between them. I do also appoint my beloved sons Jesse & Amos
executors of this my last will & Testament, & I do certify &
confirm this to be my last will & Testament revoking all
other wills heretofore by me made. In witness whereof I have
hereunto set my hand & affixed my seal this 15th day of October, one thousand eight hundred & twenty one.

Morgan Davis x his mark (seal)

Signed & sealed in the presence of us.
Abraham Summers.
Jacobs Albright.

State of Tennessee, Lincoln County Court, April Term,
1831. I, Brice M. Garner, Clerk of the Court aforesaid, do
Certify that the due execution of the foregoing will of
MORGAN DAVIS was proven in ppen Court by the oaths of Abraham
Summers & JacobsAllbright who say they heard the said MORGANₐ
DAVIS Acknowledge this to be his last will & Testament & they
believed at the timeof signing, sealing & publishing the same
he was of sound mind & memory, which is ordered to be recorded & certified, Recorded Sept. 2nd, 1831.

Brice M. Garner, Clerk.

John Rosson's last will & Testament. In the name of God,
Amen, this eighteenth day of June in the year of our Lord, One
thousand eighteen hundred & twenty five; I, JOHN ROSSON of
Lincoln County & State of Tennessee, Being weak in Body But of
Sound & perfect mind & memory & calling to remembrance the
uncertainty estate of this transitory life and that all flesh
must yield to death, whenever it shall please God to call, I
do make, ordain, constitute & declare this my last will & Testament revoking all other will or wills heretofore by me made,
or declared & this only to be Taken for my last will. And now
for the settling of my temporal estate, first that all my just
debts be paid by my executors in convenient time after my decease. I order, give & dispose of the same in manner & form,
following, to wit; I give & bequeath to my well beloved wife
Bethany Rosson three negroes, to wit, Philip & Ruth,his wife,
& George and all or so much of the household or kitchen furniture as she shall think proper for her own use, also all the

(6)

stock of every description, & the plantation utensils during her life or widowhood, provided neverless that if she see cause to give away any part of the property in her lifetime, that the same be equally divided amongst my six children hereafter named, and all the property not specially named to the legatee in this will, is at my death & the death of my wife, then to be equally divided amongst my six children to wit, Sarah S. Bagley, wife of Nathan Bagley, & Joseph Rossen. William Rossen & Mishael Cook wife of Nanie Short, & Henry B. Rosson & Candia Short, wife of John Short. Item, I give to my daughter Sarah S. Bagley one negro boy named Anthony. I give & bequeath to my son Joseph one negro girl named Nancy. I give and bequeath to my son William Rosson one negro boy named Wright. I give and bequeath to my daughter Mishael Cook 1 negro boy named Philip. I give & bequeath to my son Henry B. Rosson 1 negro Girl named Nelly. I give & bequeath to my daughter Cordia Short, 1 negro boy named Willis. I give & bequeath to my grand daughter Matilda McMaster 1 negro girl named Mary, to her & her heirs forever, Nevertheless, if the said Matilda should die without heir, then the said negro girl Mary is to return to my children, to be equally divided amongst my six children, above named. Also I give & bequeath to the said Matilda McMaster, one horse, bridle & saddle, one Bed & furniture & Bedstead, one cow & calf, one ewe & lamb,.Also the land on which I now live I give & bequeath to my two sons Wm., & Henry B. Rosson, one hundred acres each, to be divided by a line beginning in the middle of the North boundary line & running due South to the middle of the South boundary line, William Rosson to have the west end, & Henry B. Rosson to have the

(67)

east end, it is also my will that the three negroes named in the forepart of the will for the support of my wife & self during our lives & one girl named Priscilla that my three daughters have each one, Sarah S. Bagley, Mishael Cook, & Candia Short, each of which negroes is to be valued so that each one's part shall be equal & the remaining negro or negroes,, if that should be the case, are to be valued or sold, also all the household & kitchen furniture & all the Stock of every description with Plantation utensils, are to all be valued or sold, as my Executors hereafter named, shall think best, and the whole amount arising therefrom to be equally divided amongst my six children above named, to wit, Sarah S. Bagley, Joseph Rosson, William, Mishael Cook, Henry B. Rosson & Candia Short. I, also constitute, ordain & appoint my three sons, Joseph Rosson, William Rosson & Henry B. Rosson executors to this my last will & Testament, revoking & annulling all other will or wills heretofore by me made, and these my executors are to execute & perform all things according to the true intent & meaning herein contained, Signed & declared in presence of, Silas M. Clelland   John Rosson (seal)
William Cowden
John Cowder.

State of Tennessee, Lincoln County Court, Term 1831. I, Brice M. Garner Clerk of the Court of Pleas & Quarter session for said County, do Certify Certify the foregoing will of JOHN ROSSON was proven in open Court by the oaths of Silas Mc-

(67) McClelland & William Cowden who said they heard the said JOHN ROSSON acknowledge this to be his last will & Testament, & they believe that at the time of signing, sealing & declaring the same he was of sound mind & memory, all of which is recorded & Certified. Recorded 3d, Sept. 1831.
Brice M. Garner, Clerk.

(68) Sarah Stewart's Last will & So. In the name of God Amen. I, SARAH STEWART, at present of Lincoln County and State of Tennessee, Considering the uncertainty of Life and wishing to dispose of my worldly goods and estate in a just and right manner, do hereby make this my last will & testament and revoking all others by me heretofore made, first after all my justdebts are paid, it is my will that all the property should remain unsold, and kept for the use of the children to keep house as long as they see proper or as long as the youngest child should come of age, and then Mary M. Stewart is to have fifty dollars more than the rest of the children to her part of the property, and then the property is to be equally divided Between Mary M. Stewart and the rest of the children. But if Mary M. Stewart Should marry, I wish the property to be divided at that time as above mentioned. At At the same time I do make or appoint John A. Allen of the same County for a Executor of this my last will and testament, to which I have hereunto set my hand and seal or caused the same to be done, this 18th February, 1832.
Sarah Stewart x her mark.
Signed and Sealed in the presence of us.
Attest.
Josiah Roughton.
Isaac I. Roughton.

State of Tennessee, Lincoln County Court, April Term 1832. The last will and testament of SARAH STEWART was this day exhibited in open Court for probate, whereupon came Josiah Roughton and Isaac I. Roughton the subscribing witnesses thereto, who being first duly Sworn agreeably to law, say they heard the afore mentioned SARAH STEWART acknowledge the will of which the foregoing is a copy, to be her last will and testament, and that she was at the time of publishing, sealing, signing and declaring the same of sound mind & memory which is ordered to be so certified, whereupn came J. H. Allen the executor named in the will who entered in Bond with security & so. and took the oath by law prescribed. In witness whereof I have hereunto set my name this 16th April 1832.
Brice M. Garner, Clk.
By Peter R. Garner, D. C.

(69) Peter Vaugn's last will & Testament. The last will & Testament of PETER VAUGN of the State of Tennessee, Lincoln County. I, PETER VAUGN of the State of Tennessee, considering the uncertainty of this mortal life and being of Sound mind and memory, Blessed be Almighty God for the same, do make and publish this my last will and testament in manner and form following: First, that all my lawful debts be paid. Second, I give and bequeath unto my beloved wife Sarah, all my real & personal estate during her natural life or widowhood, consisting of the plantation on which I now live,

(69) negroes, Lindsey, Judith, Jenny,Washington, Dilly, Sampson,
Dick, Caroline, Jack, together with my horses, cattle, hogs,
sheep, and present standing crop, and all my farming tools,
too tedious to mention, and all my household and kitchen
furniture. Thirdly, it is my will that my wife Sarah give
to my son Wm. Vaugn, two hundred dollarsout of the said property that I have bequeathed to her, within four months from
this date, of this my will and testament. Fourthly, it is
my will and testament that at the death of my wife Sarah, or
if she should change her state of widowhood to a married State,
the above estate be divided between my children, William,
Samuel H.,Nancy, Polly and Elizabeth Vaugn, and my said wife
Sarah, lastly I do hereby appoint my wife Sarah, Executrix
of this my last will and Testament, hereby revoking all
former wills by me made. In witness whereof I have hereunto
set my hand and seal, this the 25th July in the year of our
Lord, one thousand eight hundred and thirty one. Signed,
sealed, published and declared by the above named.

                                        his
                              Peter x Vaugn, (seal)
                                        mark
Signed, sealed, published and declared by the above named,
PETER VAUGN, to be his last will and testament in the pres-
ence of us who have hereunto subscribed our names in the
presence of the Testator.
Charles McKinney
Wm. Bright
James Wilson.

(70)   State of Tennessee,Lincoln County Court,October Term,
1831. The last will and testament of PETER VAUGN was exhibited in open Court for probate, whereupon came Charles Mc-
Kinney and Wm. Bright two of the subscribing witnesses thereto, and made oath that they saw the said PETER VAUGN sign
said will, or heard him acknowledge the same to be his last
will and testament and that he was at the time of signing
the same of Sound mind and memory. In witness whereof I,
Brice M. Garner, clerk of said Court have hereunto set my
hand this 17th October 1831.
                              Brice M. Garner, Clk.
                              By Peter R. Garner, D. C.

     Samuel Jenkins last will & Testament. In the name of
God, Amen. I, SAMUEL JENKINS of the County of Lincoln and
State of Tennessee, being weak in body, But of Sound mind
and memory, do this 12th day of December in the year of our
Lord, one thousand eight hundred and thirty, this my last
will and testament. I leave to my lawful and loving wife,
Ise, the plantation on which I now live, upon, her natural
life, also the household and kitchen furniture and two feather
beds and furniture, one clay bank mare, and plantation, tools,
and one white cow, all the hogs belonging to the plantation,
at the death of my wife I give to my son George the plantation
that is left to her, containing fifty acres, and the said
man one saddle and Bridle, I also give to my Son, James,
twenty five acres of land adjoining the fifty acres on the

(70) east, I also give to my daughter Sally, one cow, and three
sheep, one feather Bed and furniture, one cotton wheel. I
give to my daughter Elizabeth, one cow and three sheep, one
feather Bed and furniture, one Cotton wheel. I leave not
any thing to my first children, knowing that I gave them a
great deal more than I have at this time to give to those
that I have had by my last wife, which is, Betsy, Jencey,
Murphy, Susannah,Cipam, Mary, Murphy, my son Joseph and Arrow.
(71) These are the names of my first children, that I consider
that I give them more by far, than I have to give these last
ones. I also leave John Smith, Esqr. and William Spencer,
my executors to the said estate.   his
Test.   Samuel x Jenkins.
Thomas Spencer   mark
James M. Spencer.
     State of Tennessee, Lincoln County Court, January Session,
1832. The last will and testament of SAMUEL JENKINS, deceased,
was this day produced in open Court for probate and thereupon
came, Thomas Spencer and James M. Spencer the subscribing
witnesses thereto, and being duly sworn according to law, said
they heard the said SAMUEL JENKINS acknowledge the same to be
his last will and testament, and that he was at the time of
signing, sealing, publishing & declaring the same of Sound
mind and memory. In witness whereof I, Brice M. Garner have
hereunto set my hand, this 16th January 1832.
                              Brice M. Garner, Clk.
                              By Peter R. Garner, D. C.

     Drewry Austin & last will & Testament. Lincoln County,
State of Tennessee. In the name of God, Amen. I, DREWRY
AUSTIN being in a low State of health, But of sound mind, do
make this my last will and revoking all others made by me
heretofore. Item, 1st, my wish and desire that all my just
debts shall be paid out of perishable property. 2nd, I give
and bequeath all my cattle, property to my grand daughter,
Annes Bolen, at the decease of me and my wife Betsy Austin.
Item 2, I give and bequeath to my grand daughter Annes Bolen
first Choice of two Beds and furniture, also 2 Stand of Curtains that She Spun and wove herself. Also a pewter dish.
3. I give to my son Harris and William Phillips, one Bed and
sheet to be equally divided between the two, at our death.
4. I give to Thomas Bolen, one dollar out of my property, 5th,
(72) I want the balance of my property equally divided amongst the
balance of my heirs at our decease, in witness whereof, I
have hereunto set my hand and seal, the day and date first
above written. Signed and acknowledged in the presence of,
Benjamin Rives.   his
Mathew Carter.   Drewry x Austin.
Henry S. Gill.   mark

     State of Tennessee, Lincoln County Court, October Term
1831. The last will and Testament of DREWRY AUSTIN was produced in open Court for probate, whereupon come Benjamin
Reeves, Mathews Carter and Henry S. Gill the subscribing witnesses thereto, and being duly sworn, say they saw DREWRY
AUSTIN sign, seal, publish, or heard him acknowledge this to
be his last will and that he was at the time of signing,

(72)   sealing and declaring the same of Sound mind and memory. In witness whereof, I, Brice M. Garner have hereunto set my hand this 25th October 1831.

Brice M. Garner, Clk.
By Peter R. Garner, D. C.

"David Reads last will & Testament." Lincoln County, West Tennessee, Sept. 6th 1831. DAVID REIDS will. In the name of God Amen. I, DAVID REED, Calling to mind the uncertain of this mortal life and being of sound mind and memory, do make and publish this my last will and testament in manner and form following,(viz) 1. That all my lawful and just debts shall be paid. 2. I give and bequeath to my son John Hamilton, my plantation on which I now live, to him and his heirs forever. 3. I give and bequeath to my daughter Martha Jane my

(73)   negro girl Anna, to her and her heirs forever. 4. I do furthermore give and bequeath to my daughter Martha Jane two Beds, together with their furniture to her forever. 5. I do give and bequeath to my son John Hamilton one bed and its furniture forever. 6. I do will that the balance of my property shall be sold after my decease to pay off all the lawful demand against my estate, and should there be any remnants over, it shall be divided between my two aforesaid Children, John Hamilton and Martha Jane, giving John Hamilton fifty dollars more than Martha Jane. 7. I do hereby appoint my Brother Wm. M. Read and brother-in-law William Hamilton, my executors of this my last will and testament. In witness whereof, I set my hand and seal this fifth night of Sept,1831. Witnesses.

Eli Taylor   David Reed, (seal).
Johnathan Anderson
Hugh Taylor

State of Tennessee, Lincoln County Court, April Term 1832. The last will of DAVID REED was exhibited in open Court for probate, and on motion of Wm. M. Read, and Wm. Hamilton the said will was exhibited in open Court for probate whereupon Come Eli Taylor and Hugh Taylor, two of the subscribing witnesses thereto, and made oath that they saw the said DAVID REED sign, seal, publish and declare the same to be his last will and testament, and that he was at the time of signing, sealing, publishing and declaring the same of sound mind and memory. Given under my hand this 17th October 1831.

Brice M. Garner, Clk.
By Peter R. Garner, D. C.

Barnabas Boyles, Senr. last will and Testament. I, BARNABAS BOYLES, Senr. of Lincoln County and State of Tennessee, wishing to dispose of what little property I may die possessed of , in such way as I think proper do make this my last will amd testament, as follows: to wit, I expect to die, and owe to no man one dollar; But if I should owe debts I wish them paid. I give to my daughter Rachael Paradise, one dollar, believing that she can do very well without any more. To my daughter Sally Reasons, I give five dollars, To my Son

(74)   Barnabas Boyles, who has always been kind to me I give my negro boy, Sam and negroe fellow Peter, to my daughter Nancy,

(74) I give my negroe girl Amanda, to my daughter Patty, I give
my negro girl Matilda, To my daughter Jane, I give my negro
boy Jacobs, To my daughter Lucinda I give my mulatto girl,
Grace, and my mulatto girl Eliza, twin Children, and further,
I give to my son Barnabas and my daughters my negro women
Epsey, and her increase if any, to be equal between them,
that is my daughters Nancy, Patsy, Jane and Lucinda, which
said negro is to remain with my daughters, last named above,
for their use and benefit, or if any one or more of them shall
marry, then the negro woman Eppie to remain herself to the exclusive use of those that remain unmarried during their lives,
and then to be equally divided at the death of those that
may remain unmarried, between the heirs of those who may
have married, if any, if not to the balance of my children,
in equal proportions. In Testimony whereof I have hereunto
set my hand and affixed my seal, this 24th December, 1830.
Signed, sealed, published and declared to be the last will &
testament of the said B. BROYLS, Senr. & in his presence, by
his request have set our names as witnesses. his
R.H.C.Bagley.   Barnabas x Boyles (seal)
C. Broyles.   mark
    State of Tennessee, Lincoln County Court, October Term,
1832. The last will and testament of BARNABAS BOYLES, Senr.
deceased, was produced in open Court for probate, and thereupon
came R.H.C.Bagley and Charles Boyles the subscribing witnesses thereto and being duly Sworn according to laws, say they
heard the said BARNABAS BOYLES acknowledge this to be his
last will and testament, and that he was at the time of sealing, signing and declaring the same of Sound mind and memory,
which is ordered to be recorded. Given under my hand this
19th October 1831. Recorded June 1832.
                                Brice M. Garner, Clk.
                                By Peter R. Garner, D.C.

(75)   Abednego Foster last will and Testament. State of Tennessee, Lincoln County, February 18th 1832. The last will &
Testament of ABEDNEGO FOSTER, I will and bequeath my soul to
them that giveth and my body to be buried in good order, and
my funeral expenses to be paid out of my estate, I desire
that all of my just debts be paid,-question 1st, I will and
bequeath all my personal and real estate to my wife Nancy
Foster, her lifetime or during her widowhood for the use and
benefit of my children. question 2nd, If my wife Nancy Foster
should marry, I wish her to have a childs part, and the balance to be equally distributed amongst all my children, question 3, I will and bequeath to my son Washington Foster two
thirds of my lands at death or marriage of my wife. question
4, I now Conclude my last will and Testament. Sealed and assigned in the presence of us & C. The day and date above
written.
Attest.   A. B. Foster, (seal)
R.I.Harrison.
Hillery C. Stokes.
John S. Johnson.
    State of Tennessee, Lincoln County Court, April Term
1832. The last will and Testament of ABEDNEGO FOSTER was this

(75) day in open Court produced for probate, and thereupon
came R. I. Harrison and Hillery M. Stokes, two of the subscribing witnesses thereto, who being duly sworn according
to law, said they heard the said A. FOSTER acknowledge the
same of which the above is a copy to be his last will and
testament, and that he was at the time of Signing, sealing,
publishing and declaring the same of sound mind and memory,
which is ordered to be so certified whereupon came John Marsh
Senr. the executor by Court appointed, and took the oath
prescribed by law, entered into bond and gave security according to law, given under my hand this 16th of April 1832.

Brice M. Garner, Clk.
Recorded June 15th 1832.   By Peter R. Garner, D.C.

(76)   John Sivily's last will & Testament. In the name of
God Amen, I, JOHN SIVELYS, Senr. of Lincoln County, State of
Tennessee, being in the full enjoyment of health, also being sound in mind, though far advanced in years, considering
the uncertainty of this present life, and the absolute certainty of death, and further wishing that there should be
no disturbance after my decease, to arise as to the distribution of what property I may leave behind, do make this my
last will and testament, hereby revoking any or all wills
made of a previous date, by me at any time. First, It is
my chief and noblest desire to give into the hand of the Cre-
ator of the universe, my immortal spirit, as his rightful
due, to be placed anywhere at his Sacred disposal, and my
body I request to be decently interred in a Christian like
manner, avoiding every thing like pomp or show, and after
all necessary expenses of my interment have been paid by the
executors whom I shall appoint, I desire the balance to be
appropriated in manner following, to wit,(viz) First, to my
beloved wife Leah Sivily, I will and Bequeath the house in
which I live with other necessary outhouse with as much of
the household and kitchen furniture as she may want. Also
50 acres of land at the lower part of my farm, around the house
house which I now live in, including as much woodland as
will answer for fire wood and also to keep the fence of the
aforesaid 50 acres in repair, also 2 horses, 2 cows, and 2
yer---, also 2 breeding sows and 3 barrows, with as many
other hogs as will do her, until she can raise a stock to
have pick of the aforesaid. Item, of all which I may have
at my death, also one plow and as many tools as she may
want to carry on the farm, provided that the young children stay with her. Also one negro girl named Dolly to wait
upon her, also as much provision as will answer for her and
the children with her, until such time as she can raise a
crop, all the aforesaid property to remain with her as long
as she lives, or as long as she remains my widow. After-
wards to be disposed of as I shall hereafter appoint. I
will and bequeath to my son Daniel Sivily, 50 acres of land,
on which he lives, to be priced at $3.00 per acre, the same
(77) which I give for it, Covering as follows, Northeast corner,
Spanish Oak,pin oak and Elm, Northwest, Spanish oak, a dogwood and Beech, unto my son John Sivily (my son) I will and

(77) bequeath 70 acres of land, on which he lives, to be priced
$150, the same which Daniels comes to, Covering Northeast
Poplar, Sugar tree, and Beech, N. West, 2 Beeches, Sugar
tree and Lynn. Also to my Son Benjamin, after my wife's
death or intermarriage the 50 acres given to her with the
improvements to be his, to be valued at $3 per acre, the
same price as the other named sons beforementioned. Unto
my son George Sivily I will and bequeath 66 acres of land,
which he now has in his possession, above where my son John
lives, to be priced at $3 per acre, Amounting to $198 unto
my sons Martin and Harrison I will and bequeath 109 acres
of land lying between the 50 acres given to my son Benjamin,
after my wifes death, or intermarriage and the land given to
my sons, Daniel and John to be equally divided between them,
and valued at $5 per acre, amounting to $545. I will and
bequeath to my son Jacob Sivily 100 acres off land lying at
the head of Short Creek, which I entered agreeably to law,
at $2 per acre, amounting to $200. Said land begins at a
poplar and Beech at the head of the Spring. All the other
land which I possess at my death I wish to be divided equally amongst the following heirs (viz) (sons) Daniel, John,
George, Jacobs, Martin, Benjamin & Harrison. (daughters)
Elizabeth, Rachael and Leah. I will and bequeath unto my
daughters above mentioned, to their bodily heirs the portion of my estate, which will come to them after an equal
division is made between the heirs before mentioned. I wish
all personal property to be sold with all other property I
may possess, not otherwise appropriated to be sold at public sale, and adding the amount of sales with the amount
of Land bequeathed, at my valuation, the whole sum to be divided equally aming my heirs, which I have mentioned before.
Also at my wife's death or intermarriage all the property
in her hands not bequeathed, I wish to be sold, and after
her funeral expenses are paid, the remainder I wish to be
divided equally among the forementioned heirs,which I
have named. Lastly, having full confidence in the interesty
(78) and honesty of my sons Daniel & John, I do Therefore appoint them my sole executors, to carry into effect everything as contained in this my last request. Also I wish
them to see that nothing is lost or wasted or squandered
away on the farm on which my wife lives. In witness whereof I have hereunto set my hand and affixed my seal this
thirteenth day of April in the year of our Lord, eighteen
hundred and thirty one. Signed & sealed in the presence.
for acknowledged before.   his
Daniel Sivily   John x Sivily,Senr. (seal)
John Stacy   mark
Jacob Tipps

    State of Tennessee, Lincoln County Court.April Term,
1832. The last will and Testament of John Sivily, Senr.,
deceased was produced in open Court for probate, whereupon
Came John Stacy and Jacob Tipps two of the subscribing
witnesses thereto, who first being duly Sworn agreeably to
law, say that they said JOHN SIVIlY acknowledged the same
to be his last will and testament, and that he was at the
time of signing, sealing, publishing and declaring the same

(78) of sound mind and memory, whereupon came John Sivily Junr.
and David Sivily, the executor named in the will, who took
the oath prescribed by law and gave bond with security on
this 16th April 1832. Given under my hand at office in
Fayetteville in the year of our Lord eighteen hundred and
thirty two.
                    Brice M. Garner, Clk.
                    By Peter R. Garner, D.C.
Recorded June 18th 1832.

(79)   Thomas Leonard's last will & Testament. In the name of
God, Amen. I, THOMAS LEONARD, of the County of Lincoln, State
of Tennessee, do make, ordain and declare this instrument
which is written to be my last will and testament, revoking
all others---Impression all my debts of which there are but
few, and none of magnitude which are to be punctually and speedily paid, and the legacies herein after mentioned, or bequeathed, are to be discharged as soon as circumstances will
permit, and in the manner directed. Item 1st, To my beloved
wife, I give and bequeath the use, interest and profits with
the future increase, if there should be any, one negro woman
named Hannah, and Moses her husband, and Nancy (commonly called)
Nanny) also all my household furniture, belonging to her room,
and all the kitchen furniture to use and dispose of as she
may think proper, also my will and desire that my wife Hannah,
Leonard, shall remain quietly in peacable possession of the
room Commonly called hers during her natural life. After the
death of my wife Hannah, to revert back to my son Griffith
Leonard. Item 2nd, To my son Robert Leonard I give four hundred dollars, which money is to be made, if not in hand, out
of my estate, hereafter bequeathed to my son Griffith Leonard.
Item 3rd, To my daughter Hannah Moore, wife of --- Moore, fifty
and one half acres of land, now in the possession of said man,
(80) situated, lying and being in the County of Lincoln, and State
aforesaid, and bounded as follows, To wit: Beginning at a white
oak on North west Corner, running thence east, one hundred and
eighty poles to a dogwood, and two bushes, a north east corner
of my tract, thenceSouth fifty poles, thence west and north to
the beginning for compliment during her natural life, after her
death my will and desire id that my grandson Thomas Delroose,
shall have the before mentioned and described tract, to his own
proper use and benefit. Item 4th, To my son Griffith Leonard,
I give and bequeath the balance of my land with the appuntenance
thereunto belonging as per deed for two hundred and thirty acres
after what has been before described for, bequeath to my
daughter Hannah Moore, as pr bound before described leaving as
per deed, one hundred and seventy nine acres and one half,be
the same more or less, also all the household furniture belonging to the balance of my house, and all my farming tools,
belonging to the plantation of every description, all the
stock of hogs, horses, cattle and sheep, wagon and geer,still
tubs and all other property belonging to me, that is not herein mentioned. If any then should be to his own use and benefit, or disposed. Item 5th, If any person being a legal heir,
not herein mentioned, my will and desire is that my son Grif-
ith pay him or them the sum of five dollars each, and lastly,

(80) I nominate and appoint my son Griffith Leonard my executor to
this my last will and testament. In witness whereof I have
hereunto set my hand and affixed my seal, this 9th day of
July in the year of our Lord, one thousand eight hundred and
twenty nine. Signed, sealed and delivered in the presence of,
Test.   Thos. Leonard,(seal)
Nacy Meeks
John Lovett
Parks Campbell.

        State of Tennessee, Lincoln County Court,April Term,1832.
The last will and Testament of THOMAS LEONARD, dec'd, was produced in open Court for probate and thereupon came Nacy Meeks,
and Parks Campbell two of the subscribing witnesses thereto,
who being duly sworn agreeably to law, say they heard the said
THOMAS LEONARD acknowledge the same to be his last will and
Testament and that he was at the time of signing, sealing,pub-
lishing and declaring the same of sound mind and memory, which
is ordered to be so certified, whereupon came Griffith Leonard,
the executor named in the will, and took the oath prescribed by
law, and entered into bond & so, this 16th April, 1832.
Given under my hand at office in Fayetteville.
                                    Brice M. Garner, Clk.
                                    By Peter R. Garner, D.C.

(81)   The last will and Testament of Henry Kelso, deceased.
In the name of God Amen. Know all men by these presents that
I, HENRY KELSO, of County of Lincoln and State of Tennessee,
being of a sound mind and recollection that all men must die,
do make this my last will and testament. That I request a
decent burial and all my just debts should be paid. My daughter Mary Street, my daughter Nancy Roabuck and my son John
Kelso, and my son James Kelso, and my daughter Elizabeth Hen-
son, and my son Jefferson Kelso, and my son Alfred Kelso, and
my daughter Jane Cunningham, and my daughter Mandana Yeates,
and my daughter Amatis Kelso, they have all got their equal
shares of my estate, except what may be mentioned hereafter,
John Kelso got his share in a three hundred dollar note given
for land,this division took place on the 24th of December 1831,
All but John Kelso, and he received his on the 5th January 1832.
As my son Henry Kelso got no share among the rest of my children, I will to him as follows, twenty six acres of land, which
the mansion house Stands entered in the name of Wm. Street, one
hundred and seventy acres of land entered in the name of Robert
Henry, one hundred and forty acres of twelve and half cent land,
entered in my own name, all luing on the south side of Elk River,
on the waters of Lees Creek, and also one third part of a two
hundred and seventy five acres of one cent land, entered in my
name. Beginning on the South boundry line of Petty and Hobbs,
five thousand acres survey, also one negroe Boy, Ned, son of
Hannah, also a filly known in the family by the name of Blaze
filly, also a good saddle,if I should die before he becomes of
age, the land is to be rented and the negro boy hired out. My
son Henry is to be educated and clothed out of the rent of the
land, and the hire of said boy, and if any overplus, it is to
be loaned out, and at the age of twenty he is to have full possession of all. I also will to my son John Kelso, one third of
two hundred and seventy five acres of one cent land,entered in

(81) my own name, and also my son Jefferson Kelso, one third of the
same tract of land, Beginning on the South boundary line of
Patty and Cobbs five thousand acre Survey, lying on the South
side of Elk River, the rest of my property not mentioned in
this will is to be sold, and my son James Kelso, first to
have one hundred dollars, then all my daughters is to receive
(82) one hundred dollars for each of them, then the balance to be
divided equally amongst all my children. I also have give my
daughter Amytis Kelso, one filly, known in the family by Idle-
kin filly, one cow and calf, one Bed and furniture, one dress-
ing table which has not been taken away. I do appoint my sons,
John Kelso and Jefferson Kelso, Executors of this my last will
and testament. In testimony of all which I have hereunto set
my hand and affixed my seal this 5th day of January, 1832.
Signed, sealed, published and declared by the said testator as
and for his last will and testament,

                              Henry Kelso, (seal)
In presence of us, who at his request in his presence and in
the presence of each other, have subscribed our names, as wit-
nesses thereto.
Nimrod Bailey.
Elisha Tomison.

     I have done as nigh right as I could, and I wish my child-
ren not to dispute in the way I have divided it, I also wish
the two graves to be walled in out of the estate.

     State of Tennessee, Lincoln County Court, April Session,
1832. The last will and testament of HENRY KELSO was this 16th
day of April 1832, exhibited in open Court for probate, and
thereupon Came Nimrod Bailey and Elisha Tomison, the subscribing witnesses thereto, who being first duly sworn, say they
heard the said HENRY KELSO, acknowledge the same to be his
last will and testament in writing and that he was at the time
of Signing, sealing, publishing and declaring the same of sound
mind and memory, which is all ordered to be so certified for
recording, whereupon came Jefferson Kelso, one of the executors
named in the will who entered into bond and took the oath by
law in such cases prescribed. In witness whereof I have hereunto set my hand at office in Fayetteville the 18th June 1832.
                              Brice M. Garner, Clk.
Recorded 18th June 1832.   By Peter R. Garner, D. C.

(83)   The last will & Testament of James M. Ferran, Dec'd.
I, JAMES MCFERRAN, Senr. of the County of Lincoln, State of
Tennessee, do make my last will and testament in manner and
form following, that is: 1st, I desire that my son James, shall
have one tract of land, Containing forty five Acres and $\frac{8}{4}$,
entered under the $12\frac{1}{2}$ cent act, and also an Entry I made, adjoining the sameno. of acres not ascertained, the place where
the said James now lives. 2nd, I desire that my daughter,
Mary Moore have ten dollars. 3, I desire that my daughter,
Margaret Pinkerton have ten Dollars, and that my bay horse
be sold to pay the two above donations. 4th, I desire that
my son John McFerran, have the tract, I now live on, with all

(83) the hereditaments, and appertanances, which contains, Seventy nine acres at the decease of my wife Nancy McFerran, and also one sorrel mare, two years old next spring, and that he still live and take care of his mother, and at her decease have all that remains of the stock of cattle, hogs, household furniture & farming tools. 5th, I desire that my wife Nancy, have my Brown Mare, and at her decease, the mare & her increase to belong to my son John McFerran. And lastly, I do hereby appoint my friend John Clark, Esqr. and Brown Parkinson, Executors of this my last will and testament. In witness whereof I have hereunto set my hand and seal, this 25th day of December in the year of our Lord, one thousand eight hundred and thirty one. Signed, sealed, published and declared to be the last will & testament of the above named JAMES M. MCFERRAN in presence of us, who at his request and in his presence have hereunto subscribed our names as witnesses the same.

Wm P. Pillian   James M. McFerran, (seal)
Thomas M. McFerran.

     State of Tennessee, Lincoln County Court, April Term, 1832. The last will and testament of JAMES MCFERRAN was on the 16th of April 1832, produced in open Court for probate, whereupon came Wm. P. Pallian & Thomas McFerran, who being first duly sworn according to law, say they heard the afore- JAS. MCFERRAN, acknowledge the said will to be his last will and testament, in writing and that he was at the time of signing, sealing, publishing and declaring the same, of sound mind and memory, which is ordered to be recorded, whereupon Came John Clark, Esqr. one of the Executors named in said will, who took the oath by law prescribed and entered into bond with security. In witness whereof I, Brice M. Garner, Clerk of said Court, have hereto set my hand.

                              Brice M. Garner, Clk.
Recorded 18th June 1832.   By Peter R. Garner, D. C.

(84)   Jacob Landiss Will. In the name of God, Amen. I, JACOB LANDISS, of the County of Lincoln & State of Tennessee, being weak in body, but perfectly Sound in mind & memory, do make & publish this my last will & testament in manner & form following (that is to say), First, I give and bequeath unto my beloved wife Marum R. Landiss & my daughter Susan M. Landiss the land wherein I now live with all its appurtenances, with all my live stock, household & kitchen furniture, also my interest in a tan yard in Jackson County, Ala. occupied by R.W.Robertson, to be sold at the expiration of partnership, now existing between him & myself. Secondly, to my son William, I will & bequeath the following property (viz), my interest in a tan yard in Hillsborough, Franklin County Tenn. to be sold at the expiration of a partnership now existing between Christopher & Robert Landiss and myself, also one horse and Saddle to be paid for out of the debts due me, and I do hereby appoint Thomas H. Shaw & William S. Smith, Executors to this my last will & testament, hereby revoking all wills by me made heretofore. In witness whereof I have hereunto Set my hand & affixed my seal, This 21st day of June 1832. Signed, sealed, published & declared by JACOB LANDISS to be

(84) his last will & testament in the presence of us who have
hereunto Subscribed our names in the presence of the testator.

Thomas N. Battle,   Jas. G. Reaves.
Felix G. Landiss.   John Landiss.
Wm, H.Setlett.
Proven in open Court, Monday July 18th 1832. Recorded 2nd,
Oct. 1832.

     Henry Hughey's last Will. I, HENRY HUGHEY of the County
of Lincoln & State of Tennessee, being in a low State of
health in body, butof sound mind, do make the following disposition of all my earthly property, both real & personal viz;
1st, All my perishable or personal property or so much thereof as will pay all my just debts to be disposed of in Such way
or manner the most best for the discharge of 2 debts, the balance if any to go to the use & benefit of my family. 2nd, The
land or real estate I wish my wife Betsy or Elizabeth Hughey,
to have or do with in any way that She may in her wisdom or
divine assistance think best, in testimony whereof I have
hereunto Set my hand & affixed my Seal this thirteenth day of
(85) March,one Thousand eight hundred & thirty two.
Signed in the presence of,   Henry Hughey, (seal)
James Askins
Jas. Henderson.
Recorded 2d, October 1832.

     Collins Campbell 's last will. The State of Tennessee,
Lincoln County. In the name of God Amen. I, COLLINS CAMP-
BELL, of the County aforesaid being of sound mind, but frail
in body- Commit to him that gave it, and that Estate here-
with providence has blessed me, I will & bequeath as follows,
first, all my just debts a re to be paid, after which, I
hereby give to my wife, Mary Ann Campbell all my real and
personal Estate and effects of every kind to her own proper
use & benefit during her natural life, after her decease.
Secondly, I will & bequeath to the niece of my wife Elizabeth
Robertson all the personal estate & effects that my wife Mary
Ann may die possessed of. Thirdly, that after the decease of
my wife aforesaid, I will & bequeath equally & jointly to
William N. Lenard and George S.C.Lenard, the sons of George
L.Leonard, all the land and real estate of which I am now
possessed. Fourth, and lastly I nominate and appoint George
L. Leonard and Joel Yowell my executor to administer &
carry into effect, this my last will & testament. Given
under my hand and seal this 19th day of September 1832.
Witness   Colin Campbell, (seal)
John Clark
Wm. Dewoody.

     Joshua Wall last Will. The state of Tennessee, Lincoln
County, in the name of God & man. I, JOSHUA WALLS of the
County aforesaid being of Sound mind & memory, do make &
publish this my last will & testament in manner & form, following: first, I give and bequeath to my beloved wife Permelia
Wall and my children, namely, Lizetta Wall, Leroy Wall, Theo-
phiba Wall, John Henry Wall, & Andrew Jackson Wall, two tracts

(85) of land lying & being in Lincoln County and State of Tennessee, on the head waters of Swan Creek of Elk river, Running

(86) as follows,beginning on a black oak on the north boundary of the school land at the South West Corner of a fifty acre tract, No. 3044, thence North with said fifty acre tract Eighty nine poles to a cherry tree and Dogwood, thence west Eighty nine Poles to a sugar tree on the line of the school land, thence East with said line Eighteen Poles to the beginning, containing fifty acres be the same more or less, the other beginning on an Ash and Ironwood eighty poles west of the Northeast Corner of the school land, thence North Eighty nine poles to a dogwood & cherry, thence east eighty nine poles to an elm, thence South eighty nine poles to an ash on T. Lewis' line, thence West passing his corner and with the line of the school land Eighty nine poles to the beginning containing fifty acres which the said above named, before wife and children are to hold with equal right and privelege until the said A. I.Wall, my youngest son becomes twenty one years of age, at which period my will is that the land be sold and the value thereof equally divided between the above named beloved wife & children. I, also will & bequeath to the said above named beloved wife & children all the household furniture, preishable property & C.,farming utensils that I am in possession of. I furthergive to my eldest daughter One dollar, I also give & bequeath to my son Major one dollar to be paid twelve months after my death, 15th May 1832.

Joshua Wall.

Signed, sealed, published & declared by the above named JOSHUA WALL to be his last will and testament, in the presence of us, who have hereunto subscribed our names as witness in the presence of the testator.

George Owen.
Nelson P. Daisy.

(87) John Watson. Recorded January 10th 1853.

Charles Collier last will. The last will and testament of CHARLES COLLIER considering the uncertainty of life, and being of sound mind and memory, blessed be Almighty God, for the same, first that all my just debts to be paid, I will and bequeath unto my son John Collier one horse colt and I bequeath unto my wife Jane Collier all the rest of my property as long as she remains my widow, and the land to remain said Jane Colliers'as long as she lives, and then to be equally divided amongst my children. I appoint my wife Jane Collier my Executrix. Signed, Sealed and declared in the presence of us, May 25th 1832.

Charles McCoy.   Charles Collier, (seal)
Joseph B. Kenneday.
Recorded January 10th 1833.

(88) Wm. Blair's last Will & testament. I, WILLIAM BLAIR of Swan Creek, Lincoln County & State of Tennessee, being of Sound mind & memory and calling to mind the Mortality of my body & that I must shortly resign & give up this mortal life, Do, therefore make, constitute & ordain this my last will & testament, in the following manner, And first, I commit my soul in the hand of God, who gave it, & next my body to the

(88) earth to be buried with a decent burial, and as to my worldly estate whereof I am possessed, I leave, demise & bequeath in the following way, And first, after the payment of my lawful debts I have demised & bequeathed unto Margaret Blair, my beloved wife, the clothes & bed & bed clothes & household furniture & the bay mare & one cow & calf & one heifer; Also the right of the plantation during her lifetime, (Second), If my two sons, John & Alexander, Continues to live on the land & gives their mother a decent comfortable support there shall be no other rent required. (Third), I leave unto my Son, John Blair, one red heifer & one red sow & her pigs, Also that part of the plantation tools he has got already. (Fourth), I leave unto my son Alexander Blair, one yearling horse colt, & the rest of the plantation tools. (Fifth), afterthe death of my beloved wife, I allow the land to be equally divided amongst my sons & daughters. (Sixth), I do hereby constitute, ordain & appoint my wife, Margaret Blair & my son William Blair, Sole Executors of this my last will & testament. In witness whereof I have hereunto set my hand & affixed my seal this 22nd, day of June A.D. 1832.
Signed, sealed & acknowledged in the presence of us.
Richard Wyatt.
John Wyatt.
Thos. Moore. Recorded, February 5th 1833.
Wm. Blair.

(89)   Robert Wilson's last will. I, ROBERT WILSON of the County of Lincoln & State of Tennessee, being weak in body but of sound memory & mind & knowing the mortality of my body & that it is appointed for all men once to die, do make this my last will & testament, that is to say, I recommend my soul into the hands of God who gave it & my body to the dust to be buried in a decent & Christian like manner & as to the worldly estate with which God has been pleased to bless me, I bequeath & dispose of in the following manner (to wit), In the first place, I allow all my just debts to be paid by my Executors, And to my beloved wife Mary Wilson, I give & bequeath all my household & kitchen furniture to be at her sole disposal & also the one half of all my money & debts owing to me in the State of Virginia & Tennessee, at the time of my decease, & to my son Charles Y. Wilson, I give & bequeath one bay horse & one Gray mare & gray filly, reserving one sorrel mare & one brown mare for the use of my wife Mary, during her life. And I also give & bequeath unto my son Charles Y. Wilson all my farming utensils & also all my Cattle, hogs & sheep & the one half of all the money & debts owing to me at my Decease, & at the death of my wife Mary, I bequeath unto my son Charles Y. Wilson the
(90) plantation whereon I now live, to him & his heirs forever, and I also give & bequeath to my daughter Jane Woodruff, the one half of all my Books & the other half, I leave to my son Charles Wilson; and I constitute my wife Mary my Executor & my son Charles, my Executor, of this my last will & testament, hereby revoking all forever will & testament. In witness whereof I have hereunto set my hand & seal, the 22d, day of April 1826. Assigned & sealed in presence of H. M. Blake, Jno. W. Blake. & Charles Thomson. State of Tennessee, December session of the County Court of Tipton County, 1832. State of Tennessee,

(90) Tipton County. I, Robert M. Stanford, Clerk of the Court of Pleas & quarter session of Tipton County, do hereby certify that the annexed paper purporting to be the last will & testment of ROBERT WILSON, Dec'd, was on this 5th July proven to be the last will & testament of ROBERT WILSON Dec'd, by the Oath of Hugh M. Blake, one of the subscribing witnesses thereto & ordered to be certified for registration, in testimony whereof I have hereunto set my hand & affixed my seal of office at office this 5th day of December 1832.
Recorded February 5th, 1833.   R. M. Lanford.

          Charles Tuley's last will & testament. In the name of God Amen. Dec. 4th 1823. I, CHARLES TULEY of the County of Lincoln, State of Tennessee, being of sound mind and thank God for his mercy that I am in tolerable health at this time, yet viewing the uncertainty of all human calculation and knowing the certainty of death, I do constitute this instrument, signed with my own hand, my last will & testament, revoking all others. First, it is my desire if I should die in debt to any person that they be paid as soon as the nature of circumstances will permit, out of my perishable property, if there is not sufficient other funds, debts due to me, ready money & C. Secondly, It is my desire that my seven Children whom I had by my first wife (viz), James Wildness Tuly, Martha Cummings Tuly, John Alexander Tuly, William Hutson Tuly, Samuel Preston Tuly, Elizabeth Caroline Tuly, Malinda Tuly, have the tract of Land now owned by me, lying on Elk river on the north side of the view five miles below Fayetteville, which tract of land Micajah McElroy deeded to me, bounded on the north by Yunts survey, containing one hundred & seventy five acres, be the same more or less, and as the situation of the land will not admit of divid-

(91) ing into number of settlement, and to prevent any contention after my decease, concerning the few legacies that I am able to bequeath my children, it is my desire that so soon as convenient after my decease that my Executors to this my last will & testament who are hereafter named, shall advertise and sell said tract of land to the highest bidder on the followingcredit, (to wit), one half of the purchase money to be paid in twelve months after the said sale, the other half in two years, and I request and direct my executors that if there is a news paper printed at that time in Fayetteville, Lincoln County, Tennessee, that advertise said land previous to selling, at least three months in said paper, and longer if thought necessary, but not to exceed six months, the printers fees to be paid out of the first instalment of the purchase money. I desire and direct that it be equally divided between my seven named children, as before mentioned. 3rd, thirdly, It is my desire that my present wife Elizabeth Tuly, live on and enjoy the benefit arising from a certain tract of land on which I now live, bounded on the South by Ephraim Drakes survey, containing one hundred & five acres, be the same more or less the same. I bequeath to my wife Elizabeth Tuly, during her natural life or widowhood, in case that she the said Elizabeth marries, then & in that case, it is my desire that the said tract of land last mentioned, be sold on a credit of twelve months & the money, when collected be divided equally, one half of it between my wife, Elizabeth

(91) Tuly & the children she may have borne or may bear by me,
& the other half of the money arising from the said land to
be equally divided among my seven children heretofore named,
in this my will (to wit), James W. Tuly, Martha C. Tuly,
John A. Tuly, William A. Tuly, Samuel P. Tuley, Elizabeth C.
Tuley, & Malinda Tuley, and in case my wife Elizabeth Tuley,
should die without marrying, then & in that case I desire
that the said one hundred & five acres of land be sold as a-
foresaid & that half of the purchase money be equally divided
between James W. Tuley, Martha C. Tuley, John A. Tuley, William
H. Tuley, Samuel P. Tuley, Elizabeth C. Tuley, & Malinda
Tuley, and the other half be equally divided between the children that I may have by my wife Elizabeth Tuley. Having gone
through the distribution of my real estate, I must proceed to
consider my perishable estate and it is my will that my daughter Martha C. Tuley, Elizabeth C. Tuley & Malinda Tuley, have
and I do hereby bequeath to them the three best beds, bed
stead & furniture that I amy die possessed of, as having been
left by their dear Mother, my beloved Polly Tuly, each to
have a bed and to have choice in the order that they are
named, and to prevent any dissatisfaction it is my will that
the said beds & C. be valued by three discreet, disinterested
men, two of which to be chosen by my seven first named children, the girls choosing one, of the boys, the other, and that
these two discreet persons choose a third person & these
three persons to value the several beds mentioned above &
each of my daughters (to wit), Martha C. Tuley, Elizabeth C.
Tuley & Malinda Tuley shall take the beds thus valued to
them at their valuation. It is next my desire that so soon
as convenient after my death, that all my other property
that I may die possessed of, not otherwise disposed of in
the foregoing bequest & distribution, be sold on a credit of
twelve months, out of the proceeds of which I direct that all
my just debts be paid & the residue to be equally divided
between my wife Elizabeth Tuley & all my children, giving to
each an equal part, except to my daughters, Martha C. Tuley,
Elizabeth C. Tuley & Malinda Tuley, from whom the value of
each of their beds shall be deducted. Now it is my will,
further that in case any of my children that I had by my first
wife, my much loved Polly, that if any of them should die
before they arrive at the proper age for making a legal distribution of their property or should die without marrying
& intestate, then & in that case, I desire that the property
that they may die possessed of, shall return to their full
Brothers & sisters, equally. Now I have an interest in my
mothers' estate, to wit, two-fifths, and it is my desire that
the proceeds of the same be equally divdied between my seven
children, James W. Tuley, Martha C. Tuley, John A. Tuley,
William H. Tuley, Samuel P. Tuley, Elizabeth C. Tuley &
Malinda Tuley. I have now gone through the several bequests,
and it is my desire that they be attended to without consti-
tion & in searching for the meaning for the several sentences,
that my meaning may not be misconstrued. Now I proceed to
appoint my good friend John Clark & David Watson of Lincoln
County, Tennessee, my executors, to this my last will & testament, as witness whereof I have hereunto set my hand & seal
this 4th day of December, 1823.

Charles Tuley, (seal)

(91) Test.
Willaim Monroe.
John Clark.

(92)   Allen F. Kennedy's Last Will & Testament. The last
will & Testament of ALLEN F. KENNEDY, made the 27th day of
June in the year of our Lord 1833. I will and devise to my
wife, Agnes Kennedy, for and during the term of her natural
life or widowhood, the two lots of ground upon which I now
reside, with my family, known and designated in the plan of
the town of Fayetteville by numbers of lots 85 and 89 together with all of the improvements and other appurtenances
thereunto belonging. I also leave to my wife Agnes, all my
household and kitchen furniture, with such Stock of provision
as may be on hand at my death, for and during the term aforesaid, provided, however, that said Agnes will receive the devises and bequeath herein contained for her benefit as a consideration for the clothing and maintenance of my five child-
until they are twenty one years of age, or such of them as
may so long live. It is my desire that William Kennedy a son
of Agnes Kennedy which was born before my marriage with said
Agnes, and my five Children herein after named, should be educated to read and write, and cypher, and study English Gram-
mer, their education, if they have the capacity to receive it
in those different branches to be as complete and as perfect
as is usually obtained in this county. It is my will & desire
that my house and lot adjoining a lot belonging to the heirs
of Vance Greer on the South and adjoining a house and lot belonging to William F. Mason & C., on the north lying on the
square in the town of Fayetteville, should be sold by my executors so soon as they may be able to do so, for the sum of
three thousand dollars or more. And I hereby authorize them
to sell the same for the sum above mentioned or as much more
as they may be able to get for it, and make such deeds in fee
simple as may be necessary to carry into effect such sale.
If my executor shall not be able to sell said house & lot for
the sum above mentioned it is my will and desire that it should
be rented out yearly until such sale can be made, the money
so raised by the sale or rent of said house and lot or the
interest thereof or sp much of either as may be necessary, I
(93) wish to be applied to the education of my children and William Kennedy, in the manner above mentioned. I desire my
stock of liquor and other groceries to be sold on a credit
of twelve months. I give & bequeath to William Kennedy, the
son of Agnes as above mentioned, two hundred and fifty dollars to be paid to him upon his coming to the age of twenty
one years. This gift is in addition to such sum as may be
necessary to educate him as above mentioned. The money which
may be raised by the sale of the property above mentioned or
by the rent of the house above mentioned or in any other manner, out of my property, not herein devised to Agnes Kehnedy,
or so much thereof as may remain after educating all the children as above mentioned, and after paying to William Kennedy
two hundred & fifty dollars. I wish to be equally divided between my five children, to wit, Mary Ann, John G. Robert A.,
Agnes and Martha, share and share alike, each child to receive
his or her proportion when twenty one years of age. If my

(93) and lot on the square cannot be sold for the sum above mentioned, I wish it to be rented until my youngest child is eighteen years of age, and then to be sold for the best price that
can be obtained for it on a credit of one, two & three years
equal annual instalments, my executors are hereby authorized
to make such deeds in fee simple as may be necessary to carry
into effect the same. I give and bequeath to James Bright,
George W. Jones, James Fulton, William Timmons and Samuel W.
Carmack, my negro man, Jeffrey, to be held by them in trust,
that he shall remain with my wife Agnes Kennedy, and by his
labor, aid her in the maintenance of her and her children
until the year 1843 or at her election, the trustee shall hire
said Jeffrey out from time to time as the said Agnes may wish,
and appropriate the money so raised by his hire to the clothing
and maintenance of her & her children, upon trust also that if
by the law of this state. It is my will and desire that he
shall be hired out until a sum of money can be obtained which
will be sufficient to send him to Liberia or to any other coun-
try he may choose to go to, where he can live as a free man.

(94) Upon trust also that if by the laws of this State, said Jeffrey
cannot be set free, and in the year 1843, or during the year
1844, he may be unwilling to leave the State, then he is forever after to remain a slave, and I wish him to remain with my
wife, Agnes or to be hired out for the purpose above mentioned,
until my youngest child is twenty one years of age, and then,
and in that event the above trust to expire and sd Jeffrey to
become the joint property of my children. Upon the death of
my wife Agnes, I devise the two lots upon which I now reside,
no. 85 and 89, to my five children, to them and their heirs
forever. I nominate and appoint William Timmons, George W.
Jones, James Bright and Samuel W. Carmack, executors of this
my last will and testament.
Attest.   Allen J. Kennedy.
A.A.Kincannon.
Davis Eastland.

        I, F. L. Kincannon, clerk of the County Court of the sd,
County, do certify that the last will & testament of ALLEN J.
KENNEDY, Dec'd, was this day produced in open Court for probate, whereupon came Davis Eastland & Andrew A. Kincannon,
subscribing witnesses thereto, who being duly sworn, say upon
their oath that they saw him sign & heard him acknowledge the
same to be his last will & testament & that they believe him
to be at the time of doing the same of sound mind. Thereupon
came William Timmons, George W. Jones & Samuel W. Carmack,
(James Bright being absent), three of the executors appointed
in said will, who entered into bond with F. L. Kincannon, Wm.
Neeld & Joel Pinson, Securities in the sum of three thousand
dollars for the faithful discharge of their duty as executors
aforesaid. The Court therefore ordered that letters testament-
ary issue to them accordingly. Given under my hand at office
this 15th day August 1833.
                          F. L. Kincannon, Clerk.

(95)   John Rutledge, Last will & testament. I, JOHN RUTLEDGE,
of the County of Lincoln & State of Tennessee, do make this
as my Last will & testament. 1st that all my Just debts be
paid. 2d, that all the balance of my property remain my wifes'
during her life or widowhood, at her death or second marriage
to be equally divided amongst all my Lawful heirs. 3, that my
wife Catherine & my son William Rutledge be appointed Executor
to this my last will & testament. Given under my hand & seal
this Eighth day of April 1833.   his
Test.   John x Rutledge.
Joseph Whitaker.   mark
Isaac Rutledge. Recorded 13th Dec. 1833.

        Mary Wilson's Last will & testament. In the name of God,
Amen, I, MARY WILSON of the County of Lincoln & State of Tennessee, being weak in body but of sound mind & memory & knowing the mortality of my body & that it is appointed for all
once to die, do make this my last will & testament. That is
to say, I recommend my soul into the hands of God who gave it
& my body to the dust, to be buried in a defent & Christian
like manner, & as to the worldly Estate with which God has
been pleased to bless me with, I bequeath & dispose of in the
following manner, (To wit), One bay Colt, two beds & furniture,
one trunk, one large kettle, one large Pot, & one small pot,
One clock & case, one dining Table, One sorrel & one brown mare,
I give & bequeath to my son Charles T. Wilson. Also one sorrel Colt, I give & bequeath to my grand Daughter, Nancy B.
Woodruff. Also I Bequeath to my two grand Sons, William J.
Woodruff & Benjamin R. Woodruff, my part of money due in the
State of Virginia & Tennessee, when collected. Also the balance of the household & kitchen furniture. And I constitute
my son Charles T. Wilson & William D. Blake my Executors of
this my last will & testament. By revoking all former wills &
(96)   declaringthis to be my last will & testament. In witness
whereof I have hereunto set my hand & seal this 20th day of
April in the year of our Lord 1830. Signed & sealed in presence Of,   her
James Blakeman.   Mary x Wilson, (seal)
John W. Blake.   mark

        Reubin Hunter Last Will & Testament. I, REUBIN HUNTER,
of the County of Lincoln, & State of Tennessee, being of
sound mind & perfect memory & being desirous to settle my
my worldly affairs in manner & form following, (to wit);
1st, I allow all my Just debts & funeral expenses to be paid.
2d, I bequeath & leave to my beloved wife Scintha Hunter, my
negro boy, James & negro girl, Polly and two of the choisest
of my horses & two cows & calves, & two head of dry cattle,
eight head of sheep, ten head of hogs, for killing, & twenty
head of Stock hogs, three beds & furniture, six chairs, two
tables, the China Press & furniturethere, and her saddle &
bridle, two plough & hoes, & two set of gears, one ox cart &
the two young work steers, two axes & one half of the kitchen
furniture & all of the Poultry of every description in fee
simple. 3, Thirdly, I bequeath & leave unto my Daughter,
Polly McElroy, wife of William McElroy, my negro woman, named,

(96) Lettie,& her two children named Patrick & Jerry, in fee simple. 4th, fourthly, I bequeath & leave unto my son Sherwood Hunter, my still & tubs, & the plantation whereon I now reside, containing about one hundred & fifty six acres, be the sames more or less, to him, my said son & his heirs forever, in fee simple, at the death of my said wife, Scintha Hunter. 5th, fifthly, I bequeath & leave to my daughter Sally Davis, wife to Elijah Davis? my negro boy, Isaac, in fee simple, & allow my Executor to sell all of the balance of my property, except my old negro man, Pompay, on a credit of twelve months, & as soon as the money is collected, to purchase a negro woman, or woman & child, worth four hundred dollars & pay over to my said daughter, Sally Davis, & the balance whatever it may be arising from my sale, to be equally divided between my three

(97) children, Sherwood Hunter, Polly M. McElroy, & Sally Davis. I do hereby appoint my son Sherwood Hunter, my executor to this my last will & testament, hereby revoking all former wills by me made, in witness whereof I have hereunto set my hand and seal this 11th August 1832.
Attest.   Reubin Hunter, (seal).
James Higgins.
Wm. Edmiston.   Recorded 15th Dec. 1833.

Joel Johnson's Last Will & Testament.   I, JOEL JOHNSON, being of Sound & perfect mind & memory, do make and publish this my last will & Testament, in manner & form, following, that is to say, It is my will that all my just debts be first paid & for this purpose that my executor sell upon a credit of twelve months such part of the tract of land on which I now live,as lies South on a line running from a point on the east boundary line of the tract of land on which I now live, due west by a school house, to the west boundary line of the same tract. After the payment of all my debts it is my will that the whole of my property, both real & personal, remain in the possession of my wife, Margaret M. during her widowhood or until my youngest child attains to the age of twentyone years, whichever event shall first happen, it is my will

(98) that my executors shall there sell upon a credit of twelve months the whole of my property, the proceeds of such sale, to the amount of twelve hundred dollars shall be equally divided between my wife Margaret M. & my children by her & the residue of the proceeds of such sale shall be equally divided between my said wife & children & my son Ambrose a horse, saddle,bridle & of the value of one hundred dollars. It is my will & I do direct my executor to furnish out of my property to the balance of my children, when they respectively, attain to the age of twenty one years or marry, a horse, saddle & bridle, bed & furniture, or such part of said articles as will be of the value of one hundred dollars. It is my will that all my children be substantially and sufficiently educated out of the annual proceeds of my farm & property, If this fund should not be sufficient quanity for the purpose, then it is my will that my sons by my present wife, taking care not to exceed the amount to which they would be entitled according to this, my will upon the division of my property between my wife & children, as herein before mentioned, I wish to have my sons well educated, should it ever require for this purpose, the whole

(98) of the property, which I have given them. I do hereby appoint my wife Margaret, guardian of all my daughters that are under the age of twenty one years, and I do appoint my friend James Franklin guardian of such of my sons as are under the age of twenty one years, at the time of my death, and I do hereby appoint James Hogue and James Fulton executors of this my last will & testament. In witness whereof I have hereto set my hand & seal this 5th day of December 1832.

Joel Johnson, (seal).

Signed, sealed, published & declared by the above named, JOEL JOHNSON to be his last will & testament, in the presence of us who have hereunto subscribed our names as witnesses in the presence of the testator.
E. M. Ringo.
Sam I. Todd.   Recorded 14th Dec. 1833.

Daniel Waggoner's Last Will & Testament. This being my last will & testament, in the name of God Amen. Being of strong mind & in my perfect Senses, after all my Just debts are paid, I give & bequeath unto my dear beloved wife Eve, one third part of my tract of land whereon I now live, including all my buildings. I also give & bequeath unto my wife one negro man named Prince & one negro woman named Dica,
(99) & one negro child named Betts. I also give unto wife three choisest cows & twenty head of choisest hogs & 3 beds & steads, & two head of my choicest horses or mares and farming tools, sufficient to that part of the farm. I also give & bequeath unto my three youngest children (to wit), Susanna & Henry & Alexander, a hundred dollar horse or mare each, to make them equal with them of lawful age, I also give & bequeath unto my dear beloved children (to wit), Catharine Michael, my oldest Daughter & to Elizabeth Bateman & to Daniel & David & Andrew & Sussana & Henry & Alexander, Seven hundred dollars each, to make them equal with my oldest son Jacob, as I give him seven hundred dollars when he went to housekeeping, after the death of my wife I give & bequeath unto my Daughter Susanna the negro named Betts, to which I left with my wife during her natural life, then to Susanna, & after the death of my wife I give & bequeath unto my son Alexander, the negro man named, Prince, to which I left with my wife her natural life & after the death of my wife, I give & bequeath unto my son Henry, the negro woman named Disa to which I left with my wife her natural life time. I do give & bequeath unto my son David Sally's child, York, negro boy & Sally to remain with David & take care of the child until he is raised so that he can take care of himself, then said Sally to be sold to the highest bidder. I do give & bequeath unto my son Andrew a negro boy named Peter. I give & bequeath unto my son Daniel a negro girl named Eada. I give unto my daughter Elizabeth Bateman, negro girl named Mary. I give unto my Daughter Catharine Michael, a negro girl named Caily, I also give & bequeath unto my daughter Catharine Michael one hundred dollars horse, to make her equal with the rest of childred. After the death of my wife I want my tract of land sold & the money equally divided amongst all my children. I want my executors hereinafter named, to sell all my property that is not named in my will & equally divide the money amongst my Children, to Jacob, Daniel, David & Andrew,

(99) Henry, Alexander, Catharine, Elizabeth & Susanna. I do appoint my two sons Daniel & David, my Executors, in witness
(100)whereof I have hereunto set my hand & seal, the 21st day of
July 1833.
                              Daniel Waggoner, (seal).
Attest, in the presence of,
Jacob E. Waggoner.
John Bateman. Recorded 14th Dec. 1833.

        "Armstead Pamplin's Last Will." The last will and Testament of ARMSTEAD PAMPLIN, of the County of Lincoln, of the
State of Tennessee, I, ARMSTEAD PAMPLIN considering the uncertainty of this life and being afflicted but of sound mind
& memory, blessed be Almighty God for the same, do make and
publish this my last will and Testament in manner and form,
following; I, ARMSTEAD PAMPLIN do put the whole estate in my
wifes power to live well on the estate, so far as this, as to
sell nothing of much value except the Legatees are all willing, not run the estate in debt any more than possible, and
if she wants the estate divided let it be done, when she wants
it done, but if she desires to keep it together and get an
overseer, she must do it, but if she spares anything to one,
let it be spared to all alike. The Legatees are those which
are to share alike, naming the oldest first, William B. Henry
H. Elizabeth, Robert, Armstead, Lucinda, Martha, Joseph, James
and Susan Waggoner, my granddaughter, I do will Jacob Waggoner five dollars for an addition to the rest he has had.
I will the whole Legacy to the legatees, and to the heirs of
their bodies forever. But if there be any of my children in
distress and she sees proper to let them live on the land, my
wife must do as she pleases in that, for I put that power in
her hands, because it is my will to do so. I choose William
Pamplin and Joseph, my sons for my executors, to see that the
Legatees are all dealt with Justly, and to keep the estate together as much as lies in their power, and to see that Susan
Waggoner has schooling as much as is common for Girls to
have , and if they have that, to see to it must come out of her
part, this my last will and testament, hereby revoking all
former wills by me made, in witness whereof I have hereunto
set my hand and seal, this the 13th July 1831.
                              Armstead Pamplin. (seal)
(101) Signed, sealed, published and declared by the above named,
ARMSTEAD PAMPLIN to be his last will and Testament, in the
presence of us who have herein subscribed our names as witnesses in the presence of the testator.
John Bailey.
Esram Loyd.
William Rutledge. Recorded 2nd, July 1834.(a copy Recd.)

        William James Last Will & Testament. I, WILLIAM JAMES,
being of sound and perfect mind and memory do make and publish this my last will and testament in manner and form following: First, I desire that all my just debts of every description be paid as soon as possible. 2d, I give and bequeath unto my beloved wife Jane B. James all my property
of every description during her widowhood, subject nevertheless, the above and all my estate to be paid to each heir,

(101) viz, on my sons arriving at twenty one years of age or on the marriage of my daughters, Sarah & Jane DeKalb to be divided equally amongst them. 3rd, I give and bequeath unto my daughter Sarah James out of the above estate a certain negro child named Harriet, nevertheless the said Sarah to have an equal share of all my remaining property with the balance of my heirs. 4th, I give and bequeath unto my daughter Jane De-Kalb James, out of the above estate a certain negro child named Adaline, nevertheless the said Jane DeKalb to enjoy and inherit an equal portion of my estate with my remaining heirs. 5th, I give and bequeath unto my sons Thomas, William, Mark, Walker & Mathias James, an equal portion of the above named estate bequeathed to my wife, Jane B. James, in common with my daughters, Sarah & Jane DeKalb, except the two negroes, Harriet & Adeline, which the said Sarah & Jane DeKalb are to have over and above an equal portion of my estate, with the remainder if my heirs. 6th, I give and bequeath unto my step-daughter Caroline Watson a horse to be valued at fifty dollars

(102) on her marriage. And lastly, I appoint my friends Thomas Massey & William M. Inge, my sole executors to this my last will and Testament. In Testimony whereof I have hereunto set my hand and affixed my seal. Signed, sealed & published in presence of us.

A. Baxter.   Wm. James. (seal).
John Duke.
William C. Kennedy. Recorded 2nd, July 1834.

Jachariah Arnold, Last Will & Testament. In the name of God Amen, I, JACHARIAH ARNOLD of the County of Lincoln and State of Tennessee, being in sound mind and memory disposing, for which I thank God, and calling to mind the uncertainty of human life and being desirous to dispose of all such worldly substance that it hath pleased God to bless me with. 1st, I give and bequeath the same in manner following: that is to say, I give and bequeath unto my beloved wife Charlotta the tract of land I now live on with all the household and kitchen furniture, the farm and farming tools, and also all the stock of horses, cattle and hogs that I now have in my possession, and as many of the stock of negroes that I now have, as she may think proper, to keep during her natural life or widowhood, and at her death or marriage the above named property to be disposed of in the following manner, viz, that is to say, all the household and kitchen furniture and all the stock, farming tools, but such as I shall hereafter mention to be sold and equally divided between my daughter Nancy (Children), and my daughter Mary, Patsy, Malinda and Melissa, I give and bequeath to my son Moses Arnold, all the tract of land he now lives, on the South side of Elk River adjoining the land of James Forsytte and also fifty acres Granted to Middleton Couch. I will and bequeath to my son Sanders W. Arnold, all the tract of land I now live on, deeded to me by James Bright, also half the Moore tract adjoining the same tract, and also twelve acres deeded to me by Hudson, also nine acres adjoining the same granted to me, I will and bequeath to my son John Arnold, one hundred dollars, and I will and bequeath to William Arnold, a son of John Arnold, one hundred dollars.

(102) I will and bequeath unto my daughter, Nancy Children, one
negro boy by the name of Mager. I will and bequeath to my
(103) daughter Malinda, one negro boy by the name of Williamson,
I also will and bequeath to my daughter Malissa one negro
woman named Lucy, and her increase. I bequeath of the personal property that I have now in my possession or may have
undisposed of , after paying all my Just contracts, to be
equally divided between my daughter Nancy Children, and my
other four daughters, that is the property I need not speci-
fy in the will, as this is my last will and Testament. And
lastly, I appoint and constitute my son Sanders W. Arnold
and my son-in-law Jarred Sirmons, Executors to this my last
will and Testament, by me assigned. Given under my hand and
seal this third day of October Eighteen hundred and thirty-
four. Signed, Sealed and delivered in the presence of us.
J. W. Hamilton   Jachariah Arnold, (seal)
W. C Jennings. Recorded 4th Dec. 1834.

Jeremiah Bryan, Last Will and Testament. In the name of
God Amen. Whereas, I the undersigned JEREMIAH BRYAN of the
County of Lincoln and State of Tennessee, though weak in body
yet enjoying a sound and perfect memory and understanding,
and considering that all must die, I have thought proper to
make, publish and declare the following to be my last will
and testament. 1st, I give and bequeath to my beloved wife
Rosamond during her natural life, and at her death to descend
to my son Newton Perry, one feather bed and furniture, one
Corner Cupboard one long pendulum clock, one dining Table, one
cotton wheel, one looking glass, two setting chairs, two bee
stands and four head of sheep. 2nd, I give and bequeath to my
sons, Newton Perry and William Carrol Bryan, one feather bed
and their furniture, each which I estimate as worth -- dollars
each. I have already given to my son James Bryan upon his
setting out upon life, one mare, one feather bed, a stock of
hogs and a small tract of Land, all of which I estimate as
worth Two hundred dollars, and as he possesses the advantage
of mature manhood whilst some other of my children are helpless minors, I give and bequeath to him the further sum of
Thirty dollars as a final settlement of all accounts, debts,
legacies, and bequeath to my daughter Jane Bolen and her
husband, Elijah, I have given already one mare, one cow and
some hogs, which I estimate as worth fifty dollars. To
(104) Kerway Bryan My son, I have already given one mare, one cow,
and one bed and furniture and some hogs which I estimate as
worth Sixty dollars. It is my will and desire that after my
decease my Executors who I hereafter appoint sell all my land
with their appurtenances on a credit of one, two and three
years, one third of the price therof I give and bequeth to
my wife Rosanah during her life, then to descend to our son
Newton Perry Bryan. In the room of her dowry in the said
land which she agrees to accept of, my stock of horses, cattle, sheep and hogs, oxen, wagon, stills and all other implements, and utensils, farming tools, household and kitchen
furniture of all and every name and description, I direct
that it or they be sold on a credit of twelve months, by my
Executors, that are not already bequeathed or herein otherwise disposed of. To Joel Swannes, I hereby give in trust

(104) my black man Jack, and direct that the said trustee allow
and permit him the said Jack, to hire his own time at Forty
dollars for each year until he, the said Jack shall pay to
my Estate the sum of Five hundred dollars over and above his
hire, then I will and direct that he acquire freedom in con-
formity to law. My slave Hetty, I give and bequeath to Robert Moore and estimate her value at two hundred and fifty dollars, and direct that Bob be sold as the other chattels of
my estate. It is my will and desire that all my debts be paid
and that the net proceeds of my Estate be divided amongst my
children, equally after such of them as are charged with an
out-fit, shall have accounted to my estate the amount already
received by them or any special gift or bequest, in this my
last will, set forth. I hereby nominate and appoint Joel
Swanner and Malakiah Reeves or either of them Executors to
this my last will and Testament. The Legacy or filial portion
of my daughter Mary, now married to William Justice. I will add
desire that my Executors retain in their hand in trust and
pay over to them the said William and Mary Justice in such sum
as a prudent necessity may require. Five hundred is all that
I require of Jack before he acquires a right to Freedom, and I
insert this item in explanation of the clause on that subject
which was made to read by interlineation as though I required
that sum over his yearly hire. Such legally or filed Portion
as may be coming out of my estate to Elijah Bolen and Jane
Bolen, I will and desire that my Executors retain in their own
hands, in Trust for their use, and pay over the same in such
sums as a pessing necessity may require. In testimony hereof
I have hereunto set my hand and affixed my seal, this fifth day
of September, 1834.
Alvin C. Oliver.   Jeremiah Bryan, (seal)
Sam'l R. Reeves.
James B. Gill: .
Nathan G. Pinson. Recorded 5th Dec. 1834.

(105)   Thomas W. Hill, Last Will & Testament. In the name of
God, Amen. I, THOMAS W. HILL, of Lincoln County and State of
Tennessee, do hereby make my last will & Testament in manner &
form following: that is to say, First, I desire that all the
perishable part of my estate be sold after my decease, and out
of the money arising thereupon together with the proceeds of the
growing crop, all my just debts and funeral expenses be paid
but should their appropriation prove inadequate, I desire full
payment to be made at the description of my executor hereafter
to be named. Secondly, After the payment of my debts & funeral
expenses, I give to my son, John William Hill, all my estate
both real and personal, to be enjoyed by him forever, and desire that he may receive and manage the same, at the age of
twenty years. Thirdly- I will that during the minority of my
son, the pplantation shall be kept up and the negroes kept together, and at work theron, and his boarding, schooling and
clothing paid for out of the money arising from the same, and
the balance, if any, returned for his use when of age. Fourthly,
I do hereby constitute and appoint my ffiend, Parker Campbell,
executor, to this my last will and Testamentm confiding in
his discretion to carry the same into full effect, and hereby

(105) revoke all other or former wills, by me heretofore made. In witness whereof I have hereunto set my hand and affixed my seal, this 19th day of July 1834. Signed and acknowledged in presence of, Thomas W. Hill, (seal).
Isham R. Howze.
Wm. S. Howze.
Wm. Campbell. Recorded 5th Dec. 1834.

Amos Davis Last Will & Testament. I, AMOS DAVIS, of Lincoln County, and State of Tennessee, being sick and weak of body but of sound mind and disposing memory (for which I thank God), and calling to mind the uncertainty of human life and being desirous to dispose of all such worldly substances as it hath pleased God to bless me with, do hereby make my last will and Testament, in manner and form following: 1st, I desire that my executors hereafter named, proceed after my decease to sell one hundred acres of Land situated, lying, and being in the County of Lincoln and State of Tennessee, and on the waters of Bradshaw's Creek, whereon Cain Acuff now resides. One hundred and fifty acres adjoining the one hundred acre tract, eleven acres and some poles adjoining the lands of John Park & William Cowden, on Richland Creek, the grist mill and all their appurtenances on said eleven acre tract, together with such perishable property as my surviving family in their judgment may not stand directly in need of the proceeds of,
(106) which to go to the use of paying my just debts, should the property named be insufficient to answer the above purpose to dispose of a sufficiency of the remainder of said perishable property or will supply the defect. 2nd, After the payment of just debts, I give and bequeath to my wife Elizabeth Davis, one negro boy named Will, one named Andrew & one named Bill, my dwelling and out houses, all of my household & kitchen furniture and as much of my Farm as she may need to raise a sufficient support for herself and her family, and as much stock as she may need, such as horses, cattle & hogs &C., and if after the sales of the before recited real & perishable property then should be a surplus left after paying my just debts, I wish such surplus to go to the use of my wife & surviving family, as I wish each of my children to have an opportunity to obtain a reasonable education, I therefore rest the management of that business in the hands of my Executors to make such provision as they may in their Judgement think proper. All of the property before recited, as given to my wife is to be her sole benefit in every respect, for and during her natural life or widowhood, in which case, provided she marries or after her decease the said property to be equally divided among all of my legal heirs. #rd, I wish my son James H. Davis to have Fifty acres of my land, including the half of a spring which William Cowden now makes use of, and the cleared land adjoining on the East of the outside cross fence, which fifty acres he is to have and hold free from any attachments, whatever, to cultivate for his own use for and during the time of his mothers life or till she be married again or the youngest heir becomes of age. 4th, I wish my sons Nathan C. Davis and Allen J. Davis to have the use of the tract of Land purchased by me of Richard Fleming, including all the cleared land on said tract, in the same manner and for the same

(106) purpose recited to my son, J. H. Davis, for fifty acres and
provided there should be any disagreement arising from any
difference of opinion on the parts, each is to have of sd
land between those, my two sons, N.C.D. & A.J.D. that my
(107) executors be vested with Authority to equitably divide the
same for them and give to each portion. 5th, I wish my sons,
Morgan A. Davis & Stephen M. Davis to continue with their
mother until they receive their education, rendering their
obedience and services to her in cultivating and improving
said farm, and after they arrive to an age capable of doing
for themselves that then my executors lay off each of them,
a suitable, equivalent or some suitable part of said premises to be occupied by them as my other sons have already
been provided for. 6th, I wish my youngest son John S. Davis
to remain with his mother during her widowhood or till after her death, which time should it take place soon, his
portion of land to be disposed of by my executors for his
benefit, if late he is not at liberty to infringe on his
mothers rights in no sense of the word, and finally, after
my wife has enjoyed the premises as is expressed, that the
said youngest son have his share of Land to include my dwelling house, spring &c. 7th, After my sons have all become
of age, on the death or marriage of their mother, the other
land to be equally as near as can be divided among my other
five sons, (viz)—I. H. Davis, N. C. Davis, A. J. Davis, M. A.
Davis & S.M. Davis, agreeably to quantity and quality, giving
no more to one than to another, in value. 8'th, I wish my
Daughter Fanny T. Davis to be provided for with her mother,
as long as she remains single ina respectable manner, in provision, clothing &c. from the proceeds of my farm, and the
labor of those hands before recited, for the use of my wife
when she marries, to have a negro girl, a horse, saddle and
bridle to be worth at least seventy five dollars, a cow and
calf to be worth ten dollars, a bed, bed stead & furniture of
a reasonable good quality. 9th, I wish my two youngest Daughters
(Viz), Sarah Ann Davis and Mary Elizabeth to remain with their
mother as their sister F.F. Davis, be provided for clothed
and fed as she was, from the same source, educated, as my
youngest sons, and after marriage to receive in value or in
property an equivalent with their sister F. T. Davis, and finally after the time arrives when this property is to be divided, either by death or marriage as is expressed in the foregoing, that there those of my sons who receives land and property, if the same cannot be done equally so as to give to each
of my daughters a fair equivalent, after taking under consid-
(108) eration what they have received in property, if any, and its
value if a defect in the portion or portions of my daughters
that the defect be supplied by my son or sons who may have received the advantage, if any heirs cannot by reason of a difference of opinion agree on the value of those effects, I
wish in that case, my executors to select two Justice ßß of
the peace for sd county, to select a Committee of Five or
more citizens, disinterested, to divide for them and give
each his or her rights. 10th, I wish my beloved Brethren and
sisters composing the Richland Baptist Church to hold in
quiet & peacable possession, the house and yard heretofore

(108)occupied by a Church, so long as they hold the religious
(tenets) they now adhere to. 11th, and lastly I do hereby
make, ordain and appoint my much esteemed nephew, Morgan
Clayton and my well beloved son James H. Davis executors to
this my last will and Testament written on one sheet of paper.
In witness whereof I have hereunto set my hand and seal this
15th day of June 1834. Signed, sealed and declared to be the
last will and Testament of the above named AMOS DAVIS in presence
of us, and at his request & in his presence have subscribed
our names as witnesses to the same.
Test
A. Young   Joshua Davis
Isaac Moore   James Poole   Recorded 5th December 1834.
                                       Amos Davis, (seal).

       Soloman Reese Last Will & Testament. Whereas I, SOLOMAN
REESE of the County of Lincoln and State of Tennessee, being
at this time laboring under sickness of body though of sound
mind and memory in order to prepare my Temporal affairs in the
(109)best manner, Do make, publish and declare the following to be
my last will and testament. First I give and bequeath unto
the seven children of my first wife or survivors of them all,
my lands in Lincoln County and my negro man, also I give unto
them the proceeds of the sales of the following horses which
I direct my executors to sell on a credit of twelve months, one
large sorrel mare and mother of the stud, one stud horse, one
leopard filly or mare, one bay horse Peter, one young horse, a
colt of the old sorrel mare, another horse named Fox, the proceeds to be equally divided amongst them. And I give and bequeath unto my beloved wife Mahala and her three children if
she should be mother of so many within nine months after my decease, all my lands in Carroll County and one old spotted Leopard mare, and her two youngest fillies, one sorrel horse and
one mare and her colt, Got of Sugg, during her natural life,
and at her death, to descend unto her three children, the fruit
of our marriage. All my other Estate of whatever name and description in which the same does exist excepted, I direct to
be sold by my Executor and the proceeds thereof to constitute
a fund for the payment of all my just debts, and legal liabilities, and if the same shall not be all exhausted in that way,
the same to be equally divided between my wife and ten children. The beds and bedding is already known by distinctions,
such are known as my present wife's, I give to her and her
children and such as are now known in the family as belonging
to my first seven children, I give to them and must not be sold
under any consideration. I nominate and appoint Cullen E.
Sugg, to be Executor to this my last will and Testament. In
testimony whereof I have hereunto set my hand and affixed my
seal this 11th day of October 1834.
William Wafford.   Soloman Reese, (seal).
C. T. Reese.
Willie Wingo.
N. G. Pinson.   Recorded 6th Dec. 1834.

(109)   William A. Davis Last Will And Testament. I,WILLIAM
A. DAVIS, of the County of Lincoln and State of Tennessee,
do hereby make my last will & Testament in manner and form
following, that is- 1st, I desire that all my perishable property not otherwisw disposed of to be immediately sold after
my decease, and out of the money arising therefrom all my
just debts and funeral expenses be paid, should the perishable part of my estate prove insufficient for the above purpose, then I desire that my executors hereafter named, may
sell some part of my real estate and out of the proceeds of
the money arising therefrom pay and satisfy such of my just
debts as remain unpaid out of the perishable part of my estate.
2nd, After the payments of my debts and funeral expenses, I
give to my wife. Polly Davis all my possession of lands for
the purpose of supporting the family, and educating my children until my youngest children shall become twenty one years
old, provided my wife remains a widow, but if she marries, she
no longer shall be entitled to any part of my landed estate,
And further, it is my desire that my wife Polly shall have
possession of all that part of my premises except that part
bought of William Jones, during her widowhood or until my son
Newton C. Davis arrives at the age of twenty one years, then
my said son Newton C. to have two thirds of the above named
premises, and my wife Polly the other one third part during
her natural life or widowhood, and at her death or marriage
her one third part to descend to my said son Newton C. Davis.
The balance of my land, namely, that tract bought of William
Jones, I give and bequeath unto my two sons, namely Cadwallader
C. Davis and Rufus Columbus Davis to take possession of the
same at the age of twenty one years, without back rents. Cad-
walled C. Davis to have that part of the tract where said Jones
once lived to be divided between my sons by persons disinterested, as soon as Cad. W. C. shall arrive at 21 years. I also
(110)give to my wife Polly David a certain negro woman named Mary,
during her natural life or widowhood, and at her death or marriage the said negro or the value thereof to be equally divided amongst my Girl children, to be enjoyed by them and their
heirs forever. 3rd, I give to my daughter, Adaline Davis, a
negro girl named Susan, to be enjoyed by her and her heirs forever. 4th, I give unto my Daughter Eliza Ann Davis, a negro
girl named Harriet, to be enjoyed by her and her heirs forever.
5th, I give unto Daughter Narcissa P. Davis a negro boy named
Joe, to be enjoyed by her and her heirs forever. 6th, I give
unto my daughter Theodocia B. Davis, a negro boy named Lewis,
to be enjoyed by her and her heirs forever. 7th, I give unto
my daughter Margaret Elizabeth Frances Davis, a negro boy
named Henry, to be enjoyed by her and her heirs forever. 8th,
I give unto my Daughter Arena Josephine Davis, a negro girl
child named Ann, to be enjoyed by her & her heirs forever.
9th, I require that my two negro men, namely, Prince and Sam,
remain in the family to labor for the support of my children
that continue in the family or are minors, until my youngest
son Rufus C. Davis is twenty one years of age, then I wish the
said negro men to belong to my above named three sons, that is,
I wish my son Nathan C. Davis, to have Sam, and pay over an
amount in money, so that my said sons shall have them or the

(110) value thereof equally amongst them, and further, as my said
negro man Prince is of turbulent, unruly disposition, shall
(111) he prove to remain unmanageable in my family, I request that
he be hired out annually, and the money arising from the hire
to go to the above named three sons, when the youngest shall
be twenty one years old, that is that the two negroes or the
value thereof shall be theirs in the manner above suggested.
10thly, I give unto my wife Polly Davis a certain bay mare,
named Mag, to be enjoyed by her and her heirs forever. 11th,
I give unto my daughter Adaline Davis, a certain sorrel filly
two years old last spring, to be enjoyed by her and her heirs
forever. 12thly, I give to my Daughter Eliza Ann Davis a certain bay filly two years old past, to be enjoyed by her and her
heirs forever, each of the above mares to be valued at seventy
five dollars. 13thly, I give unto my son Newton C. Davis a
certain old sorrel mare for which he shall allow sixty dollars,
and the young colt of said mare I give unto my daughter Narcissa
P. Davis for which she shall be charged thirty dollars. My wagon
and large Oxen, I leave with my family for their support and
benefit, so long as they may remain. 14thly, I request my Executors hereinafter named, to sell all my perishable property
that they may think not necessary for the immediate benefit of
my family, and the money arising therefrom to be equally divided among my children, considering the value of those horses as
part of said money in reference to a certain negro woman named
Mary, given to my wife, her increase, should there be any,
shall descend to my children and be equally divided among them.
And lastly, I do hereby constitute and appoint my friends,
Pleasant Bearden & Thos. W. Hays, executors of this my last
will and testament, hereby revoking all other or former wills
or testaments by me made heretofore. In witness whereof, I
have hereunto set my hand & seal this 17th day of September, in
the year of our Lord, one thousand eight hundred & thirty four.

                                    his
                        William x A. Davis, (seal)
                                    mark

Signed, sealed, published and declared to be the last will &
testament of the above named WILLIAM A. DAVIS in presence of us
who at his request, and in his presence have hereunto subscribed
our names as witnesses to the same.
Attest.
Obidiah Pinson.
John P. Davis. Recorded 6th day of December, 1834.

(112)   John Marr, Last Will and Testament. In the name of God,
Amen. I, JOHN MARR of the County of Lincoln and State of Tennessee, being now on a bed of sickness, but being Sound in mind,
have thought it proper and necessary to arrange my worldly affairs, and dispose of the property wherewith God has blessed me
in this world, as seems to me and proper, therefore I have
adopted this my last will and Testament. 1st, I bequeath my
body to the grave, with suitable interment, and my soul to God
who gave it. 2nd, I will that all my property both real and
personal be sold, except such as hereafter reserved, on the
folllwing terms, viz, My tract of Land on Cane Creek, the same
whereon I now live, containing two hundred and sixty acres or

(112) thereabouts, must be sold to the highest bidder, on one, two and three years credit, the purchaser securing the payments fully, the personal property in like manner to be sold on twelve months credit, to the highest bidder, the above terms to be computed from the court as a notification of sale. 3rd, All notes, hands and accounts that may be due or owing to me at the time of my decease, and such as may fall due thereafter, are to be collected as soon as the law will permit. These sums, viz, the amount of the sales of my property as above and the debts due me as above, together with the ready money I may die possessed of, is to form a capital which is to be laid out in the following manner, viz, my debts are first to be paid, after which three thousand dollars are to be laid out in purchasing young negro slaves, between the age of fifteen and twenty years, the balance whatever it may be is to be laid out in purchasing a tract of land at such place as my executrix may designate, said negroes and land to be placed under her sole direction, & control, until my youngest child shall arrive at full age, it is nevertheless to be understood that the profits arising from the culture of said tract of land which may be purchased, and the labor of said slaves are to be appropriated to the support of the family and education of my children, or so much as may be necessary for that purpose, and if there shall remain a surplus, it may be loaned out or applied in any other way that my executrix may think proper to vest it, yet so as not to waste the same. 4th, I reserve the following property from being sold, viz, my negro boy Jim, two head of horses, two cows and calves,

(113) two feather beds with their furniture and as much provision as will be sufficient for the maintenance of the family, one year from decease. %th When my youngest child shall arrive at full age, there shall be an equal division of the land and negroes amongst my children that are now single, and my wife is to have a childs part and over and above a childs part. I bequeath to her the said negro boy Jim, who at her death may be set free if she so wills. 6th, When my executrix may think proper she is privileged to lay off to each or either of children, John M. B. Marr and Eliza Marr such a portion of the estate as she may deem expedient, but in no case to exceed their proportionable part of the estate. And when either of those who are now of non age, shall have attained to the age of twenty one, She may so lay off to them any part of the estate, which shall be charged to them and considered as so much paid to them at the general division. 7th, I ordain and appoint my well beloved wife, Sarah Marr, sole executrix to this my last will and Testament, hereby revoking and annulling all former wills by me made, either written or verbal, and fully ratifying and establishing this as my last will and testament. In witness whereof I have hereunto set my hand and affixed my seal, this 27th day of July in the year of our Lord, one thousand eight hundred and thirty four.

John Marr, (Seal).

Signed in the presence of us.
William B. Benge.
J. J. Todd.
Wm. C. Blake.   Recorded 8th December , 1834.

(113)   James Blackburn Last Will and Testament. I, JAMES
BLACKBURN, in my proper mind, make this my last will and
testament, world without an Amen. 1st, I wish at death, my
present crop of cotton sold to pay my debts. 2nd, It is my
will that my two cows and calves and heifer, and a sufficiency of my hogs be left for the use of my family, for meat and
stock, and the remainder be sold and that be appropriated to
the discharging of my debts, if my cotton should fail, if there
be a surplus it is to be appropriated to the education of my
(114)   children. 3rd, I leave my sorrel mare and side saddle to my
beloved wife Ellinor, also all my household and kitchen furniture, to her during her natural life or widowhood, the all to
be divided equally between her and my five children. 4th, I
also leave to my beloved Ellinor to raise my children, with
one plough, one hoe, one pair of gear, clevis and swingletree,
one large & 1 small ax, one bee hive. 5th, My corn and fodder
I give for the use of my family. 6th, If there is twenty bushels of wheat, I wish it for the use of my family, if any over
twenty bushels I wish it sold. 7th, And all the rest of my
property, not mentioned I wish sold and the money put to the education of my children. It is my wish that David Blackburn,
and Ellinor Blackman be executors. This 4th day of October, in
the year of our Lord, one thousand eighteen hundred and thirty
four.   his
Test.   Jas. x Blackburn.
W. N. B. Gracy.   mark
Jefferson Kelso. Recorded 9th Dec. 1834.

        William Patterson Last Will. In the name of God Amen.
I, WILLIAM PATTERSON, of the County of Lincoln and State of
Tennessee, being weak as to body, but of sound memory and calling to mind the fatality of Human nature- Believing that we are
all born to die, do make and ordain this my last will & testament. First of all, I recommend it to Almighty God, who gave it.
Secondly, I wish to be buried in a decent like manner at the
discretion of my Friends. I expect there will be money & notes
found among my papers to discharge all my just debts, if not
I want them first paid out of the property which God has been
pleased to bestow on me in this life, at the discretion of my
Executors hereafter mentioned. It is my will and bequest that
the balance of the property both real and personal, shall remain in one joint stock, until my Eldest son now living, arrives at the age of twenty one years of age, which is John C.
Patterson, or Maria H. Patterson marries or becomes of age at
which time or times I bequeath all my property to be valued
and divided equally between my beloved wife Rachel and each of
them surviving heirs, after which it is my request that all
the balance of the lots set apart should again fall into one
(115)   common stock and remain so until some of the Heirs should arrive of age or get married, as before stated, observing that
when any of the female heirs gets married they are intended to
be allowed an Equal part of the estate at that time, except
four hundred dollars which is intended to be applied to a
negro girl, one horse, bridal and saddle, which negro girl,
that I intend and have given to her, her life time, and then
to the heirs of her body forever. I give and bequeath to my
daughter Martha Eliza, one negro girl, named Judean, one horse,

(115) bridle and saddle, on the same condition that I allowed Maria
Henderson Patterson, as above stated, they being the only two
surviving daughters at this time. My sons John C. Patterson,
William B. Patterson, David S. Patterson, James H. Patterson,
and Logan M. Patterson are to have equal shares of the estate,
with their mother, and to be at their disposal after they arrive of age or after the intermarriage of the widow, should
any of my children die before being married or arriving of age,
then the property is to be equally divided among the living.
I appoint my well beloved wife Rachel and my son John C. Patterson as Executrix and Executor of this my last will and
Testament. Witness my hand and seal this 17th April 1833.
                                    William Patterson, (Seal)
Signed, Sealed and delivered in presence of us.
For the probate of the above (see minute Docket) at January
Term 1835. Page 196. Recorded 23rd Feby, 1835.

        I, WALTER B. SHARP, of Lincoln County and State of Tenne-
essee, being in a low state of health, tho of perfect mind
and memory, and knowing the uncertainty of this mortal life, and
the certainty of death, do make, ordain and publish the following, as my last will and testament, hereby revoking all former,
or other wills by me made. First, It is my wish and desire
that after my death that I shall be buried in a decent and order-
ly manner, and that the expense of my funeral be in proportion
to my pecuniary circumstances. Second, It is my will that all
my just debts (which there are but few) be paid out of my notes,
Stock, tools & crop of corn & wheat now on hand, and that as
soon after my death as practicable, and if there should be any
(116) over what will pay my debts, it is to go to my mother, to be
disposed of as she may see proper for her own use. Third, It is
my wish that my negro boy, Alfred, remain in the possession of
my mother, and for her use during her life, and if she should
die before Alfred arrives at thirty one years of age, then &
in that case he is to be hired out by my executor until he arrives at sd, thirty one years of age, and the proceeds to be
equally divided between my brother and sisters, but if my mother should live until Alfred arrives to thirty one years of age,
she is still to have the use & possession of him during her
life and at her death to be freed or if she should die before
he is thirty one, then he is to be free at that age. Alfred is
not to be hired to the highest bidder, but privately by my executor. Fourth, It is my will that my tract of land adjoining
that on which my mother now lives, containing fifty acres &
a half, go to the use of my mother forever, and to be disposed
of as she pleases. Fifth, I give and bequeath to my brother
Benjamin F. Sharp, my negro woman, Malinda, and the child she
is now with- and her son Caleb I give to my sister Elizabeth H.
Sharp- the same negroes that was given to me by my Aunt Nancy
Guyder, and if the said negro woman Malinda should have any
other increase than the one she is now with, then and in that
case the whole of Sd increase, after the one she is now with
is to be equally divided between my brother, Benjamin and my
sister Elizabeth. I also give my bed and furniture to my sister Nancy, & my clock to my brother Benjamin, my candle stand
to my sister Elizabeth, the same bed, clock & candle stand
that was given to me by my Aunt Nancy Guyder. My yearling colt

(116) I give to my brother Benjamin, and my mare I give to my mother.
Lastly, I do hereby constitute and appoint Sam(l Todd, Executor,
of this my last will and testament. In witness whereof I have
hereunto set my hand and affixed my seal, this eighteenth day
of October, in the year of our Lord, one thousand eight hundred
and thirty four.

Walter B. Sharp, (Seal).

Interlined before signed.
Test.
Sam'l Todd.
Hugh Thomason.
Elijah Davis. For the probate of the above will, see minute
docket at January Term 1835. Page 213. Recorded 23rd Feby,1835.

(117)   William Howard's Will. State of Tennessee, Lincoln County,
April 2nd, 1827. In the name of God Amen, And be it remembered that I, WILLIAM HOWARD, being weak in body but of sound &
perfect mind and memory, thanks be to the Almighty God for the
same, and considering the uncertainty of this mortal life, do
make & publish this my last will & testament, in manner and
form following, to wit, that is to say, I will & bequeath to
Benjamin Howard, my youngest son, aged nineteen years old, yet
a minor, the tract of land I now live on with all its appurtenances, containing four hundred & fifty acres, be the same more
or less. I also will and order that he shall remain in possession of one negro man named Richard, also one negro girl named
Vain, also one negro boy, named Samuel, also two horses named
Charley & Roan, also two plows and two pair of gears, also one
mule which is his own right of property, also to remain in possession of all my tools and to have the profits arising from the
use of said negroes & tools, until he becomes twenty one years
of age, which will be the 22nd day of February 1831. Also I
will & bequeath unto the said Benjamin my wheat fan. Also I
Will & order that he shall remain in possession of my oxen &
cart, also to remain in possession of all my cooking utensils,
also choice of my beds and furniture, and choice of my milk cows,
until he should become of age as before stated. And then the
executor of this my last will amd testament shall call a sale,
by giving thirty days notice, and sell the three above named
negroes, & one horse and oxen and cart, and all the farming u-
tensils. I will and decree a title to the rest of the above
named property to the said Benjamin, also I will & order that
the said executrix to this will, shall after my death call a
sale & sell all my personal property & also make a speedy col-
(118) lection of all money due me. and I will & order that the executor shall pay over to Faner Parker, my youngest daughter, a
negro girl aged between twelve & fifteen years of age, which
shall be purchased with the first money he may collect, also I
will & order that all payments shall be made so as to make equal
legacies between Christopher Howard, my oldest son, also Sarah
Boone, my oldest daughter, also Faner Parker, my youngest daughter, whereas I have paid to Christopher Howard six hundred &
sixty dollars, also I have paid to Sarah Boone five hundred and
ten dollars, and I will & order that the said Christopher & the
said Sarah & the said Faner shall be made equal as heirs at law
in my estate, including the several sums paid heretofore mentioned, and I will & order that which several legacies or sums of

(118) money shall be paid to the respective legatees, agreeable to
this my last will and testament, hereby revoking all former
wills by me made. In witness whereof I have hereunto set my
hand & seal, the day and date before written.   his

                      William Howard,**x** (seal).

                        mark

Signed, published & declared by the above named WILLIAM HOW-
ARD, to be his last will and testament in the presence of us
and at his request have hereunto set our names as witnesses
to the same.
Obadiah Burnet.
William A. Tucker.
N.B. Also I appoint Christopher Howard and Benjamin Howard
whole sale executors to my estate. For the foregoing will
see minutes at April Term 1835.

(119)   Leonard Miles Will. The last will and testament of
Leonard Miles. In the name of God Amen. I, LEONARD MILES,
of the State of Tennessee and County of Lincoln, being weak
in body but of sound mind, do make & ordain this my last will
and Testament, revoking all & every other- First, That all my
just debts and contracts be justly and truly paid. Secondly,
I give and bequeath the whole of my estate, both personal &
real, unto my beloved wife, Mary Miles, during her natural life.
Thirdly, After her death, I do give & bequeath to my children
as follows: To Polly Caruthers one dollar. To Elizabeth Atwood
one dollar, one feather bed and trunk. To Sally Martin, one
dollar. To Nancy Gee, one dollar. To William Miles one dollar.
To Leonard Miles, one dollar. To Patsey Lindsay & heirs, one
hundred & fifty acres of land, including the plantation where
I now live, & one feather bed to her daughter Polly Lindsay.
Fourthly, I do appoint William Atwood my executor to settle all
my earthly business. Sealed & acknowledged this first day of
April A.D. 1835.

                Leonard Miles, (Seal).

In presence of us.
William F. Smith.
John Loyd.
The foregoing will was proven & ordered to be recorded at
April Term 1835.

(120)   Cornelius Darnell last Will. In the name of God Amen.
I, CORNELIUS DARNELL, of the State of Tennessee and County of
Lincoln, knowing & believing that it is appointed for all men
once to die, and after that a Great and General Judgment, but
being weak in body, but sound in mind and memory & knowing
that my exit or departure from this world of trouble must come,
do make and constitute this to be my last will and testament,
in the following manner, viz, 1st, I commit my soul to God,
who gave it. 2nd, And my body to its Mother dust, to be buried
in a decent manner, by my friends or executor. I then will,
futhermore that all my property both real & personal estate,
that the Lord hath blessed me with in this world, I will that
it should be sold, the land to be sold on one, two and three
years pay: the negro or negroes to be sold on one years' pay,
for the sake of not parting my negro from her husband,

((120)If Henry Tolly will give within twenty five dollars of what
she or they are worth, he is to have them, otherwise to be sold
to the highest bidder. All my personal property to be sold on
twelve months credit, then I will that all my lawful debts be
paid out of the same and the balance of the money of said estate, after giving my beloved children, common English schooling, be put on interest until my beloved sons and Daughter comes
of age, Calvin R., John B. and Mary Ann Darnell, for them to
have an equal part of the estate, as they come of age, the same
to be divided by my lawful Executor, John Broadway, whom I do
nominate and appoint for that purpose. In testimony whereof I
have affixed my hand and seal this 21st June 1835. his
                                    Cornelius Darnell,x
                                                   mark. (Seal)

Assigned in presence of us,
William Beavers.
William Hopper. Admitted to probate at July Term, 1835.

(121)   Noah Ryals' Will. I, NOAH RYALS, of Lincoln County,and
State of Tennessee, being on a bed of sickness, but of sane
mind, do make and ordain this my last will and Testament, for
the disposal of that property, both real & personal, wherewith
God has blessed me, and which I find myself now possessed.
First, I bequeath my soul to God, who gave it, & my body to the
Grave with suitable interment. Secondly, to my beloved wife,
-----Ryals, I bequeath the tract of land whereon I now live,
during her natural life or widowhood, together with the appurtenances thereto belonging, the profits and unoberments arising
from which is nevertheless to be applied by her to the decent
support & education of our children, after a sufficient subsist-
ance for herself, but at her death or if she shall again marry
I wish the land sold to the highest bidder, on terms that may
be thought the most advantageous, and the money thus arising
to be put out in safe hands on interest until pur youngest
child shall have attained the age of twenty one, the proceeds
to be equally divided among my seven children, Mahala, Nancy,
William, Mary Ann, Martha Lane, Eliza & the youngest child, yet
un-named, the balance of my property I wish sold on 12 months
credit, to the highest bidder, except such as may be absolutely
necessary for the use of the family, & after my debts are all
paid, I want the balance of the money thus arising, to be used
for the support and education of my children. I do hereby revoke, annul and make void all other wills by me heretofore
made & do fully ordain and establish this my last will and Testament. I do hereby constitute my wife, Rebecah Ryals sole
executrix to this my last will and testament, and do not wish
the Court to bind her to security. In witness whereof I have
hereunto set my hand & affixed my seal this 22d, of October 1835.
Test.   his
W. B. Baye   Noah x Ryals, (Seal)
Cas I Claiborne   mark
       Proven at October Term 1835.

(122)   William R. Warren's Will. In the name of God Amen.
I, WILLIAM R. WARREN, of the State of Tennessee and County
of Lincoln, being of sound mind & perfect recollection, do
make this my last will and Testament. And first, I do bequeath and give my Soul to God who gave it, and in the second place, that all my just debts be paid. 3rd, I do bequeath & give all my real and personal Estate to my beloved
wife, Sarah Warren, for five years and as my boys come of
age, that each of them have a fifty dollar horse, viz,Robert
Warren, William Warren, James Warren, Peter Warren, Samuel
Warren, I do will and bequeath to my beloved wife Sarah Warren, all my land during her natural life or widowhood, to
raise the children. I do will to my daughter Mary Warren,
out of my estate what will make fifty dollars, also Sarah Warren fifty dollars, and to my daughter Elizabeth Warren, sixty-
five dollars, and to my daughter Martha Warren one hundred
dollars. And at the death or marriage of my beloved wife
Sarah Warren, all my property, real & personal, to be equally
divided among the named heirs of my body, except to William
Warren to which I bequeath out of my estate fifty dollars more,
and all the rest of the named boys, twenty-five dollars more,
and if there is more property than will make my daughters more
than my daughter Nancy Gean has had,for her to have an equal
share with them, this done and subscribed to in the year of
our Lord, 1835, August 28th.
Witness.   Wm. R. Warren.
John Gilbert
John Cooper.   Proven at Oct. Term 1835.

(123)   Frederick Conaway Will. State of Tennessee, Lincoln
County, December 1st, 1835. In the name of God, Amen I,
FREDERICK CONAWAY, being in alow state of Health, but of
sound mind and memory, and being desirous to dispose of my
worldly goods before I die. 1st, After paying all my just
debts, I give to my loving wife, Minney, all my land & plantation to support her, her natural life or widowhood, & do
also give her all my household & kitchen furniture, I also
give her a choice cow and calf, & I give her my bay mare & a
choice sow & pigs, also eight hundred pounds of pork and 30
barrels of corn for her support until she makes a crop, also
1000 bundles blades, and 1000 bundles oats, also all my stock
of sheep & poultry, I give her my family bible & all the above
named property I leave my wife during her widowhood or lifetime, & if she marries, all the above property to be sold &
equally divided among my lawful heirs. Item the 2nd, I have
portioned off my loving sons John and Wiley with each a horse
and cow and calf & bed & furniture, which is all they are to
have during their mothers life or widowhood. Item 3d,I have
also given my loving son Dunsey, a horse equal to John and
Wileys', he is also to have a bed and furniture and cow and
calf, equal to the others, or $10 in lum of the cow and calf.
Item 4th, I have also portioned off my three oldest daughters,
I give my loving daughter Matilda, a bed & furniture, cow and
calf, sow and pigs, and the other two, equal with her, which
is all their portion during their mothers lifetime or widowhood. I give my loving daughter Peruna Ann a bed & furniture,

(123) and a cow and calf now, and a sow and pigs when she marries.
Item, 6th, I give my loving son, Green B. Conaway, a grey filly
& twenty dollars to make her equal to the other hogs, horses,
a cow & calf, bed & furniture. I also give him the one fourth
of the present crop of corn & fodder, for making & taking care
of it. Item, 7th, I give my loving son Benjamin B. Conway a
bay horse colt & $25. when he is 21 years of age, to make his
horse equal with the rest. I also give him a feather bed &
furniture when he marries or comes of age, also ten dollars in
hire of a cow & calf, when he comes of age or marries. Item 8th,
Lastly, I appoint my loving son, to wit, namely, Wiley W. Conaway and Soloman P. Simpson, my true and lawful Executors to
this my last will and testament. Signed in presence of us, the
above written.   Frederick Conaway. (Seal)
James W. Cooke.
Jesse McClure.   Proven at January Term 1836.

(124)   Robert Moore's Will. In the name of God Amen. I, ROBERT
MOORE, of Lincoln County, Tennessee State, do (in my common
mind and memory) make and constitute the following my last
will and Testament, viz. First, of my goods and chattels pay
my debts, if any. 2nd, I give to my wife all my property, during her natural lifetime, and then to return to our children
except what I shall hereinafter mention. 3rd, I give to my son
Washington Franklin Moore when he comes of age or shall marry,
one half of the tract of land on which I now live, one negro
lad named Alley & one negro girl named Nan & her increase, one
wagon, one set smith tools, one horse, saddle & bridle, worth
one hundred dollars, and one fourth part of all the sheep, hogs,
cattle & farming utensils at that time. 4th I give & bequeath
to my daughter Amanda when she becomes of age or marries, one
negro girl Matilda, and her increase, one negro boy named Portes-
field, one bed,stead and furniture, one bureau,chest and table,
one fourth part of all the horses, cattle and sheep and hogs,
farming tools and wagons not named. 5th, I give to my daughter
Martha Hefizeba Moore when she comes of age or marries, one
negro girl named Temp and their increase, one bedstead and furniture, one bureau chest and table, one fourth part of all the
horses, sheep,cattle, hogs and farming tools and wagons not
before named. 6th, and I constitute my wife Joanah, Executrix,
and James Fulton Esq., Executor. Given from under my hand
and seal on the 4th day of October in the year of our Lord,1832.
Signed in presence of,   Robert Moore, (Seal).
William A. Reavis.
John Enochs
Jacob Silvertooth. Proven at January Term,1836. 14th April 1835.

(125)   Elijah McClure's Will. I, ELIJAH McCLURE, of Lincoln County and State of Tennessee, being in sound mind and memory, do
make this my last will and Testament, revoking all others, In
the first place, I bequeath to my beloved wife Susannah McClure,
my land and household furniture of every kind, likewise my stock
of every kind & farming utensils, during her natural life or
widowhood. I also empower my brother Jesse McClure to pay all
my just debts, and to collect all debts coming to me. I also
empower my brother Jesse McClure to bargain, contract or sell

(125) all or any part of my property so as to go to the benefit of
my wife or children during her life or widowhood or remaining
in good credit. I desire my wife to enjoy all my property as
long as she lives or remains in good credit, but if she marries
or forfeits her credit, then I want whatever part of my estate
should be left or at her death, I desire all my property to be
disposed of in the following manner, I desire my son Aaron to
have 12 months schooling or all my succeeding sons, then I desire all my property to be equally divided among my children.
I desire my brother Jesse McClure to see to the care of my family, and to be paid for his services. In witness whereof I
hereto set my hand and seal this 26th of April in the year of
our Lord, 1831.   his
                Elijah x McClure, (Seal).
                mark
Signed, Sealed and delivered in presence of us.
Thomas McClure.
Aaron McClure. Proven at January Term 1836.

(126)   Isaac Rutledge's Will. This being my last will and Testament. In the name of God Amen. Being of sound memory and
in my proper senses, as follows: After all my just debts & funeral expenses be paid, I wish all my lands to be equally divided
among my heirs, including my Grand daughter, Ann Rebeccah Rutledge, also my perishable part of my estate, I wish equally divided among my heirs. And wish my granddaughter as above named,
to have an equal part in the same, but will leave the matter
discretionary with my heirs, those that are my children,whether
to sell or divide the above named Estate. I wish to be understood respecting the situation of my grand daughter above
named, that is I wish my executors to see to her raising and keep
her & do all other acts as I was bound by law to do as a guardian for said grand daughter above mentioned, and as her estate
is in my hands is the reason I give her an equal share with my
heirs, after her raising, expenses is to come out of her part
& all other expenses be paid, but should my Grand daughter Ann
Rebeccah Rutledge be taken from my executor before the law will
make her a guardian so she can act for herself or be of lawful
age, then I wish her part in my estate to relinquish & wish my
executor only to pay to her what I am bound for as a guardian
for her cash and not to the amount of $808.75 I also wish equal-
ly divided among my heirs as above mentioned. I appoint Mark
Whitaker Jr. and Abner Steed as my Executors. In witness whereof I have set my hand this 23d, day of October 1835.
Attest.   his
J. E. Waggoner.   Isaac x Rutledge, (seal)
Wade I. Morris.   mark
        Proven at January Term 1837.

(127)   Elizabeth Hughey Will. I, ELIZABETH HUGHEY, of Lincoln
County and State of Tennessee, being mindful of my mortality,
do this 23d day of May in the year of our Lord 1836, make &
publish this my last will and Testament, in manner following:
First, I give & bequeath to my Eldest daughter Polly, the rents
& profits arising from my land for the present year, also one
loom, bed & furniture, and I further give & bequeath one cow,

(127) and one Ewe, also I give & bequeath to my eldest son Washington, all my stock of hogs and one yearling calf. Also I give and bequeath to my second son Robert, one yearling calf, and two head of sheep. Also I give & bequeath to my daughter Jennetta, one bed & furniture & two head of sheep. Also I give & bequeath to my son Isaac two head of sheep. Also I give & bequeath to my youngest daughter Peggy, one bed & furniture and two head of sheep and I also desire that my land should be sold on a credit of one and two years, and the money arising from the sale, to be equally divided among all my children, after paying all my just debts. And I do hereby constitute & appoint James Wilson sole Executor of this my last will and Testament. In witness whereof I have hereunto set my hand and seal, the day & year above written. her

Test.   Elizabeth x Hughey.
Mathew Wilson.   mark
Joseph Henderson.
Washington Wilson.

(128)   John Murdock, Senr. Will. I, JOHN MURDOCK, Senior, of the County of Lincoln and State of Tennessee. Farmer, do make and ordain this my last will and Testament in order to dispose of those things which God in his infinite Goodness has bestowed upon me while sojourning here upon Earth, hereby revoking and annulling all other wills by me at any time made, either written or verbal. And 1st, I bequeath my body to the ground, with suitable interment, and my Soul to God who gave it, the expenses of my burial to be paid out of the first money that may come into the hands of executor from my estate, after my decease. 2nd, I bequeath to my son John Murdock, my tract of land whereon I now live, with all the emoluments arriving, or belonging thereto, with this provision only, that my wife Isabella Murdock shall have her maintenance therefrom during her life, as also my daughters Nancy Murdock, Eliza Murdock, and Rachel Murdock are to have an equal portion of the proceeds arising from my farm, so long as they shall see proper to remain upon the premises, but if they marry or shall leave the premises, then their portion to be with held from them, & go to the exclusive benefit of my son John Murdock. 3rd, After all my just debts are paid, I bequeath to my children, John Murdock, Nancy Murdock, Eliza Murdock & Rachael Murdock all my personal estate of whatever kind it may consist, to be equally apportioned to them. 4th, When my mother Molly Murdock dies, if living, I would be sole heir to her estate, which consists principally of money, but out on interest to Col. Jas. Caruthers & Major Wm. Caruthers, of the County, all of which I bequeath to my son John Murdock & my three daughters, Nancy, Eliza, & Rachael Murdock, who have faithfully waited on & attended to my said Molly Murdock during her old & infirm state, to be equally divided among them at her decease. 5th, I bequeath all the debts that may be owing to me at my decease to my son John Murdock, and lastly, I appoint my friend William B. Berry, sole executor to this my last will & testament. These things being done may my soul rest in peace. In witness whereof I have hereunto set my hand & seal, this 6th day of August in the year of our Lord, 1836. Signed & sealed & acknowledged to be the last will & testament of the Testator in presence of us.
Samuel Wakefield   John Murdock, x his mark.

(128) Ezekiel Sanders. Proven at October Term, 1876.

(129)   Anthony Mulling' Will. In the name of God Amen. I, ANTHONY DAVIS, of Lincoln County, State of Tennessre, being very sick in body but in perfect mind and memory, thanks be given unto God for all his mercies, calling to mind the mortality of my body & knowing that it is appointed for all men once to die, dothmake this my last will & Testament, principally & first of all, I give & bequeath my soul to Almighty God, who gave it, & my body I recommend to the earth in a Christian like manner,   as touching my worldly estate I give & bequeath the same in the following manner: 1st, I do give & bequeath to my beloved wife, Sarah Mullins 50 acres of land, 25 acres formerly the property of Wainwright,the other 25 acres of a late entry joining said tract, the line to run from White Summers lower line to Noah Locks line east course, to include said 50 acres, to her & to her use during her natural lifetime with all my stock & my debts due or coming, & all my movable property after my debts are paid. At her death the land and property then in her custody to be sold & equally divided among the legatees. Item 2, I do will that all my other lands be sold at public sale to the highest bidder, agreeable to law, at one year credit, & equally divided among my children & each to receive an equal part,viz, Elizabeth Smith, oldest, Mary Luicity second,Margaret Price, William Mullins, John Mullins, Sarah Byles, Aaron Mullins, Milly Mullins, Patsy Mullins,Walter Mullins,Martin Mullins, George Mullins, Polly Mullins, Milly Mullins, Nancy Ricks, Vincent Mullins, Thomas Jefferson Mullins, Pleasant Mullins, Eliza Mullins, and I do nominate & appoint my trusty friends Jesse Bonner, Samuel W. Clay & William Stephens to be my executors, of this my last will & testament, & do utterly revoke & dis-annul all & every other will, and bequeath, ratifying & confirming this to be my last will & Testament, in witness whereof I have hereunto set my hand & seal, this 5th day of October, 1824.

his

Anthony x Mullins.(seal)

mark

Signed, sealed & delivered in presence of us.
John Paul.
Thomas Gilospie.
John Vickers, Senr.
John Vickers, Jr. x his mark.

(130)   Robert R. Allaup, Will. I, ROBERT R. ALLSUP, of the County of Lincoln and State of Tennessee, do make & publish this my last will and Testament, And first I direct that my body be decently interred, and that my burial be conducted in a manner corresponding with my estate and situation in life. And to such worldly estate as it has pleased God to intrust me with, I dispose of the same as follows: 1st, I direct that all my debts & burial expenses be paid as soon after my decease as possible, out of the first money that shall come into the hands of my executors from any portion of my estate, real or personal, I also direct should there be a sufficiency to pay my debts without selling my personal property that it all remain in possession of my wife during her natural life or widowhood,then to be equally divided between all my children, sons and daughters. I also

(130) direct that should there be enough money left with what will arrive from the sale of my present growing crop, after paying my debts, that it be appropriated in paying for the tract of land on which I now live, which shall remain in possession of my wife during her natural life or widowhood, then to be divided or sold & the proceeds equally divided between all my children as aforesaid. I also direct that so soon as my three youngest sons, Robert H. Alsup, Brin M. G. Allsup and Thomas H. Allsup, have each of them so soon as they come of age, a horse, equal in value with the horses I have given my three oldest sons. I also direct that when my youngest daughter comes to the age of 21, that each of my daughters have a horse equal in value with my sons, if it can be done without distressing my wife, should she be then living, should she die before my youngest daughter comes of age, then my daughters are to have a horse each equal in value with my sons. And I do hereby make & ordain my son Ephraim S. Allsup & David C. Cowen executors of this my last will and Testament. In witness whereof I, ROBERT R. ALLSUP, the testator, have to this my will, writ on one sheet of paper, set my hand & seal, this 22nd day of August in the year of our Lord, 1836.

Robert R. Allsup, (Seal).

Signed, Sealed & delivered in the presence of us, who have subscribed in the presence of each other.
B. M. G. Allsup.
Joseph L. Tharp.

(131) Zealos Milstead Will. The last will and Testament of ZELOS MILSTEAD, Senr. of the County of Lincoln and State of Tennessee. After the payment of my just debts, I give & bequeath the balance of my property in the manner following, viz, To my daughter Sally Milstead, I give one cow and calf, she to have choice of my stock, one bed-stead & bed clothing, she to choose the same. I have already given my son Aaron Milstead all my horses and hogs. To my wife Elizabeth, I give the balance of my property, consisting of household and kitchen furniture and all other things which belong to me, and at her death it is to fall to Sally. Given under my hand this 22nd day of September 1836. his
Ephraim Dickey   Zelos x Milstead, (seal)
Samuel Lauderdale.   mark
Proven at November Term, 1836.

(132) James Scott, Will. I, JAMES SCOTT, of the County of Lincoln & State of Tennessee, being of sound mind & memory, do hereby make this my last will & Testament in the manner and form as hereafter detailed, first, I give unto my wife Jane Scott during her life all that portion of my land lying on the east side of the east fork of Mulberry Creek, including all the buildings & appurtenances thereon, also my negro man named Ned, and negro woman named Mary, to be her property during her lifetime, & bed and furniture, one table and cupboard, bureau, & embracing all articles used in the cupboard, also kitchen utensils sufficient to answer her purpose, also chairs, one large Bible, and such other books she may wish to keep, also two head of cattle, such as she may choose, also a sufficient quantity of grain for her support for one year, embracing fodder &C., say all the grain & fodder on hand, also all the bacon on hand & fifteen head of hogs of her own choosing, & ten head of sheep,

(132) and all the poultry. I give unto Elizabeth Jobe, my daughter, one negro boy named Hal. I give unto Isabelle Turley, my daughter, one negro girl named Mariah. I give unto my daughter, Mary Ferguson, one negro girl named Martha. I give unto my daughter, Rossetta McDonald, one negro girl named Suke. I give unto my daughter, Nancy Mitchell one negro girl named Harriet. I give unto my daughter, Rachel, one negro girl named Ellen, two beds, and furniture, also one horse beast, bridle & saddle as she may choose, to be third choice, one bureau. I give unto my son John, one horse beast, to be fourth choice, also a note of two hundred dollars, which is to be counted of his share in the division. I will my land to be sold at the death of my wife, to the highest bidder. I will my son William Scott, $350. to be taken out of my land when sold & collected, also my son John Scott, $350. in the same way of my son William. I will that my son William Scott, shall have the use of the land he has heretofore occupied, during his mothers lifetime. I will that part of my land west of the creek which is not occupied by my son William to be rented out from year to year, during the lifetime of my wife. I will that all my property not disposed of heretofore in this my will, to be sold on a credit of twelve months & to be equally divided between the whole of my children, after deducting $200. out of my daughter Marys' part, an amount of a horse estimated at that price my son John having received $200. heretofore specified to be counted out in the same way as my daughter Marys' is to be & C. I will that when my land is sold that an equal division be made between the whole of my children, having due regard to all the Clauses specified Viz, an amount of my son John, & daughter, Mary, I do hereby appoint William Moore & Charles Bright, my executors to this my last will & testament, given under my hand this 24th day of March 1836. I will that the property willed to my wife be sold at her death & divided equally as other property. Present.
Carter Walkeer   James Scott.
David Cooper. Proven at May Term 1836.

(133)   Davis Eastland's Will. I, DAVIS EASTLAND, of the County & State of Tennessee, do make & ordain this my last will & Testament, as follows: to wit, 1st, I give & bequeath to my sister Ann L. Eastland whichever one of my two mares, Rose & June, she may choose to take. 2nd, I give & bequeath to my brother Cyrus Eastland my watch. 3rd, I give & devise to my father Ezekiah Eastland all the residue of my property, both real & personal, charging such residue with the payment of all my debts. And I appoint my father sole executor of this my last will, & request that no security may be required to be given by him for the execution of the same, by the County Court. In witness whereof I have hereunto set my hand this 9th day of March 1838.
Signed in presence of,   Davis Eastland.
Charles McKinney
S. W. Carmack.
     In addition to the above it is my request that the County Court may not require my father to return any inventory or amount of sales. I also authorize my father to dispose of such part of my property as may be necessary to pay my debts, either at public or private sale, or in such way as may seem to him best. I, also request that the County Court may not require my father

(133) to make settlement with Commissioners or otherwise, an amount of his executor of my will. In witness whereof I have hereunto set my hand this 19th, March, 1838.
Charles McKinney,   Davis Eastland.
S. W. Carmack.   Proven at April Court 1838.

(134)   Ann Means' Will. State of Tennessee, Lincoln County. In the name of God Amen. I, ANN MEANS, of the State & County aforesaid, widow, being of Sound & perfect mind & memory, do make & publish this my last will and Testament in manner & form following: First, I give and bequeath to my Nephew, Alfred S. Templeton, one negro boy named Andrew. Also give & bequeath to my nephew, Leander Templeton, one negro girl named Milly. Also give & bequeath to my nephew Howard Templeton, one negro girl named Amanda. Also, I give & Bequeath to my nephew Hugh M. Templeton, one negro girl named Hannah. I also give & bequeath to my niece Minerva W. Templeton, one negro girl named Caroline. I do also give and bequeath to my niece, Evaline A. Templeton, one negro girl named Emaline. I do also give and bequeath to my nephew & niece, Archibald & Polly Templeton two negro children named Elizabeth & Jane, to be theirs their lifetime, and then to be left to their youngest child, William W. Templeton, and do also give & bequeath unto Elizabeth Craig, John Shulos, Margaret Craig, Nancy Curry & to Robert Shulos the sum of thirty dollars each, the above sum to be paid to the respective parties, by my executors hereinafter named, out of the personal property devised hereinafter mentioned, to my residuary legatees, for the purpose of buying each of them a suit of mourning at my death, and it is my wish that Henry & Kez should be free at my death, provided the laws of this State would admit of their staying in it, or if they shall be at liberty to do so, and if not, they & their increase to be left to Polly Templeton until her death & then they shall be equally divided among the heirs of her body. I do also give & bequeath to Minerva & Evaline Templeton my two beds & furniture. And lastly, as to all the rest and residue & remainder of my personal estate of what kind & nature soever,

(135) after my just debts & funeral expenses are paid, the remainder shall be equally divided between the heirs of Archibald & Polly Templeton. And I now appoint & nominate John Wilson & Cyrus Cathey sole executors of this my last will & Testament, hereby revoking all former wills by me made. In witness whereof I have hereunto set my hand & seal this July 1835. her
                            Ann x Means.
                            mark
Signed, sealed, published & declared by me ANN MEANS to be her last will & Testament, in the presence of us who have hereunto subscribed our names as witnesses in the presence of the Testator.
Witness.
John McDaniel.
John I. Crawford.
     In addition to this my last will, it is my wish that Archibald Templeton shall be the Guardian of his children until they come of age.   her
              Ann x Means.
              mark
John I. Crawford.

(136)   Moses Chambers' Will. Memorandum, that I, MOSES CHAM-
BERS, of the State of Tennessee, being in my perfect senses, &
right mind, & contemplating that it is appointed for all men
once to die, I do make this my last will & testament in the words
following: First of all being impressed of the rights of men,
being entitled to freedom, I do as an act of Justice & Humanity,
emancipate & set free from bondage my mulatto man, Stephen, at
my decease & do hereby emancipate the said Stephen from my heirs
Executors, Adm. or assigns from all slavery forever. I do give
& bequeath all my worldly Goods & Chattles in the following manner: Imprinus. I give and bequeath to my wife Jean a plentiful
support out of my estate, with a young negro to wait on her during life, then to be sold & equally divided. I give & bequeath
to Julia Parks a part of my tract of land joining the part that
I formerly gave her, the same more or less, beginning at my
south boundary line & running up the creek with the Meanders, to
the road & with the road to her line, a southeast course, the
balance of my estate I wish to be sold, both real & personal, &
equally divdied with my Grand Children, John Cook, Catherine
Chambers, Jobe Parks, & Elizabeth Jean Parks. I wish them to receive their portion when they become twenty one years of age, or
when they marry. I do hereby appoint Daniel Sivally & John Sivally as my Executors & Executrixes, of this my last will and
testament, hereby revoking & dis-annulling all other wills & testaments or covenants, desiring this & only this to be my last will
& testament, & no other. In witness whereof I have hereunto set
my hand & affixed my seal this 9th of August, 1837.
Signed & sealed in presence of us.   Moses Chambers, (seal)
Test.
John S. Johns
John T. Brown
Daniel Spuk x his mark.
     As I deem it necessary for giving my reasons for not laying
off a dower, they are that I did not think her capable of manag-
ing such, for she has been insane for some twelve years or more.
And furtherthought proper to will her a plentiful support, if it
took the half of my estate or even all, it is not my intention
to wrong, but to right her. This September 15th 1837.
                              Moses Chambers.
The above will proven at November Term 1837.

(137)   Robert Stephens' Will. The last will & Testament of
ROBERT STEPHENS, of the County of Lincoln & State of Tennessee.
Considering the uncertainty of this mortal life & being in
Sound mind & memory, thanking Almighty God for the same, I do
make this last will & testament in manner & form following: viz,
I will that all my just debts as shall be by me owing at my
death, with my burial expenses, shall in the first place be paid.
I give & bequeath to my beloved son, Jerman Stephens the tract
or parcel of land that I now live on, containing 177 acres, also
30 acres lying bounded by William Rollin & Benjamin Noles. I give
& bequeath to my second son, James Stephens, one negro woman Rar-
ecy & her two children, Robert & Mary. I give & bequeath to my
third son, Josiah Stephens one negro man, Peter & negro woman Silva.
I give & bequeath to my fourth son Henry Stephens, three hundred
dollars in money. I give & bequeath to Robert Randolph Stephens,

(137) son of James Stephens, one hundred dollars in money. I give & bequeath to my grand daughter Sarah Ann Franklin, the daughter of David Franklin, one negro girl Eliza, with her offspring, and if Sarah Ann Franklin shall depart this life before the age of eighteen years or her marrying, then the said girl shall be the property of Theophilus Franklin, the son of David Franklin. I will that Sarah Ann's mother Sarah Franklin, the wife of David Franklin shall have the use of the girl Eliza, during Sarah Ann's minority, or death. Also I give to the said Sarah Ann one bed, bedstead & furniture, & one bureau. I give & bequeath to my daughter, Sarah Franklin, the wife of David Franklin, twenty dollars in money. I give & bequeath to my grand son Theophilus Franklin, the son of David Franklin, one bed, bedstead & furniture. I give to my negro woman Letty one hundred dollars in money, also the said Letty to have the liberty of living with any of my children that she may like best. I give to my negroes, Ned, Peter, Silva & Raney, ten dollars each in money. I will that my negro Ned shall be sold

(138) to the highest bidder on a twelve months' credit. Also I will that all my stock of all kinds with all farming utensils, with household & kitchen furniture to be sold on twelve months credit. I will that if there be a residue of money left, this money shall be equally divided between Tennessee Stephens & Mary Stephens, the daughter of Jerman Stephens & Charity Ann Stephens, the daughter of Joniah Stephens. I do nominate & appoint Charles Bright of the County of Lincoln & State of Tennessee & John Moorehead of the County aforesaid, Executors of this my last will & Testament, hereby revoking all former will by me made. In witness whereof I have hereunto set my hand & seal this November the 10th 1835.

Robert Stephens, (seal).

Signed, sealed, published & declared by the above named ROBERT STEVENS, to be his last will & Testament, in the presence of us, who at his request & in the presence of him, have subscribed our names as witnesses thereto.　　　his

Henry x Warren, (seal)

mark

J. B. Ramsey, (seal)

The foregoing will of ROBERT STEPHENS was established at the June Term 1837, of the Circuit Court of Lincoln County.

(139)　　　Hiram Culberson's Will. I, HIRAM CULBERSON, of the County of Lincoln & State of Tennessee, do make & publish this my last will & Testament, & first I direct that my body be decently interred. And as to such worldly Estate as it has pleased God to entrust me with, I dispose of the same as follows: First, I direct that all my debts be paid as soon after my decease as possible, also I direct that my wife Nancy Culberson shall have & hold all my property for the support of herself & children, during her natural life or widowhood. Also wish so soon as it is or may be thought best by my executor or executrix, that they shall dispose of so much of my property as they think can well be spared, & appropriate the money, with the money in hand, to the following use, viz; in buying a tract of land, which land shall remain in the hand of my wife, Nancy during her natural life or widowhood, then to be equally divided or sold, & the proceeds equally divided between all my children, viz; Parthena, Abi, James S., William C., Mary Ann, Thomas, Sarah E., Hiram F. L. Culberson. My two oldest

83

(139) sons have had a horse, saddle & bridle, & as soon as the balance come of age or so soon as they may need it, I wish them to have one each, of equal value. After the death or marriage of my wife, then I want all my property that is in hand now, with its proceeds & what may come into her hands as a legacy to me, to be equally divided between all my children as aforesaid, & I do hereby ordain & appoint my wife Nancy Culberson, James S. & Wm. C. Culberson, Executrix & Executors of this my last will & testament. In witness whereof I, HIRAM CULBERSON, the Testor, have to this my will written on one sheet of paper, set my hand & seal this 28th day of April 1836. Signed, sealed, & delivered in presence of us, this day & date above written.
Jesse Holbert.
Morgan Holbert.

I wish all this business to be transacted without any security or responsibility on any one of the Executors. I also request that D. Hightower be called on by my Executor or Executrix, for any advice or assistance they may need from him, & my request is that he lend them all the aid & assistance in his power, without the responsibility of our Executor.
Jesse Holbert.   Hiram Culberson,(seal).
Morgan Holbert.   Proven at September Term, 1837.

(140)   Margaret McCoy's Will. In the name of God Amen. I, MARGARET McCOY, of Lincoln County & State of Tennessee, having attained to an advanced age, and being weak in body, but through the mercy of God, of sound mind & memory, do make, ordain, publish & declare this my last will & Testament, revoking all others, that is to say, First, it is my will & desire that all my just debts & funeral expenses be paid. "nd, I give & bequeath to my grand daughter, Candess Delina McCoy, my negro woman Dica, aged about 50 years, also one bed, bedstead & furniture, also one yearling heifer & increase from this time. 3rd, I give & bequeath to my children, named Spruce S. McCoy, David Billings, Samuel Williams & Elizabeth Wilson, the whole of the balance of my property, including my tract of land & negro man, Harry, & all other description of property to be sold & the proceeds equally divided between them. It is also my desire that my friend John C. Taylor should enter in as my Executor & dispose of the property agreeable as set forth above. In witness whereof I have hereunto set my hand & seal this 14th day of May,1837.
Signed, sealed in presence of,   her
Ira McKinney.   Margaret x McCoy, (seal).
John Wood.   mark
        The foregoing will proved at Sept. Term, 1837.

(141)   William Hobbs Will. In the name of God Amen. I,WILLIAM HOBBS, of the County of Lincoln & State of Tennessee, being of sound mind do make this my last will & testament, as follows; (viz), Item first, I will & bequeath to my sons, Nathaniel Hobbs & William Hobbs, my negro boy Dick, to be equally divided between them after my death, also I will to my son Nathaniel Hobbs, my wagon and two head of horses for the trouble & expense he has been at in removing me from the state of North Carolina to Tennessee. Also I will that my son William have his equitable part in paying my mediaal bill & funeral expenses

(141) with my son Nathaniel, to be paid out of his part of said negro boy Dick. Item 2nd, I will that my negro woman Phillis, be sold after my death & the price of said negro to be equally divided between my two daughters, Nancy & Sally, and my grand daughter, Caroline George & that my grand daughter receive her part of said negro woman when she arrives at the age of eighteen years, & if it should so happen that she should die without a lawful heir, I desire that it come back to my own heirs. Item 3rd, I desire that my grand son Lorenza Don Porter receive five dollars in cash out of my estate, after my death. I have given to my two sons Jesse & Alfred their full proportion of my estate, for which I have put them in full possession of, before I left Carolina. Also I will my bed & furniture to my grand daughter Susannah Alfred Hobbs after my death. I also appoint my son Nathaniel Hobbs my lawful executor. December, 7th, 1836.

Attest

Thomas Fortune

David W. George

his

William x Hobbs

mark

This will was proven at January Term, 1837.

(142) John Whitaker's Will. In the name of God Amen. I, JOHN WHITAKER, of the County of Lincoln & State of Tennessee, being weak in body, but of sound mind, & knowing that man has once to die, do make this my last will & Testament, revoking all others. 1st, I will my body to the earth & my Soul to God who gave it, and that all my debts be paid. 2nd, I will that all my estate both real & personal be equally divided among all my children, except such part as is hereinafter disposed of, & that my beloved wife Nancy be made an equal heir with them. I give one negro woman, Caty to her to do as she may think proper with, also one horse of her choosing in addition to her dower in the land & childs' portion. 3rd, I give to my grand daughter Nancy W. Sebastian, a negro girl, Judea. 4th, I will that my negroes be lotted off equally among all my heirs, to my wife, Nancy, the heirs of William Whitaker, I. I. Whitaker, Joseph Whitaker, the heirs of Nancy Sebastian, Benjamin Whitaker, Thomas Whitaker, Daniel Whitaker, Martha King, Madison G. Whitaker & Newton Whitaker, & that my land be sold on a credit of one, two, & three years & that the rest of my property of every description be sold on twelve months credit, except one third of all the household & kitchen furniture, which third is reserved & given to my wife, with one years provision. 5th, In order to equalize my property among all my heirs herein named, I here record the amount they have severally received. I have heretofore given my son William, twelve hundred & ninety four dollars($1,294.) to my son John, I have given nine hundred & eighty six dollars($986) to my son Joseph, eight hundred & seventy nine dollars ($879.) to my son Benjamin, nine hundred & fifty dollars.($950.) to my daughter Nancy, twelve hundred dollars. ($1,200.) to my son Thomas, nine hundred dollars.($900.) to my son Daniel, nine hundred dollars.($900.) to my daughter Martha, one thousand & ninety five dollars. ($1,095.) to my son Madison G., nineteen hundred dollars. ($1,900.) to my son Newton, fifteen hundred dollars.($1,500.) 6th, It is my will that all my heirs be made equal as before named, that they all receive nine hundred dollars, with the amount already received before further division is made,

(142) and those whose sums are small or under $1900. receive interest on the deficit, from this time until the division is made. 7th, It is my will that my friend William Moore, with my two sons, John I. Whitaker & Newton Whitaker, be my Executors. Signed & sealed this 31st day of January 1837. In presence of, John Whitaker, (seal). John Bailey. William Moore. This will proven at July Term, 1837.

(143)   John Gray's Will. I, JOHN GRAY, of the County of Lincoln & State of Tennessee, knowing the uncertainty of this mortal life & the certainty of death, at the sametime enjoying usual health & sound mind & memory, do make, ordain & publish this as my last will & Testament. First, it is my will & desire that after my death, I shall be buried in a plain decent Christian like manner. Second, it is my will that after my death all my just debts (if there be any) be paid & settled as speedily as. Third, it is my will that all my property, both real & personal of every description remain in the possession & be under the control & management of my wife, Mary R. Gray, for the purpose of raiding & supporting my three children, which I have had by her, to wit, Elizabeth, Mahala & Frances until the youngest one of them arrive at the age of eighteen years, at which period it is my will that all my property of every description, both real & personal, consisting of land, negroes & other property which I shall leave at my death, be sold & the proceeds thereof equally divided between my children which shall then be living & the grand children by those who shall then be dead, that is to say, the whole of my grand children by any one of my children, to have a share or portion equal to one of my children, they inheriting that portion which my child should have inherited, had it been living, my present wife having an equal share or childs' part or dower in the land if she chooses, & a childs part of the negroes & other property. Fourth, it is my will that if my wife Mary R. Gray should marry before my youngest child arrives at the age of eighteen years, then & in that case, it is my will that all my property both real & personal be sold & equally divided between my wife & my children & grand children, who shall then be living, that is to say, all my grand children together of any one of my children to have a childs' part, unless my wife should choose to have her dower as aforesaid, in that case she is to have an equal share or childs part of the other property. Fifth, That in case my wife should die before my youngest child should arrive at the age of Eighteen years, it is then my will

(144) that all my estate both real & personal be sold & the proceeds thereof equally divided between my then living children & grand children if my daughters by my present wife should marry before the youngest arrives at the age of eighteen years, it is my will that upon their marriage they be furnished out of my estate or property, so left in the hands of my wife, a good cow & calf, a good feather bed & furniture, & such other necessities toward housekeeping as can be conveniently spared & furnished by their mothers, as near as may be to the amount furnished my other children upon their marriage. I hereby nominate & appoint my wife Mary R. Gray executrix & James Bright, executor of this my last will & Testament. In witness whereof I have hereunto set my

(144) hand & seal this 16th day of October in the year of our Lord, 1832, & of the Independence of the United States, the fifty-seventh. Acknowledges in presence of us this 5th day of November, 1832.   John Gray, (seal).
John King
John Copeland.
The foregoing will Established at the June Term 1837, of the Circuit Court.

(145)   Aaron McWorter's Will. State of Tennessee, Lincoln County In the name of God Amen. I, AARON MCWORTER of Lincoln County & State of Tennessee, being weak of body & knowing that all men must die, do make & constitute this my last will & testament, in the first place, recommending my soul to God who gave it, in hopes of its Eternal will being through the merits of a crucified Savior, and my body to be buried in a decent manner without pomp or unnecessary expense. And my worldly property I dispose of in the following manner; that is, I give & bequeath to my well beloved wife Rebecca her bed & furniture, also one little pot & skillet, tea kettle & coffe pot, bread dish & coffee mill & one drab iron & likewisw the one half of my dresser,furniture & cooking utensils & also one hundred & fifty weight pork & two barrels of corn, one spinning wheel, one brown cow & the remainder of my movable property to expose to sale, to pay all my just debts & if there be any money remaining after my debts are paid, to be equally divided among my three children,(viz),Betsy,McWorter, Hugh B. McWhorter, & Matilda McWhorter, & likewise my real estate to be offered at public sale by my executors & the money arising from such sale of my plantation to be equally divided among the aforesaid three children & not to any of the rest of my children & I likewisw nominate & appoint my trusty friends, William Strong & Cordell Sheffield, executors of this my last will & testament. In witness whereof I have set my hand & affixed my seal this 4th day of April, 1837.
In presence of,   Aaron McWhorter,(seal)
Joseph Joins
Elizabeth Moore,x her mark. This will proven at July Term 1837.

(146)   Anna McConnell's Last Will. In the name of God Amen. I, ANNA MCCONNELL, of the County of Lincoln and State of Tennessee, being of sound mind and disposing memory do make and ordain this my last will and Testament in manner & form following: First, I direct that all my just debts be paid. Item, I direct that after my death my body be decently buried and all necessary funeral expenses be paid out of my estate. Item, I give and bequeath unto my daughter-in-law Patsy McMcConnell during her natural life for the support of herself and family, my boy Sam, and if her son Robert McConnell should survive his mother, then at the death of said Patsy I give said boy Sam to Robert McConnell, duing his natural life, and at his death the said boy shall have his freedom, and in the event that the said Patsy McConnell should survive her son Robert, then my will is that Sam shall be not be sold in any event, either by Robert McConnell or any other person to pay and satisfy any of the debts contracted by said Robert, either before or after he may get possession of said boy, Sam. Item. I give and bequeath to Robert McConnell my bureau.

(146) Item, I give and bequeath to Sarah T. McConnell my bed and furniture. Item, I give and bequeath to John Perry McConnell, all my interest due and owing me for the hire of Sam for twelve months, at eight dollars per month, from the estate of John P. McConnell, deceased, to be paid to him so soon as the same may be collected, also my family Bible to be delivered to him at my death. Lastly, I constitute and appoint Elijah M. Rings & A. Bradshaw, my Executors of this my last will and testament. In witness whereof I have hereunto set my hand and seal, this the eighth day of July, in the year of our Lord 1834. Signed,sealed and published by the testator as her last will and testament, in the presence of us. her
A. Yell.   Anna x McConnell,(seal).
John T. Morgan.   mark
This will proven at June Term, 1838.

(147)   Abner C. Heath's Will. I, ABNER C. HEATH of the County of Lincoln, and State of Tennessee, planter, do make and publish this my last will and testament, hereby revoking and making void all former wills by me at any time heretofore made, and first I direct that my body be decently interred at, in said County in a manner suitable to my condition in life. And as to such worldly estate as it hath pleased God to entrust me with, I dispose of the same as follows: First, I direct that all my debts and funeral expenses be paid as soon after my decease as possible, mout of any money that I may die possessed of, or may first come into the hands of my executors from any portion of my estate, real or personal. Secondly, I give and bequeath my home and farm to my beloved wife, during her natural life, amd at her death it is to be equally divided between my children, and I want as much of my perishable property sold as will pay my just debts, and the balance to be for the use of my wife and children. I do hereby make and ordain and appoint my esteemed neighbors and friends, Samuel Young and John Copeland executors of this my last will and testament. In witness whereof I, ABNER C. HEATH, the said testator have to this my will written one sheet of paper. Set my hand and seal this thirtieth day of June in the year of our Lord one thousand eight hundred and thirty eight. Signed, sealed in presence of us.
James Sorrell.   Ab. C. Heath, (seal).
James Frame.
Proven at the August Term 1838, of the County Court of Lincoln County, Tennessee.
          C. Boyles, Clk.

(148)   William S. Hall's Will. I, WILLIAM S. HALL, being in a low state of health, but being in sound mind do make this my last will and Testament. First, I bequeath my soul to God who gave it. Second, I wish and desire that my funeral expenses & all my debts be paid as soon after my death as possible, out of any money that I may die possessed of, or may first come into the hands of my executors. Third, I give and bequeath to my beloved wife, Rebecca, one mare and colt, named Jude, two cows & calves, one bed and furniture, one cupboard, one bureau, one loom, and such other household and kitchen furniture as my executors think she will need for her comfort and convenience, and as much corn, fodder, wheat and oats, beef and pork, as my said

(148) executors think sufficient for one years support for her and her family. Also it is my desire that my wife Rebecca, shall have the entire use and control of my plantation to enable her to live comfortable and maintain herself and children during her natural life. She shall have the privilege of renting it out, cultivating it, or in any other way using it for her own advantage, by and with the consent of my said executors. Fourth, I give and bequeath to my daughter Lucinda A. Hall, one be and furniture. Fifth, it is my desire that my executors shall as soon as possible after my death, proceed to sell all my effects on a credit of twelve months, except what is heretofore provided for and close my business as soon as possible. Sixth, it is my request that after the death of my wife Rebecca, that my said executor shall proceed to sell the whole of my real estate and the appurtenances thereon, on such terms as the law directs, and shall as soon as possible divide the proceeds equally among my lawful heirs. Seventh, and lastly, I do hereby nominate and appoint William Thomas, my executor. In witness whereof I do to this will set my hand and seal this the 2nd day of August, 1838. Signed, sealed and published in our presence, and we have hereunto set our names. This 2d,August, 1838.
J. L. Stone.   Wm. S. Hall, (seal)
John N. Hayes. Proven by J.L.Stone, Sept. Court, 1838.
         Proved at Oct. Term 1838.

(149)   State of Tennessee, Lincoln County, I, SAMUEL BUCHANAN, do make and publish this as my last will and Testament, hereby revoking and making void all other wills by me at any time made &C. First, I direct that my funeral expenses and all my debts be paid as soon after my death as possible, out of any money that I may die possessed of, or may first come into the hands of my executors. 2,Secondly, I give and bequeath to my beloved wife, Sallt Buchanan, the profits of my plantation for the purpose of raising my children, and then to have her third part during her life, also to have the use of my household & kitchen furniture, and as much of the stock as will be necessary for their benefit of raising them, though to be under the control of my executors, and likewisw to have all my furniture, tools for the benefit of the farm. Thirdly, I wish my negroes to be kept under the care of my executors for to help to raise my children, then to be divided equally amongst all my children, my wife to have her part the number of my negroes is as follows: one negro woman & five children, two boys and three girls. Fourthly, I wish my sons, James M. Buchanan & Simpson Buchanan for their labor in helping to raise the rest of the children, I wish my Executors to pay them what they think is right, out of the crop or stock that they raise, to be paid yearly to them and not charged to them in their part of the legacy, and my younger son William Buchanan, to have the same allowance when able to work with the rest, and make a hand. I wish my negro woman Luanne to remain in the family for the purpose of raising my children. Fifthly, I allow my daughter Mary's two children, James Tooley & Preston Tooley, to have an equal part with the rest of my children, counting what she received, I allow all to share equal in the division. I do hereby nominate and appoint William H. Taley, & James M. Davis my executors. In witness whereof I do to this

(149) my will, set my hand and seal this twenty third day of May, one
thousand eight hundred & thirty eight.
Test. signed in presence of us,   Samuel Buchanan, (seal).
Thomas Hines.
Thomas H.N. Gaugh.
Samuel Buchanan.
Thomas Massey.   Proven at October Term 1838, County Court.

(150)   In the name of God Amen. I, JOSEPH LONG, of the County of
Lincoln and State of Tennessee, being weak in body, but of perfect sound mind and memory, do make and constitute this my last
will and testament. First, that my body be decently buried in
Christian like manner. Secondly, that my worldly goods and effects that God has blessed me with, I will, give, bequeath and
dispose of as follows: to wit; First that all my just debts be
paid. Secondly, I give and bequeath to my beloved wife Matilda,
one negro woman named Myra, one negro man named Moses, and the
two negro children named Martha and Mary, together with my saddle horse, household and kitchen furniture, two cows and calves,
and such of provisions on hand as will support the family one
year, and such as sugar, coffee, flour or other things needful,
as is not on hand, they must be procured. All the balance of my
perishable property, such as stock, provisions, farming utensils,
&C., I wish to be sold on twelve months credit, my negroes to
be kept in the tan yard, and on the farm, under some tanners and
curriers, that be procured by my Executors hereafter mentioned,
until the crop is secured, that together with the stock sold &
the stock of Leather now in the yard is tanned out, all of which
stock of Leather I wish sold at private or public sale, as my
said executor may deem most advisable. Thirdly, I give and bequeath to my beloved wife Matilda, and to my four children (viz)
Mary Ann, Robert W. William R. and Albert J. an equal division
of my personal estate, after the above distribution, my lands,
and tan yard to be rented and negroes to be hired out until the
children become of age. My said wife to have her dower of one
third of the real estate for life, and when my said children arrives to lawful age, their estate to be divided between them
equally by division or sale, the way most satisfactory. My
children to be raised and educated from the hire, rent and interest. I hereby appoint my brother William F. Long and Rufus K.
Flack, my Executors to this my last will and testament, hereby
revoking all former wills by me heretofore made. In testimony
whereof, I have hereunto set my hand and affixed my seal, this
5th day of September, 1838.
Witness.   J. Long, (seal)
B. H. Berry.
D. M. Beatie.
John H. Taylor. Proved at October Term 1838 County Court.

(151)   I, JOSHUA GIBSON, of Lincoln County and State of Tennessee, being sick and weak of body, but of sound mind and disposing memory (for which I thank God) and calling to mind the
uncertainty of human life and being desirous to dispose of all
such worldly substance as it hath pleased God to bless me with,
I give and bequeath the same in the following manner: that is
to say, I give and bequeath to Newton M. Buchanan, the son of

(151) Samuel S. Buchanan, the tract of land that I now live on, it
being a tract of land that   bought of Robert Bradon, on the
waters of Cane Creek. I give and bequeath to Andrew J. Buchanan, the son of Samuel S. Buchanan, the tract of land that I
bought of John H. Gibson, on the waters of Buchanan Creek,187
acres more or less. I give and bequeth to William S. Buchanan th
the son of Samuel S. Buchanan, my negro man Dick. I give and
bequeath to Samuel S. Buchanan all my interest and claim I
have in a tract of land that Samuel S. Buchanan and myself
bought of Francis L. Kincannon on the waters of Cane Creek, a-
bout a ninety acre tract, the said Samuel S. Buchanan must pay
his son John M Buchaman, or cause it to be paid, the sum of
three hundred dollars for my interest in the above named Kincannon tract of land. It is my will and desire that all the
remainder of my perishable property be sold immediately after
my decease, and that my executors hereinafter named, after paying my funeral expenses and what debts I may owe, do equally
divide the surplus, if any, among Sam'l S. Buchanan's four
daughters, Louisa, Margaret, Julia and Mary Ann. It is my will
and desire that my executors as aforesaid do equally divide all
the money I may die possessed of, and all money which may be
due me at my death, so soon as it can be collected, equally a-
mong Samuel S. Buchanan's four daughters. And finally, I do
hereby constitute and appoint James Fulton and Samuel S. Buchanan executors of this my last will and testament by me heretofore made. In witness whereof I have hereunto set my hand
and seal this thirty first day of January in the year of our
Lord, one thousand eight hundred and thirty seven, in presence of the Subscribing witnesses. his
                                    Joshua x Gibson, (seal).
                                           mark
        Signed, sealed, published and declared to be the last
will and testament of the above named JOSHUA GIBSON in presence of us who at his request and in his presence have hereunto subscribed our names as witnesses to the same.
James Toole.
David Buchanan.
Juan J. S. Edmiston. Proved at October Term 1838,County Court.

(152)   In the name of God Amen. I, ABRAHAM SUMMERS of the County of Lincoln, and State of Tennessee, being weak of body, but
of sound mind and disposing memory, for which I thank God, and
calling to mind the mortality of the body and the uncertainty
of human life, do make, ordain, constitute and appoint this my
last will and testament in manner and form following; principally and first of all I give and bequeath my soul into the
hands of Almighty God who gave it, and my body I recommend to
the dust to be buried in a decent Christian burial, at the discretion of my Executors, and such worldly estate as it has
pleased God to bless me with. I give and bequeath in the manner and form following: first it is my will and desire that all
my just debts be paid and funeral expenses out of my perishable
property. Secondly, I give and bequeath to my beloved wife
Nancy, my negro woman Patsy and her youngest child James, during her natural life, and at her death, the said negro woman,
Patsy to descend to my beloved dauhhter, Margaret Coble, for
herself and heirs forever, and it is my will and desire that

(152) my beloved wife have her maintenance on my plantation so long
as she sees proper to live on the same, and retain as much of
my household and kitchen furniture as she sees proper, and if
the said negro woman Patsy have any more children in the lifetime of my beloved wife Nancy, then it is my desire that the
value of the said children, including James, shall equally be
divided amongst my beloved children and their heirs. Thirdly,
I give and bequeath to my beloved son Thomas P. Summers, and
Abraham M. Summers, my plantation whereon I now live, to be
equally divided between them, agreeable as to quality and
quantity, so as to divide the basin spring for themselves and
their heirs forever.

    Fourthly, I give and bequeath to my beloved son William G.
Summers, my black boy Arthur, for himself and his heirs for-
ever. Fifthly, I give and bequeath to my beloved son, Thomas
P. Summers, my black boy, Robert, for himself and his heirs forever. Sixthly, I give and bequeath to my beloved daughter Mary
Williamson, my black girl, Silvy for herself and her heirs forever. Seventhly, I give and bequeath to my beloved son Abraham
M. Summers, my black boy, Green for himself and his heirs forever. Eighthly, I give and bequeath to my beloved grand daughter
Nancy Summers,---- dollars to be paid to her by my other children between now and the time she comes to the age of twenty
years, if she should live to arrive to that age, and not otherwise. And lastly, I do hereby constitute and appoint my beloved sons, William G. Summers and Thomas P. Summers and Abraham M. Summers, executors of this my last will and testament,
hereby revoking all others or former wills or testaments by me
heretofore made. In witness whereof I have hereunto set my
(153) hand and seal this day, in the year of our Lord, one thousand
eight and seventy.
                Abraham Summers, (seal).

    Intestinal before signed, sealed and declared to be the
last will and testament of the above named ABRAHAM SUMMERS in
presence of us who at his request, and in his presence have
hereunto subscribed our names as witnesses to the same.
Proven and ordered to be recorded at November Term 1838.

    I, DAVID HOLMAN, of Lincoln County, and State of Tennessee,
being old and infirm in body, but of sound mind and memory, and
knowing that it is appointed for all men once to die, do make
and ordain this writing to be my last will and testament, viz,
In the first place, my will and desire is that my funeral expenses, and just debts be first paid, and as touching such
worldly goods and effects as may remain thereafter, I give and
dispose of in the following manner. In the first place, I give
and bequeath to my sons Isaac, James and Hohn, the land and
plantation whereon I now live, with all the improvements thereon,
belonging, containing about one hundred and forty acres to be
equally divided between them. 2nd, I give and bequeath to my
daughter Sally Haggard, a negro girl named Caroline which I
have heretofore given her, and which she is already in possession of. I also give to her my negro girl Emmaline, which
she is to have and be in possession of after my death. And
that all my property that may remain at my death, both real &
personal (except the land before named) be sold on a credit of
twelve months, and that a part of the children of my son Hardy,

(153) (deceased), namely, Patsy (now the wife of James S. Holman)
James, Willis and Nancy have One eleventh part of the net
proceeds of such sale. Only that my grand daughter Patsy,
(154)(wife of said James S. Holman, as aforesaid) have thirty
dollars more than the aforesaid James, Willis and Nancy, in
consideration of thirty dollars loaned by the said James S.
Holman to the father of said children, in his life time, which
has never been replaced to the said James S, Holman. The
balance which may arise from such sale, I desire to be equally divided between my three sons aforesaid, namely, Isaac,
James, John and the children of my daughter Polly,(now the
wife of Harrison Davis),formerly the wife of John Hughes,de-
ceased.(except her child Jesse, which she has had since her
inter-marriage with said Davis, and such other child or children as she may hereafter have by the said Davis. And if it
should so happen that either of the said children of my son
Hardy,dec'd, as mentioned above, should die without issue or
before they may become of lawful age, that their part or parts
should be equally divided between the surviving balance of
said children before mentioned, and further should my daughter Polly Davis be living at the time the money arising from
the sale as aforesaid may fall due, my will is that my executors hereafter named may present her with twenty dollars, arising from the sale as aforesaid. I hereby appoint my son
Isaac Holman and William F. Long executors of this my last
will and testament. In witness whereof I have hereunto set
my hand and seal, this 12th day of October 1829. "Note", Davis-
may fall due & her inheritance before assigned. his
Witness.   Daniel x Holman(seal)
I. Long.   mark
John Brown.
Wm. Brown.
Jacob Hamilton.

     Codicil. In consequence of my daughter Sally Haggard,
having deceased, I hereby revoke and make void that part of
this my foregoing will by which I have devised to her my negro girl Emmaline, and in lieu thereof, my will and desire is
that my Executors make sale of the said negro girl Emeline on
a credit of twelve months, and the net proceeds of the money
arising from such sale, when collected, to be equally divided
between three of the children of said Sally Haggard, namely,
Sally Johnson, Dorcas who I understand is married, but to whom
I do not know- and Joel Haggard. In witness whereof I have
hereunto set my hand and seal, this first day of December 1830.
(155) J. Long.   his
D. Bryant.   Daniel x Holman,(seal)
John Brown.   mark

     The foregoing will was established by the verdict of the
jury and judgment of the Court at the October Term 1838, of
the Lincoln County Circuit Court.

(155)   Arthur Albertson's Last Will.   In the name of God, Amen.
I, ARTHUR ALBERTSON, of the County of Lincoln & State of Tennessee, being weak in body, but through the mercy of God, of
sound mind & memory, do make, ordain, publish & declare this my
last will and testament, revoking all others, that is to say;
First, it is my will & desire that all my just debts be paid.

Second, I give & bequeath to my brother, John Albertson, of
the State of Indiana, his heirs & assigns forever, all my right
title, claim & interest as heir at law, of Caleb Albertson,dec'd,
of, in & to a certain tract of land containing 640 acres,granted
to the University of North Carolina, founded upon a warrant
which was issued for the Military service of said Caleb Albertson in the Revolutionary war, & was Excheated by act of Assembly
of said state, & is said to be located In the county of Obion in
the State of Tennessee.

Third, I give & bequeath to my beloved wife, Elizabeth Albertson, for and during the term of her natural life, the whole
of my Estate, both real & personal, consisting of & including
the tract of land with all its improvements upon which I now
live, with the whole of my household & kitchen furniture, my
negro man, Jim, my stock of every description, and all other
property rights, & credit, that I may be in possession of, at the
time of my death.

Fourth, after the death of my said wife, it is my will &
desire that my estate be disposed of in the following manner,
that is to say, I give & bequeath to my friend Robert W. Rags-
(156dale during his natural life, from and of the death of myself &
wife the following described land, being part of the tract on
which I now live, & bounded, that is to say, beginning at the
Northeast corner of my tract of land, on Swan Creek, running
thence west with Sally Childress' south boundary line, to Mary
Barclay's east boundary line, thence South with Wm. Barclay's
line to Wm. Barclay's Spring branch, thence east with the meanders of said branch to its mouth into Swan Creek, thence up
the meanders of said Creek, to the beginning, supposed to be
between 20 & 30 acres, provided always that this tract or parcel of land, at the death of the said Ragsdale, this land shall
descend to & be subject to the same disposal of the balance of
said tract, or revert & be disposed of with the balance of my
estate.

Fifth, It is my will & desire that my said wife Elizabeth
Albertson shall have the sole & absolute disposal of the whole
of my estate, and she is hereby vested with full power & authority at or before her death to dispose of the same by will in
such manner as to her shall seem right, with the exception,how-
everof a life time estate in the before mentioned premises to
Robert W. Ragsdale. And I hereby declare that the last will &
Testament of my said wife Elizabeth Albertson, when the same
shall be made, is & shall be considered as part of my will & the
disposition of the property aforesaid by her shall be valid &
efficient.

Sixth, I hereby constitute my said wife Elizabeth Albertson my sole executrix to this my last will & Testament, & hereby request that she be permitted to enter upon the execution of
the same without being required to give bond & security, as is

(156) usually required in such cases, In witness whereof I have
hereunto set my hand & seal, this 5th, day of December 1836.
Signed, sealed, published & declared in presence of, his
Ira McKinney   Arthur x Albertson.
Abraham Barnew   mark
This will duly proved at February Term, 1839.

(157)   John Rhea's Will. I, JOHN RHEA, of the County of Lincoln
& state of Tennessee, do make, ordain & publish the following
as my last will & Testament.

First, It is my will & desire that my Just debts (which I
have taken especial care, shall be few in number & small in a-
mount) shall be settled & paid out of my personal estate as
speedily as possible.

Second, I give & desire to my son William B. Rhea all that
part of my tract of land with its appurtenances situated in said
County of Lincoln, lying on the waters of Norris Creek & bounded as follows: to wit, Beginning in the east boundary of my said
tract of land twenty poles south of a dry branch or creek, which
runs through old Wm. Shaws land, from thence to run a direct line
westwardly down said branch or creek & paralel with the general
course thereof so far that by running northwardly will run with
the direction of the east line of the ferrel of the large field
next to & adjoining Wm. Moffitts farm, to where a cross fence
joins the same, thence westwardly to a cherry tree, lately
marked J.R. thence due north to William Moffitts line thence
with his line east to my North East Corner thence South with my
east boundary line to the beginning, I also give & bequeath to
my son Wm. B. Rhea a negro boy, now in his possession named,
Isaac.

Third, I give & desire to my beloved wife Sally Rhea, the
use of my dwelling house with all the building & appurtenances
thereto belonging, together with all that part of my tract of
land lying east of Main Norris Creek, not devised to William B.
Rhea, which said tract of land embraces my said dwelling house
& out Houses, during her natural life. It is further my will
& desire that the profits & benefits arising from my farm so
devised to my wife Sally Rhea shall go to the support & maintenance of her & my three children, namely, Mary B. Rhea, Susan
M. Rhea & Brice M. G. Rhea, so long as they shall remain with
their mother in the same manner as if I were living. It is also my will & desire that after my said son Brice M.G.Rhea shall
arrive at the age of twenty one years, provided he shall not
marry before that period, that he still remain with his mother,
if she should then be living, and aid & assist her in carrying
on the farm. But if my said son should be desirous he may at
(158)his option have & occupy all my said farm except a fifteen acre
field in the forks of the creek, & a Twenty acre field adjoining Wm. Soloman (commonly called the cotton field) which is set
apart for my wife Sally Rhea during her natural life, together
with the orchard & orchard field with all the Houses on said
farm. It is also my will & desire that my grand daughter Frances E. Smith shall remain with her grand mother & be supported
& maintained from the proceeds of the farm, but in case her
father should take her away, then that support & maintenance to
cease. I also give & devise to my wife Sally Rhea during her
natural life or until my son Brice M. G. Rhea shall arrive at age

(158) the following negroes, to wit, Harry, Lewis, Manuel, Grace,
& her child Chaney & her increase who are to remain & be kept
on the farm or hired out as my said wife shall think best &
the profits & benefits arising from said negroes are in like
manner to go to the maintenance of my said wife & Mary B.,
Susan M., Brice M.G. Rhea & my grand daughter Frances E.Smith.
I further give & bequeath to my wife Sally Rhea all my stock
of every description & my farming utensils, household & kitch-
en furniture of every description, with full power & authority
to give, devise & convey such patt thereof to such of my children as she may think proper, or to sell & dispose of the same
or any part thereof for her or their benefit.

Fourth, I give & desire to my son Brice M.G.Rhea, all that
part of my tract of land lying on the east side of main Norris
Creek & not devised to William B. Rhea, subject nevertheless, to
the life estate of my wife as herein before states.

Fifth, It is my will & desire that all that part of my tract
of land lying on the west side of Norris Creek be sold upon a credit of one & two years or rented out & the proceeds thereof to
be equally divided between my daughter Allamira Isom for her use
& her children by James Isom, Sally Ann Broyles, Mary B. Rhea &
Susan M. Rhea.

Sixth, I give & bequeath to my daughter Mary B. Rhea my negro boys, Ned & Tom.

Seventh, I give & bequeath to my daughter Susan M. Rhea my
negro boy named Robert, & negro girl named Nancy. It is my
wish & desire that the before named negroes, Ned & Tom & Robert
& Nancy remain with my wife Sally & be under her control & management during her natural life or until my said daughters Mary
B. & Suaan M. shall marry, & then each said negroes to be deliv-

(159) ered over to them, respectively. I also give & bequeath to my
daughter Susan M. Rhea a young bay mare I got from Joniah Burrow.

Eighth, I give & bequeath to my son Pleasant V. Rhea a negro boy named Peter.

Ninth, I give & bequeath to my daughter Allamira Isom & her
children by James Isom, a negro boy named Caswell.

Tenth, I give & bequeath to my son Brice M.B. Rhea my negro
men named Harry & Manuel, which negroes it is my will he shall
have possession of at the death of my wife, or at his arising at
the age of twenty one years.

Eleventh, I give & bequeath to my daughter Sally Ann Broyles
a negro woman named Harriet & her child named Walker & her increase.

Twelfth, I give & bequeath to my two grand children Rufus
K. Smith & Frances E. Smith, a negro girl named Mary & her child
Dorcas & their increase, to remain in possession of my wife &
be under her control & management during her life or until they
shall arrive at the age of twenty one years, to be hired out or
remain on the farm & to be under her control & management & at
her death if they or either of them should be living my son,
William shall have & take charge & management of said negroes.
I give to my son Wm. B. Rhea my blacksmith tools. I give & bequeath to my grand children Rufus K. & Frances E. Smith one hundred dollars each to be loaned out upon interest and the same
applied to their schooling & other necessary expenses, and the
principal paid over to them as they shall severally arise at the

(159) of twenty one years. I give & bequeath to my daughter Mary B.
Rhea my negro boy named Ransom, I also give her my roan horse
called Blue Skin. I give & bequeath to my daughter Susan M.
Rhea, my negro boy named Isaac. I give & bequeath to my daughter Allamira, three hundred dollars to be held & paid over by
my executor as she may need it. It is my will that the grain
& forage now on hand remain & be for the use of the family.
Upon the death of my wife it is my will that the four following
negroes be equally divided between my sons, Pleasant V., Wm. B.,

(160) Brice M.C. & my daughters, Mary B. Susan M., Sally Ann, & Allamira & my grand children, Rufus K. & Frances E. Smith, that portion of said Allamira to be for use & benefit of her children
by James Isom, to wit Lewis, Grace, Dave & Chaney, & the increase, if any. I give to my son Brice M.C. my still. I give
to my son William, one hundred & thirty seven dollars & 50cts.
due from Henderson Robertson. I give to my daughter -- one
hundred dollars due from Joseph Hinkle. I give to my daughter
Sally Ann Broyles one hundred dollars due from James M.Collins.
I give to my daughter Susan one hundred dollars, due from Joseph Miller. I give to my wife Sally Rhea five hundred dollars.
        It is my will that the residue of my money, notes & all
property or things not herein before specially disposed of, be
converted into money, & the same placed in such bank as my Executor shall think best & the principal & interest to be equally
divided among all my children at such time & in such terms as
my said Executor shall think best for the interest & benefit of
my said children. I hereby nominate & appoint James Bright, as
Executor of this my last will & Testament, revoking all former
wills by me made. In witness whereof I have hereunto set my
hand & affixed my seal, this 29th day of December 1838. Signed,
sealed & published in presence of,
Andrew Buchanan.   John Rhea, (seal).
Hugh Shaw.
Charles McKinney.
        This will was proved at the March Term 1839, of the County
Court.

(161)   James B. English's Last Will. In the name of God, Amen.
I, JAMES B. ENGLISH, of the State of Tennessee, Lincoln County,
calling to mind the uncertainty of life and wishing to settle
my worldly affairs suitable to my own wish before this change
shall come, and now being of sound mind & judgment make this
my last will & testament, viz, I will & bequeath to my beloved
wife Martha, two beds, bedsteads & their furniture during her
life time & at her death she may dispose of them as she may
think proper. I do also will & bequeath to my son Samuel Lewis
the plantation on which I now live, to him & his heirs forever,
upon the condition of him taking care of & providing for the
comfortable support of his mother during her life. I do also
will & bequeath to my beloved wife Martha, one cow & calf of
her own choice, wheels & cards, & large pine chest, & also all
the household & kitchen furniture & pot ware. I also will &
bequeath to my son-in-law William Gragg, one hundred acres of
the same 500 tract lying along George Wests' 100 acre tract &
Wm. Dyer 100 acre tract. I do also will & bequeath to my son
E. E. English, one hundred acres of the same 500 acre tract to

(161) be run off square with the other. I also will & bequeath to
my son Eleazer E. English my clock. I also will & bequeath to
my son Montgomery, my broad axe, brace & bit, chest & all the
tools belonging to it except those tools necessary for Samuel
Lewis to keep up the farm with. It is my will & desire that
the remainder of my Barren land be sold wherever the legatees
may agree among themselves & equally divided as to the profits,
among all my children. I also will & bequeath to my son S. L.
English my old yoke of Steers. I, also will & bequeath to my
sons Eleazer & Montgomery English my young yoke of oxen upon
the condition of their letting son L. have the use of them in
heavy hauling. I also will & bequeath to my beloved wife three
(162) of the choice stock hogs for her use & all the other hogs to
be sold, one lot of cherry lumber to be sold to the highest bidder. I also will & bequeath to my son S. L. English one bed &
furniture & bedstead. It is also my will and desire that after
all my just debts are paid, & funeral expenses, that the over-
plus, more or less, be given to my beloved wife Martha for her
use. And I do now appoint my three sons, Eleazer, Montgomery,&
Samuel L. English, the executors of this my last will & Testament, as now written & signed befpre these witnesses.
Henry Bryson.   J. B. English,(seal)
A. McMullen.
Samuel L. English.
This will was proven at the June Term, 1839, of the County Court
by Henry Bryson & Samuel L. English.
                              C.B.

(163)   Edward Harris Will. The last will & Testament of EDWARD
HARRIS, of. Fayetteville Tennessee. Know all men that I,EDWARD
HARRIS, of Fayetteville, Lincoln County,Tennessee State. Considering the uncertainty of this life & being of sound mind &
memory, do make & publish this my last will & Testament in manner & form following: First, I will that all my just debts as
shall be owing by me at my death, together with my funeral expenses be paid and then my will is that all the residue of my
property, lands, stock, household furniture &C, be held by my
beloved wife, Catharine for the benefit of my children and that
she have the sole management of the matter, but that she be subject to the direction of the executors of this my will, the
whole to be held by her for the benefit of my children until
she shall again marry or until the oldest child shall be of age
& my will further is that my property shall be equally divided
among my children, Martha Ann, Eliza, Mary Jane, Rebeccah, Agnes & Casandra Louise, allowing my wife Catherine, an equal division with the children together with the advantage that may
arise from the use of the property, shuuld my wife remain single
it is my wish that each one of my children should receive their
portion as they come of age, should she marry, it is my will that
(164) the property is retained for the benefit of my children as above
directed. I further will that no public sale of my property be
made, but that my wife, by the direction of with the consent of
the executors sell such articles as may be deemed necessary.
It is finally my will that Harmon Cummins & Arnzi Bradshaw be
the Executors of this my last will & testament, this 10th day of
August 1836.

(164) Signed in presence of,
John S. Morgan.   Edward Harris, (seal).
Edmond M. North.
This will was proven by the oath of John S. Morgan at July
Term, 1839.
                    C. B.

        Branson D. Caple Will. State of Tennessee, Lincoln
County, August 8th, in the year of our Lord 1839. Know all
men by these presents, that I, BRANSON D. CAPLE. of the County & State aforesaid, do make my last will & Testament. First,
I give & bequeath my soul to God who gave it. My will is
that my Executors sell my house & lot in Lewisburg at twelve
months credit & that this place I now live on be sold in the
same way. My will is that my wife shall have all my household & kitchen furniture, books & farming utensils, & two cows
& one bay mare named Jewel. My will is that my son William,
shall have a certain filly that he claims & that my executors
buy him a saddle this year, & that he shall have his part of
(165) my estate at twenty years old. Also that my daughter Nancy,
shall have a gray mare, called Nell, & that my Executors buy
her a saddle this year. Also my will is that William,Willis,
Davey & Craig shall have an equal part of my estate at twenty
years old. And my will is that Nancy & Malvina shall have an
equal part of my estate at 18 years old. William & Nancy to
be charged by my executors with the value of their horses &
saddles, so as to make each child equal. My will is that all
just debts shall be paid when the money is collected, the balance of my estate to be equally divided between my wife & children, also she shall have her part when collected. My wish is
that Daniel Whitaker & Pleasant Holbert be my Executors of this
my last will & testament. In witness whereof I have hereunto
set my hand & seal.
Test.   Bransford D. Caple, (seal)
James Fulgum.
Eli Evans. Duly proven at Sept. Court 1839.

(166)   Hezekiah Jordan's Will. In the name of God Amen, I,
HEZEKIAH JORDAN, being very sick & likely to die, though in
perfect sound mind, do make the following bequests as my last
will & testament.
        In the first place, I commit my soul into the hands of
Almighty God who gave it.
        Second, my body to be decently buried & funeral expenses
paid.
        Thirdly, All my just debts to be paid out of my property.
        Fourthly, All the remainder of my property I leave to my
beloved wife Martha to keep & make use of during her life time,
then to be divided as named, as follows, among her children.
giving unto Spencer Leatherwood & his wife Clay, one half to
John H. Norton & his wife Polly, one fourth unto Barnet Burton
& his wife Malinda one forth, which includes all.
Fifth & last, that John H. Norton & Spencer Leatherwood be my
Executors to this my last will & Testament. In testimony whereof I have hereunto set my hand & seal this 11th day of April,
1830.

(166) Attest.   his
David Byers.   Hezekiah x Jordan, (seal)
Edmond D. Parker.   mark
Proving by the subscribing witnesses legally in open Court,
At October Term 1839.

C. Boyles, Clk.

(167)   Robert Stewart Will. The last will & testament of ROB-
ERT STEWART, of the State of Tennessee, Lincoln County. I,
ROBERT STEWART, considering the uncertainty of this mortal
life & being of sound mind & memory (Blessed be Almighty God
for the same) do make & publish this my last will & testament
in manner & form following: that is to say,
First, I give & bequeath to my son James One saddle, now
at Morgans shop in Fayetteville, worth twenty dollars, & furthermore, I will that his schooling the present session be paid
out of the money on hand, belonging to the estate. I also give
& bequeath to my daughter Mary, eighty dollars & one side saddle, worth twenty-five dollars. I also give & bequeath to my
youngest son Bryson, eighty dollars & also five dollars that I
am due him, besides this five dollars to be paid when called for
it being due. I also will & bequeth the saddle that I now
have to my youngest son Bryson. I also authorize & allow my executor to this my last will & testament to sell all my estate,
both perishable and real. And I will & bequeath to my beloved
wife, Mary Stewart, after the above portions are paid, one third
of the balance of the estate, and my children namely, John,
Arthur, James, Mary and Bryson to have the balance of said estate, equally divided among them. Furthermore, I appoint-----
sole executors of this my last will & Testament hereby revoking
all former wills by me made, in witness whereof I have hereunto
set my hand & seal this 30th day of August in the year of our
Lord, 1839.
Robert Stewart, (seal).
Signed, sealed & published & declared by the above named Robert
Stewart to be his last will & Testament in presence of us who
have hereunto subscribed our names in the presence of the Test-
ators, as witnesses.
Test.
James Stewart.
    his
David x Black. Proven at November Court, 1839.
    mark   C. Boyles, Clerk.

(168)   Henry B. Smith's Will. State of Tennessee, Lincoln County.
In the name of God Amen. I, HENRY B. SMITH, being weak in
body, but of sound and perfect mind and memory, blessed be Almighty God, for the same, do make and publish this as my last
will and testament in a manner and form following, (that is to
say) First, I give and bequeath unto my beloved wife, Cynthy Ann
Caroline, all my personal property during her natural life or
widowhood, except my colt and seven or eight wethers, which is
to be sold to pay my just debts, and the over plus to go to the
use of the family. Now at the death or marriage of my wife, the
property shall be sold and equally divided among my children,
my wife having a childs' part. I hereby appoint William Beavers
sole Executor of this my last will & testament, and hereby revoking all former wills by me made.

(168) revoking all former wills by me made. In witness whereof I
hereunto set my hand & seal this the 12th of June 1840.
Test.   his
William Harris.   Henry B. x Smith, (seal)
Thomas Mathis, x his mark.   mark
Proven at August Court 1840.
          G. W. Jones, Clk.

          William Gunter's Last Will. In the name of God Amen. I,
WILLIAM GUNTER, of the County of Lincoln and State of Tennessee,
being sick and weak of body, but sound in mind and disposing
memory (for which I thank God) and calling to mind the uncertainty of human life, and being desirous to dispose of all my
worldly substance, as it hath pleased God to bless me with.
          First, I give and bequeath to my son Joshua Gunter one dol-
lar. my reason for so doing having given him his part before-
hand. Also to my son Hiram Gunter I give one dollar, for the
(169) same reason above mentioned. I also give and bequeath to my beloved wife Phoeba Gunter the residue of my estate both real &
personal, during her natural life or widowhood, and after her
decease all the property bequeathed to my said wife to be sold
ona credit of twelve months or longer, if my under-named Executors think it best for the heirs, and equally divided between
my other children, (viz) Polly Hughes, James Gunter, William
Gunter, George W. Gunter & Rebecca Gunter, but provided my said
wife Phoeba does marry, the above named property to be sold as
above named, and to be divided so as my said wife will have an
equal share with the above named children.
          And lastly, I do constitute and appoint my friends, Joshua
Gunter & Malcolm F. Hughes, my executors of this my last will
and testament, hereby revoking all other or former wills or
testaments by me heretofore made. In witness whereof I have
hereunto set my hand and affixed my seal this 12th day of August, Eighteen hundred and forty. Signed, sealed & delivered
in the presence of,   his
Samuel Ramsey, x his mark.   William x Gunter, (seal)
John Ramsey.   mark
Proven at September Term 1840.

          Abraham Cunningham's Will. In the name of God Amen. I,
ABRAHAM CUNNINGHAM, Sr. of the State of Tennessee and County
of Lincoln, being weak of body, but of sound mind and disposing
memory, do make and ordain this to be my last will and testament, revoking all others and as touching the estate and effects
it has pleased God to bless me with, I leave, devise and bequeath in the following manner, (viz).
          1st, my will and desire is that all my just debts be col-
lected, and all the just debts I am now owing or expenses
which hereafter may arise, be paid.
          2nd, I give unto my wife Nancy Cunningham, my sorrel mare
Nipp, one choice cow and calf, four head of sheep, four hundred pounds of fat pork, fifteen barrels of corn, fifteen bushels of wheat and fifty dollars in money and one feather bed &
furniture, one cupboard, now in my possession, and the furni-
(170) ture that is in it, and as much of the pots or casting ware as
she will need for her own use, all which property to be hers

(170)forever.

      3rd, my will and desire is that all the land I am now in possession of and all the residue of my property of every description, be sold on a twelve months credit and the money thence arising together with the money arising from debts owing to me, be equally divided between my following named children, except as hereinafter mentioned,(viz),

To Samuel Cunningham, one ninth part.

To John Cunningham, one ninth part.

To Nancy Grace, one ninth part.

To James Cunningham one ninth part.

To Joel Cunningham, one ninth part.

To Wilson Cunningham, one ninth part.

Mary Bearden, one ninth part.

To George Cunningham, one ninth part.

To Abraham Cunningham,Jr. one ninth part.

      4th, My will and desire is that my daughter Jane's two sons, to wit, Jeremiah O. Coulter and Hardy H. Coulter have twenty dollars a piece to be paid to each of before the above divisions be made.

      5th, my will and desire is that my son John Cunningham, and my friends Abner Steed be my Executors to this my last will and Testament, believing they will see it properly executed. September 8th, 1840. Signed, sealed, published & pronounced to be the last will and testament of ABRAHAM CUNNINGHAM Sr. in presence of us.

Travis Ashby.

Wilson Grace. Proven at the October Term 1840.

(171)   Henry Moore's Will. Be it remembered that I, HENRY MOORE, of the County of Lincoln and State of Tennessee, being weak in body, but of sound and perfect mind and memory, considering the uncertainty of this mortal life and being of sound mind, blessed be Almighty God for the same, do make & publish this my last will and testament in manner and form, following (that is to say),

      First, the following property to be sold for the purpose of paying all my just debts; the horses all sold but the gray mare and the chestnut sorrel mare, also all the largest hogs that can be spared from the family, and the balance kept for next year, also thirty head of sheep and all the cattle that will not be needed for the use of the family, also the wagon and the rifle gun, also those leasers living on the land to have the specified time according to contract. Furthermore, I wish my beloved wife Frances H. Moore to keep the land and all the property not above specified until Jordan R. Moores comes of age, and then be made equal with William H. Moore,and Mary L. Bean, land with what is coming from his grand fathers estate.

      The rest of the children to have as they come of age or marry two hundred dollars, a good horse, saddle and bridle. a cow and calf, bed and furniture, and other property in proportion. I wish my wife to keep all the property, only the above mentioned to be sold, during her widowhood, and should she marry, then an equal division to be made of the property among all the children of both families. I wish my wife and William H. Moores, my son to be the Administrators and Administratrix

(171) of the estate. In witness whereof I have hereunto set my hand
and seal, the 12th day of Sept. in the year of our Lord 1840.

his
Henry x Moore, (seal).
mark

Signed, sealed, published and declared by the above named,HENRY
MOORE, to be his last will and testament, in the presence of us
who at his request and in his presence have hereunto subscribed
our names as witnesses to the same.
Joel L. Reese.
John Bell.
Jas. D. Cole. Proven at October Court 1840, by Reese & Cole.

(172)   Henry Swinebroad Will. I, HENRY SWINEBROAD, do make and
publish this as my last will and Testament hereby revoking and
making void all other wills by me at any time made,
        Lst, I direct that my funeral expenses and all my just debts
be paid as soon after my death as possible, out of any money I
may die possessed of.
        2nd, I give and bequeath unto my dearly beloved wife Elvira
the whole of my real and personal estate, subject to her management and control during her natural life or widowhood, but if my
wife, the said Elvira should at any time marry again,then and in
that case, it is my will that she should have out of the estate
thus bequeathed, the following articles only, one horse, saddle
and bridle, one cow and calf, one bed, bedstead and furniture,
one cupboard and furniture, one bureau, two sows and pigs, also
one choice of the spinning machines.
        3rd, At the death or marriage of the said Elvira it is my w
will and desire that Ehat my Executors hereinafter mentioned
shall enter upon the discharge of his duty by taking the whole
of my estate into his hands, first selling apart to the said
Elvira the above named property upon the conditions aforesaid,
and secondly sell or otherwise divide amongst my children, the
(173)whole of my estate both real and personal.
        Lastly, I do hereby nominate and appoint Boon Wilson,Davis
Smith and Wm. B. Wright, Executors to this my last will and testament. In witness whereof I do to this my will, set my hand and
seal this 20th day of September 1840.

Henry Swineboard, (seal).

Signed, Sealed and published in our presence and we have sub-
scribed our names hereto in presence of the testator.
Ira McKinney.
S.D.Milliken.
John Kennedy.   Proven at November Court 1840,by McKinney&Kennedy.

        Ephraim Dickey's Will. Know all men by these presents,
that I, EPHRAIM DICKEY, of the County of Lincoln and State of
Tennessee, calling to mind that it is appointed for all men
once to die, and feeling my bodily powers failing, although my
mind is clear and unimpaired and sound. I constitute this my
last will & testament.
        And 1st, I commit my soul to Almighty God who gave it,and
my body to the dust to be buried at the discretion of my friends.
        2nd, I will that my funeral expenses be punctually paid out
of my estate and also all my other just debts.

(173)   3rd, I will that my beloved wife Elizabeth Dickey have my plantation on which I now live, her natural life time to be managed and conducted at her will and pleasure, I also will and bequeath to my beloved wife Elizabeth my chestnut sorrel mare her life time, also my household and kitchen furniture, also my present crop of grain. The household and kitchen furniture to be disposed of at her death as she may think proper.

4th, I will that my daughter Mary have my sorrel horse to have and dispose of as she may think proper, provided my debts can be paid without selling him for that purpose.

5th, I will that the remainder of my stock consisting of my cattle and hogs be sold to pay my debts, also all my other property, consisting of my farming tools, blacksmith tools &C. This I constitute and ordain my last will and testament. Signed in the presence of us this the 16th day of September, in the year of our Lord, 1840.
Test.   Ephraim Dickey, (seal).
Alexander Edmiston.
Samuel Bell. Proven at the November Court 1840.

(174)   James M. Dean's Will. In the name of God Amen. I,JAMES M. DEAN, being in my right mind and proper senses,

1st, I wish my body to be decently buried.And 2nd, I wish for all of my just debts to be paid and 3rd, I give and bequeath unto my dear and beloved wife Ann Dean the sum of three hundred dollars, provided there is that much collected after paying my debts, also my gold watch, 1 Bureau and small candle stand, I also bequeath and give to my brother Alvin M. Dean a certain lot of books that is now in the upper drawer of my bureau. And I wish my father Henry Dean to take my stock of horses and dispose of them at private sale and account to the executors for the same. And should ther be more than three hundred dollars left after paying all just debts, I will and bequeath the same to my brother Harvey M. Dean, and I wish the same to go for his education, and I wish Thomas Dean of Bedford County and B. H. Berry of this Lincoln County to be my Executors this Sept. 20th 1840.
Witness.   Jas. M. Dean.
Wm. G. Rountree.
Jas. A. Berry.
Proven at October Court 1840, but entered nime protune at December Court 1840.

Minty Alexander's Last Will. I, MINTY ALEXANDER, do make and publish this as my last will and testament, hereby revoking and making void all other wills by me at any time made. First, I direct that my funeral expenses andall my debts be paid as soon after my death as possible, out of any money that I may die possessed of or may first come into the hands of my Executors.

Secondly, I give and bequeath to my son James A. Alexander my servant boy Simon, and thirdly, I give and bequeath to my daughter Milly Susannah Alexander my servant girl Mary,and Fourthly, I give and bequeath to Temple Taylor my servant girl

(174) Harriet, and lastly, I do appoint and hereby nominate Temple Taylor my executor. In witness whereof I do to this my will set my hand and seal this the 3rd day of September 1840.

her

Minty x Alexander.

mark

(175) Signed, sealed and published in our presence, and wa have subscribed our names hereto, in the presence of the testator this the 3rd day of September 1840.

T. S. Williams.

his

John x Keller.   Proven at December Term, 1840.

mark

Fielding McDaniel's Will.   State of Tennessee,Lincoln County.

This is my written will & testament. I, FIELDING MC-DANIEL,Sr. do make and publish this aw my last will and testament, hereby revoking and making void a ll other wills by me at any time made.

First, I direct that my funeral expenses and all my debts be paid as soon after my death as possible out of any money that I may die possessed of or may first come into the hands of my executors.

Secondly, I direct that all my children that I have hot given property to, that is those of them that have not left me or come of age, to have an equal portion with those of my children which have left me or come of age, that is to say, one horse, bridle & saddle of as nearly an equal value as can be with those which I have given to the other children, also one bed, and furniture, one cow and calf, two head of sheepp with other little things which they can recollect, a ll of which is to be as nearly of an equal value as possible- moreover that Evan, my 3rd son to have another bed and furniture or its value,about $18 or $ 20. Also one other horse or its equivalent $70 or $75. And that Agnes, my second daughter to have her mothers' bed and other clothing, together with the cupboard, and one certain set of cups & saucers, which was her mothers request.

Thirdly, my will is that after the above donations, and divisions are made, that all of the rest and residue of my property and effects both personal and real estate, to be equally divided among all, each and every one of my children, by consent if possible, if not as directed by law, these are my children, Elizabeth, John, Ambrose, Evan. Agnes, Fielding, Charles, William & Coleman, nine in number. Ambrose my second son being dead, I wish John my first son to be appointed the guardian of his (Ambrose's) two children, John and Robert, and that he, the said John to receive the portion of Ambrose and keep it for the sole benefit of his, Ambrose's, two heirs, John and Robert,and to be given to them where and ax they come of age, and expressly that it, Ambrose's legacy or part of my estate shall not go directlt or indirectly into the hands of Rosetta, Ambrose's wife and their mother.

And lastly, I do hereby nominate and appoint Thomas Wakefield my son-in-law and John, my first son, my executors. In witness whereof I do to this my will set my hand and seal or cause it to be by mark, this 23rd day of July, 1839.

his
Fielding x McDaniel. (seal)
mark

Signed, sealed and published in our presence, and we have
subscribed our names hereto in the presence of the testator
this 23rd day of July, 1839.
Hugh Shaw.
Wm. H. King.   Proven at the January Term 1841, of the County
Court and Recorded January 7th, 1841.

G. W. Jones, Clerk.

Alexander Ashby's Will. —In the names of God Amen. I,
ALEXANDER ASHBY, of the State of Tennessee and County of
Lincoln, being at this time of sound mind, and disposing memory, do make and ordain this to be my last will and testament
revoking all others, and as touching the property and effects
that it has pleased God to bless me with, I leave and bequeath
in the following manner (viz).

1st, I leave in possession of my wife Lavina Ashby all my
property of every description during her natural life or widowhood, except as herein after mentioned.

2nd, I have given my son John L. Ashby, a saddle, and
when he arrives at lawful age he is to receive a horse and shot
gun, now in my possession.

3rd, I give unto my daughter Rachel E. Ashby, a feather
bed and furniture, a cow and calf, a cotton wheel and cards,
when she arrives at lawful age or marries.

4th, I give unto my daughter Frances S. Ashby, a feather
bed and furniture, a cow and calf, a cotton wheel and cards,
when she arrives at lawful age or marries.

5th, I give unto my son Nathan A. Ashby a horse, bridle
and saddle, and a shot gun when he arrives at lawful age.

6th, I give unto my daughter Minerva Jane Ashby a feather
bed and furniture, a cow & calf, a cotton wheel and cards,
when she arrives at lawful age or marries.

7th, I give unto my daughter Nancy A. Ashby a feather bed,
and furniture, a cow and calf, a cotton wheel and cards, when
she arrives at lawful age or marries.

8th, I give unto my daughter Mary Ashby a feather bed &
furniture, a cow and calf, a cotton wheel and cards, when she
arrives at lawful age or marries.

9th, My will and desire is that the above named property
to be given to my sons and daughters be valued at the time
they receive it, and if it is not equal at that time, to be
made equal in the general division of my property, as I want
my daughters as well as sons to share equally alike in my property of every description.

10th, My will and desire is that my executor sell the land
I once sold to Burwell O. Quinn, containing about twenty seven
acres in any way they see proper, in order to enable them to
comply with the above gifts.

11th, My will and desire is that the debts I now owe, together with my future expenses, be paid out of the money owing
to me, but if that should not be sufficient, any property that
can be best spared from my family discretionary with my executor
be sold on a twelve months credit, and the money thence arising

(177) to finish paying my debts and expenses.

  12th My will and desire is that should my wife Lavina
Ashby, alter her way of living by a second marriage, she can
take her choice, either to take a childs part of my land as
hers forever, or a third part during her natural life, in
either case my will and desire is that the balance of all the
land and property left be sold on a twelve months credit, immediately, except the land which must be sold on a credit of
one, two and three years, and the money thence arising be e-
qually divided between my above named seven children.

  13th, And lastly, I do appoint my friends Travis Ashby,
and Abner Steed, my Executors to this my last will and testament, believing they will the said properly execute.

             Alexander Ashby, (seal).
Signed, sealed, published and pronounced to be the last will
and testament of ALEXANDER ASHBY, in presence of us, August,
24th 1840.
William Ashby.
Chloe Steadman. Proven at the January Term 1841 of the Lincoln
County Court, and Registered January 7th 1841.
             G. W. Jones, Clerk.
Copy delivered to T. Ashby, 18th August, 1841.

  The last will and testament of James Campbell. I do give
and bequeath unto my wife Margaret Campbell all my right title
and claim and interestof the tract of land on which I now live
containing one hundred and thirty six acres to have and to hold
during her life, and at the death of my wife Margaret, it is my
will that my son-in-law Lewis Womack shall havethe said tract of
land provided he will pay each of my daughters fifty dollars,
Elizabeth Lucinda, and Mary Ann & Lucinda, where and provided my
(178) son-in-law Lewis Womack does not pay each of the above named
heirs it is my will and desire that the above named tract of land
shall be sold all together to the highest bidder, and the money
to be equally divided between the four named heirs, whereas I
have hereunto set my hand and seal. Nov. the 30th, 1840.
Attest.   his
Paul Ingle.   James x Campbell, (seal).
R. B. Ramsey.   mark
Proven at the March Term 1841, of the Lincoln County Court.

(179) In the name of God Amen. I, JAMES GRANT, of the county of
Lincoln and State of Tennessee, being weak of body but of sound
mind and disposing memory, for which I thank God, but knowing
the uncertainty of life and the certainty of death, do make and
ordain this to be my last will & testament, revoking and rescind-
ing all other wills by me heretofore made.

  Item 1, I will and bequeath that all my just debts be immediately paid, and discharged. I will and bequeath to my daughter Nancy Russell & Charlotte Merrill, the tract of land adjoining, the same whereon I now live, to be equally divided between
them in such manner that an equal portion or as near as can be
equal portion of the bottom land, be given to each one, giving
to my daughter Charlotte, the half whereon the house I now live
in stands, and I will that after my decease the land be divided
and the portion being allotted to my daughter Nancy Russell be

(179) sold on a credit of one, two and three years, and the proceeds of the sale of the land to go to the benefit of my
daughter Nancy.

Item 2, To my daughter Nancy Russell I give and bequeath
a negro girl, now in her possession, named Cynthia, also my
my small bureau, two beds and two bedsteads and furniture,five
chairs, one hundred dollars in cash to be paid to her by my
executors, out of the proceeds of the sale of such property as
will be sold.

Item 3, To my daughter Charlotte I give and bequeath my
negro girl Sarah, also two beds and furniture, also including
the bedsteads, the said beds being the same that was made for
Charlotte and her brother Asa, also two milk cows and calves,
to be of her own choice out of my stock, also my young sorrel
mare, also my loom and all harness belonging to same. Also my
spinning wheel and the balance of my household and kitchen
furniture. Nancy Russell to be paid eight dollars out of the
proceeds of the sale of the perishable property to compensate
her for one-half of the cupboard.

Item 4, To my grandson James Franklin, the son of my
daughter Charlotte, I give and bequeath one bed and bedstead,
and furniture, to remain in the possession of his mother until he becomes of age or shall require the use of same. I
also will and bequeath to him my negro boy Mike, to be hired
out by my executor yearly, and a sufficient amount of the proceeds of sd. herein to be appropriated to the schooling ofhim
until he becomes of age, when the balance, if any, will be
paid over to him, and together with the boy become his own forever.

(180) Item 5, It is my will and wish after my decease, my negro
man George and his wife Viny, be put up together and valued and
not to be separated under any circumstances, and also my negro
girl Haley, to be valued likewise, by two disinterested men and
my two daughters draw lots for choice.

Item 6, I give and bequeath the negro property that may
fall to the lot of Nancy Russell to be her own personal property during her natural life.

Item 7, My daughter Charlotte to have my clock as her own
property. I also bequeath that all my perishable property not
otherwise disposed of, that is to say my horses, cattle and
farming utensils be sold agreeable to the laws of our state,and
that the proceeds of the same be equally divided between my two
daughters viz, Nancy Russell and Charlotte Merrill, by my executor. I constitute and appoint Benjamin Whitaker and Josiah Mc-
Cracken, my sole executors to this my last will & testament
which I have signed, sealed and published on the 19th of March
in the year of our Lord, one thousand eight hundred and forty
one. In presence of,   his
Jas. McCracken.   James x Grant.
R. B. Matlox.   mark
Josiah McCracken.
Proven at the May Term 1841, of the Lincoln County Court. Recorded May 5th, 1841.

(180)   Elizabeth Albertson's Last Will. In the name of God
Amen. I, ELIZABETH ALBERTSON, of the County Of Lincoln and
State of Tennessee, being weak in body, but through the mercy of God of sound mind and memory, do make, ordain, publish
and declare this my last will and testament, revoking all others, that is to say:

First, It is my will and desire that all my funeral expenses and all my debts be paid as soon after my death as may
be practicable out of any money that I may die possessed of or
may first come into the hands of my Executors.

Secondly, I give and bequeath to my nephew John Crawford &
Henry Crawford sons of Elias Crawford of Randolph County, North
Carolina, and to Elizabeth Russell, wife of Ransom Russell, of the
same County and State aforesaid, I give to them each, one hundred dollars to be paid by my executor hereinafter mentioned.

Thirdly. It is my will and desire that the remainder of my
estate both real & personal, with the exceptions before and after mentioned, be equally divdded between the following persons;
that is to say, my niece Sally Arnold, widow of Daniel Arnold;
and to my brother Elias Crawford and to the children of my deceased niece Elizabeth Taylor, all of North Carolina, that I
give one third of my estate, with the exceptions before mentioned, to Sally Arnold, one third, to my brother Elias Crawford,
and the remaining third to the children of my deceased niece,
Elizabeth Taylor.

Fourthly, It is my will and desire that Sally Arnold, in
(181) addition to the one third of my estate should have one bed, bedstead & furniture, but if she should prefer the proceeds of said
bed & furniture she must direct my executor to sell the same for
her benefit and account to her for the proceeds thereof.

Fifthly, It is my will and desire that the whole of my personal estate be sold, excepting that part of the same disposed
of otherwise, and also excepting my negro man Jim, be sold by my
Executor on a twelve months credit, and the proceeds thereof applied to the use and purposes above mentioned.

Sixthly, It is my will and desire that at my death, should
my trusty negro man Jim, be then alive, that he should have one
horse beast, the choice of my stock, and that my executor shall
superanuate said negro Jim, set apart a small portion of the
farming land for his own support during his life time, and further to see that he is reasonably supplied out of the rents, profits of said land, and at my death that my said Executor shall
rent yearly, the balance of my farm for and during the life time
of said negro Jim, and at his death to sell and dispose of said
tract of land to the best advantage and apply the proceeds thereof as well as rents as before stated.

Seventhly, I hereby constitute and appoint my neighbor &
friend Abram Barnes, my executor to this my last will & testament. In testimony whereof I have hereunto set my hand and seal
this 26th day of March 1841.   his
                       Elizabeth x Albertson, (seal).
                       mark
Signed & sealed in presence of,
Ira McKinney.
Joseph Clarke. Proven at the May Term 1841, after-L.C.C.

(182)   Phillip Fox Last Will. I, PHILLIP FOX, of the State of Tennessee, and County of Lincoln, being weak of body, but of sound mind and disposing memory, do make and publish this as my last will and testament, hereby revoking and making void all other wills or testaments by me heretofore made.

First, I desire that my funeral expenses and all my just debts be paid as soon after my death as possible, out of any money that I may be possessed of or may first come into the hands of my executors.

Second, I give and bequeath unto my beloved wife Ailey,the use, occupation and enjoyment of my tract of land whereon I now live, together with all other property I may die possessed of, except such property as is otherwise bequeathed, all of which property I wish her to have during her natural life or widowhood.

Thirdly, My will and desire is that not one of my children shall have more of my effects than another, and for remedy whereof, I have given unto my son Benjamin, six hundred dollars, a feather bed and covering, as his portion of my estate until after my wife's death.

Fourthly, I have given unto my son John, six hundred dollars, and when he marries, he is to have a feather bed and covering.

Fifthly, I have given unto my son Enoch, six hundred dollars, and when he goes to housekeeping, is to have a feather bed and covering.

Sixthly, My will and desire is that my following minor heirs, viz, Nancy Ann, Rebecca, Daniel and Morgan, as they become of lawful age or marry, have each of them six hundred dollars, including a horse, saddle and bridle and blanket, valued to them at a fair valuation, and a feather bed and furniture each.

Seventhly, My will and desire is that if there should be any property that my wife will not immediately need or should not be considered by my executors as needful to be kept in the estate, it may be sold on a twelve months credit, and the money thence arising to be appropriated to the use, benefit and comfort of my wife and minor heirs, if they should need it, if not (183) be thrown back into the estate.

Eighthly, My will and desire is that all money I may leave or money arising from collection of notes be put out at interest, and be solely managed by James W. Holman, my Executor, as being best calculated to manage the same, until it is called for by the provision of this will.

Ninethly,My will and desire is that if my wife Ailey, should alter her way of life by another marriage, in that case, she may, at her discretion take a widows' dower during her natural life , or an equal part as a legatee forever.

Tenthly, My will and desire is that after my wife's death that my land all be sold on a credit of one, two and three years, and the payments well secured, and that my other property be sold on a credit of twelve months, and money arising from the whole be equally divided between my above named children (to wit) Benjamin Fox, John Fox, Enoch Fox, Nancy Ann Fox, Rebecca Fox, and Daniel Fox, and Morgan Fox, or their legal heirs.

Eleventhly, and lastly, I appoint my wife Ailcey Fox and James W. Holman Esqr.,the Executors to this my last will and

(183) testament, believing they will see it properly executed.
July 31st, 1841.
                            Phillip Fox, (seal)
Signed, sealed and published in our presence, and we have
subscribed our names thereto in the presence of the testator.
This 31st day of July 1841.
Thomas Flack.
Abner Steed.   Proven at the September Term 1841, of the Lin-
coln County Court. Recorded Sept. 7th 1841.
                            G. W. Jones, Clerk.

(184)   Stephen Cole's Last Will. In the name of God Amen. I,
STEPHEN COLE, of the County of Lincoln & State of Tennessee,
being of sound mind and perfect memory, blessed be God, do
this 9th day of April 1838, make & publish this my last will
and testament, in the following manner(viz)My body to be buried after Christian like manner without pomp or parade.
      2nd, I give unto my loving wife Elizabeth Cole during her
natural life & after her death, the following property, if any
remains, to my son Isaac R. Cole (viz), all my household &
kitchen furniture, except two beds & furniture in the west room
of the house I now live in, all my stock, consisting of horses,
cattle, hogs and sheep.
      3rd, I give unto my son Isaac R. Cole one bed & furniture.
      4th, I also give unto my son Felix G. Cole one bed and
furniture.
      5th, I give unto all my other heirs a proportionable part
of my property which they have received.
      6th and lastly, I nominate and appoint John Cole and Zeb-
ulan Parr executors of this my last will and testament. In
witness whereof I hereunto have set my hand and seal the day
and date above mentioned.
Test.   Stephen Cole.
Jesse M. Rowling.
John Maddox. Proven at September Term 1841, of the Lincoln
County Court, Tennessee. Recorded September 7th 1841.
                            G. W. Jones, Clerk.

      Samuel Dobbins' Last Will. I, SAMUEL DOBBINS, of the
County of Lincoln in the State of Tennessee, having attained
to advanced age and knowing that it is appointed for all men
to die, and being by the blessing of God, of sound mind & memory, do make, ordain, publish and declare this my last will
and testament, in form following, that is to say;
      First, It is my will and desire that all my just debts be
paid, for which purpose I direct the sale of such property as
can be most conveniently spared, not otherwise disposed of.
      2nd, I give and bequeath to my dearly beloved wife Susan-
(185) na Dobbins, six negro slaves, to wit; my negro woman Patsy now
about thirty six years of age, together with five of her children, to wit, Sam, about twelve years old, Eliza, about seven,
Ethelburt, about five, Marcus about three, and Alfred about one
year old, and also if the said Patsy should become the mother
of other children, such child or children, I also give to my
said wife, her will to be absolute, including the right to sell
and dispose of said slaves to her will and pleasure.

(135) 3rd, I give to my son John Dobbins, two hundred and fifty dollars. I also give to my said son John Dobbins three negroes, to wit, George & Ellis about sixteen years old. Matilda about ten years old,lastly,I give and bequeath to the said John Dobbins the half of the plantation on which I now reside, And to the children of my deceased, the consort of Samuel Hall, seven hundred and fifty dollars, which said money is to be paid so soon as the same can be collected out of such cash notes as may
(186) be due for the land purchased of John Brackenridge.

4th, I give to my wife the said Susannah Dobbins, for and during her natural life the use of my land and plantation whereon I now live, with all the issues and profits thereof, including my household and kitchen furniture, together with two work horses and farming tools, three cows and calves, the choice of my stock, and the whole of my stock of other description.

5th, All the balance of my estate both real and personal, not otherwise disposed of including the reversionary property set apart for the use of my wife, I give to my son John Dobbins, and to my daughter Elizabeth Pinson and to the heirs of my deceased daughter, consort of Samuel Hall, to be equally divided between them and their heirs, hereby intending that the plantation on which I now reside to be equally divided between my son John Dobbins and Elizabeth Pinson with all the improvements thereon, the balance to be equally divided between the three, John, Elizabeth and the heirs of my deceased daughter,consort of Samuel Hall, together with all property which I may hereafter acquire, including all receipts and credits of every description which may remain at death.

6th, Any and all property by me heretofore given and advanced to any of my children, or which I may heretofore give or advance to any in my lifetime, is and will be intended as a gift and no child or children shall be required to refund or account for such advance, but the balance shall be disposed of under this my last will and testament in the same manner as if no such advance had been made.
(187) 7th, I hereby revoke all former wills and request that this my last will be faithfully executed, according to the true intention and meaning thereof, without intervention or appointment of Executors or Administrators, but should the same become necessary I leave them to be appointed by the court of the county. In witness witness whereof I have hereunto set my hand and seal this 28th of December 1839. Signed, sealed, published & declared in presence of,
Test.   Samuel Dobbins, (seal).
Ezekial Sanders.
P. W. Harper. Proven at the Lincoln County Court. Recorded 8th October 1841.

Martha Thwing's Last Will. I, MARTHA THWING, of the County of Lincoln and State of Tennessee, do make and publish the following as my last will and testament.

First, It is my will that all my just debts and funeral expenses be paid as speedily as possible out of my personal property.

Second, I give and bequeath to Mrs. Mary E, Wheeler, wife of David Wheeler, and her children all the residue of my person-

(187) personal property of every description to be exclusively for the use and benefit of her and her children, and not to be subject to the payment of said David Wheeler's debts.

Third, I give and desire to the said Mary E Wheeler during her natural life, and then to be equally divided amongst her children, the tract of land whereon I now live, with all (188) the appurtenances thereunto belonging or in any wise appertaining together with all the profits and benefits arising therefrom, to be for the sole use and benefit of her and her children, and not to be subject in any manner to the payment of said David Wheeler's debts, nor to be subject to his control even in his lifetime, but the same shall remain to the said Mary E. for her sole and separate use as though she was unmarried, and shall in no wise be subject to the control or debts of said David Wheeler.

It is further my will that five acres of my land be set apart for my faithful old servant Peter, to be laid off in some convenient part of the tract, so as to have firewood and timber to fence it, which he is to have and enjoy during his natural life, and then to remain with the balance of the tract. I also give to said Peter my Carpenters tools. It is my will and desire that the best of my clothing and trinkets and jewelry be sent to my grandchildren, and equally divided amongst them.

I nominate and appoint James Bright sole Executor of this my last will and testament, hereby revoking and making null and void all former wills by me made. In witness whereof I have hereunto set my hand and affixed my seal this thirteenth day of January, 1840.   her
                    Martha x Thwing, (seal).
                            mark
Signed, sealed and acknowledged in the presence of us,
John J. Ramsey.
Elisha Bagley.

For good and sufficient reasons I make the following alterations in my last will and testament, as within set forth, that is to say, that instead of devising my land to Mary E. Wheeler (189) during her natural life, and then to her children. I give and devise to her alone said tract of land which she may sell and dispose of as she may think best, and the proceeds after paying all my just debts, is to be for the sole use and be under the entire control of the said Mary E. Wheeler, and not to be subject in any manner to the payment of David Wheeler's debts. In witness whereof I have hereunto set my hand and seal this 23rd, day of May 1840.   her
                    Martha x Thwing, (seal).
                            mark
Signed and acknowledged in our presence.
J. J. Ramsey.
Elisha Bagley. Proven at the Term 1841, of the Lincoln County Court. Recorded 8th October 1841.

Archibald McElroy's Will. This my last will and testament, made this 3rd day of December, Eighteen hundred & thirty nine. I give to my beloved wife Elizabeth my negro boy Harry, and his wife Lucy, negro boy Cook, and girl Malinda, during her lifetime. I also give my wife the house that I now occupy for five years, the balance of my property to be equally divided

(189) divided amongst my children, after paying my debts. I appoint my wife and Amos Hurley guardians for children, and I also want them to administer upon my estate.

W. Bonner.   Archibald McElroy.
John M. McGaugh.
May Buchanan.
Anthony Delaney.   Proven at the Oct. Term,1841, of the Lincoln County Court.   Recorded 8th October, 1841.

(190)   Thomas Childress' last Will.   I, THOMAS CHILDRESS, of the County of Lincoln & State of Tennessee, do this 17th day of November, eighteen hundred and thirty six, make and publish this my last will & testament, revoking all othersheretofore by me made.

I give to my daughter Nancy, my brown horse that I bought of Lum Nobles.   I give to my son Thomas D. my razor and other shaving utensils.   I give to my daughters Hannah, Polly & Nell one dollar each, to be paid by said Susannah & Nancy.

I give all the balance of my estate, both real and personal, after paying my just debts, to my daughters Susanah & Nancy, to be equally divided between them.   Witness my hand the day and year above written.   his
Test.   Thos. x Childress, (seal).
Wm. Stephens.   mark
James Hayes.
Eli L. Hodge.   Proven at the Term 18-- of the County Court of Lincoln County.   Recorded 8th October 1841.

(191)   William Blairs' Will.   Lincoln County, State of Tennessee, September 3rd, 1841.   In the name of God Amen.   I, WILLIAM BLAIR, of the County and State aforesaid, being in sound mind and judgment, but calling calling to mind the frailty of man and the uncertainty of my day, and wishing to make a disposition of my worldly affairs before this change comes, I hereby make this my last will and testament.

1st, It is my will that after my decease, all my just debts be paid.

2nd, I give and bequeath my beloved wife Ann Blair the tract of land where she now lives, with all the other property for to raise the children on, and to be at her disposal, as she thinks best, and I also appoint John Wyatt and Hugh Taylor, the Executors of this my last will and testament.his
Test.   William x Blair, (seal).
Jesse Morton.   mark
John Blair.
Richard Wyatt.   Proven at the October Term 1841, of the Lincoln County Court.   Recorded October 16th 1841.

Charles Thorp's Will.   I, CHARLES THORP, of the County of Lincoln and State of Tennessee, do make and publish this my last will and testament.

First, I direct that all my debts and funeral expenses be paid as soon after my decease as practicable, out of the money now on hand.   Also I give and bequeath unto my brother Joel Thorpe all my lands lying in Lincoln County and State of Tennessee, on Bradshaws' Creek, a north branch of Elk River, to him

(192) and his heirs forever, giving him, the said Joel Thorp, the power of selling or trading the same at will. And all the money on hand after paying my debts and funeral expenses together with what may be collected from notes due me and to become due to me, and also all money collected from accounts due or to become due, I give and bequeath unto my two brothers, William Thorp and Hardin Thorp, to be equally divided between them or their heirs, if either of them should die before me.

I also direct that all my stock, consisting of two head of horses, besides one mare, I have given to my brother William Thorp, one yoke of oxen and one half of the stock of hogs now on hand owned by my brother Joel and myself jointly, after selling enough of the pork hogs for cash to pay Ridding Maddox, one hundred and ten dollars, after the hogs are fattened next fall out of the crop raised this year, by said Maddox and Joel. Then all the balance of said stock to be sold and the proceeds to be equally divided between my two brothers, William Thorp and Hardin Thorp, or the property as before named divided between said William Thorp and Hardin Thorp equally as they may think fit. All the balance of the crop raised this year by my brother Joel and said Redin Maddox, after fattening the pork hogs next fall, I give to my brother Joel Thorp.

Also I direct and say there shall be no executor to this my last will and testament, but appoint and direct my brother Joel Thorp so soon as practicable after my death to hand over to my (193) two brothers, William Thorp & Hardin Thorp or to their executors or administrators all the money and other proceeds as directed in the body of the foregoing will. In witness whereof I, CHARLES THORP, the testator have to this my will written on one sheet of paper, set my hand and seal this the fifteenth day of February, one thousand eight hundred and forty.

Charles Thorp, (seal)

Signed & sealed in the presence of us who have subscribed in the presence of each other.
Test.
David C. Cowan.
James Thorp. Proven at the March term 1840, of the Lincoln County Court. Recorded 26th October 1841.

Joseph Kennedy's Will. Lincoln County, Middle Tennessee, December 29th 1839. In the name of God Amen. I, Joseph Kennedy of the County & State aforesaid, being in sound mind & judgment but calling to mind the frailty of man & the uncertainty of my days here, & wishing to make a disposition of my worldly affairs before this change comes, I hereby make this my last will and testament.

1st, It is my will that after my decease all my just debts be paid, then it is my will that my beloved wife Lucinda have the tract of land whereon she now lives, during her life time or widowhood, then it is to be equally divided between the boys. I also allow my father a small piece of land to work for to make his support while he stays her, and all the over-plus to go to the widow, & if she changes her way of living it is all to return to the heirs to be equally divided among them.

And I also appoint Hugh Taylor & William Wyatt the executors (194) of this my last will and testament, being signed, sealed and

(194) delivered in the presence of,   his
James E. English.   Joseph x Kennedy,
John H. Reece.   mark
Andw M. English.
Proven at the term 1841 of the Lincoln County Court. Recorded
26th of October 1841.

John Allbright's Will. State of Tennessee, Lincoln County.
I, JOHN ALLBRIGHT, being of sound mind and perfect memory, but
in a very low State of health, and knowing that it is appointed
unto all men once to die, do make and publish this my last will
& testament, as follows:
I first direct that all my just debts be paid out of any
money that I may die Siezed of, or may first come into the
hands of my executor.
Secondly, I give and bequeath unto my beloved wife Margaret all that part of my farm east and south of the big road during her natural life or widowhood, also my gray horse Brandy,
and my claybank mare Nell, my wagon & harness.
Thirdly, I bequeath unto my son John ten dollars in cash.
Fourthly, I bequeath to my son Jacobs' daughter,Mary five
dollars in cash.
Fifthly, I bequeath to my son William my Soloman horse.
Sixthly, I bequeath to my son Mathews my horse Peter.
Seventhly, My son Alexander shall have my bay filly. My
son Barney Monroe shall have the Peter colt, the balance of my
land I give and bequeath to my six sons equally, that is, William, Matthew, Alexander,Barney, Monroe, James, Isham & Harvey.
I order and bequeath unto my Manson twelve hundred dollars in
(195) cash. And to my daughter Mary Ann, four hundred and fifty dollars. I also bequeath unto my beloved wife Margaret all my
household and kitchen furniture, and the balance of my property
I order to be sold on a credit of twelve months.
Lastly, I do hereby nominate and appoint Robert Drennan,my
executor. In witness whereof I do to this my will set my hand
and seal this sixteenth day of December 1839.his
                                John x Allbright,(seal).
                                        mark
Signed, sealed & published in our presence and we have subscribed
our names in the presence of the testator, this sixteenth day of
December, 1839.
Test.
James Roach.
Hamilton Cochran. Proven at the term 18-- of the Lincoln
County Court. Recorded 26th day of October 1841.

Last will of Isaac Gattis. In the name of God Amen. I,
ISAAC GATTIS, of the State of Tennessee, and County of Lincoln,
being at this time weak in body, but of sound mind and disposing memory, do make and ordain this to be my last will and testament revoking all others, and as touching what worldly estate
it has pleased God to bless me with, I give and bequeath in the
following manner,(viz):
1st, My will and desire is that the fifty acre tract of land
I purchased of William Braden be sold on a credit of twelve months
and the money thence arising, to help pay my just debts.
2nd, My will and desire is that my three youngest sons,to

(196) wit, Newton, James and Thomas have the sole benefit of the balance of my land and premises until James and Thomas become of lawful age, and at that time said land to be equally divided according to quantity and quality, between my five following sons, viz; William, Wilson, Newton, James and Thomas.

3rd, My will and desire is that my two sons James and Thomas have two colts which they have claimed, and James to have a saddle, worth twenty-five dollars, Thomas having already had his saddle, a cow each, two sheep a piece, and the hogs they have marked in their own mark, all three of them a plow and gear each, James and Thomas also to have the cooking utensils and cupboard ware, and a years' provision to be laid off to them by John Dusenberry and James W. Holman, and moreover, that Wilson, James and Thomas, have feather beds and furniture.

4th, My will and desire is that my four following daughters, to wit, Sophia, Polly, Eliza and Julian, have two sheep each, and Elizabeth to have a cow.

5th, My will and desire that my horse called Jack, and my mare called Pigeon, be left with Thomas and James, until they become of age, and Elizabeth is to have a colt from the mare if they can raise one, and at that time the balance of the horses with the increase that may be left, be thrown into the estate for a general division amongst my daughters.

6th, My will and desire is that whereas my son-in-law Daniel E. Yarbrough has taken a lease of me, and has been in possession of it one year, my desire is that he have said lease four years longer.

7th, My will and desire is that all my property of every description, not mentioned in this will and that what is mentioned to be sold when Thomas and James become of lawful age, be sold on a credit of twelve months, and the money thence arising, after finishing paying my just debts, be equally divided between my nine daughters, (viz) Jane Waggoner, Elizabeth Cashion, Sarah Brown, Nancy Gattis, Sophia George, Martha Brady,

(197) and Polly Yarbrough, Eliza Allen and Julian Brady. The balance of the property left except what is left with Thomas and James, to be sold immediately, the others to be sold when they become of lawful age.

8th, And lastly, my will and desire that my son William Gattis, and my son-in-law Abner Bready be Executors to this my last will and testament, believing they will see it properly executed.

Isaac Gattis, (seal).

Signed, sealed, published and pronounced to be the last will and and testament of ISAAC GATTIS, who by his request and in his presence, and in the presence of each other, have witnessed the same.

Abner Steed.

N. Gattis.

Charles Gattis. Proven at November Term 1841. Recorded Nov. 23rd, 1841.

Robert Wilson's Last Will. In the name of God Amen, September 17th 1839, I, ROBERT WILSON, considering the uncertainty of this mortal life and being in a sound mind and memory, (Blessed be Almighty God for the same) do make and publish this my last will and testament, in manner and form as follows; viz,

(197)   First, I direct that my funeral expenses and all my
just debts be paid as soon as possible out of any money I
may die possessed of, or may first come into the hands of my
Executor.

Secondly, I give and bequeath unto my eldest daughter,
Elizabeth T, Wilson five dollars.

Third, I give and bequeath unto my second daughter Narcissa L. Sawyers, five dollars.

Fourth, I give and bequeath unto my eldest son Vinson A.
Wilson, five dollars.

Fifth, I give and bequeath unto my second son Matthew T.
Wilson, five dollars.

Sixth, I give and bequeath unto my youngest son Robert W.
Wilson, five dollars. And I give unto my beloved wife Hannah
B. Wilson all my real and personal estate to dispose of at her
will and pleasure.

And lastly, I do hereby nominate and appoint my wife Hannah B. Wilson and William Wyatt, my Executors. In witness
whereof I do to this my will and testament set my hand and seal
(198) this 17th day of September in the year of our Lord, Eighteen
hundred and thirty nine.

                    Robert Wilson, (seal).
Signed and sealed in the presence of us.
Adam Nipp.
John Wyatt.
Proven December Court 1841. Recorded December 10th, 1841.

John Pryor Senr. Last Will. In the name of God Amen. I,
JOHN PRYOR, Senr. of the County of Lincoln and State of Tennessee
being quite unwell and weak in body, but sound in mind and
know that it is appointed for all men to die, and wishing to
dispose of what worldly goods it hath pleased God to bless me
with, I do make, publish and declare this to be my last will
and testament.

First, I wish all my just debts to be paid by my executor
as early after my decease as is convenient. My daughter Mild-
red in her life time receive what I intended for her, except
the value of two negro boys, John and Henry, which is with my
sons John and Nathan. I wish the two boys valued at cash valuation, and the amount equally divided between Mildreds' two
daughters. I have also given my son William what I wish him to
have at present. My son John has also received what I wish
him to have at present, except a negro girl Martha, which is
his. My daughter Ann has not received her part of my negroes
which I wish her to have, they are Pheba and her children, and
Anthony and Clarissa, also two cows and calves, two beds and
furniture, and such other articles as will be necessary for
housekeeping, also a good saddle horse with three thousand dollars, the first of January next, to make her portion equal with
my other children. My son Nathan has also received what I wish
him to have at present. My daughter Mary has also received
what I wish her to have at present. I wish my beloved wife Mary
Pryor, after my death to have the free use of all my negroes, that
I have not given to my children, with the use of all my farm and
houses, and household and kitchen furniture with the stock of all
kinds, farming tools, with all my notes and cash so long as she
(199) may live, and after her death I wish all my property of every

(199) kind not before disposed of, to be equally divided between my
five children, William, John,and Nathan Pryor, Ann R. Estill,
and Mary Estill, except my negro Tom, he shall be at liberty
to choose his master amongst the heirs, and I do hereby appoint
my three sons, William, John and Nathan Pryor, my Executors,to
this, my last will and testament. In testimony I have hereunto
set my hand and seal, this the 24th day of September, 1841.
Charles McKinney.   John Pryor, (seal).
William Bonner. Witnesses.
Proven at the January Term,1842,of the County Court. Registered January 11th, 1842.

          Nancy Cunningham's Will. In the name of God Amen. I,
NANCY CUNNINGHAM, of the State of Tennessee,and County of Lincoln, being weak of body, but of sound mind and disposing memory, do make and ordain this to be my last will and testament,
revoking all othersby me hitherto made. And as touching what
estate it has pleased God to bless me with, I leave, give and
bequeath in the following manner,(to wit).
          1st, My will and desire is,and I give and bequeath unto
Rebecca Allen, a young woman I have principally raised, one
feather bed, one bolster, one pillow, one under sheet, one blanket, and a checked counterpane, and two bed quilts, eight dollars in money.
          2nd, I give unto my son-in-law John Cunningham, nine dol-
lars which he has already received, and I give unto my daughter
Polly Cunningham, a part of my wearing clothes.
          3rd, I give unto Nancy Cunningham, my daughter, part of
my wearing clothes, and part of bed clothes, and five dollars
in money and my saddle.
          4th, I give unto Cincinnati Grace, my daughter-in-law,
part of my wearing clothes. I give unto John Grace my son
thirty three dollars and some cents, being the amount of a
note I have on him.
          5th, I give unto Elizabeth Howell, my daughter, a part
(w200)of my wearing clothes and part of my bed clothes.
          6th, I give unto my granddaughter Nancy Howell, daughter
of James Howell, my cupboard and whats in it.
          7th, My will and desire is that my beds and bed clothes,
that are not otherwise disposed of, be dividedas heretofore
mentioned, between, John Grace, Elizabeth Howell and Rebecca
Ashby, without a sale.
          8th, My will and desire is that all the balance of my
property be sold on a credit of twelve months, and the money
thence arising, together with the money owing me after paying
my just debts and expenses, be equally divided between my son
John Grace,Rebecca Ashby and Elizabeth Howell,my daughters.
          9th, My will and desire is that my son-in-law Travis Ash-
by, and my son,John Grace, be my executors to this my last
will and Testament, believing they will see it properly executed.
December the 12th 1841.   her
                         Nancy x Cunningham, (seal).
                              mark
Signed, xealed and pronounced to be the last will and testament of NANCY CUNNINGHAM, who at her request, and in presence
of each other have witnessed the same.

(200)   Witness.
        Abner Steed.
    Alex Bready.   Proven at the January Term 1842, of the Lincoln
        County Court.   Recorded January 11th, 1842.

  Aaron Well's Will.   I, AARON WELLS, of the County of Lincoln and State of Tennessee, do make and publish this my last
will and testament, hereby revoking and making void all former
wills by me at any time heretofore made.
  First, I direct that my body be decently interred in a
manner suitable to my former course of life.   As to such worldly estate as it has pleased God to intrust me with, I dispose
of the same as follows:
  Firstly, I direct that all my just debts and funeral expenses be paid so soon after my death as possible, out of any
money that I may die possed of, or may first come into the
hands of my Executors, from any portion of Estate, real or personal.
  Secondly, I gave and bequeath to my dear beloved wife,
Mary Wells, her peacable possession of my dwelling-

house and a comfortable and Sufficient of support of my home
Plantation with the household and Kitchen furniture and my
Negro Man and woman Joshua and Venus during her natural life
or widowhood-But should my wife at anytime intermarry with any
other Man-My wish is that she have one half of my household and
Kitchen furniture with my first choice of Cows and calves and a
like portion of my sheep and hogs.

Thirdly I gave and bequeath to my grandson Alex Don F.Dobbins
My plantation whereon I now live including a small part of the
tract of Land that I purchased of William B.Wright lying in the
forks of the Main Swan Creek and the west fork of Swan Creek -
bounded with said Creek to a cut off and the Main Swan Creek
to line of my home Plantation and Alex Don F.Dobbins to keep his
grandmother Mary wills in a peacable possession of the portion
alloted her.

Fourthly. I gave and bequeath to my grand daughter Narcissa M-
Kinney and to heirs of her body the tract or piece of land lying
on the Fayetteville road below the ford on Swan Creek being the
tract of Land I purchased of James Bright agent for Polk.

Fifthly I gave and bequeath to my grand daughter Josephine Wood
and to the heirs of her body the plantation that I purchased of
William B.Wright Excluding the part take from said tract and attached to the home Plantation.My tract of ridge land lying on
the chesnut ridge north of Enos Sackey to be equally divided
between A.F.T.Dobbins and Josephine wood and the heirs of her
body.

My wish and desire is that the before Allotted tracts of land
shall be valued by W.B.Wright,Jacob Wright,Moon Wilson and -
Davis Smith the said tracts of land to be made equal by the
Claimant paying to each other the difference in Valuation.

Sixthly .as I have heretofore given to Narcissa M Kinney a
negro girl I do now allot to the balance of my grandchildren a
Negro girl as follows to Alex Don F.Dobbins ,Tilda and child and
to Josephine wood and to the heirs of her body Pitter to Adeline
Dobbins and to heirs of her body Alec and to Calidonia Dobbins
and to the heirs of her body Rachael.

Seventhly.I gave and bequeath to Adeline Dobbins and to the heirs
of their body an equal portion of My negroes to make their parts
equal in value to the parts given in land to Narcissa M Kinney
Alex D.T.Dobbins and Josephine Wood.

Eightly. I gave and bequeath to my daughter Sally Dobbins My -
Negro Girl Ann during her Natural life or widowhood.

Ninthly. The remaining portion of my Negroes if any after the
portion already given,to be equally divided between Alexander
Don F.Dobbins,Narcissa M Kinney Josephine wood, Adeline Dobbins
and to their heirs and the heirs of there body.

Tenthly.As I wish no portion of my perishable to be sold no -
further than is actually Necessary upon the account of the heirs
not of age I give and bequeath the whole of my stock including
horses.Cows,Hogs,and heep to be equally divided between Alex
Don F.Dobbins,Narcissa M.Kinney,Josephine Wood,Adeline and -
Caledonia Dobbins and to their heirs and the heirs of their bodies.

Eleventhly.I do give and bequeath in addition to what I have
given to Alexander D.F.Dobbins the whole of my farming tools including My waggon also all my Mill tools.

And as Issac Heaven has now set in to oversee_for me the present
years.I wish him to be Continued agreeable to our contract.

Lastly I do hereby make and appoint My grandson Alexander D.F.-

Dobbins and my two grandson in law Ira McKinney and John Wood my executor to this my last will and testament.
In witness whereof I Aaron Wells the said Testator have to - this my will written on one sheet of paper Set my and affixed my seal this the 24th. day of January one thousand eitht hundred and forty two.

Aaron Wells   (seal)

Signed, sealed and published in the presence of us who have subscribed in presence of the Testator and of each other. Proven by Davis Smith & Boone Wilson, April Term of the Lincoln County Court 1342.

Recorded April 12th 1842,
G. W. Jones, clerk.

Davis Smith
Wilson B. Wright
Boone Wilson
Amos Harley
Isaiah Nerren

(203)

State of Tennessee, Lincoln County. To all whom this may concern.

I, Philip Koonce, being of sound mind and memory do make and publish this my last will and testament in manner and form following (to wit) I give and bequeath to my beloved wife all my land and plantation that I am now in possession of during her natural life and at her death to be equally divided between my four youngest daughters that is to say, Burdotty Juily Woods, Sophia Ann, Patsey Pina, I also give to my wife my negro boy Sam and Charles and Charles and negro woman Malinda during her natural life and at her death to be equally divided between my four youngest daughters as above stated, I give and bequeath to Andrew McCartney and Amos Small fifty Dollars each to be paid out of my stock and other perishable property all the balance of my worldly goods that I am seized with at this time to be sold for to pay my debts and the remainder whatever that may be I give to my wife during her natural life, and at any time if she should think proper to do so, to give to the children any part of the above property that she may think just and so to do, I wish to be understood that I do not want any more property sold than a sufficiency to pay all my just debts whatever they may be. I hereby appoint William McGee and my beloved wife sole Executrix and Executor of this my last will and Testament hereby revoking all former Wills by me made. In witness whereof I have hereunto set my hand and affixed my seal this 5th day of March in the year of our Lord one thousand Eight hundred and thirty three.

Philip Koonce   (seal)

Signed, sealed published and declared by the above Philip Koonce to be his last Will and Testament in presence of us the subscribing witnesses.

George W. Dennis
Andrew MCartney

Proven and admitted to recorded at the April Term 1842 of the Lincoln County Court and Recorded April 12th 1842.

G. W. Jones, Clerk

State of Mississippi.Marshall County.The last will and -
(204) Testament of ROBERT HAIRSTON . I Robert Hairston consid ring
the uncertainty of this mortal life.and being of sound mind and
memory Blessed be Almighty God for the same,do make and publish
this my last will and testament in manner and form following.
That is to say,First I give and bequeath unto my beloved wife
Margaret Hairston one negro woman by the name of Lile about
thirty years of age.also one other negro woman by the name of
Vina about seventeen years of age.also five hundred Dollarsin
Cash.I also bequeath to my daughter Mary Meek and the heirs of
her body a certain tract or parcel of land being and lying in
Range four township six and the Northeast quarter of section
Eight.Known as the place on which the said Hairston now lives
Calling for one hundred and sixty acres More or less and also
five hundred Dollars in Cash.I also bequeath to my Nephew -
Robert Meek a certain tract or parcel of land being and lying
in Range four Township six and the Northwest quarter of section
Eight west of the bases.Calling for one hundred and sixty acres
more or less.

I also bequeath to my nephew Robert Hairston five hundred Dollars in Cash.I also bequeath to my two sons (to wit)Manly M.-
Hairston and James N.N.Hairston also my real and personal both
in the State of Tennessee and also in the State of Mississippi.
that is to say all my property consisting of the rise of one -
thousand Acres of land lying on Elk River in Lincoln County -
Tennessee and the balance of Land lying in DeSota County and -
State of Mississippi.Together with all the negroes belonging to
the said Robert Hairston not bequeathed to his beloved wife -
Margaret Hairston.Also all the balance of money and notes after
taking out the services aforesaid Amounts.
Also all the stock of every descriptions that is to say,Horses
Cows,Hogs,Sheep,and sofourth.Together with the household and K
Kitchen furniture after all my debts are paid,which aforesaid
amounts is to be equally divided between my two sons Manly M.
Hairston and Jmaes H.Hairston My Administrator to settle and
arrange all my business.
In witness whereof I have hereunto Set my hand and seal this
(205) the twelfth day of August in the year of our Lord one thousand
Eight hundred and forty one.

Robert Hairston

Signed sealed and Published & declared by the above named
Robert Hairston to be his last will and testament in the presence of as who have hereunto subscribed our names as witness in
the presence of the Testator.

J.J.Meek
Robert Jackson
I.F.Davis.

The State of Mississippi Marshall County.Probate Court -
October Term 1841,This last will and testament of Robert Hairston
late of this County Decd was this day exhibited and duly proven
in open Court by the oathes of J.J.Meek and Robert Jackson two
of the subscribing witnesses thereto and ordered to be recorded
Given under my hand and the seal of said Court at office the 25th,
day of October 1841.

Gordentia Waite Clerk.

The State of Mississippi Marshall County.I Gordentia Waite clerk of the probate Court of Said County hereby Certify the fore going to be a rue and perfect transcript from the records of my office of the last will and testament of Robert Hairston Decd. and the probate thereof in our said Court.Given under my hand and the seal of said Court at office the 24th.day of November A.D.1841.

Gordentia Waite Clk.

The State of Mississippi Marshall County.I Jesse Seivellen Judge of this Probate Court of sd_County & State do hereby certify that Gordentia Waite whose signature is annexed to the foregoing Certificate is and was at the date thereof clerk of the sd Cour t that full faith & credit are due to his official acts & that his Certificate & allertation are in due form of law.Given under my hand & seal this 18th.January 1842.

Jesse Seivellen (SEAL)

Admitted to record by the Lincoln County Court February .

(206)   William Collins Last Will.

I WILLIAM COLLINS of the County of Lincoln in the State of Tennessee having attained to advanced age and knowing that is appointed for all men to die,and being by the blessing of God of sound mind and memory.do make ordain,publish and declare this my last will and testament in form following that is to say.

First It is my will and desire that all my just debts be paid by my executors herein after mentiones out of any moneys on hands or may first come into their hands.

2nd.I give and bequeath to my dearly beloved wife Catharine-Collins for and during her natural life or widowhood the use of my home Plantation is so much thenof as may be within the following bounds.Beginning at Jacobs Wrights fence on my west boundary line running thence East with the cross fence near the branch , thence a Southern direction and eastward with the Meaders of said fence including the South eastern field and to the east boundary line of my last then North with the Vanier Meaders of said line to my North east corner thence West with the line of thesame to the South west Corner of a tract of land belonging to the Heirs of John Dobbins-thence running South western direction to Jacob Wright land and with his and with his and my fence to the beginning with the further privilege of timber out side of said bounds to keep up the fencing of the same.I also give to my said wife Catharine during her natural life time or widowhood the use of three Negro slaves to wit,Jesse Henry and a negro woman Dilly also the use aforesaid her two choice horses,also there Cows. and Calves,the choise of my stock,also the one fifth of my stock of hogs,I also give upon the terms aforesaid to her the use of all My household and Kitchen furniture together with the whole of my farming tools of every descriptions.Also twenty bushels of wheat also Sixty barrels of Corn and ten stands of bees and yoke of Oxen.

3rd.I give and bequeath to my daughter Nancy Collins My negro girl Adeline and at the death of my daughter Nancy Collins. It is my will and desire fer her son Robert T.Collins to have

(207) the said Negro Girl Adeline and her increase.

4th.I give and bequeath to My son Wright P.Collins my Negro boy Allen Toney aged 7 or 8 years.

Fifthly,I give and bequeath to my son Samuel D.Collins My -
Negro boy Loyd about 5 or 6 years of age.

6th.I give and bequeath yo my daughter Missouri Ann Collins
My Negro Girl Jane age 8 or 9 years.

7th,I give and bequeath to my son Alexander F.Collins My
negro boy Daniel aged about two years.also to the same My -
Silver watch.

8th.I give and bequeath to my Grandson Robert T.Collins the
proceeds or value when sold a certain bay filly known as his My
Executors to collect the same & hand it over to Wright P,Collins
and that the place the same or interest yearly until the said
Robert T.become of lawful age and then to be given to him with
interest.

9th.All the balance of my property not previously disposed
of I direct to be sold at my death and the proceeds thereof together with all moneys on hand or due me by note or otherwise,
I give and bequeath to be equally divided between My five children
Namely Nancy Wright P.Samuel D.Missouri Ann,and Alexander F.Collins
except Wright P Collins having heretofore given to him a Horse
worth fifty Dollars which he is to be charged with or in other-
words the four other Children are to have fifty Dollars More.
than he the Wright P.Collins.

10th.I give to my three sons during the life time of my wife
the use of all the balance of my land in equal portions of the
same.

11th.At the death of my wife Catharine I direct the sale of
all the land or a division of the same if Practicable to be made
equal between my five Children which is hereby given to them -
absolute.I also direct the sale of all the riversionary property
now set apart for the use of my wife including the Slaves Jesse
Henry and Dilly together with her increase to be sold and the
proceeds thereof to be equally divided between my five Children
above named.
If either of the above Named Negroes should die which has been
given to either of my Children and the said woman Dilly should
(208)   become the Mother of another child or Children upon that contingency the said child loosing by death shall be supplied with one
of said black children.

Lastly I hereby revoke all former wills and request that this
My last will be faithfully executed accordingly to the true intent and meaning thereof.I do hereby Nominate and appoint my -
friends Thomas McAfee and Ira M.Kinney Executors to this My last
will and testament.
In witness whereof I have hereunto set my hand & seal this 8th.
day of July 1842.

Wm.Collins (SEAL)

The within will was executed by William Collins in our presence
& in presence of each of us on the 8th.July 1842.

A.F.Dobbins
Jacob R.Wright.
Henry Turney

The foregoing will of William Collins proven at the August
term 1842 of the Lincoln County Court by the oath of A.F.Dobbins
and Henry Turney and ordered by the Court to be recorded.
Recorded August 9th.1842.

G.W.Jones Clerk.

(208) Mark Whitaker Sen. Ill.State of Tennessee Lincoln County - October 30th.1841.

    I MARK WHITAKER SENIOR, calling to mind that all men have once to die, and feeling the infirmity of old age,but feel thankfull to God,for that strength of Mind which enables me to make this my last Will and testament as follows;

    1st.I will my soul to God who gave it and that my body be decently buried.

    2nd.I will that all my estate both real & personal be equally divided among all my children (as the law directs,Namely Rebecca, Isard,,Nancy Hammonds,John Whitaker,Mary Lucas,Sarah Basinger Martha Pegram,Benjamin I Whitaker,Judah Prewitt,Mark Whitaker Jr, and Perlina Purton and their heirs except the following special provision which circumstances seem to require to be made,as my beloved wife Catharine is far advanced in years and feeble.I will

(209) that she have the use of one negro woman of her own choosing and as much household furniture as she may need, also the use of five hundred Dollars,All to be Managed for her Comfort by the assistance of my Executors.

3rd.I will and appoint and do ordain Benjamin I Whitaker Special agent and attorney in fact for Martha Pegram and her heirs to receive and hold for their special benefit all of my estate agreeable to this will to which she may be entitled to deal out as in his Judgement her necessities May require.

    4th.I further more will ordain and appoint Mark Whitaker the special agent and attorney in fact for Judah Prwitt (as above) to receive hold and deal out that part of my estate which may fall to Judah Prewitt and her heirs.

    5th,I consider My children near equal in my former gifts to them except Sarah Basinger who have received one hundred and - fifty Six Dollars which is to be accounted for with the other-hheirs bearing interest from the time received My son Mark will also account for two hundred Dollars which is due Me for land. In order to carry the above into effect I hereby ordain and - appoint my two sons Benjamin I Whitaker and Mark Whitaker My Executors.

    In testimony whereof I have hereunto set my hand and seal in presence of

                                   his
                             Mark X Whitaker (SEAL)
                             mark

John J.Whitaker
William Moore
Joseph Whitaker
Proven at October Term 1842 of the Lincoln County Court.
Recorded October 13th.1842.

(210) Wiley C.Newman's Last Will.

    I Wiley C.Newman do make and publish this as my last will and testament hereby revoking and making void all other wills by me at anytime made.

    First I direct that my funeral expences and all,and all my debts be paid as soon after my death as possible out of any money that I may die possessed of or May first come into the hands of my executors.

    Secondly I give and bequeath to my son Wiley M Newman the six pewter plates and three white sheets.

Thirdly I give and bequeath to my son Wiley M.Newman the full power and authority to take into his possession all the balance of my Estate and stay on the place where I now live with my family for at least and Keep the estate so near as practicable ,all together and at any time after that period the Estate may be equally divided between my son Wiley M.Newman,My son Moses H. Newman,My son Martin W.Newman and My wife Mary M - Newman.

Lastly I do hereby nominate and appoint my son Wiley M.Newman my executor .

In witness whereof I do to this my will set my hand and seal this 26th.day of August 1842.

(210)

W.C.Newman   (SEAL)

Signed,sealed and piblished in our presents and we have subscribed our names hereto in the presence of the testator this 26th.August 1842.

Eli Couch
Obd Holloway

Proven at the October Term of the Lincoln County Court 1842
Registered October 13th.1842.

(211)   John Gragg's Last Will.

In the name of God amen.I JOHN GRAGG.SENR.of the State of Tennessee Lincoln County calling to mind the Mortality of all men and the shortness of time here & wishing to arrange all My earthly affairs before this change may come;And being now in my right mind do hereby make this my last will and Testament And in doing this,it is my will that after my decease all my just and lawful Debts be paid.I also will and bequeath to my beloved wife Jane Gragg as hers forever My Negro Man named - Adam & Negro woman named Lucy & her son Robin & one hundred and fifty Dollars which she now holds in Cash,this property to be execlusively her own,& at her desposal at any time as she may think proper,either during her life time or at her death - And I do also will and bequeath to my beloved wife all the Plantation on which I now live together will all the stock of every kind plantation tools & wagon,& household and Kitchen furniture & My negro man Gilford to be hers during her natural lifetime or widowhood,I also will & bequeath to my two daughters Eliza Jane Gragg & Elizabeth Gragg one horde and saddle apiece to be given to them out of the property left to my beloved wife when they may Marry or leave their Mother,or at their Mothers death should she die before this,& also one bed & furniture,I also will & bequeath to my son John W.Gragg this Plantation on which I now live to (be) his after his Mothers death.provided he may then at that time choose to give the sum of six hundred & fifty Dollars for this place.the whole of the money to be paid within two years after his Mothers death,his own part of their money excluded or not to be paid over to the other legatees but if he doed not choose to take this land at this price,it shall be sold & an equal division made of it.And I also will that after my beloved wife's death all the stock of every Kind and all the Plantation tools,household & Kitchen furniture be sold & the proceeds of this together with the price of the land be equally - divided among all my children & also my negro Man Gilford to be sold & disposed of as to his price in the same way among the Children. And I appoint my son John W.Gragg & wife Jane Gragg the Executor & Executrix of this my last will & testament

This Feby 9th.1842.

John Cragg.

(212) This will is now signed in the presence of the presence of the
following Witnesses Henry Bryson

Robert M.Calla.

Proven by Henry Bryson at the November Term 1842 of the Lincoln
County Court.

James Russell's Last Will.
I JAMES RUSSELL make and publish this as my last will and
testament hereby revoking and making void all other wills by me
at any time made.I direct that the law of the land shall be
my will except first that the property of which I die possessed
instead of being Sold as directed by law shall be divided
among the heirs.
Secondly that Mary my wife shall have an Absolute right to
the negro slaves Tom & Maria and also a right for her natural
life to the negro girl Celia,and a sufficiency of the stock
and also to have at her disposal all the household and Kitchen
furniture and the farming utensils.
Thirdly that my son William Alexander shall have one thousan
dollars less than the remaining heirs.
Fourthly that my daughter Christiana Jane shall receive one
hundred Dollars and John Cowan and David Whitfield shall together receive one hundred and .
Seventy five Dollars more than the remaining heirs.
In witness whereof I do to this My will set my hand and seal
this 24th.October 1842.

James Russell (SEAL)

Signed and acknowledged. in our presence to be the last will
and Testament of James Russell Senr.the date above written.

William B.M.Collum
John Gray
Proven and admitted to record at December Term 1842.of the
Lincoln County Court.

(213)

Josiah Brandon's Last Will.
In the name of God Amen.I JOSIAH BRANDON of the County of -
Lincoln in the State of Tennessee being of sound Mind and disposing Memory but fully aware that it is appointed for all men
once to die do make this my last will and testament hereby revoking all other and former wills by me made.
Item 1st.It is my will and desire that at my death my body
be decently intered in a plan decent manner my immortal soul -
being constantly dedicated to God who gave it me.
Item 2nd.It is my will and desire that the expenses of my
burial be immediately be immediately paid by Executors with all
my just debts.
Item 3rd.It is my will and desire that my wife Rachael -
Brandon be supported and have full and absolute control of all
my effects both real and personal during her natural life shoul
she survive Me and at her death and her remains are disposed
of in a decent manner it is My will and desire that my son -
Lemuel Brandon have all my lands the here ditamenis thereto
belonging forever.

Item 4th.It is My will and desire that my son Logan D.Brandon
Keep the Money of mine due from Judge William Smith and all he
may owe me until my death and the death of his Mother my wife
and pay Me annually 8 percent interest on the amount and should
my wife survive Me he must pay the interest to her or dispose of
it to her benefit and then it is my will and desire that the amount
that may be in My son Logan D's hand due me.My Executor after
the said son Logan is fully satified for all his trouble about
My estate.shall divide the residue among My daughter that are
living and the children of those that May be dead My sons Thomas
and William Brandon are sufficiently wealthy without my aid I pre-
sume would not desire any part of My estate.
It is specifflcally understood that it is my will and desire that
my Executor shall exercise their own residue of Money above mentioned among my indigent daughters.

(214)   Item 5th.It is my will and desire that My Executor whenever
it is convenient to them to give my grandson Lemuel S.Woodard
one hundred Dollars to be raised out of my effects not to be -
given until after the death of both my wife and myself as a special legacy,and I now hereby appoint my sons Lemuel Brandon and
Logan D.Brandon Executors of this My last will and testament.
     Given under my hand and seal 4th.day of January 1840.

                                    Josiah Brandon (SEAL)

Test
B.B.Brandon
Daniel Scivally
William Frame
Proven and admitted to recorded at the December Term 1842 of the
Lincoln County Court.

Joseph Hester's Last Will.
     I Joseph Hester of the County of Lincoln and State of Tennessee
do make and publish the following as my last will and testament
having made no other or former wills.
First I give and bequeath to my son Wilson W.Hester My Negro boy
Davey (a blacksmith) three choice mules & bay horse which he is
to have possession of on the first day of January next which is
  intended to be infull of his proportion of my estate it is also
my will that the expences & the schooling of the present session
also the expences of his return to this County is to be paid put
of My personal estate exclusive of the above named bequeats.

     Secondly I give and bequeath to my beloved wife Mary Hester My
Negro man named Ned.I also give to her during her Natural life
or widowhood the sole Management and control of all My personal
property of every description consisting of Negroes, Stock of -
every Kind household and Kitchen furniture and farming utensils
of every description to be used and disposed of by her as she
may think best for the useand benefit of her and my children ,as-
-nt as herein after mentioned,that is to say it is my will,that
      My children shall se verally arrive at the age of twenty one
          that they shall have a negro that shall be of about and -
             value of the Negroes then on hand and that such one shall
be put in possession of the same.
(215)   Thirdly.It is my will that my children receive a liberal -
education and that an equally portion out of my estate be applied
to each of my children for that purpose,unless it should be dis-

covered that anyone or more of them were not disposed to receive
such education,then and in that case such portion as intended
for that purpose shall be otherwise Sit apart to such as may
not be disposed to receive such education.and it is my will that
all the support of my family shall be applied towards the education of my children as above stated.but if there.should not be a
sufficiency for that purpose,then it is My will that such Negroes
or Negroes as can be best Spared,be sold for that purpose.
It is my will that the tract of land whereon I now live,shall be
subject to the control and Management of my wife,and the proceeds
arising from the Cultivation thereof,be applied to the support of
My family.And that said land remain so subject to the Cohtrol and
Management of my wife for the purposes aforesaid so long as she
may desire to live on the same.And if she should desire to leave
said tract of land and should desire it to be sold.It is my will
that said land be sold,and that my friend John J.Whitaker (who
is hereby requested and empowered so to do) Sell the same at -
private sale on such terms as he shall deem most beneficial to
the interest of my family-It is further my will that if my land
should be sold as herein before stated that the proceeds arising
from such sale of my tract of land be laid out in the purchase
of another tract or tracts of land lying north of the thirty -
fifth degree of North Latitude,and that my said wife is hereby
authorised to purchase said lands and it is my request that my
son Wilson with such others as my friends as my wife shall request
will aid and assist her in making an advantageous and judicious
purchase and that the said John J.Whitaker or such other person
as shall hold the proceeds of my said tract of land shall pay the
same one to the person from whom said land shall be so purchased
And it is my will and desire that in case my said tract of land
be sold that the title be retained until the purchase money is p
paid.It is further My will that if my said tract of land shall not
be sold during the lifetime or widowhood of my wife.that upon the
(216) happening of either that the same be sold upon a credit of one
two and three years and the proceeds together with all other estate shall be sold and the proceeds equally divided amongst my
heirs.share and share alike,except my son Wilson as herein before
stated.
It is alsomy will that if it should be desired by my wife that
said tract of land be sold that it shall be at her option whither
said tract of land be sold upon a credit or for cash.
It is my request that James Bright Senr.shall be guardian for my
children so long as they shall remain in the County and if they
should remove then it is my request,that my son Wilson shall be
their guardian.
It is also my request,that said James Bright Senr.aid and Assist
my wife in the execution of this my last will and testament.
It is also my will that all debts due and owing me be Collected
and the same be applied as herein before stated.
It is my will that at the marriage or upon the death of my if -
wife,the Negroes which shall remainand not herein before devised
shall be equally divided amongst my children,Except my son Wilson
as herein before stated.
Lastly I hereby nominate and appoint my wife Mary Hester sole -
Executric of this my last will and testament.
In witness whereof I have hereunto set my hand and seal this twenty
fifth Day of October in the year 1842.

                              Jas.Hester (SEAL)

Signed ,sealed and acknowledged in the presence of us
J.Bright
H.B.Bonner
Jacob Broyles

Proven by the oathes of .J.Bright and Jacob Broyles and admitted
to record at the December Term 1842 of the

Lincoln County Court
G.W.Jones Clerk.

(217) Cyrus Cathey's Last Will.
    I CYRUS CATHEY of the County of Lincoln in the State of
Tennessee.Knowing that it is appointed for all men to die,and
being by the blessing of God of sound Mind and Memory do make
ordain,publish and declare this my last will and Testament in
form following that is to say.
    1st.It is my will and desire that all my just debts and fun-
eral expences be paid by my executor and executrix herein after
mentioned out of the proceeds of Notes and other claims on -
hand which may be due me but should said Notes & Money thus due
be not sufficient further purpose then and in that case I direct
the sale as such personal property as can be most conviently spared as shall be sufficient to Pay the balance of my debts and other
expences.
    2nd.All the balance of my Estate both real and personal of
every description I give and bequeath to my dearly beloved wife
Nancy Cathey the use and control of the same during her Natural
lifetime or widowhood,and at her death it is my will and desire
that the whole of said estate of every description be equally -
divided between my six children that is to say William A.Cyrus
L.H. Mary E,Sarah C.George J.F.and John T.Cathey.
    4th.But should My said wife Nancy Catheys any other person
then and in that case I direct the whole of my Estate both real
and personal of every description to be then sold or a division
of the same if praciticable to be made equal between my said wife
Nancy Cathey and our six children as above named which parts or
portions thereof.I hereby give to them absolute.It being my will
and desire that my said wife Nancy Cathey be entitled to one seven-
the or childs part of my said estate upon the happening of the
Contingency as above stated.Lastly I hereby revoke all former -
wills and request this my last will be faithfully executed accordd-
to the true intent and meaning thereof I do hereby nominate and
appoint my wife Nancy Cathey and my brother
(218) Alexander Cathey my Executrix and Executor to this my last will
and testament.I witness whereof I have hereunto set my hand and
seal this 25th.day of September 1842.
                              Cyrus Cathey (SEAL)
The above will was executed in our presence of Cyrus cathey and
in presence of each of us.
                              John Wood
                               Ira McKinnoy
                              Wm.F.Zimmerman.

Proven at the February Term of the Lincoln County Court 1843.

John O.Griffin Last Will.
    I John O.GRIFFIN of Fayetteville,Lincoln County Tennessee do

make this my last will and testament .

First I desire that all my just debts be paid as soon after my decease as

(218) possible.

Second.I give and bequeath to my wife Martha M.the whole of my property both real and personal to have and to hold the one morty thereof to her & her heirs & assigns forever and to have & to hold the other moiety of the same to her during her natural life and after her death the same to be equally divided amongst all the children of my brothers & sisters then Living.

Lastly I do appoint Moses H.Bonner & John Cowan executors - of this my last will and testament.In witness whereof I have here unto set my hand and seal this 21st.day of December 1842.

John O.Griffis(SEAL)

Attest
L.Gullett
       his
William   Smith
      mark
William A.Griffis
Proven at the February Term 1843 of the Lincoln County Court.

(219) George Martin's Last Will.

In the name of God Amen-I GEORGE MARTIN of the County of Lincoln and State of Tennessee being in advance age and laboring under great bodily infirmity in view of the approaching dissolution do make publish and declare My last will and testament as follows(to wit)

First I give and bequeath to my two sons St.George Martin and William J.H.Martin and their heirs and assigns my tract of land on which I live at this time in said Lincoln County supposed to contain one hundred and forty eight acres valued at seventeen hundred and seventy six Dollars being eight hundred and eighty eight Dollars to each one.

Second.I give and bequeath to my Daughter Martha J.A.Timius during her life and at her death to her children the heirs of her body,my negro boy Jacob Valued at seven hundred Dollars.

Third.I give and bequeath to my daughter Celia Ann Martin my negro boy named Henry valued at six hundred & fifty Dollars.

Fourth.I give and bequeath to my grand children Ann Eliza, Mary Catharine ,Francis Virginia and two infants twins,in all five the children of my son C.K.V.Martin recently deceased my two negro boys Named Peter and Lewis valued at five hundred and fifty - dollars.

Fifth.I give and bequeath to my son Robert Martin My negroes Dick,Lydia,Jane,Benjamin and anthony valued at Eight hundred and fifty Dollars.
In order to make the legacy to each of my children above named equal,it is my will and desire that my son St.George pay over to Martha J.A.Timmorius fifty four Dollars and thirty three cents
  to my daughter Celia Ann Martin Seventy nine Dollars and - three cents.And that my son William J.H.Martin pay over to ren of my son C.K.V.Martin aboved named one hundred and hree Dolllars and sixty cents and that my son Robert -
(220) pay over to my daughter Celia Ann Martin twenty five Dol-
lars also that my son Robert Martin pay over to the children of my son C.K.V.Martin before designated seventy dollars and sixty

six cents. I have heretofore given to my daughter Mary V.Houston
and to my daughter Elizabeth M.L.Proutly each property which I
consider equal in value to the property herein bequeathed to my
other children respectly.
I constitute and appoint my sons St.George Martin and William J.-
H.Martin Executors of this my last will and testament.
In testimony whereof I have hereunto subscribed my name and affixed my seal this 11th.day of November 1840.

George Martin (SEAL)

George Martin,signed sealed Published and declared the above or
foregoing to be his last will and testament and also acknowledged
that he executed the same for the purpose therein contained all
of which was done by the said George Martin in our presence the
day the same bears date.
George W.Jones.
Samuel Bell.

Proven at the March Term 1843 of the Lincoln County Court.

Thomas Atwood Last Will.

    I THOMAS ATWOOD of the State of Tennessee and County of
Lincoln being weak of body but of sound mind and Memory do make
this my last will and Testament I give unto my son John Atwood
the tract of land on which I live containing forty acres my reson
for giving my land to my son John to the exclusion of my other
children is because he has always lived with me and is not calculated to make a living in the world as My other children and I
therefore appoint my friend George Renegar to be guardian for my
son John and he is hereby empowered to rent or sell said Land
or use it as he in his judgement may think best for the benefit
of John I give to my wife Nancy all the ballance of my property
of every description after my debts and funeral expences are paid
and I hereby appoint My friend Enos Wilson to be my Executor to see
that this will is come a unto effect.
Signed sealed and delivered in presence of this 12th.day May 1843.
John J.Whitaker
Enos Wilson
George Renegar

His
Thomas X Atwood
mark

(221)   I JOHN VICKERS,of Lincoln County and State of Tennassee do
make and publish this as my la t will and testament hereby revoking and making void all other wills at any other time made.
    First.I direct that my funeral expences and all my debts
be paid as soon after my death as possible out of any Moneys
that I may die possessed of or that my first come into the hands
of my executors.
Secondly.I give and bequeath to my wife Nancy Vickers during her
lifetime all my land all my stock of every description all my
household and Kitchen furniture,My Plantation tools of every description and all other property whatever of any and every discription,Lastly I do hereby nominate and appoint Jacob Nipplin and
Uty.Sherrell my Executors.
In witness whereof I do this my will set my hand and seal this
28th.day of Fenruary 1843.
Signed sealed and acknowledged in the presents.

his
John X Vickers
mark

Martin Graves
Aron Doyd.

I JAMES PYBAS of the state of Tennessee and County of Lincoln being weakley of body but of sound mind and disposing Memory do by these presents make and ordain this to be my last will and Testament revoking all others and as touching what wordly estate it hath pleased God to bless me with I give leave and bequeath in the following manner (viZ)

First my will and desire is that all my property of every discription be left with my wife Sarah J.Pybas during her Natural life or widowhood in order for her own Mentainance and comfort and the Maintainance and education of my children except as herein after named.

Second my will and desire is that My Executors collect all the debts that are owing to me and pay all the just debts against me therewith if there should not be enough to pay My debts Executors to sell my property they May see proper and the Money thence arising to finnish paying my debts.

Third My will and desire is that at my wife death all my land and other property to be equally divided between My two sons - Keneth M.Pybas & William J.Pybas the land to be

(222)

equally divided between them the other property to be sold on a credit of twelve months and the money thence arising to be equally divided between them both.

Fourth.My will and desire is that if my wife should alter her way of living by a second Marriage in the case my will and desire is that my wife shall have all my household and Kitchen furniture

Fifth my will and desire is that at my wife second marriage all my land shall fall to my two sons immediately and to be equally divided between them when they come of age and all my perishable property except My household and Kitchen furniture to be sold and the Money thence arising to be equally divided between my two sons

Sixth my will and desire is that if my household & Kitchen furniture should get destroyed by fire or some other unavoidable accident then in that case my will and desire is that my wife shall have a pooportionable part of the perishable property with my two sons.

Seventh my will and desire is that if my two sons should decease leaving no heirs nor have made no sale of the land my will & desire is that my wife shall hold my land during her natural life together with all the perishable property.Eight and last my will and desire is that if my two sons should decease leaving no heirs and have made no sale od there interest in the land then in that case my will and desire is that Lucinda Pybas my Neice that now lives with me shall have one half of the land at the decease of my wife the other half I leave with my wife to make such deposition of as she may think proper.

Ninth.I do hereby appoint My Trusty frind John Landess my executor and Sarah J. Pybas my Executrix to this my last will and Testament beleiving they will see it properly executed.
Signed sealed Published and Pronounced in presents of us this 1st. day of August 1840.

James Pybas (SEAL)

John Cunningham
Polly X Cunningham
    her mark

(223)   I PURLINA PURTON of the County of Lincoln & State of Tennessee this 8th of August 1843 being weak of body but of sound mind and

Memory do make this my last will and Testament my will and desire
is all my just debts and funeral expences be paid.
That my negro woman Matilda together with all my other property
of every description except one bedstead and furniture be sold
to the highest bidder on a credit of twelve months.

My desire is that all my children shere equal in the proceeds
of my property both of the sale and what is coming from my Fathers
estate except the bed and furniture above named which I give
to my daughter Susan Catharine over and above what I give to the
boys.

I do hereby appoint My brother Mark Whitaker guardian to my
four sons Francis Marion,Patrick Henry Mark.& William and that
he take charge of them and what is coming to them and he is authorised to bind them out to learn trades or to such persons as he
is in his descission may think proper,and my will is that he be
not required to give security as guardian and my will is that my
sister Juda L.Pruitt be and is hereby requested to take charge
of and rase & school my daughter Susan Catharine and call on my
executor for funds as she may need.

My will is that my brother Benjamin I Whitaker be and he is
requested to be my Executor and that he be not requested to give
security.Signed sealed and delivered in the presents of day and
date above written.
                                                her
                                    Perlina X Purton
                                                mark

Test.
John J.Whitaker
Martha Pigram
George Waggoner

(224)   I ALEXANDER HUGHY do make and publish this my last will and
testament hereby revoking and makingvoid all other wills by me
at anytime made.

First I direct that my funeral expences and all my debts be
paid as soon after death as possible out of any monies that I may
die possessed of or may come into the hands of my executor by the
sale of a sufficent quantity of my personal property to do the -
same.

Secondly I give and bequeath to my wife Mary Hughy all of the
balance of my property both personal and real to be hers to support her children on her lifetime or widowhood and if my wife -
Mary should marry I will and bequeath that she have a childs -
part of my property that should be in her hands at the time of
her marriage and the balance to be equally divided between my
beloved children heirs of my body (viz)Elvira J.Hughy,Parthena
Mary C.Franklin A Rober Sariah A Martha L Williams L.Williams
Henry Hughy. My Executor is witnes whereof I do this my will
set my hand and seal
Alexander Hughy. This 11th.day of March 1843.

I also appoint my beloved wife Mary Hughy my Executrix to
this my last will & Testament.
Signed sealed and published in our presents and we have subscribed our Names hereto in presence of the Testator.

Test
Wm.B.Wright
J.N.Keith.

(225) Mathew Price Last Will & Testament.

    In the name of God Amen. I MATHEW PRICE of Lincoln County -
State of Tennessee becoming old and infirm but being of sound
mind and disposing memory for which I thank God and calling to
mind the uncertainty of human life and being desious to dispose
of all My wordly substances it has pleased God to bless me with
my will and wish is that when it pleased God to take me from this
world that My body shall be intered in the earth in a decent and
christian like manner.

    First I give and bequeath unto my beloved wife Elizabeth Price
the benefit and use of all my land negroes and all other property
that I may be in possession of during her natural life or widowhood after making sale of Perishable property sufficint to pay all
to pay all debts that I may owe, and after the death of my wife -
Elizabeth My will and wish is that all my property and possession
both real and personal shall be sold by me Executors.

    And I give and bequeath unto Anna Gowan my daughter if living
if not to her children two hundred and seventy five dollars and
also unto my daughter Sarah Roundtree if living if not to her
Children two hundred and seventy five dollars and what My remain
to be equally divided between my four children (to wit) Anna-
Gowan ,George Price to this will this 28th. February 1829.
his
Martha K Price
mark

Signed in presents
of Gundna Pearson Thomas Blythe
John Newton.

(226)   JAMES K.NEICE last Will & Testament.
In the name of God this being my last will and Testament being
weak in boddy and strong in mind I bequeath unto my beloved Mother
after paying all my just debts and burial expences My Mare and a
saddle and bridle and stock of hogs and ore year old colt.one note
of hand on W.W.Reese for forty dollars due Decr.1843 one on David
Felps for about twelve dollars and all my rights and title in the
tract of land that I am intitled to by decent on which she now -
lives also the money I am entitled to in the hands of Jesse Neice
my guardian,And will appoint my Mother Huldy Neice My Executor to

settle and wind up my business In testimony whereof I have hereunto caused my hand and seal to be affixed in the presents of
these witnesses this the 9th.day Sept.in the year of our lord
one thousand eight hundred and forty three   his
James K.Neice (SEAL)
mark

Test
W.W.Gill
W.W.Reese
Jesse Neis
Hardy W.Neis.

George Cathey's Last Will.State of Tennessee Lincoln County.
    This is my written will and testament.I GEORGE CATHEY,do
make and publish this as my last will and testament hereby revoking and making void all other wills by me at anytime made.
    First I direct that my funeral expences and all my debts be
paid as soon after my death as possible out of any moneys that I

(226) may die possessed of or may first come into the hands of my Executor, or if there be not enough of that out of such of my property as my Executors may think can be best spared by my family.

Secondly, I will and bequeath all of the rest and residue of my property of what kind soever, together with my negro girl Mary, to my beloved wife Elizabeth, during her lifetime or widowhood, to support, raise and educate my two heirs, Frances S. C. and Robert A. Cathey or any other heir which my wife, Elizabeth may have by me.

(227) Thirdly, I will that after my wife Elizabeth's death, that my estate be equally divided between my children, that may then be living, but if she should marry again I will that she have an equal part with my children, of all of my estate, and lastly, I do hereby nominate and appoint William F. Zimmerman, Executor, with my wife, Elizabeth Cathey, Executrix to this will. In witness whereof I do to this my will set my hand and seal. This 26th, of June, 1843.

George Cathey, (seal).

Signed, sealed and published in our presence, and we have subscribed our names hereto in the presence of the Testator, this 26th, June 1843.

John McDaniel.

Alexander Cathey. Proven & admitted to Record at the November Term 1843, of the Lincoln County Court.

John B. Leatherwood. Last Will. I, JOHN B. LEATHERWOOD, do make and publish this my last will and testament, hereby revoking and making void all other wills by me at any time made.

First, I direct that my funeral expenses and all my debts be paid as soon after my death as possible, out of any money that I may die possessed of, or may first come into the hands of my executor.

Secondly, I give and bequeath to my wife Sally Leatherwood, during her life, my negro boy, Charles, my negro woman June, my negro boy Jim, and my negro girl Betsy. I also give her during life, all my land, with the privilege of my son Elisha to live on it. I give him my mare Boney, and one other horse which she may choode. I give her all my household furniture of every description whatever. I give her my wagon, and as many of my farming tools and utensils as she wishes to keep. I give her as many kitchen utensils as she may choose to keep. I give her my loom-I give her as much of my stock of every description as she chooses to keep. I give her all my

(228) crop of corn & fodder.

Thirdly, I give and bequeath to my son Jesse Leatherwood, to my son Spencer Leatherwood, and to my son Elihu Leatherwood each two hundred dollars.

Fourthly, I give to my son Norris Leatherwood, two hundred dollars.

Lastly, I do hereby nominate and appoint Norris Leatherwood my executor. In witness whereof I do to this my will set my hand and seal. This twenty eightth day of October, eighteen hundred and forty three.

John B. Leatherwood, (seal).

(228) Signed, sealed and published in our presence, and we have subscribed our names hereto in the presence of the testator. This 28th day of October 1843.
Uty Sherrell.
Spencer Leatherwood.
Proven & admitted to Record at the November Term 1843, of the Lincoln County Court.

Elizabeth Blake's Last Will.   I, ELIZABETH BLAKE,do make and publish this my last will and testament, hereby revoking and making void all others by me at any time made.

First, I direct that my funeral expenses and all my debts be paid as soon after my death as possible, out of any money that I may be possessed of or may come into the hand of my executor.

Secondly, I give and bequeath to Jane Caroline Blake, my young mare, saddle and bridle, & my best bed & clothes, & white stand of curtains.

Thirdly, I give and bequeath to Sarah Penelope Mary hinay, my negro woman Hannah, her boys Squire & Elby.

Fourthly, I give and bequeath to John W. Blake, my negro woman Mary, and her children.

Fifthly, I give and bequeath to Margaret Scales heirs, Lacky & Eliza.

Sixthly, I give and bequeath to William D. Blake, Liddy, Jim, & Jenny, for which he is to pay my funeral expenses.

Lastly, I do hereby nominate and appoint John W. Blake & William D. Blake, my Executors.

In witness whereof I do to this my last will set my hand
(229) and seal this 1st day of December 1843.

Elizabeth Blake, (seal).
Signed, sealed and published in our presence, and we have subscribed pur names hereto in the presence of the testabor,this 1st day of December 1843.
Joseph McMillen.
David P. McMillen.

Reuben Washburn Last Will. State of Tennessee, Lincoln County. Being Vigorant in intellect, but indisposed in body, and knowing life to be uncertain and wishing to make such a disposition of my worldly goods, as to me seems equitable and just, with a conscience void of offence toward all men. I make this my last will and Testament,and for the sectilude of my course I appeal to the Great Judge of all the earth, Amen.

Art. 1st, In the fear of God, I bequeath my soul to Him who gave it, and dispose of all things.

Art. 2, I will to my son Abram, my two daughters, Mary Elizabeth & Louisa Jane, and my grand child,Charlotte Moaning, the farm and tract of land where I now live, and all my property, both real and personal, during the space of seven years to come, in consideration of which my said son, Abram is to reside at the dwelling, and now do take care of and support my said daughters, Mary Elizabeth & Louisa Jane, and support and educate my said grand child Charlotte Moaning, during the above stipulated time.

Art. 3rd, I will that any money or property which my son

(229) Abram may accumulate by his own industry on the farm, after
defraying the above named expenses, be his to all intents
(230) and purpose, but provided that any money or property arise
from the rents of the said land or otherwise not herein named at
at the end of seven years, to be equally divided between my
said son Abram, and my two daughters, Mary Elizabeth & Louisa
Jane.

Art. 4, At the expiration of seven years to come, that
my land in lots, and all my effects whatsoever after all my
just debts are paid, be equally divided between my several
children, and grand child, Charlotte Moaning, with the exception that my two daughters Mary Elizabeth & Louisa Jane,
have each a horse worth fifty dollars, fifteen dollars
worth of cattle, ten head of sheep, bed and furniture, and
every thing that they may make by their own industry during
the said seven years,more than the rest of my heirs, and also that thirty three dollars each be taken from the shares
of my son John & Abram, making in all sixty-six dollars and
be given to my grand child Charlotte Moaning.

Art. 5, I will and request that my friend James Thompson
be, and is hereby appointed my executor to this my last will
and testament, and that the said Executor take the money or
property of my grand child Charlotte Moaning, and to do the
best he can with it until she arrives at the age of twenty-
one years of age, when she will be the legitimate owner.
In Testimony whereof I subscribe my name and affix my seal,
this the 20th day of February in the year of our Lord,eigh-
teen hundred and forty four.

Reuben Washburn, (seal).
Signed, sealed & published in our presence and we have sub-
scribed our names in the presence of the testator.
February, 20th 1844.
F. W. Teidbitter.
John S. Dollins.

(231)   John Gibson Last Will. I, JOHN GIBSON, of the County of
Lincoln and State of Tennessee, being of sound mind and disposing memory, for which I thank God, and calling to mind
the uncertainty of human life and being desirous to dispose
of all such worldly substance as it has pleased God to bless
me with, do make and declare the following to be my last will
and Testament.

1st, I give and bequeath unto Margaret Gibson, my wife,
during her natural life, the use of the farm, on which I now
live, including the mansion house building, and all the improvements, after deducting therefrom the portion hereafter
bequeathed to my son Albert G. Gibson, for her support and
for the support of my two daughters un-married, and living
with her so long as they remain single with her. Futhermore,
it is my will that my wife Margaret, shall have such portion
of the stock of every description of which I may die possessed, as she may choose and judge proper for support, and shall
have all the kitchen and household furniture for her own proper use and behalf, and for her own absolute disposal during
her life, and at her death I also give and bequeath unto my
said wife Margaret, during her natural life my slaves,Alexander,

(231) Calvin and Harriet, for her use, with the exceptions hereafter specified.

2nd, I give and bequeath to my son Albert G. Gibson,for
his own proper use and behalf forever, that portion of my land
on which I now live, which is east of a line beginning on the
North Boundary line of said tract of land, at a point due north
(232) of the spring house, which my family obtains water and running
thence south through said spring, thence down said spring branch
on water mark as it now runs to the South boundary line of the
aforesaid tract of land. I also bequeath as aforesaid to said
Albert G. Gibson, my negro man slave named Alexander, from and
after the death of my wife Margaret, mother of Albert.

3rd, I now declare as my will that after the decease of my
wife Margaret, that portion of my land bequeathed for her use
as above, I give and bequeathed to my daughters, Nancy and Margaret for their use and benefit, if living and unmarried at
that time provided they reside upon the premise so long as they
remain unmarried and will reside thereon but in case of the mar-
maried and will reside thereon but in case of the marriage or
death of either the other shall have the use and benefit of it
so long as she remains single and reside upon the premises or
death then it is my will that son Albert G. Gibson shall have the
aforesaid tract or portion of land for the sum of four hundred
dollars to be paid in two payments of two hundred dollars each
in one and two years from the date of such relinquishment and it
is furthermore my that the said sum of two hundred dollars each
shall be qually divided among my daughter Lucinda Dolly Jenttea
Calinda Manay and Margret for there own proper use and behalf
forever.

4th I give and bequeath to my son Parke Gibson in addition to
what he has heretofore recd ten dollars.

5th I give and bequeath son John H. Gibson in addition to what
he has heretofore received ten dollars.

(233) 6th I give and bequeath to my son Felix G. Gibson inaddition
to what he has heretofore received ten dollars.

7th I give and bequeath to my son in law John W. Smith ih
addition to what he has heretofore received his note of hand executed to mr for fifty five dollars dated September 20th 1819, a
and also to my daughter Loucinda his wife ten dollars.

9th I give and bequeath to my son in law Samuel Drofford in
addition to what he had heretofore received ten dollars.

10th I give and bequeath to my son in law Orchibald Hunter
in addition to what he as heretofore received ten dollars.

11th I give and bequeath to my daughter Eliza Dicky one negro
girl slave named Martha and also to my son in law Alfred C
Dicky her husband ten dollars.

12th I give andbequeath to my daughter Nancy R.Gibson one
negro boy slave named Calvin and a negro girl slave named Jane.

13th I give and bequeath to my daughter Margret A Gibson one
negro boy slave named Henry which she is to take possession of
and my deceased and also one negro girl slave named Harriett
which she is to take possession of at the decease of her mother.

14th my will is that such portion of the stock of every description of which I may die possessed may remain after the se-

lection of my wife Margret as provided in the first section of
of the will shall be sold by me executing at public sale on a
credit of twelve months out of the proceeds of which the money
legacies before mentioned shall be paid and the

(234) balance if any shall be divided equally between my wife Margret
and my two daughters Nancy R Margret A and also it is my will
that the crop on hand at the time of deceased growing or gathered shall go for the sole use and benefit of my said wifes Margret
and my daughters Nancy R and Margret A.

I do hereby appoint my sons Albert G. Gibson and Felix G.
Gibson executor to this my Last will and Testament disanulling
and hereby revoking all former wills by me heretofore made and
confirming this my last will and Testament.

In testamony whereof I here unto set my and affix my seal
this the fourth of June in the year of our Lord one Thousand
eight hundred and forty.

John Gibson(Seal)

Signed sealed and declared to be the last will and Testament
of the above named John Gibson in presence of us who at his request and in his presence have hereunto subscribed out named as
witness to the sum this 4th day of June 1844.

Isaac Southworth,Joseph B.Hill
Napoleon Ward

Proved and admitted to record at the June Term 1844 of the
Lincoln County Court.

(235) JOHN COLE- Last Will and Testament I John Cole being in a
low state of health but being in sound mind do make <u>tis</u> my last
will and Testament.

1st I bequeath my soul to God who gave it. 2nd I wish & desire that my debts be paid as soon as possible after my death
out of any money that may first come into my Administrators
hands.

3rd I leave to my son William the Colt that he now claims as
his part fourth I give to my son Joseph the Colt that he claims
5th I give to my Daughter Emeline one heifer which she claims
as hers. 6th I give to my daughter Money one heifer which she
also calls hers. I give to my beloved wife Nancy the entire use
and control of my plantation to enable her to maintain herself a
and children during her natural life I also give to her all my
corn bacon my horses cattle and sheep hogs and working tools
household and kitchen furniture my intention is that she have
the use and benefit of all my property except what has been here
tofore provided for my request is that after the death of my
wife my administrator shall proceed to sell all my real estate
and the appertainces therein on suvh terms as the law directs &
also such other property of mine as may be in her hands at her
death and she shall as soon as possible divide the proceeds equa
lly among my lawful heirs in.

In testamony whereof I do to this will set my hand and seal
this 3rd day of June 1844.

Test: Josiah Norwood,Pinkney Pikant   John Coal(Seal)

The following will was proved and admitted to be recorded at
the June Term 1844.

(236)   Henry Robertson Last Will.   I, HENRY ROBERTSON, of Lincoln County, Tennessee, do make and publish this my last will
and testament.

First, I direct that my funeral expenses and all my debts
be paid as soon after my death as possible, out of any money
that I may die possessed of, or which may first come into the
hands of my executors.

Second, I give and bequeath to my wife E lizabeth, during
her natural life, three hundred and twenty acres of land in one
tract, the same to be selected by her out of any of the land of
which I may die siezed, wherever situated.

Third, I give and bequeath to my wife Elizabeth during her
natural life, twenty slaves, being an average lot of such slaves
as I may own at the time of my death, to be set apart by executors at the death of my wife. I give and bequeath said twenty
slaves and their increase, together with said three hundred and
twenty acres of land to my children, Lucy R. Bonner, David F.
Robison, Henderson F. Robinson, Ann F. Bonner, Eliza C. Robertson and Mary Robertson, to be equally divided amongst them, and
to be held by them, respectively, during their natural lives,
and at the death of any of them, their share in said property,
and its increase to be equally divided amongst the children of
the deceased parent, and should any of my said children die
leaving no issue living at the time of his or her death, the
share of such deceased child shall be equally divided amongst
my said other children, and should any of them be then dead, the
issue of such deceased child shall take the share of such deceased
child in said property, should any of my said children die in
the life time of my wife, the issue of such deceased child shall
take the share, to which the deceased parent, if living at my
wife's death would have been entitled.

Fourth, I give and bequeath to my said wife, such part of
household and kitchen and kitchen furniture, as she may select.
(237) Also a sufficient quantity of stock of every description, to
stock her farm, including work mules, together with a sufficient
quantity of provisions to support the negroes, stock and farm
for one year, to be set apart by my executors.

Fifth, I give and bequeath to my grandson Henry H. Robertson, child of my deceaded son William H. Robertson, ten slaves
being an average lot of such slaves as I may own at the time of
my death, to be selected and set apart by my executors, who
shall hold the same, and their increase upon the following trust;
that is to say, said executors shall hire out said slaves annually, publically, or privately, at their discretion, until my said
Grandson arrive at the age of twenty five years, and shall dispose of the hire of said slaves, together with all interest accrueing thereon as folllws: 1st, said executors will retain a
reasonable compensation for their trouble in executing the trust
for the benefit of my said grandson. 2nd, they will pay to the
mother of my said grandson, annually during her widowhood, the
sum of fifth dollars. 3rd, They will pay the necessary expenses
of supporting and educating my said Grandson until he arrives at
the age of twenty one years, at which time, should this remain
undisposed of any part of the hire of said slaves & interest

(237) thereon, the same shall be paid by my executors to my said Grandson. The hire of said negroes accrueing after my said grandson arrives at the age of twenty-one years, and until he attains the age of twenty five years, shall be paid him annually, by my executors. So soon as my said grandson arrives at the age of twenty one years, or at his death, should that happen, du-

(238) ring his minority, the annual payment of fifty dollars to his mother before mentioned shall cease. When my said grandson arrives at the age of twent-five years, my executors shall deliver to him the said ten slaves and their increase, to be held by him during his natural life, and at his death, said slaves and their increase shall be equally divided amongst the children of my said grandson, and should he die leaving no children or the decendant of such living at the time of his death, them the said ten slaves and their increase shall be equally divided amongst my six children before named, and if, all or any of such deceased child shall take that portion of said property to which the deceased parent, if then living would be entitled under this will.

Sixth, I give and bequeath to James Shores, brother of my wife, the saddle horse, saddle & bridle which I may have at the time of my death, and which I may be accustomed to use before my death.

Seventh, I give and bequeath to my son Davis F. Robertson, my rifle gun, shaving apparatus, red travelling trunk, Sword Cane and gold collar button.

Eighth, I give and bequeath to my son Henderson F. Robertson, my silver watch and pistol.

Ninth, I give and bequeath the residue of my property of every description whether real or personal, as well as that which I now have, and that which I may hereafter acquire, wherever the same may be situated, to be equally divided amongst my six children, before named, and the slaves and their increase and the land to be held by them respectively, during their natural lives, and at their death to be equally divided amongst their children respectively, and should any of my children die

(239) leaving no children or the issue of such living, at the time of their death, the slaves and their increase & the land hereby given to such deceased child, shall be equally divided amongst my said other children, and if they or any of them be then dead, the children and issue of such deceased child shall take that portion of said property to which the deceased parent, if then living would be entitled under this will. Should any of my children or my said grandson die leaving no children or the decendant of such living at the time of their death, and in that event the property heretofore bequeathed to them should be divided amongst my children as before directed. It is my will that if any of my then surviving children should die leaving no children or the decendant of such living at the time of their death, the property thus acquired shall be equally divided amongst my said other children and the decendant of such as may be dead, the decendant taking the share to which my deceased child if living would be entitled under the will. It is hereby declared to be my intention that my said grandson shall in no event take anything under the provision of this will, except the ten slaves, their increase heretofore given him.

Tenth, I have heretofore given to my children, Lucy R. Bon-

(239) Lucy R. Bonner,David F. Robertson & Henderson F. Robertson,and Ann F. Bonner each,about three hundred and twenty acres of land of second quality, and eight slaves being an average lot of such slaves as I now own. I intend in my lifetime to give property of the like kind & of the same value to each of my daughters,Eliza C. & Mary, should I fail to do so,it is my will that my executors allot or set apart to my last mentioned daughters (before making a division of my property among my children as

(240) heretofore provided for) three hundred and Twenty acres of land to each of them of the quality aforesaid,in like manner to each of them,eight slaves being average lot of such slaves as I may own at the time of my death. Should any of my children die in my lifetime,the devise & bequest made to them by this will shall not thereby lapse,but the descendants of such deceased children shall take the property to which such deceased child,if living at the time of my death would be entitled under this will,& if any of my children should die in my lifetime leaving no children or the descendant of such living at the time of their death,the property heretofore given to such child shall be divided among my other children as heretofore provided for and as if such child had died after my death. In alloting and setting apart, as well as in divideing the slaves under this will,I desire that the families of slaves be separated as little as possible, to avoid which,if necessary where I have given a certain number of slaves,that number may be increased or diminished in all instances,however giving to the legatee slaves altogether of the value of those mentioned in the bequeath.

Lastly, I do hereby nominate and appoint Moses H. Bonner and David F. Robertson executors of this my last will and Testament. In witness whereof I have hereunto set my hand and seal this 9th day July 1844.

Henry Robertson.

Signed,sealed and published in our presence and we have subscribed our names hereto in the presence of the testator,this 9th day of July,1844.

James Fulton.

James Goodrich.

John Goodrich.

Wilson W. Hester. Proven at the September Term,1844,and admitted to record.

(241) Will. I, JONAS LEATHERMAN,of advance age,but of sound mind and disposing memeory do make and publish this my last will and Testament hereby working and revoking & making void all other wills by me at any time made.

1st,It is my will and desire that my funeral Expenses be paid,and Just debts,if any.

2nd,I give and bequeath unto my beloved wife,Martha Leatherman,forever and absolute,the following property;All of the beds and bedclothing about the house,also one half of the household & kitchen furniture,also pne half of the stock of cattle, to include one yoke of oxen,also one pair of wheels or truckels, also one half of the stock of hogs, also the whole of the stock of sheep, one sorrel mare, also the first choice of

(241) one other of my stock of horses, also the whole of my farming utensils of every description. I also give and bequeath to my wife during her life time, the use & benefit of two negroes, Boys, Lewis & Wilson, also the use of that part of my plantation south of the lane towards Sally Ruth, including buildings, garlling, together with one half of what is called the mill field, Also one half of the orchard. It is my will also that she shall have the whole of the corn, wheat & oats that may be on hand at my death.

        3rd, I give and bequeath unto my only Daughter Nancy Wilson, the whole of my property, both real and personal, of every description, excepting always that portion of property set apart for my wife.

        Lastly, I do hereby nominate and appoint Boon Wilson, Daniel Leatherman and George Reed my executors to this my last
(242) will. In Testimony whereof I do to this my will set my hand and seal, this 20th day of September, 1840.

                                      Jonas Leatherman,(seal)

        Signed, sealed & published in pur presence, and we have subscribed our names in the presence of the Testator.
Isa M. King.
Davis Smith.   Proved at the Sept. term of the Lincoln County Court. Recorded Sept. 9th, 1844.

        Robert Cunningham Will. I, ROBERT CUNNINGHAM, Senr, of the County of Lincoln and State of Tennessee, being weak in body, but of a sound mind, do this twenty ninth day of April Eighteen hundred and forty four, make & publish this my last will & Testament, in manner following: that is to say:

        First, I give to my beloved wife Sarah, all my property that I may have at my death, both real and personal, and all my money, notes & accounts,NC,to have and to hold the same during her natural life.

        Second, I give to my two sons, John & Enoch one hundred acres if the tract of Land on which I now live, to be taken off of the south end of said tract so as to include my present dwelling house, and at the death of my son John, I give to my son Enoch the entire right fo said one hundred acres of Land.

        Third, I give to my said son John my negro slave Adam, during his life, and at his death I wish the said slave Adam to be sold, and the proceeds of said sale to be equally divided among my other children.

        Fourth, At the death of my wife Sarah, I wish all my prop-
(243) erty, personal and real, to be sold and the proceeds to be equally divided between my children viz, Francis, Rebecca, Lucinda, Robert & John, Mary, James, Enoch and Sarah, except the Special Legacies which are above named. I wish it to be specially understood that said special gifts are not to take place until the death of my wife Sarah, and lastly I do make and appoint my son Wilson, and my son-in-law Francis Bearden, Executors to this my last will & testament. In witness where-of I the said ROBERT CUNNINGHAM Senr, have hereunto set my hand and seal this day and year above written.

                                  Robert Cunningham (seal)

(243) Signed, sealed and published in presence of us.
W. F. Zennaman.
H. R Hamilton.

Proved at the August Term of the Lincoln County Court, &
Recorded September 14th 1844. (This is upon the will of ROBERT
CUNNINGHAM,& record by request at the same time).

We, the undersigned Legatees of ROBERT CUNNINGHAM Senr, deceased, do hereby acknowledge that in the executing of the several ---- mentioned, that the name of Wilson Cunningham was omitted
through mistake and the said will was intended to be written so
as to include the Wilson Cunningham named, and to give him an e-
qual share of said estate with the rest of said legatees, and we
hereby acknowledge and request that said will shall be so con-
strued and understood as to give the said Wilson Cunningham his
equal share of said estate. It is also the understanding of said
(244) trustees that this conveyance is not to interfere with the
special legacies named in the above will. Given under our hand
and seal --- 3rd, 1844.

Francis Bearden, (seal)
Lucinda Bearden, (seal)
Sarah Cunningham, (seal)
John Cunningham, (seal)
Enoch Cunningham, (seal)
James Cunningham, (seal)
Mary Bearden, (seal)
John Bearden, (seal)
G. W. Sawers, (seal)
Rebecca Sawers, (seal)

Signed in presence of us.
Wm. F. Zennaman.
Hugh R. Hamilton.

Proved by the oaths of Wm. F. Zennaman & Hugh R. Hamilton,
at the August term of the Lincoln County Court. Recorded
Sept. 14th 1844.

David Buchanan Will. I, DAVID BUCHANAN of Lincoln County,
and State of Tennessee do make and publish this as my last will
and Testament, hereby revoking and making void all other wills
by me at any time made.

First, I direct that my Funeral expenses and all my debts
be paid as soon after my death as possible, out of any money
that I may die possessed of or may first come into the hands of
my executors.

Secondly, I give and bequeath to my wife, Margaret, my four
negroes, Ellick or Alexander, Jinny, John and George during her
life time. I also give and bequeath to my wife all of my stock
of every description during her life, except so much as shall be
necessary to be sold by my executors to pay all my debts, imme-
(245) diately or as soon as practicable after my death, on twelve
months credit. I also give and bequeath to my wife all of my
crops of every description at my death, and all my farming tools,
household and kitchen furniture, and at the death of my wife
Margaret it is my will and desire that all of the above named

(245) negroes that may then be living, and all the stock and property that may be left at her death to be sold by my Executors
on twelve months credit, & when the money is all collected to
be divided equally among my four daughters, Martha, Joannah,
Mary and Isabella, except the part that will be coming to
Joannah. I give and bequeath to S. S. Buchanan and David Buchanan Junr, her part to have and to hold the same in trust for
the sole and separate use and benefit of my daughter Joanah,
wife of Park Gibson, during her natural life, so that the same
shall not be subjected to his debts or contract, if it should
be that Joanah wish to receive her part just as she should need
it or all at once by her giving her receipt to S.S. Buchanan &
David Buchanan, she can have it. Now if my wife Margaret at
any time after my death should think proper to give up any portion of the property I have left her, into the hands of my executors to sell amd for them to make a distribution as above
named, she ca do so, and lastly I do hereby nominate and appoint
Samuel S. Buchanan & David Buchanan Junr, my executors. In witness whereof I do to this my will set my hand and seal, this
12th day of August 1844.

              David Buchanan, (seal)

    Signed, sealed and published in our presence, and we have
subscribed our names hereto in the presence of the Testator,
this 12th day of August 1844.
Test.
Thomas W. Buchanan.
Felix G. Gibson. Proved at Sept. Term 1844, & Recorded Sept.

(246)   In the year of our Lord,one thousand Eight hundred and
forty four. I, JOHN MCMILLEN, of the County of Lincoln and
State of Tennessee, being of a sound mind & recollection, do
this day make this my last will & testament.
    First, I desire that my executors pay all my just debts,
after that is done, I will and bequeath to the children of my
daughter Elizabeth Parkes, Fifty dollars. Also to my daughter
Frances Davidson Robertson, fifty dollars, and to my son Doak's
children, one Hundred dollars each, to be used in schooling
them, also to my daughter Charlotte Hardin one hundred dollars,
and to my son William Brown, fifty dollars, and to myson John,
Fifty dollars, also to my son Constant Thomas, fifty dollars,
and to my daughter Eliza Ann, One hundred dollars, and all my
household and kitchen Furniture, also my cow & calf, my stable
horse known by the name of King Hiram, which equally belongs to
Andrew C. Woods of Bedford County, Tenn. and myself. I allow
my half of him to be sold on a credit of twelve months, also all
the rent corn that I have coming for the rent of Land this year,
also my part in a lot in Fayetteville, Lincoln County, I believe
NO. 14, the same that Soloman Gullit once owned and occupied my
Interest, is the same that Hiram Buchanan had in and to said lot.
And the plantation contains 291 acres, I wish sold on a credit

(247) of one, two & three years, to be sold as soon as the law will
allow my Executors to do it, and after all my just debts are
paid, and all the different sums, bequeathed to my children,and
grand children, if there be any money left from the sales of

(247) property, I allow it to be Equally divided between my sons William Brown, John & Constant & Thomas. It is also my will and desire, and I do appoint William T. Ross & Woodruff Parkes, my executors to this my last will and Testament, whereunto I set my hand and seal this 21st day of August, the year above written.

In the presence of,   John McMillen, (seal)
E. M. Ewing.
W. mA. Russell.   The named Gullit, the word (be) Enter lined before signed and the word)(sold).

          John Davis Will. I, JOHN DAVIS of the County of Lincoln & State of Tennessee, being in a low state of health, and knowing the uncertainty of this mortal life, and the certainty of death, do make. ordain & publish the following as my last will & testament.

          First, It is my will after my decease, I shall be buried in a plain & Christian like manner, and that my funeral expenses be in proportion to my circumstances.

          Second, It is my will that all my just debts & funeral expenses be paid out of personal estate as soon after my death as practicable.

          Third, I give to my beloved wife, Sarah Davis during her natural life, that portion of my tract of land whereon I now live, described as follows: Beginning at my lower Corner on Norris Creek, running thence up the same with my line, to the cross fence, that runs a little south of my barn, thence with that line of fence, so far that by running Northwardly thence Westwardly, will include four acres around said Barn, thence continuing with the direction of said cross fence Northwestwardly will run with the time of fence between my pasture land,

(248) and the land now cultivated by Edward Johnson, to my South boundary line, thence Eastwardly to the beginning, including my dwelling house, and other houses within said bounds. I also give my wife two cows and one heifer to be of her choosing, also my horse called Baily, & my mare called Dolly. I also give to my wife during her natural life my negro woman named Anny, unless she should become unmanageable, in that case she is to be sold by my executor upon a credit, at the option of my said executor, & the proceeds loaned out upon interest, which interest is to be applied to the benefit of my wife. I also give to my wife two beds, bedsteads & furniture of her own choosing. I also give to my wife my china press, together with my china ware & table furniture, together with as much of my kitchen furniture as she may need. I also give to my wife one of my Bureaus.

          Fourth, It is my will that the residue of my land be rented out by my executor until such time as she may think it advisable to sell the same, & then to sell the same upon such credit as she may think best for the estate. It is also my will that that portion of my land laid off for the use of my wife during her life, be also sold by my executors upon the death of my wife, upon such terms and credit as he may think proper, unless my wife should choose to let the same be sold during her lifetime, and at the time the residue of my land should be sold, and to take in money as stipulated price for the same.

(248)   Fifth, I give & bequeath to my daughter Martha Jane & Margaret Elizabeth, five hundred & twenty five dollars each, in cash to be paid them by my executor.

      Sixth, I give and bequeath to my daughter Sarah Johnson & her heirs of her body four hundred & eighty dollars, out of the first money that shall come to the hands of my executor, after paying my debts & expenses which is to be paid by my said executor in the purchase of a negro woman for my said daughter Sarah Johnson & the heirs of her body.

      Seventh, I give & bequeath to my said daughter Martha Jane, and Margaret Elizabeth each, a feather bed, bedstead & furniture.

      Eighth, I give & bequeath to my son Campbell N. Davis, five hundred & twenty five dollars in cash, to be paid him by my executor, if my said son should be living, and apply for the same,

(249) if not, then the same is to be equally divided between my four daughters now living & my two grand children, being the children of my daughter Madeline McMallen, deceased, the two together to have an equal share with one of the others or one fifth part of the said five hundred & twenty five dollars. I also give to my said two grand children one hundred & fifty dollars each.

      Nin th, I give & bequeath to my son Leroy Davis fifty dollars.

      Tenth, I give and bequeath tp my two grand children, being the daughters of my son Hiram Davis, dec'd, fifty dollars each.

      Eleventh, I give & bequeath to my son-in-law Fielding Parks, four hundred & fifty dollars.

      Twelfth, It is my will that my negro man Jim remain on my farm the ensuing year, for the purpose of making a crop, which crop, when made is to be sold by my executor. It is further my will that my said executor hire out my said negro man Jim, until such time as he may think it best to sell him, & then to sell him upon such terms & credit as he may think best.

      Thirteenth, It is my will that all my stock of horses, cattle, sheep & hogs, except what is herein bequeathed to my wife, together with all the residue of my kitchen furniture, farming tools of every description and every other thing or specin of property not herein specially bequeathed, be sold by my executor, and proceeds applied to the payment of the legacies herein before mentioned.

      And lastly, It is my will if there should be anything remaining after paying off the legacies herein before named, the same is to be applied & equally divided between my three daughters, Caroline Parks, Martha Jane & Margaret Elizabeth.

      I hereby constitute, nominate & appoint my son-in-law Fielding Parks sole executor of this my last will & testament.

      In witness whereof I have hereunto set my hand & seal this ninth day of August in the year of our Lord, one thousand eight hundred & forty-four.

Hugh Thomison.   John Davis, (seal)
A. J. Cunningham.

(250)   William Rowell's Will. I, WILLIAM ROWELL, do make & publish this my last will and testament, hereby revoking & making void all other wills by me at any time made.

      First, I direct that my funeral expenses and all my debts be paid as soon after my death as possible, out of any money I

(250) may die possessed of or may first come into the hands of my
executor.

Secondly, I give and bequeath to my beloved wife Katharine,
all my land which I now live on, also the negroes (to wit) May
Joe, Allen, Jimmy & Miles, & all the perishable property, all of
my household and kitchen furniture, after all of my debts are
paid out of said property.

Thirdly, I give and bequeath to my daughter Esther Mary,
two negroes, to wit, Grace and Mill, also one cow and calf, one
bed & furniture which she has received, that being all that I
intend for her or her heirs out of my effects to have.

Fourthly, I give and bequeath to my son Jacob William, the
tract of land he now lives upon, worth five hundred dollars,
two horses and saddle, worth eighty dollars each, three cows
and calves, worth --- each, one gun worth fifteen dollars, one
bed and furniture.

Fifthly, I give and bequeath to my son David James, one
tract of land worth three hundred and twenty-five dollars, one
saddle, worth sixteen dollars, and ten dollars in cash, one cow
& calf, worth eight dollars, and bed and furniture.

Sixthly, I give and bequeath to my son John Wesley, one
tract of land worth five hundred dollars, one horse, worth fifty dollars, one saddle, worth eight dollars, one bed & furniture.

Seventhly, I give and bequeath to my daughter Mericah, one
horse worth thirty-five dollars, two cows & one calf, worth
eight dollars each, one bed & furniture.

Eightthly, I give and bequeath to my son Samuel Milton, one
tract of land worth three hundred dollars, and one cow and calf,
worth eight dollars, one horse, worth sixty dollars, one saddle
worth sixteen dollars, one bed & furniture.

(251) Ninthly, I give and bequeath to my daughter Eliza Jane, one
horse worth thirty-five dollars, one cow and calf, worth eight
dollars, one bed and furniture.

Tenthly, I give and bequeath to my daughter Martha Caroline, one horse worth thirty dollars, one cow and calf, worth
eight dollars, one bed and furniture.

Eleventhly, All the above named property has been received
by the above named heirs, and which valuations I wish to remain
unaltered, & to be a set off of their distribution share of my
estate, at the death of my wife, Katharine, without any accru-
ing interest thereto. It is my wish that all the property be
sold at the death of my wife, and my heirs made equal, namely,
Jacob, Williams, David James, John Wesley, Mariah Ann, Samuel
Milton, Eliza Jane, & Martha Caroline.

Lastly, I do hereby nominate & appoint David James Rowell,
John Wesley Rowell & Samuel Milton Rowell, my executors.

In witness whereof I do to this my will set my hand & seal
this 4th day of September, 1844.

William Rowell, (seal).

Signed, sealed & published in our presence, & we have subscribed our names in the presence of the testator, this
4th day of September, 1844.
William Bland.
Samuel J. Bland.

(251)   State of Tennessee, Lincoln County.   I, JOHN MOORE, being
in a low state of health, but of sound mind, do make and ordain this my Last will & Testament, viz;
     First, I wish all my Just debts to be paid.
     2nd, It is my will that my whole Estate both real and per-
sonal, be equally divided between my two children (viz) Eli
Moore & May Hinds, after disposing of the following Item in the
following manner, I give to William Johnson, two hundred dollars, and his choice of my Grey fillies, I hereby confirm contract with William Ely Smith, and to convey to him my girl,
Jane, for the sum of five hundred dollars, to be paid on when
called for, say $250. and two hundred & fifty dollars to be
(252) paid twelve months after my death.   I do also will that my old
and faithful servant Dicy, be liberated and set free, and hereby appoint William Fly Smith her Guardian agent to do and perform all that the law of Tenn. may require, to perfect the same,
and place her in his possession at my death.   It is my wish
that my beloved children above named Eli Moore & Mary Hind, divide the balance of my slaves equally between themselves, and
such other property as may suit them, after which sell the balance and divide equally as above specified, and to carry the a-
bove into effect I appoint my son Eli Moores, my son-in-law
Thomas Hinds, and my friends Doc Williams & F. Smith my executors, this 22nd, day of October 1844.
                                   John Moore, (seal).
Signed & sealed in presence of,
William Moore.
B.M.G. Rhea.   Recorded November 21, 1844.

     State of Tennessee, Lincoln County.   I, HENRY LANDESS, be-
ing of sound mind, do make and publish this my last will and
testament, revoking all others.   In the name of God Amen.
     First, It is my wish after my death, to be buried in a de-
cent and respectable manner.
     Second, I will that my burial & funeral expenses together
with all my Just debts be paid.
     Third, I give and bequeath to my beloved wife Gracy, my
tract of land where I now live, my negro woman Amanda, and as
much of my household and kitchen furniture, and of my stock of
all kinds and provisions on hand, as she may think fit or proper to have and to hold during her natural life.   The stock,
furniture and provender to be designated previous to the sale.
     Fourth, I give to my daughters, Hannah Ford, Polly Green,
and George E. Tally, fifty dollars, and to the children of my
(253) daughter Ann, who inter-married James F. Smith (and has since
died) Twenty-five dollars each out of the first money collected.
My daughter Susan Eaton I consider received her portion of my
estate in the sale of a tract of land I heretofore sold her husband, Alfred Eaton.
     Fifth, I gave to my two sons John and Joseph Thompson, each
one hundred and twenty dollars, to make them equal with my son
Henry Harman, for a certain sorrel horse which he took with
him when he left this County, which I consider worth that
amount.
     And lastly, that my negro man Jackson together with the re-
mainder of my household and kitchen furniture, stock, provenderNC,

(253) after my wife's selection, be sold as soon as convenient after my death, and the land and negro woman Amanda together
with that portion of household & kitchen furniture, stock
that be living NC. to be sold after the death of my wife and
equally distributed between my three sons, John Henry, Har-
man and Joseph Thompson. And I do hereby appoint my son John
Landess to execute and carry into effect this my last will and
Testament. Signed, sealed and acknowledged in presence of us.
This 21st day of October, 1844, in the year of our Lord,1844.
Attest.   Henry Landess,(seal).
Wm. C. Blake.
D. R. Smythe. Recorded 21st, Nov. 1844.

(254)   In the name of God Amen. I, JOSHUA GUNTER, being in
sound mind and memory, do make and publish this my last will
and Testament, in manner and form following: (viz), I wish all
my lands sold on a credit of one, two and three years, all of
my personal property sold on a credit of twelve months, and the
proceeds of said property to be equally divided amongst (the
following named) my beloved sons and daughters, after the payment of all my debts & burial expenses (iv) Franklin Gunter,
Wesley Gunter, Clayburn Gunter, Elizabeth Ann Gunter, Susan
Adeline Gunter and Joseph Gunter. I give and bequeath unto my
beloved son & son-in-law, William Gunter & John Ramsey, the
sum of one dollar each, my reasons for giving them no more are
these: they have had as much or more than I have to give to the
above named six children. It is my request that Clayburn Gunter, Elizabeth Gunter, Susan Adeline Gunter, & Jasper Gunter be
bound out to some good human person or persons that will do a
good part by them, also do hereby appoint my friend Alfred
Beardin, my sole Executor, to carry into effect the above will
& Testament, and my will is I do hereby expressly declare that
my said Executor or Executors, shall not charge or be chargeable with or accountable for more of the aforesaid money than
he or they shall actually receive, come to his or their respective hands, by virtue of this my will or with or for any
loss which shall happen, of the said money, so as such loss
happen with his or her wilfull default & neglect.
                                    Joshua Gunter, (seal)
Signed in our presence this the 4th of December 1844.
Test.
A. G. Dowhing.
Robert H. Wheeler.

(255)   I, GEORGE WAGGONER, do make and publish this as my last
will and testament, hereby revoking and making void all other
wills by me at any time made.
     First, I direct that my funeral expenses and all my debts
be paid as soon after my death as possible, out of any money I
may die possessed of or may first come into the hands of my
Executor.
     Secondly, I give and bequeath unto my beloved wife Mary,
the use, occupation and enjoyment of my tract of Land whereon
I now live, together with all other property I may die possessed of, which consists of, negroes, horses, cattle, hogs, crop
and provision on hand, farming tools, all of which I wish her

(255) to have during her natural life, with the privilege of selling any of my stock, such as horses, cattle, hogs or sheep,
and converting to her own proper use for the support of herself and Family, if she thinks proper to do so, together with
three hundred dollars in money, ahd after my wife's death, to
be disposed of in the following manner:

    Thirdly, My will and desire is that after my wife's death,
that my son Peter Waggoner have the tract of Land whereon I
now live, and wish him to have that amt. more than the rest of
my children, in consequence of his being an invalid.

    Fourthly, My will and desire is that after my wife's death
all of the property that I may die possessed or may be then remaining, be sold upon a twelve months credit, and the proceeds
thence arising from such sale be equally divided amongst all my
heirs,(viz,namely),Margaret, Barbary, Elizabeth, Mary, Fetty,
George, John Lewis, Jesse,Peter and the heirs of my son Jacob
Waggoner.

    Fifthly & Lastly, I appoint my two sons Jesse and Peter
Waggoner, the Executors to this my last will and testament, believing they will see it properly executed. In witness whereof I have hereunto set my hand and affixed my seal this the
thirteenth day of October in the year of our Lord, one thousand
(256)eight hundred and forty two.   his

              George x Waggoner
                mark

Signed, sealed and published in our presence, and we have subscribed our names thereto, in the presence of the testator the
day and date above written.
James W. Holman.
Bill Jones.

    Codicil. I, GEORGE WAGGONER, having heretofore made and
published my last will and Testament do make and declare this
as a codicil thereto, to wit; that so much of the fifth art+
icle of my will as appoints my son Peter Waggoner an executor
to my last will, I hereby revoke, and my will is that my son
Jesse Waggoner, above named, tend to the execution of the same,
it is my desire that this Codicil be attached to and constitute
apart of my will to all intents and purposes of my will, given
under my hand and seal this 24th day of November, 1844.

              his
           George x Waggoner, (seal).
              mark

Signed, sealed and published in our presence, and we have subscribed our names in the presence of the testator, the day and
date written.
James W. Holman
William J. Brazur. Proved according to law at the April Term,
1845.
    H. Kelso, Clk.

(257)   I, THOMAS MASSEY, of Lincoln County, in the State of Tennessee, do make, ordain, publish and declare the following to be my last will and testament, hereby revoking all former wills or testaments by me heretofore made.

First, It is my will and desire that so soon after my demise as practicable, my executors hereinafter named, out of the first money that comes into their hands, of my estate, pay all my just debts.

Second, I give to my children Willard R. John B. William P. and Christiana H. Massey, all the real estate that descended to my former wife Polly, from her father John Rains, which lies in Davidson County, Tennessee, to be valued to them by suitable & disinterested persons who may live near enough to said land to estimate its value, to be appointed by my Executors. Also in like manner an unimproved lot in the City of Nashville.

Third, So soon after my death as convenient I direct that my executors select a suitable member of freeholders uncomniated with the parties to set apart, lay off and value my wife Priscilla R. Massey's dower, which shall embrace my dwelling house, and out houses, and place her in possession of the same & which when so done shall (vist) in her an estate for her natural life.

Fourth, I will and bequeath to my son Thomas J. Massey, and to my daughter Jane Eliza Clark each a part of the tract of land on which I now live, running east & west across the tract and embracing a portion or the whole of the dower directed to be set apart to my wife, and to be subject to the encumbrance of the dower, and to be laid off of the Southern of the original tract or tracts, in such manner as to make each share equal in value to each share of the land lying in Davidson County, willed to some of my other children, as above mentioned, which shall be laid off & valued by suitable and disinterested man as directed in laying off my wife's dower.

(258)   Fifth, I will and direct that my executors, so soon after my decease as convenient, lay off the residue of my land on Cane Creek into six lots as nearly equal in value as they can, and have the same valued by three or more disinterested men, all of whichlots of land I give & bequeath to my six children above named, one lot to each of them to be ascertained by lot by my executor.

Sixth, I will and direct that my Executors sell the balance of a tract of land belonging to me on Cold Water Creek in Lincoln County, containing one hubdred & ninety-two acres more or less at public sale, to the highest bidder on a credit of one, two and three years, provided the same shall not be sold for a less sum than four dollars & fifty cents per acre.

Seventh, It is my will that my faithful and trusty negro woman named Rachel shall at my death have her freedom, under such rules and regulations as the law prescribes. And it is my desire that she live with my son Thomas J. Massey, and that he will protect her in her rights.

Eighth, I will that my executors sell all my personal property of every description, except my slaves, upon a credit of twelve months.

Ninth, I will that all my slaves except Rachel, be valued by three disinterested men.

(258)   Tenth, I will that after my executors have paid all my just debts, they pay to my daughter Elizabeth Doke or her children as they may need it, the sum of one thousand dollars, my executors or such person as the court may appoint to be her or their guardian.

Eleventh, It is probable that my wife is now insunt,and should she have one or more children, I will that it or they be made an equal heir or heirs with my other children.

Twelfth, I will that my Executors divided my negroes and lands equally, to valuation as above provided for, among my wife and all my children (except Elizabeth Doke) in such manner as will give my wife a childs' part of all the personal estate, and proceeds of sales of personal estate, and among my children (except Elizabeth Doke) in such manner as will make their shares all equal in land or negroes or money, including or embracing all the property mentioned on this will, my heirs or children to whom the above devises are made are my wife, Thomas J. Massey, Jane Eliza Clark, Wilford R. John R.,William P.,Christiana H. Mary I. & Sarah B. Massey, & those unborn (if any).

Lastly, I constitute and appoint my friends Thomas Hines & Joseph Clark Executors, to this my last will and testament.
(259) In testimony whereof I hereunto set my name and affix my seal this 15th day of January in the year of our Lord, eighteen hundred and forty-four.
Attest.   Thomas Massey, (seal).
William L. Pamplin.
Thomas Chiles.
B. W. D. Carty.   Recorded 10th July 1845.

I, THOMAS CHAPMAN, do make and publish this my last will and testament, hereby revoking and making void all former wills by me made at any time.

First, I direct that my funeral expenses and all my debts be paid as soon after my death as possible, out of any money that I may die possessed of, or may come into the hands of my Executor.

Secondly, I give and bequeath to my wife and Companion,
(260) Mary Chapman, all the following described property, to be owned and enjoyed by her to all intents and purposes during her natural life or widowhood, namely: The tract of land on which I live, all the household and kitchen furniture, one certain gray mare, one yoke of oxen, Two cows and calves, six sheep, twenty choice hogs, Fifty barrels of corn, twenty bushels of wheat, and a thousand pounds of good bacon. I also bequeath to my wife Mary Chapman, one negro man named Ben, one negro woman named Vicey, and one negro girl named Martha-but I make this bequest that should the above mentioned negroes or may one of them prove sofractory or unmanageable and complaint being made to the executor by the said Mary Chapman, then the executor shall have full power to sell said slave or slaves, and when they are sold, the money arising from the sale of said slave or slaves shall be put to interest, which

(260) interest the said Mary Chapman shall be entitled to receive yearly. The above bequeath is made upon condition that the said Mary Chapman remain in a state of widowhood. I do hereby direct that upon her inter-marriage with any one, that all of the above mentioned property shall be sold, after giving due notice thereof, and an equal division be made of the proceeds, between all of my children, But in the event that she, the said Mary Chapman is never allied by a second marriage with any one, then I bequeath unto her, the said Mary Chapman, a Certain negro girl named Martha, and mentioned in the above enumeration, to be her own individual property with the power to dispose of the same, as in her judgment she may deem proper. But she is not authorized to dispose of any other property above enumerated save the negro girl, but the same disposition shall be made of it at her death as is above directed, in case of a second marriage of the said Mary Chapman.

Thirdly, To my daughter Katharine Wakefield I bequeath a certain tract of land in the state of Illinois, containing eighty acres, the same upon which she has been living. I also bequeath to my daughter Katharine Wakefield, one Thousand dollars in Cash.

(261) Fourthly, To my daughter Delila Brown, I bequeath a certain tract of land that was sold under a deed of trust in June 1843, when I became the purchaser, and known as the tract upon which John S. Price Esq. now residing, Provided, however that said land is not redeemed according to the redemption laws: and in the event that said land should be redeemed, then I bequeath to her the said Delia Brown, the redemption money with interest thereon- I also bequeath to my daughter Delia Brown, Three hundred dollars in cash.

Fifthly, To my daughter Harriet Scott, I bequeath a certain negro girl named Sylvia.

Sixthly, I bequeath to my daughter Mary Ann Kymes a certain tract of land, the same upon which she is now living, containing Seventy-four acres adjoining the land of William Carithers, and Claborne Andrews, and known as the Rust Place. I. also bequeath to my daughter Mary Ann Kymes a certain negro woman anmed Mary and her three children, to wit, Albert, Rachel and Jerry. I also bequeath to my daughter Mary Ann Kymes, Three Hundred Dollars in cash- But I bequeath unto my daughter Mary Ann Kymes all the real estate above enumerated upon this condition, that she leaves upon her death an heir of her own body, should she die without such heir, then the above mentioned land and negroes, with their increase shall rescind back and be equally divided between my other children.

Seventhly, I bequeath to my son Jesse, One Thousand Dollars in Cash.

Eighthly, I direct my executor to proceed to advertise and sell on a credit of twelve months, Two negroes, to wit, Frank and Henryn and I do further direct the executor to advertise and sell likewise, all and every species of property of which I am possessed, that is not included in the above enumeration, in a reasonable time after my death, and I further direct that an equitable division be made between all of my children, of all money, not only of what I have by me, but also the proceeds of any or property sold as above directed, but

(261) such division shall not take place until the foregoing bequests shall have been paid off, which I direct to be done as soon as possible.

Lastly, I do hereby nominate and appoint John Kymes, my son-in-law, my Executor. In testimony whereof I have hereunto set my hand and affixed my seal, this the 29th of July, A.D. (262) One thousand, Eight hundred and forty-four.

I do acknowledge the above enumerations in these words, "that is not included in the above enumeration". This the day and date above written.   his
                                    Thomas x Chapman, (seal)
                                             mark
Signed, sealed and published in our presence, and we have sub-scribed our names hereto in the presence of the testator, This 29th day of July 1844.
Theo Harris.
William Beavers
Howell Harris.   Recorded 11th July 1845.

Know all men by these presents, that I, RALPH SMITH, of the County of Lincoln and State of Tennessee, do covenant and make this my last will and testament, whereas I will to my companion & lawful wife Cynena Smith, one cupboard and falling leaf table, and also one bedstead & furniture. Alfred Smith, one Clay-bank colt and Clarina Smith, one bed and furniture, & Elizabeth Smith, one bedstead & land to remain in the present situation for my Companion and children, as they become of age, to be equally divided, and it is my request that the negroes be sold, with my cash and cash notes to be equally divided be-tween my Companion and my lawful heirs, before mentioned, and (263) some Horses & some pork Hogs and some cotton, with some other property not necessary for the support of the family. All the necessary things about the house and kitchen for housekeeping, I want left for the use of the family, my will is that John Smith assist my son Alfred to collect my notes & accounts, and to selling such other property as I have mentioned heretofore, and Alfred can choose by assistance her own guardian, and for my daughter I wish John to attend to them or have some good safe man to be appointed, so as to save their estate. This the year of our Lord 1845, April the 12th.
Samuel Hawkins.   Ralph Smith.
Joseph B. Smith.   Recorded 11th July 1845.

In the name of God Amen.   I, JOEL E. BROWN, of the County of --- and State of Tennessee, being of sound mind and memory, but belonging under affliction and knowing the certainty of death, and the uncertainty of what time it may take place, do make this my last will and testament.

1st, I request that all my just debts be paid.

2nd, I give and bequeath to my four daughters, vix, Eliza-beth Brown, Sarah Brown, Martha Jane Brown and Minerva Brown, all my estate that I may be possessed of at my decease, con-sisting of six hundred and twenty-seven dollars and ninety-five cents. Two hundred and twenty dollars off the above amount being in Missouri money, one wagon and gear, and three head of

(263) horses to be sold on a twelve months credit. The amount of the above to be equally distributed between my four above named daughters. I do hereby constitute and appoint Tunstall
(264) Gregory my Executor, to this my last will and testament,whereunto I have set my hand and seal this 28th of May 1845.

Joel E. Brown, (seal).

Signed and sealed in presence of,
William B. Woodroof.
Fenton Gregory. Recorded the 11th July 1845.

I, JOHN SUMMERS,of the County of Lincoln and State of Tennessee, do hereby make my last will and testament in manner and form following, that is:

1st, I direct that immediately after my decease, my sorrel filly amd young Black horse be sold at a price that may be agreed upon among my children, and if they fail to give upon a price satisfactory with all, this said horses to be sold to the highest bidder. Also I desire that all my hogs that may be suitable for pork this fall, be fatted out of the present growing crop of corn, and after setting apart a sufficient quantity for my wife Rebecca Summers, the balance to be sold to the best advantage, and the money arising from the sale of the above property, after paying my just debts and burial expenses, I give to my wife Rebecca Summers.

2ndly, I give to my Grandson, two male calves to belong to him and his heirs forever.

3rdly, I give to my wife Rebecca, my old sorrel mare,and after her decease, to descend to my daughter, Jane Summers, to belong to her and her heirs forever.

4thly, I give to my grandson, Abner Summers, the present young colt to belong to him and his heirs forever.

5thly, The remainder of my live stock,with the exception of one three year old steer, I give to my wife Rebecca. Also all my farming tools, household and kitchen furniture I give to my wife Rebecca Summers. The above named steer to be sold and the money, after my debts are paid to belong to my wife,
(265) Rebecca.

6thly, I give to my daughter Sally Roden, twenty six acres of land adjoining said Roden's land, and including the improvements, to belong to her and the heirs of her body forever. But provided that she may desire to sell it with their other land she shall do so, and convey it accordingly.

7thly, I direct that the remainder of my land belong to my wife Rebecca, during her natural life, to have the sole power and control, so far as she may choose, and rents, profits,and all advantages that may arise therefrom shall be hers, so long as she lives, or desires to have the same, and when she is done with it, to descend to my other seven children, to wit, Margaret Sellers, Joseph Summers, Jane Summers, Polly Shelton, Robert Summers, Andrew Summers and Rebecca Williamson, to be sold and equally divided among them for them and their heirs forever.

8thly, I direct that the one half of the part falling to my daughter Jane, be given to her daughter Eliza Reed.

9thly, I further desire and direct that after the decease

(265) of my wife,Rebecca, that all the money and other property of which she may die possessed, be equally divided among all my children.

And lastly, I do hereby constitute & appoint my son Robert Summers, Executor of this my last will & testament, by me heretofore made. In witness whereof I have hereunto set my hand and seal, this 18th day of May 1845.his

John x Summers. (seal)
mark

Signed, sealed, published and declared to be his last will & testament of the above named John Summers in presence of us, who at his request and in his presence have hereunto subscribed our names as witnesses to the same.
Davis Smith.
Pleasant Bearden.

(266)   I, THOMAS BLAIR, of the County of Lincoln and State of Tennessee, Planter, do make and publish this my last will & testament, hereby revoking and making void all former wills by me at any time heretofore made, and as to such worldly estate as it hath pleased God to entrust me with, I dispose of the same as follows:

First, I direct that my Executors sell my girl Adeline, and pay all of my debts.

And secondly, I bequeath to my wife Milly, all of my land, my stock, my household and kitchen furniture. Also two negro men, Dick and John, one woman, Poll. one boy Tom Isom, and Alfred, during her natural life, hereby I will and bequeath to my son Louis C. Blair, one hundred acres of the land whereon I now live, including the mansion house, and also a negro boy Dan.

And I do further will and bequeath to my daughter Nancy a negro girl named Genney, and also a bed and furniture, cow and calf, and the saddle she now has, and a roan filly that is now on the premises, and all of my estate that is not specially willed to my children at the death of my wife, to be divided equally among all of my children. I do hereby make, ordain and appoint my sons Harrison and John W. Blair executors of this my last will and testament. In witness whereof I,THOMAS BLAIR, the said testator have to this my will set my hand and seal, this 5th day of June in the year of our Lord, one thousand.eight hundred and forty-five.   his

Thomas x Blair, (seal)
mark

Signed, sealed and published in the presence of us who have subscribed, in the presence of the testator, and of each other.
John Smith.
Allen Pool. Recorded July, 15th 1845.

(267)   I, ANTHONY BAITS, do make and publish this my last will and testament, revoking and making void all other wills made by me heretofore.

1st, My desire is that my funeral expenses and all my just debts may be paid out of any money that may first come into the hands of my executors.

2nd, I give to my wife Catharine Baits, all the land I

(267) am possessed of, and my wish and desire is that my son Alexander Baits, move and live in the house with her for the purpose of assisting to paying my debts and helping his mother to take care of the children. I leave in possession of my said wife, all of my property of every description, except such as is hereafter named.

3rd, I give to my son Alexander Baits one horse and saddle, bed and furniture, worth $100. which he has already reed.

4th, I give to my son George Baits one horse and saddle, bed and furniture, worth one hundred dollars, which he has already received.

5th, I give to my daughter Mary Ready, forty-one dollars in a bed and furniture, cow and calf, trunk which she has received.

6th, I give to my son Anthony Baits one hundred dollars in property, horse and saddle.

7th, I give to my son Doak Baits, one hundred dollars in a horse and saddle, bed and furniture when he arrives at lawful age.

8th, I give to my son Jasper Baits one hundred dollars in a horse and saddle, bed and furniture when he arrives at lawful age.

9th, I give to my daughter Jane Baits forty-one dollars in a bed and furniture, cow and calf &C, to be valued to her by my executors.

10th, I give to my daughter Tennie Baits, forty-one dollars in a bed and furniture, cow &C, when she arrives at lawful age or marries.

11th, My desire is at the death of my wife that the balance of my property, if any, together with my land be sold by my Executors, my land sold on a credit of one, two, and three years, and the money equally divided among all my children, first making my youngest sons equal with them that has rec'd, and likewise my youngest daughter equal with the daughters that has received.

(268) 12th, My desire is that Travis Ashby and my son Alexander Baits be my Executors to this my last will and testament. Signed, sealed and acknowledged in the presence of us, on the 1st. of July 1845.

```
Test.                          his
M. W. Yount.        Anthony x Baits, (seal)
Peter Ashby.                   mark
```

State of Tennessee, Lincoln County. I, EPHRAIN KING, being in a low state of health, but of sound mind and disposing memory, do make this my last will and testament, hereby making void all other wills by me made at any time.

First, I direct that my funeral expenses and all my just debts be paid as soon after my death as possible, out of any money that I may die possessed of or may first come into the hands of my executors.

Secondly, My will and desire is that my wife Jane King, have all my property that I amy die possessed of, during her natural life or widowhood.

Thirdly, My will and desire is that Martha C. King, Susan C. King, Eleanor M. Sorrda, Ephrain C. King and Washington A.

(268) King, have each a horse, bridle and saddle, cow and calf, bed & furniture, and after her death, my will is that all the balance of my real and personal estate be sold and the money be equally divided between my heirs.

4th, and lastly, I do hereby nominate and appoint my son James G. King and James B. Hudson, my Executors, to see this my will be carried into effect. In witness whereof I do to this my will set my hand and seal this 10th day of January 1845.

his

Ephrain x King, (seal)

mark

(269) Signed, sealed and published in our presence, and we have subscribed our names in the presence of the testator, this 10th day of January, 1845.

John Landers.

Joseph P. Harkins.

July 23rd, 1845. I, BENJAMIN KNOWLES, of the County of Lincoln and State of Tennessee, being old and infirm, and in a low State of health, but of sound mind, do this day make and ordain this my last will and testament.

1st, I consign my body to the earth to be buried in a decent & Christian like manner, and my soul to God who gave it, and in Relation to my Earthly property, it is my will that it should be left to my beloved wife and children, in the following manner, after my executors shall make sale of so much of my perishable property as may be necessary to defray the expense of my funeral, and discharge all the Just debts which I may in any way be owing to any person or persons whatsoever:

2nd, I give and bequeath to my beloved wife Ann Knowles, to be hers for the use of herself and for the support of my two daughters, now living with us, which said daughters shall remain single, and are disposed to live peacably with their mother, all and singular, my lands and Tenements, household and kitchen furniture, one horse of her own choosing, all cattle, all my hogs and sheep, and all of any stock or article which may not be herein mentioned, after the sale of my executors as above mentioned, to her and to the only proper use of her during her natural life or widowhood, and at her death, said lands and Tenements to be disposed of in the following manner.

(270) 3rd, To wit, I give and Bequeath unto my Two daughters, Martha Knowles and Elizabeth Knowles all the lands and tenements above mentioned to be Equally Divided between them to be theirs and to their only proper use for themselves and their heirs forever.

4th, I give and bequeath to my eldest son Jesse Knowles, one dollar, out of my Estate when collected by my Executors, over and above what he has heretofore Received of me in Token of the Live I leave to him.

5th, I Give and bequeath to my Eldest daughter Rebecca, wife of Joseph Campbell, one dollar, if she is living, to be paid by my said Executors out of my estate, over and above the property she has heretofore Received of me in Testimony of the love I have for her.

(270) 6th, I give and bequeath to my beloved Daughter,Nancy, wife of William Thompson, one dollar, to be paid by my exe- cutors, out of my estate when collected over and above the bed and furniture, which she received of me when she was first married, and left my house, in testimony of the love I have for her.

7th, I Give and bequeath to my daughter Mary, wife of Shelton, one cow and calf or other property 6f the stock on the farm to the amount of Ten dollars, which property shall be paid by my executors to said Mary Shelton previous to the sale above mentioned in Testimony of my love to her.

8th, I Give and bequeath to my daughter Cynthia, wife of Mathews W. Carter, Ten dollars to be raised out of my estate, and paid over to her in place of the land which I sold to Mathews Knowles, out of her share of the said land.

9th, I appoint and ordain my two Trusty Friends,Crofford Carter. and my son Mathews Knowles, Executors of this my Last will and testament. In Testimony whereof I have unto set my name and affixed my seal, the day and date above written.

his
Benjamin x Knowles.
mark

Test.
James Hagen.
A. J. Eslick. Proven at Sept. Term, 1845.
Recorded Sept. 18th 1845.

I, DANIEL HOLBERT, being weak of Body, but of sound mind, do hereby make and publish this my last will and testament, thereby revoking and making void all wills by me at any time made.

First, I Give myself into the hands of God who made me.

Secondly, I wish to be decently buried in a situation agreeable to my former or course of life.

Thirdly, My wish is that all my Just debts with my funer- al and burial Expenses be paid out of the first money that may come to hand or may be on hand at the time of my death.

Fourthly, as to my worldly affairs I do give and bequeath to my dear and beloved wife Mary Holbert, all my personal & Real Estate during her natural life, and at her death, my wish is the property that is left to be equally divided among my lawful heirs, in proportion, taking in consideration some of them has already got.

Fifthly, and lastly, I do leave my wife Mary Holbert, the Executrix of this my last will and testament. In Testimony
(271) thereof I have hereunto set my hand and affixed my seal, this the 9th day of May 1844.   his
Signed and sealed in the   Daniel x Holbert, (seal)
presence of,   mark
Davis Smith.
Henry Robinson. Recorded 15th Sept. 1845.

(272) William Solman. In the name of God Amen. I, WILLIAM SOLMAN: of the state of Tennessee, and County of Lincoln,be- ing of sound mind and disposing memory and calling to mind the uncertainty of life and certainty of death, do make and ordain this to be my last will and testament, revoking all

(272) others, and as touching the property that it has pleased God
to give, I leave and bequeath in the following form, viz:

1st, My will and desire is that my Executors to be hereafter named, shall collect the debts owing to me and pay all my
Just debts.

2nd, My will and desire is that all my property of every
description be left in the hands of my wife Hasley Solman &
my Executors, in order for her maintenance and education of
my children &C, except as hereafter provided in the following
form.

3rd, My will and desire is that when my nine following
named Children, to wit, William Calvin, John Rhea, James
Madison, Mary Louisa, Julia Ann, Elizabeth Jane, Augustus
Marion, Bonnet Franklin and Joseph Hamilton, severally arrives
at lawful age, there shall be a portion of property valued by
three disinterested men, and Given to each of them so as to
make them all equal from first to last, in the division of all
my property, except as hereafter mentioned.

4th, If my wife Hasly Solman should alter her way of living by a second marriage, my will and desire is that she shall
not have any of my property, provided, nevertheless, if she is
not willing to let this will stand, then all my property of
every description shall be immediately valued, except as hereafter mentioned, and equally divided between her and the above
(273) nine named Children, giving her one tenth or a Child's part,
with the following exceptions.

5th, But if my wife Hasly Soloman should continue single
and let this will stand, when my youngest child shall arrive
at lawful age and have its part of property valued to it, there
shall be a sufficient quantity of property left in her hands
for her maintenance during her life, and what property she may
have in her hands at her death, the negroes to be valued, and
the balance to be sold, and equal division to be made between
my above nine children, with the following exception.

6th, If it should so happen that I should have another
heir after my death, whether a son or daughter, my desire is
that in every Instant, it shall have an equal part with the
balance of my other children, and my wife's part would in
that event be one Eleventh of my estate.

7th, My will and desire is that my negro woman Lucy and
her youngest child, Lucinda, and all their future Increase, fr
from the date of this will be forever free, that neither my
heirs, Executors, administrators, assigns nor any other persons or persons, wheresoever, shall ever hereafter have any
claim ti them or their increase as above stated.

8th, My will and desire is that the above Lucy's children to wit, Manerva, Dinah and Clinton, be jointly sold in
one lot on a credit of twelve months, and the money thence a-
rising to be equally divided among all my legal heirs or put
to any use for my family, if needed and my will and desire is
that all the property of my estate of every description which
falls to my daughters, I give ti them, and the heirs of their
Body forever.

9th, My will and desire is that as respects the Lots and
property of mine, where Jordan Soloman, my Brother lives, that
they be sold on a credit of twelve months, and that what I

(274) paid for said property together with Legal Interest and Taxes, and other damages I have paid, be deducted out of the price arising from the sale of said property, and the balance, if any to be to said Jordan Soloman. and his legal heirs.

10th, And lastly, my will & desire is that my friebds, James Fulton, James Bright, John V. McKinney & Abner Steed be my executors, to execute and see this my last will and testament executed. believing they will attend to the same Correctly.

Wm. Soloman, (seal)

Signed, sealed, published and pronounced to be the last will and testament of WILLIAM SOLOMAN, in presence of us this 16th of January 1833.
Samuel Rosbrough.   Proved Sept. Term 1845.
A. J. Rosbourgh.   Recorded Sept. 18th 1845.

I, JAMES R. BLAIR, of the County of Lincoln and State of Tennessee, do make and publish this my last will and testament, hereby revoking all former wills by me at any time made heretofore.

And first, I direct that my Body be decently Interred in a Christian like manner, first it is my will that all my Just debts and funeral expenses be paid out of any money that I may have or that may come in the hands of my executors.

Secondly, I will and bequeath to my beloved wife, Lavina, the tract of Land on which I now live, containing one hundred and seventy acres, also the tract of Land that I purchased of Thomas Blair, of a tract, one hundred and sixteen acres, unless my executors should think it best to sell the last mentioned tract of Land, then it is my will that they advertise the said
(275) tract of Land, find a public place in the County and sell it on, one and two years credit, taking bond with two approved security, and divide the proceeds Equally between my children. I will to my wife, one negro boy, Calvin, one negro woman, named Mariah, and her child George, and her increase, if any, to be hers during her natural life or widowhood, and at her decease or marriage I want my executors to proceed to sell the above named tracts of land and negroes, on a twelve months credit & taken bond with approved security, and the proceeds to be equally divided between my children, namely, Josiah H. Yolman, William B. Martha E. John M. Lewis J. Elizabeth A. Cassena M. James E. W. & Lanina, my wife to have a childs part of the whole. I want my executor to sell off and set apart horses sufficient to cultivate the land and cattle, hogs sufficient for their support and propagation, all the household and kitchen furniture I wish to remain for the benefit of my family. I want my executors to proceed to sell to the highest bidder, on a credit, my stock of Jennets and all such property as my executors should deem necessary to be sold and after all my debts is paid, the proceeds to be equally divided between my heirs above mentioned. I do hereby appoint James F. McCowan, William C. Bland and John Fowler, my executors to this my last will and testament, in witness whereof I have herein set my hand and seal, this first day of September, in the year of our Lord, one thousand, Eight hundred and forty-five.

J. R. Blair, (seal)

(275) Signed, sealed and published in the presence of us who have
subscribed our names in the presence of the testator, and
each other.
W. B. Robinson.
Samuel J. Bland.   Pronounced the 6th day of Oct. 1845.
Recorded the 25th of Oct. 1845.

    Tennessee, Lincoln County. I, COLONEL JAMES DUFF, of the
State and district, County aforesaid, being in health of body,
and of sound and disposing mind and memory, do make this my Last
will and testament, in manner and form as follows:
    1st, I will and bequeath all and singular, my negro slaves,
both male & female to the American Colonization Society, to be
by them transported to the African Colony of Liberia to be forever free and independent.
    2nd, My will is that until it shall be convenient for the
above named Society to transport my negro slaves, so to set free
that they shall be hired out by the family and the proceeds
thereof or such part thereof, as may be necessary, be applied
towards having the Children, both male and female to read with,
and cipher, and the residue or remainder, if any to be applied
in aid of their transportation to the African Colony of Liberia,
(276) there to be forever free.
    3rd, My will is the residue or remainder of my estate, real
or personal, if any, be by my Executors or Administrators ex-
posed to public sale and the proceeds or money arising therefrom be put out to interest until the time of transportation of
my negro slaves, so set free by the above named Colonization
Society, at which time each one of my negro slaves so set free
shall receive the sum of fifty Dollars, if so much there be.
    4th My will is that my sister Margaret Smith receive out
of the residue of my money arising as above directed, fifty dollars, also the sum of fifty dollars to my sister Elizabeth
Campbell. Signed, sealed and acknowledged in presence of us who
at his request and in his presence, and in the presence of each
other have signed our names as witnesses.
Carson Sloan.   James Duff, (seal)
William Taylor, x his mark.

(277)   Vincent Hearalson Will. I, VINCENT HEARALSON, being weak
in body and of sound mind, do make and ordain this my last
will and Testament.
    1st It is my wish that my land and negroes remain in poss-
ession of my wife Mary G. and my three Children James C. Ephrain
L. and Elizabeth W. Herralson, and all my other property with
the exception of as much as my executors may find necessary to
sell to pay my Just debts.
    2nd, It is my desire if my wife Mary G. should marry again,
then for my property to be equally divided between her and my
three children, James H. Ephrain L. and Elizabeth Heraldson, or
that it may be divided equally between them as directed above,
when the oldest child shall become of age or when any or either
of them marries, my wife Mary G. taking a childs part, of land

(277) negroes and all other property, and do as she may see proper
with it.

       3rd, I appoint my wife Mary G. Heralson and John L.
Henderson, my Executors to this my last will and testament,in
witness whereof I have hereunto set my hand and seal,December
the 30th 1845.

Witness.   Vincent Haraldson, (seal).

M. H. Bonner.

Lewis Shipp.

Proved and admitted to record at February Term, 1846.

(278)   John Austin Will. In the name of God Amen. I, JOHN
AUSTIN, do make and publish this as my last will & testament,
hereby revoking and making void all other wills by me at any
time made.

       1st, I direct that my funeral expenses and all my just
debts be paid as soon as possible after my death, out of any
money that I may die possessed of or may first come into the
hands of my executors.

       2nd, I give and bequeath to my beloved wife Elizabeth
Austin, twelve acres of lamd in Lincoln County, where my dwelling house stands and all my personal property that is left after paying expenses and debtsm besides what I have given to my
children.

       Thirdly, I give and bequeath to my daughter Sally Thornton,
one dollar more than what she has had out of my estate.

       Fourthly, I give and bequeath to Hardy Birmingham,one tract
od land lying in Giles County, on the waters of Sushing Creek,
containing forty-seven acres on which Lecel Thornton now lives,
the said property to be held by said Hardy Birmingham, upon the
following Trust, that he permit my daughter Sally Thornton,wife
of Lecel Thornton, to have the possession and use of said land
during her natural life for her comfort and support, and the
support of her children, so that the same or the proceeds thereof shall not be subject to the Control, debt or contract of
her husbamd, and at the death of said daughter I bequeath said
land or property to her children, to be equally divided amongst
them, shoukd said Trustee at any tbme think that the ease and
comfort of any said daughter and her children could be promoted
(279) by renting said land, he is at liberty to do so, and pay the
proceeds to my said daughter for the purpose aforesaid,should
the execution fo this trust at any time become inconvenient to
the trustee, he may, with the consent of my said daughter sub-
stitute some other suitable prson in his stead or place.

       Fifth, I give and bequeath to my son Andrew W. Austin,all
the remainder of my land in Lincoln and Giles County, also if
there should be anydf the property as mentioned secondly, at
the death of my wife, I leave it to my son Andrew W. Austin.

       Also, lastly, I do hereby nominate and appoint Hardy
Birmingham, my Executor. In witness whereof I do to this my
will, set my hand and seal this 28th March 1845. his

                                   John x Austin,(
                                    mark.

Signed, sealed and published in our presence, and we have subscribed pur names hereto, in the presence of the testator.

(279) Test.
Spencer Leatherwood.
B. B. Leatherwood. Proved & admitted to record at Feb. Term 1846.

(280)   Last Will and Testament of H. Warren. I,HENRY WARREN,of
the County of Lincoln and State of Tennessee, being in a low
state of health, but of perfect sound mind, do make and ordain
this my last will and testament, in manner and form following,
(To wit), I Give and bequeath to my eldest son John E. Warren,
one negro Girl by the name of Milly, who is now in his possession, and valued at five hundred and fifty dollars, & also a
negro Boy by the name of Edward, valued at eight hundred dollars,
which two negroes amount to one hundred and thirty-three dollars
and 42 cents more than his equal Division of my estate, which
it is my will that he pay into my estate, on the reception of
the Boy Edmond.
     Item 2nd, I give and bequeath unto my son William Warren,
my boy Cato, who is now in his possession and valued at Eight
hundred dollars, also my boy Isaac, valued at two hundred and
fifty dollars, which two negroes by valuation will amount to
ten hundred and fifty dollars, and also one hundred and sixty-
six dollars and fifty-eight cents to be paid to him by my executors, so soon as they shall be able to collect the same out
of any money due to my estate not otherwise appropriated.
     Item, 3rd, I give and bequeath unto my beloved Daughter,
Elizabeth, wife of Joseph Stephens, my negro woman Dice,valued
at three hundred dollars, and my girl Luiza,which is now in
her possession and valued at three hundred dollars, which two
(281) negroes I give to her, the said Elizabeth, and the heirs of her
body forever, the said two negroes amounting to six hundred
dollars, and also one note, executed to G. W. Payne for twelve
dollars & fifty cents, also six hundred and four dollars &
Eighty cents to be paid to her by my executors out of anymoney
of my estate not otherwise appropriated.
     Item 4th, I give and bequeath to my beloved Daughter Mary,
wife of James P. D. Rosebrough, my Girl Rosannah, now in her
possession, and valued at four hundred and twenty-five dollars,
and also my Boy, Jacob valued at four hundred & Twenty-five
dollars, which two negroes I Give to her, the said Mary and the
heirs of her body forever, the said negroes amounting to Eight
hundred and fifty dollars, and also one note of hand executed
by J. P. D. Rosebrough to G. W. Payne, for Twelve dollars and
fifty cents. I also give and bequeath to James P.D.Rosebrough,
husband of Mary a note of hand, executed by him to Henry Warren, Junior, the balance of which is about three hundred and
ten dollars, and also one mare of the value of fifty dollars,
which is now in his possession.
     Item 5th, I give and bequeath to my son Thomas R. Warren,
my negro Girl, Manda, valued at five hundred and fifty dollars,
and also my negro Boy, James valued at eight hundred dollars,
the said Girl now in his possession which amounts to their ten
hundred and fifty dollars, which two negroes amount by valuation to one hundred and thirty-three dollars and forty-two
(282) cents more than his equal portion of the estate which one hundred and thirty-three dollars and forty-two cents I will that

(282) he pay into the estate on the reception of said Negro James.

Item, 6th, I give and bequeath to my daughter Sarah, wife of Beckworth J. Lettes, my negro Girl Malvina, now in her possession, valued at four hundred and Eighty dollars, and also one note of hand Executed by herself to me for one hundred dollars, and lot no.4 containing sixty-eight acres of Land valued at six hundred and Eighty dollars, which land and negroes I give and bequeath to her, the said Sarah and the heirs of her body forever, and also Thirty-six dollars and fifty-eight cents to be paid to her by my executors, out of any money not otherwise appropriated.

Item 7th, I Give and bequeath to my daughter Nancy, wife of Thomas J. Payne, my negro Girl Elvira, now in her possession, and valued at five hundred & fifty dollars, and Lot no. five of Land, containing Sixty eight acres and valued at six hundred and Eighty dollars, which land and negroes I Give and bequeath to her the said Nancy and the heirs of her body forever. I also Give and bequeath to Thomas J. Payne, husband of Nancy, one note of hand executed to me by himself for Eighty-four dollars, & ninety-eight cents, the above land and negro & note amounting to thirteen hundred and fourteen dollars and 98 cents, which amount is ninety-eight dollars and forty-seven cents over their portion of my estate, and for which sum the said Lot of Land may be rented out after my deceased, until the said sum of money shall be raised and paid into my estate.

Item 8th, I give and bequeath to my son Henry Warren, my negro Girl Eliza, valued at five hundred and fifty dollars, and my negro man Dick and his wife Ruth, valued at seven hundred and fifty dollars, the Girl now in his possession, which three negroes do amount to thirteen hundred dollars, which sum amounts to eighty-three dollars and forty-two cents over his porportion of my estate, which I will that the said Henry Warren pay to my Executors on the reception of said property.

Item 9th, I Give and bequeath to my son Benjamin Warren a tract of Land, Lot No. two, containing ninety acres and valued at nine hundred dollars, and also one half of one other tract of land by survey, containing Twenty-two acres, which I Give to him for Lumber to support the farm of the ninety acres, also the (283) half of one other tract of land by survey, eighty acres for timber, which Eighty acres tract lies in the hills on the east side of Mulberry Creek, and also one negro boy named Alick, valued at two hundred and fifty dollars, and also one negro Girl by the name of Malinda, valued at three hundred and twenty-five dollars, and I also Give and bequeath to said Benjamin, the privilege of cutting fire wood and hauling it for his own proper use, off the north end of the two lots, No.4 and 5, free of charge, the chargeable property herein named, amounting to fourteen hundred and seventy-five dollars, a sum of two hundred and fifty-eight dollars, and forty-two cents, over and above his proportionable part of my estate, which sum it is my will (284)that the said Benjamin, pay to my executors in Equal payments of one, two and three years after my Decease.

Item 10th, I give and bequeath to my two single daughters, Emeline Warren and Caroline Warren, the balance of my estate in the following manner and form, to wit, to my daughter Emeline, I give and bequeath one negro woman named Flora, and her child,

(284) Ellen, valued at seven hundred and fifty dollars, and one tract off Land NO. 3, containing forty-five acres and valued at four hundred and fifty dollars, and also one-fourth of a tract of land containing twenty-two acres, and also one fourth part of one other tract of land, containing Eighty acres, all of which property I Give to her and the heirs of her body forever. I also give and bequeath to her the said Emily, the privilege of Cutting so much wood as shall be sufficient for her fire-wood, of the North end of Lot No.4 &5, that at any time if the said Emily should be disposed to sell her land to any of her Brothers or Sisters, and convey the same (free of encumbrance) by a good and sufficient Deed, the amount of the above property by valuation,amounts to twelve hundred Dollars, which is sixteen dollars and fifty-eight cents less than her proportional part of my estate, which sixteen dollars and fifty cents it is my will that my Executors pay to her the said Emily, out of any money of my estate not otherwise appropriated.

(285)   Item 11, I give and bequeath to my daughter Caroline Warren one negro womwn named Judy, and her child Luiza, valued at seven hundred and fifty dollars, and also one tract of Land, Lot No. 1, containing forty-five acres and valued at four hundred and fifty dollars, and also one fourth part of one other tract of Land, containing twenty-two acres, and also one fourth part of one other tract of Land Containing Eighty acres, on the east side of Mulberry Creek, the above named property I give and bequeath to the said Caroline, for the only proper use of herself and her heirs of her body forever. It is also my will that the said Caroline shall have the privilege of cutting and using so much wood off the North end of Lot No. 4 and 5, as will be sufficient for her fires. It is also my will that at any time, if the said Caroline shall be disposed to sell any of the above property to any of her sisters or Brothers, she may do so and Convey the same by a good title, clear of encumbrance, the above mentioned property by valuation amounts to twelve hundred dollars, a um of sixteen dollars and fifty-eight cents less than her proportionable part of my estate, which sum it is my will that my Executors pay to her out of any money of my estate not otherwise appropriated.

     Item 12th, I also give and bequeath to my two single daughters, Caroline and Emeline to each of them one Good Horse, saddle and Bridle, also one cow and calf each, and one Bed and bedstead and furniture each, and one Good Bureau each. It is also

(286) my will that my said two daughters shall remain in the House, and Benjamin Warren tract of Land and shall be self ported out of the proceeds of my estate for the Term of two years, if they shall live single for that length of Time.

     Item 13th, It is also my will further, that my son Benjamin aforesaid have a Cherry Corner Cupboard which stands in my house, for his own Benefit.

     Item 14th, I further will that my Negro Girl Masouri be sold to the highest bidder among my family on one and two years credit, and if the said Girl will not sell as aforesaid for two hundred dollars, it is my will that each of my heirs lose in proportion to the loss of the sale.

     Item 15th, it is also my will that my executors sell to

(286) the highest bidder on twelve months credit, all my household and kitchen furniture not willed to my heirs and the money to be appropriated to the payment of my Just debts and my funeral expenses.

Item 16th, It is further my will that all my negroes, stock, of all kinds and of every description, of farming utensils, and what soever may be for the benefit of the farm, shall remain on the farm under my son Benjamin aforesaid, until the crop of 1846 be gathered in, but nevertheless it is my will that my executors make sale of all my hogs, cattle and sheep, after the first day of August next, either for cash or on Credit as they may think proper, also it is my will that after the crop aforesaid shall be gathered in, my executors advertise and sell all my remainder of my stock and utensils of every description, on Twelve months

(287) credit, the purchases in all cases giving Bond and approved security, and the proceeds first to go to the payment of my Just debts and the balance to be equally divided among my heirs, and lastly, I make and ordain my friend James Bright and my two sons Benjamin Warren & Thomas R. Warren, my executors to this my last will and testament, in witness whereof I have hereunto set my hand and affixed my seal this Twenty-Third day of January in the year of our Lord, one Thousand eight hundred and fortysix.
Signed & sealed in the presence of,   his
Test.   Henry x Warren, (seal).
James Hagen.   mark
Thos. James.

Codicil. February 24th 1846. I, HENRY WARREN, do continue weak in Body, but of sound mind, and in consequence of the Great Trouble and expense which I have been to my three children, Benjamin Warren, Emeline & Caroline, my two Daughters, I give and bequeath to the three above mentioned Children my negro Girl, Masouri, to dispose of amomg themselves Jointly, as they may think proper, and the 14th Item in my above last will and testament is hereby made null and void, and no other part thereof to be in anyway affected by this alteration. In witness whereof I have herein set my hand and seal this day and year above written.   his
Test.   Henry x Warren.
James Hagen.   mark
Thomas James.   Recorded April Term 1846.

(288)   I, ALEXANDER FORBES, Senior, of Lincoln County, in the State of Tennessee, do make and publish this as my will and testament, hereby revoking and making void all other wills by me at any time made.

First, I direct that my funeral expenses, and all my debts be paid as soon after my death as possible, out of any money that I may die possessed of or that may first come into the hands of my executors.

Secondly, I give and bequeath to my daughter Ann Patterson five dollars.

Thirdly, I give and bequeath to my granddaughter Lucinda Forbes, the daughter of James Forbes, Deceased, five dollars.

Fourthly, I give and bequeath to my daughter Lucy Murry,

(288) five dollars.

Fifthly, I give and bequeath to my son Absolam Forbes, five dollars.

Sixthly, I give and bequeath to my daughter Polly Rainy, five dollars.

Seventhly, I give and bequeath to the children of my son, Schuyler Forbes, deceased, five Dollars.

Eighthly, I give and bequeath to my son Alexander Forbes, five dollars.

Nineth, I give and bequeath to my daughter Martha Gillehand, five dollars.

Tenthly, I give and bequeath to my wife Catharine Forbes, all my land, all my stock of Horses, Cattle and sheep and hogs, all my household and kitchen furniture, all my plantation tools, all the crop that may be possessed by me at my death, with any other property that I may possess for ever, with the exception
(289) of the above named eight Legacies of five dollars each are not to be paid till after the death of my wife.

Lastly, I do hereby nominate and appoint my friend Samuel Parker my executor. In witness whereof I do to this my will set my hand and seal this thirteenth day of March, Eighteen hundred & forty-three.

Alexander Forbes, (seal).

Signed, sealed and acknowledged in the presence of us.
Aaron Boyd.
Bazel Leatherwood. Recorded April 1846.

Hannah Evans Last Will. I, HANNAH EVANS, do make this, and publish this as my last will and testament, hereby revoking and making void all other wills by me at any time made.

First, I will and Bequeath my soul to God.

Secondly, I direct that my funeral and burial Expenses, and all my debts be paid as soon after my death as possible, out of any money that I may die possessed of or may first come into the hands of my executors.

Thirdly, I Give and bequeath to Malinda Evans, the wife of John Evans, Jr. my cotton wheel and cards and Reel, and Iron potrack, & one pot and my Trunk and all my clothes, only what may hereafter be mentioned, also I give my bed and bedclothes, & bedstead and two smoothing Irons, and one set of pewter plates, and one dish and one washing Tub & one churn and two chairs.

Fourthly, I give to Dellingtine Evans, two calico Frocks & one blue check cotton frock, and one plain white counterpin.

Lastly, I do hereby nominate and appoint Enoch Hamilton, my executor. In witness whereof I do to this my will, set my hand and Seal this 28th day of March 1846. her

Hannah x Evans, (seal)
mark

Signed, Sealed & published in our presence, & we have subscribed our names in the presence of the Testator, this day and date, March 28th 1846.
Test.
John H. Taylor.
John Hamilton. Admitted to Record June 1846.

(289) I, BENJAMIN THURSTON, of Lincoln County, Tennessee, Being of
Sound mind and disposing memory, & knowing the uncertainty of
life & the Certainty of death, do make and publish this, my
(290) last will and testament, hereby revoking all former wills or
testaments by me made.

First, I direct that my funeral expenses and all my Just
debts be paid as soon after my death as possible, out of any
money I may die possessed of or may first come into the hands
of my executors.

Secondly, I give and Bequeath unto my nine grandchildren,
viz, Elizabeth Thomison, Pathena S. Isham, Mary C. Summerford,
Martha D. Roach, Catharine S. Parkes, Aaron Parkes, Oney Parkes,
William Parkes & Joel Parkes, childres of my deceased daughter,
Polly Parkes. The negro woman Hiziah & Daphne, which I have
heretofore loaned to my said deceased daughter, said women,
their children and future increase, to be equally divided be-
(291) tween my Said Grandchildren, when the youngest one of them arrives at the age of twent-one years.

Thirdly, It is my will and desire that my friend Samuel C.
Gilleland, have the Control & possession of my old negro man
Peter & that said Gilleland, shall See that he is properly and
humanly treated, and that Peter have the benefit of his own
labor.

Fourthly, It is my will and desire that one-eighth of an
acre of land, of the tract on which I now live, which I have
chosen & set apart as the burial ground for myself and wife, be
reserved from Sale forever, and that the Same be Suitably en-
closed by my executors.

Fifthly, I give & bequeath unto my dearly beloved wife, all
of my property, both real and personal of every name, kind &
description, not herein before disposed of otherwise, during
her natural life, and at her death I give and bequeath unto
Benjamin Thurston Parkes, the negro boy Gilbert, now in the
possession of William Parkes, which boy I loaned to my Said deceased daughter, and also the Tract of Land on which I now live,
except the one-eighth of an acre, reserved as aforesaid, to him
and his heirs forever.

Sixthly, I direct that my executor, at the death of my
wife, sell all the rest of my property of every description, not
herein otherwise disposed of, on Such a credit as they may
think most for after the interest of all concerned & that Said
Executors divide the proceeds of Such Sale together with the
proceeds of two bonds or Notes which I hold on Samuel E. Gille-
(292) land, one of them for Six hundred dollars, the other for two
Thousand, Six hundred dollars. Said bonds were executed to me
by Said Gilleland for negroes which I sold to him, equally a-
mong my nine Grandchildren mentioned by name in the Second
Item of This will.

Seventhly, I do hereby nominate and appoint my friends,
James Bright & Hugh Thomison my Executors to this my Last will
& testament. In witness whereof I have hereunto Set my hand &
seal This 11th day of July, 1843.

B. Thurston, (seal).

Signed & published by the above named BENJAMIN THURSTON, as &
for his last will and testament, (the word herein being erased)

(292) in the presence of us, who in his presence and in the presence of each other, have hereunto Subscribed our names as
attesting witnesses thereto, The Same day and date above written.
E. M. Ringo.
G. W. Jones.
Jno. C. Rogers.

　　　　Codicil. I, BENJAMIN THURSTON, having heretofore made,
and published the foregoing as my last will and testament,do
make and declare this as a codicil thereto, to wit:
　　　　First, I give and bequeath the one-half of the Legacy
heretofore by me given to my Granddaughter Martha, to my Grand-
daughter Cathrine S. Parkes,and the other half of the legacy I
loan to my said grand-daughter Martha, during her natural life,
and at her death I give and bequeath the same to her children
to be equally divided between them.
　　　　Secondly, I give and bequeath the one-half of the legacy
heretofore by me given to my Grand-daughter, Mary C. to my
grand-daughter Elizabeth, during her natural life, and at her
death, the Same to be equally divided, the other half of that
legacy I leave to my Grand-daughter Mary C. during her natural
life, & at her death to be equally divided between her children.
　　　　Thirdly, I revoke that portion of my will whereby I ap-
(293) pointed Hugh Thomison, one of my executors, and I hereby appoint James Bright and Andrew Buchanan, my executors.
　　　　Lastly, it is my desire that this codicil constitute a
part of my will to all intents and purposes, this 19th day of
July 1844.
　　　　　　B. Thurston, (seal).
Signed, Sealed and published in our presence, and we have sub-
scribed our names hereto in the presence of the testabor, this
19th July 1844.
James Fulton.
John Goodrich.
　　　　Established by the Circuit Court at the June Term 1846,of
the Circuit Court.

　　　　Milton Hodges Last Will. To all who shall See these pres-
ents- Greetings- Know ye that for divers good causes & consideration, I, MILTON HODGES, of the State of Tennessee, and County
of Lincoln, have nominated, made, constituted and appointed,
and by these presents do make, nominate, constitute and appoint
my Brother, Joseph Hodges, of the State of Mississippi, and
County of Leek, my true and Lawful Attorney, for me and in my
name, sworn & stead to take possession of Eighty acres of land
lying in the State of Louisiana, and parish of Lebane.including
the place whereupon Daniel Ritchie now lives,including all the
buildings on Said land, with every improvement whatsoever,
which land and premises I give and bequeath to him and his
heirs forever, and for his better ascertaining the bearing, dis-
(294) tance and Location of Said Land, he may find it herein Recorded in the Clerk of the Parishes' office, in said Parish or nop-
chihac, his,and I further nominate, constitute, make and appoint my said attorney for me and in my name sworn and Stead to

(294) collect, ask for, demand, receive and receipt for all money
due to me by note, bil, bond, assignment and indorsment or
book account, which may be owing to me within said parish, or
anywhere else, in the States aforesaid, or what other place
my debts as may have or moved to and Such money when received
I give, lease and bequeath to him to dispose of as he may see
proper, and to do everything necessary, both with said Land,
and premises and debts as tho I were present personally, acting
for myself. In testimony whereof the said MILTON HODGES, hath
hereunto set his hand and seal this 2nd, day of August 1845.
Attest.   Milton Hodges, (seal).
Abner Steed.
Thomas Roe.
Samuel Boone.
Joel Reese. Proved at the July Term 1845, by Samuel Boone and
Joel Reese, and admitted to Record.

  The Last Will and Testament of Robt. Buchanan. Whereas,
I, ROBERT BUCHANAN, of the County of Lincoln, Tennessee, being
of Sound mind and memory, doth make this my last will & Testament in the form and manner following, that is to say:
  First, I will and bequeath unto my Son Pryor Buchanan, the
plantation that I now live on, Supposed to be four hundred &
Thirty acres.
(295) Secondly, I will to my son Milton Buchanan, a certain
tract, on Said Buchanan Creek above the old factory place, containing about two hundred and ninety acres, to Run the line
between him and Moses Buchaman, agreeable to a Conditional
line before made between them.
  Thirdly, I will to my three Daughters, Elizabeth Woodward, Jane Buchanan and Mary Buchanan, five negro women, with
their female children, but Elizabeth Woodward to make allowance for one negro girl She has Received Some time ago.
  Fourth, I allow all my male Slaves, except Andrew, to be
divided between my two Sons equally, Andrew to be Pryor's
property, the Balance of my property, after my Just debts are
paid, to be divided equally between all my children. I wish
Hiriam Buchanan and Alfred Smith to attend to Business.
March 5th 1839.
Test.   Robert Buchanan.
Samuel Buchanan.
Established by the Circuit Court June Term, 1846, as to the
present property.
     N
  Andrew McCARTHEY WILL. In the name of God Amen. I,
ANDREW McCARTHEY, being of sound will and disposing mind and
memory, blessed be God, but believing that the day of my deso-
lation is well nigh at hand, do make, ordain, publish and de-
clare this to be my last will and Testament, in manner and
form following:
  I will and bequeath to my Seven Sons and Three Daughters,
(viz) Council, Andrew C. William W. George, James, Thomas and
Rufus Carlines heirs, Mahala and Mary an Equal distribution of
(296) all and every part and parcel of my Estate. Council having
Received fifteen hundred & forty dollars, William, nine hundred,

(296) Andrew, thirteen hundred and seventy-five. George, six hundred and seventy-five. Caroline, Six hundred and Sixty-five. Mahala, fourteen hundred and thirty, and Mary, Five hundred, and ninety dollars. Now my will is that each and every one of my children be made equal to Council, he having received fifteen hundred and forty dollars with this addition to Thomas, that is (Harry) to him as a nurse, and the residue of my Estate to the Support of Thomas during his life with two hundred dollars to Mahala Stonebraker, for the ensuing year as a Compensation to her for her trouble with Thomas, and at the death of Thomas, this residue of my property to be Sold and equally divided between my nine Children.

And I do hereby nominate, Constitute and appoint Jacob Stonebraker my executor to this my last will and testament, this 13th day of August 1846.
Test.   Andrew McCarthey.
Charles H. Edmondson.
James Locker. Admitted to record, Sept. Term 1846.

(297)   I, JOHN W. LEMOND, do make and publish this as my last will and testament, hereby revoking and making void all other wills by me at any other time made.

First, I direct that my funeral expenses and all my debts be paid as soon after my death as possible, out of any money that I may die possessed of or may first come into the hands of my executors.

Secondly, I give and bequeath to my beloved wife Betsey, the Land where I now live, for the support of her and her children, during her natural life or widowhood, and the land at her death to be sold and the proceeds divided or the Land divided at the discretion of the heirs. I give and bequeath to my beloved wife Betsey a Sorrel mare, named Fan, also one Sorrel mule. I give and bequeath to my beloved wife Betsey, all the balance of my property, consisting of horses, Cattle, sheep and hogs, household and kitchen furniture, farming utensils & with the corn crop now Growing, the oats and wheat crop.

Lastly, I do hereby nominate and appoint John M. Daniel, my executor. In witness whereof I do to this my last will and testament, Set my hand and seal. This 14th July 1846.
                                    his
                            John x W. Lemond.
                                    mark
Signed, sealed and published in our presence and we have subscribed our names in the presence of the testator. This 14th July 1845.
Test.
Samuel D. Milliken.
Wade H. McRee.
Anderson Boone. Proven and admitted to Record at Oct. Term 1846.

In the name of God Amen. I, WOODY TAYLOR, of the County of Lincoln and State of Tennessee, knowing that it is appointed for all men once to die, mindful of my departure from this mortal State and the happiness of the off-spring of my body, that may be left behind, and being in sound mind and memory, do make

(298) and publish this my last will and testament, hereby making all former wills void. In the first place it is my will, after my decease, that my body be decently Buried in the Dust from whence it came, and that my funeral charges and Just debts be punctually paid by my Executors, hereafter named, out of my Estate, then it is my will, and do hereby give and bequeath unto my present wife, Nancy Taylor, now living with me, all my living Stock of every description, animals of every kind, and all my household furniture of every kind, and all my farming tools of every kind, and the use and occupation of so much of my plantation wherein I now live, as to support herself and two daughters, named Louizer and Caroline Taylor, also the use of six of my negroes, namely, Hester, Soloman. Pinkney, Milly, Hester and Emeline. My land herein after willed to my son, John H. Taylor, but for my wife Nancy Taylor, not to be dis- possessed of any of the property left to her, whether real or personal, without leave of my executors, all of which said es- tate to her Bequeathed. It is my will that she possess and en- joy after my death, retain and contain in possession of the same, and the use and benefit thereof, during her natural life, or widowhood, only for the purpose of raising, providing and supporting of my two daughters, aboved named, so long as they remain single and with their mother, and at her death or mar- riage, the said property left to her and the increase of it to be equally divided among my six children hereafter named, by my

(299) executors (viz), William, Elizabeth, John, Polly, Louizer and Caroline, which I have had born to me by the said Nancy. I do hereby give and bequeath unto my son Wm. A. Taylor, five hun- dred dollars, which I have delivered to him, also one negro boy named Hollen, which named negro, at my decease, is to be the property of my son above named, Wm. A. Taylor, with an e- qual share of the balance of the above named property. I do give and bequeath unto my daughter Elizabeth, my negro boy, George, and to descend to her heirs forever, which boy I have delivered. I give and bequeath unto my son John H. Taylor, all my right title and interest to the tract of Land wherein I now live, Containing about one hundred and thirty acres of land, by deed of Conveyance from James Curtis, to me, but it is my will as above stated that my wife Nancy have the possession of it, or so much thereof, as may be sufficient to support her during her natural lifetime or widowhood, and the Support of my two daughters, Louizer and Caroline, so long ad they remain un- married, and with their mother.

I do give and bequeath untoo my Daughter Polly, my negro boy named Aaron, and to descend to her heirs forever, which boy Aaron is delivered. I do give and bequeath to my daughter Louizer my negro boy named Moses, which boy is to be delivered when she marries or at my Decease, which boy is to descend to her heirs forever, and if said Boy, Moses dies before he is delivered to Louizer, then at my death for her to have four hundred and fifty dollars, out of my Estate, also two Beds and furniture, with the one Bedstead, which is delivered, two horses known by the name of Mark and Pete, which horses is de- livered, and if Louizer dies without an heir, then the above named property to be equally divided among the surviving

(300) Balance of my children. I do give and bequeath unto my daughter, Caroline, my two negroes, Girls, named Judy and Sally, which negroes, if they die before they are delivered to Caroline, then she is to have four hundred & fifty dollars, of my Estate at my death, and if one of them dies, she is to have two hundred and twenty-five dollars out of my estate, at my decease, which property is to descend to her heirs forever, two Beds and furniture with one Grey mare. Pigeon, which property say, bed and stead and beast is delivered, and if Caroline dies without a lawful heir, the above named property to be equally divided amongst my surviving children.

I do hereby nominate, ordain and appoint my son William A. Taylor, of Franklin County, and Joseph A. Adkins, of Lincoln County, the Executors of this my last will and testament. In testimony whereof I have hereunto set my hand and seal this thirteenth day of June, one thousand eight hundred and thirty-two.

     Woody Taylor, (seal).
Signed in presence of,
John W. Hamilton.
A. C. Hamilton. Proven and admitted to record at Oct.Term 1846.
     Henry Kelso, (clerk).

(301)   Last Will & Testament of Thomas H. Jones. I, THOMAS H. JONES, being of a Sound mind, do make and ordain this my last will.

    1st, I give and bequeath to my mother, Leah Jones, my part or half of a tract of Land owned by myself and Edmond C. Jones, her natural lifetime, and at her death I give it to my Brother, Edmond C. Jones.

    2nd, I give to my mother, Leah Jones, my Grey mare.

    3rd, I give to my Brother, Edmond C. Jones my Bay Horse.

    4th, I give to my sister Julia F. Jones, my Grey Colt.

    5th, I want all my notes of hand, on different individuals to be appropriated to the payment of the land bought by myself and Brother, Edmond C. Jones.

    6th, I want my wages for this year applied to the payment of my debts.

    7th, I appoint Griffith Cunningham, my executor to this my last will. In witness whereof I have hereunto Set my hand and seal.   Thomas H. Jones, (seal).
Witness.
M. H. Bonner.
Griffith Cunningham. Recorded November 1846.

(302)   I, CORNELIUS SULLIVAN, being of Sound & perfect mind, and memory, do make and publish this my last will and testament in manner and form following:
First, I give and bequeath unto my beloved wife Mary, during her natural life or widowhood, my Negroes, viz, William, Jane Looner, Amos, George, Frank, and also my plantation, as to all the rest of my personal Estate, residue and Remainder, I wish to be sold, and all my debts to be paid and should there be anything remaining, I want it equally divided with all my children, so as to make all equal, with what I have heretofore given them.

(302)   I herebt appoint Constant Smith, my sole Executor of this
last will and testament, and hereby revoking all former wills
by me made, in witness whereof I have hereinto set my hand and
affixed my seal, this 25th day of October, 1846.
Test.   C. Sullivan, (seal).
John Wood.
Robert E. Edmondson.
Joshua Hughes.   Recorded Nov. 1846.

(303)   State of Tennessee, Lincoln County. Know all men by these
presents, that I, JOHN SEBASTIAN, of the State & County, aforesaid, being of sound mind and intellect, though weak in body,
do make and publish this as my last will and Testament.
     Imprinis- I bequeath my soul to Almighty God, who gave it.
     Item, I direct my executors hereafter named, after paying
my funeral expenses and all my just Debts, to dispose of my
property as follows- to wit:
     I give and bequeath to my Brother Joseph Sebastian, a
tract or parcel of Land belonginh to me lying on Big Creek, in
Philips County, in the State of Arkansas.
     Item, I bequeath to my nephew, William, son of Joseph
Sebastian, my Trunk and all my apparel.
     Item, I bequeath the residue of my property of every des-
cription, to the following named persons, to wit, Joseph
Sebastian, Jacintha Huey, Martha Hornsby, Sarah Hughes, Isaac
Grizzard & Hetty Polk, to be equally & Equitably divided among
them, and I do hereby appoint John J. Whitaker and Wiley
Grizzard, my executors, of this my last will & Testament. In
testimony whereof I have hereunto Set my hand and Seal this
Eighteenth day of November, in theyear of our Lord, one
Thousand Eight hundred & forty-Six.
                         John W. Sebastian, (seal).
Signed and sealed in presence of us, the undersigned witnesses
who have hereunto Set our hands in presence of the testator,
and of each other, the day & date above written.
Jno. F. Whitaker.
William L. Moore.   Proven at Dec. Term 1846.

(304)   John Henderson. Last will & Testament. In the name of
God Amen. I, JOHN HENDERSON, do make and ordain this my last
will and testament, revoking all others made by me.
     First. I do give and bequeath to my loving wife, my house
together with the land which I have generally cultivated, during her natural life. Also my negroes namely, George,Alfred,
Lucy and her youngest child, Martha, during her life. I give
her all my stock of every description that she may choose to
keep, also all my household and kitchen furniture to be divided
as she thinks proper.
     To my Daughter Mary, I give the following described Land,
beginning at the Creek running straight with the orchard fence
to the upper corner thence straight to Sherrils line, not to
intrude on John L. -- improvements. all my land South-East of
said line to be hers, her lifetime and to be hers her lifetime,
and to be hers children. I also give my negro man, George to
my Son John L. I give all my land North-west of Said line by his

(304)   paying to James W. Henderson. two sons, E. F. & W. A. Henderson, six hundred Dollars, to be paid twelve months after the death of my widow. I also give my son John L. my negro boy Alfred. I give to the above named heirs of J. W. Henderson, the proceeds of the following property, Aaron & Harriet to be sold on Twelve months credit, by the Executor, and after the death of my widow, Lucy & Martha, and all the other property to be sold and Equally divided Between Mary, John L. Henderson and James W. Henderson Heirs. I will that Enough of my Crop & Stock be Sold to pay all my Just debts, and my (305) widow to have all the balance that she may choose to keep.

   Lastly, I do appoint and nominate my son John, Executor to this my last will and testament, also it is further my will and desire that John L. Henderson, be Guardian for my Son, James W. Henderson Heirs. Witness my hand and seal this 5th September, 1846.

Test.   John Henderson, (seal).

E. M. Shelton.

Norris Leatherwood.   Proven Dec. Term, 1846.

   I, James Hague, of the County of Lincoln and State of Tennessee, do make this my last will and testament, in manner and form as follows, to wit:

   I give to my wife Ann Hague, that part of my real Estate and personal, that may remain after all my just Debts are paid during her natural Life, and also a Reasonable Support out of my Estate, until the Same shall fully pass into her hands. I also Give her into Immediate possession, a negro woman named, Ginney. My will is that the whole of the above property of every description, be placed in her hands, subject to my Just debts. After the partnership is closed with William S. Hague, what may remain is to be delivered over to her, which is to be for her support during her life, & after her death to pass into the hands of my children, equally to be divided between them, and Teir representatives, and further my will is That my children who have heretofore Received a portion to be chargeable for the Same on a settlement so as to make them all Equal.

   I hereby appoint C. M. Ringo and my son Robert Hague, my (306) Executors, to this my will, Given under my hand and seal this 11th day of January 1847.

Witness.   James Hague, (seal).

Wm. L. Hague.

Charles Bright.   Proven July Term, 1847, and admitted to Record.

   In the name of God Amen. I, WILLSON SCOTT, of Lincoln County and State of Tennessee, being frail in body, but of Sound mind and disposing memory, Thanks be to God for the same, the frailty of my body calling to mind the mortality of the same, I therfore make and ordain this my last will and testament.

   First of all, I commend my Soul to God who gave it, and my body to the earth, in a decent Christian like manner, and as Touching such worldly Estate as it has pleased God to bless me with, I do hereby bequeath and dispose of in the following manner, to wit:

   1st, I desire that my funeral Expenses be paid out of the

(206) first money that may come to the hands of my executors.

2nd. I desire that my executors expose to Sale on one and two years credit, my 47, forty-Seven acre tract of Land adjoining John Buchanan, on the North and West, Walker Hodgepeth, on the South & East for the purpose of paying all my debts.

3rd, I give to my beloved wife, Althoney Scott, all the Balance of my real Estate and all perishable and personal property of every description, during her natural life or widowhood.

(307) 4th, In case she inter-marries it is my desire that she have an equal portion with my children.

5th, I hereby appoint Constant Smith, my executor to this my last will and testament. In witness whereof I have Set my hand and Seal this 5th day of February 1847.

William Scott, (seal).

Signed, sealed and published in presence of us.
H. N. Reeves.
John Williams.   Proved and admitted to Record, March Term 1847.

February 9th, 1846. I, WILLIAM B. SHELTON, do this day, make this my Last will and wish to dispose of my property in the following manner.

First, that my Brother Dr. E. M. Shelton divide our property that belongs to us both, according to an agreement, after that is done it is my will that my wife Mary B. Shelton have all my property to keep and dispose of as she may think best, it is also my desire that she keep our children and educate them together as well as she can, first paying all my Just debts which I hope will be done as soon as convenient.

I Leave my Brother E. M. Shelton my executor to this my last will and Testament.

witness.   W. B. Shelton.
Joseph F. Brown.
James Dunlap.
John J. Clarke.   Admitted to Record March Term 1847.

(308)   I, JAMES MILLS, of the State of Tennessee and Court of Lincoln, being at this time weak of body, but of sound mind and disposing memory, do make and ordain this to be my Last will and testament, revoking all other wills. And as touching the Estate property or effect it has pleased God to bless me with, I Leave, bequeath and give in the following manner,:

First, I desire that all the money that is owing to me be collected by my executors and all my Just debts be paid, the money I now have on hand to also go to settle up my business and pay my expenses.

Second, my desire is that my wife Elinor, have all the property she brought here, to wit: a cow and calf, Bed and furniture and one bedstead. I have Given her a Black mare which she claims and twenty-five Dollars in money, she can also either take choice of a cow and pigs or Bureaus.

Third, My desire is that all my Land be sold on a credit of one, two and three years, and all my other property of every description be sold on a twelve months' credit, and the

(308) money therein arising, be equally divided between my children, to wit: Sarah Cunningham, Eliza N. Ashby, James W. Mills, Nancy C. Mills, Margaret Adeline Mills and Elizabeth Ann Mills, subject to the following deductions, viz, Sarah Cunningham has had a twenty-five dollar saddle, three Dollars in a bureau and five Dollar bedstead, a cow and feather bed to be deducted from her part. Eliza N. Ashby has had a bedstead, bed and furniture, a twenty-five dollar Saddle and a cow to be deducted from her part. James W. Mills has had a twenty-five Dollar saddle to be deducted from his part and Nancy C. has had a twenty-two dollar saddle to be deducted from her part.

Fourth, my will and desire is that Henie Johnson and Samuel Brown Esq. execute this will May 31st 1847.
Acknowledged upon us the day it bears date.
Jesse Stockell   James Mills, (seal).
Abner Steed.
Admitted June Term 1847.

(309)   February 22, 1847. In the name of God Amen. I, SAMUEL COLEMAN, of the State of Tennessee and Lincoln County, calling to Remembrance the shortness and uncertainty of my life, and now being in my proper mind and wishing to dispose of my worldly possessions, in a manner which may be agreeable to my own will, do now make this my last will & testament, revoking all others.
        Lst It is my will that so much of the property after my decease be sold as shall be sufficient to pay off all my Just debts and after this the whole of the remainder of my Estate, Land and property of every kind, I will and bequeath to my beloved wife Rebecca, during her life, and at her death to be disposed of among our children as she may think best, except she would be disposed to enter into the marriage relation again & should she ever do this, the property shall then all be sold and an equal distribution be made between her and each of the children, and I also Leave at the executor & executrix of this my Last will and Testament, my beloved wife Rebecca & my son George Coleman. As witness my hand and seal this 22nd, day of February 1847.
Witness.   Samuel Coleman, (seal).
Henry Bryan.
George Coleman.
H. J. Anderson. Proved and admitted to Record June 1847.

(310)   I, MILLY BARKER, of the County Of Lincoln and State of Tennessee, being of sound mind and memory, but in feeble health, and calling to mind the mortality of the body and uncertainty of life, have this day ordained and constituted this my Last will and Testament, that is first I will and request that my body be decently buried and that my soul return to God that Give it. I will and bequeath that so much of my personal property be sold by my executor as may be necessary to pay all my Just debts, and burial expenses, then I will and bequeath to each of my three sons, McKindsee Whittenberg, Norman H. Whittenberg and Joseph Whittenberg, one good feather bed and

(310) furniture, to be delivered to each of them when needed or
called for.

I will and bequeath to my two daughters, Margaret E.and
Rebecca A. my stock of horses to be equally divided between
them. I will and bequeath to my son Charles H. all the remainder of my stock, consisting of Cattle, hogs & sheep together with all the household and kitchen furniture to be kept
by him for common use and benefit of himself and his two sisters, Margaret E. and Rebecca A. until the said Rebecca A. becomes of the age of twenty-one years, then all the before recited property to be equally divided between Charles H.
Margaret E. & Rebecca A. and the profits or proceeds of the
Stock, during that time to be divided as follows, Charles H.
to have one half, and Margaret E. and Rebecca A. one fourth
each, provided nevertheless, if the said Margaret E. or
Rebecca A. should marry before the time set apart for division
in the foregoing clause, then in that event the furniture and
Stock on hand may be divided so as to set apart to the one so
married, their proportion of Said Stock & furniture.

I also will and bequeath to my Son Charles H. all my farming tools now on hand, including wagon and gearing to be kept
and used for the benefit of the family. I further will and bequeath to my son McKindee W. Whittenburg, sixty Dollars, out
of my estate to be paid in the following manner, as I hold a
note on him, the said M. W. Whittenberg, for Eighty dollars due
the 21st day of November 1841- with a credit of forty dollars
now I allow the said note to be Given up without calculating
Interest and the remaining twenty Dollars to be paid by my Son
Charles out of the proceeds of the Stock or any money may come
into his hands, to be paid soon as convenient or whenever applied for and Lastly I nominate and appoint my Son Norman H.
Whittenberg my Lawful executor to this my Last will and testament.

In witness whereof I have hereunto set my hand and Seal
this 2nd day of April one Thousand Eight hundred and fortyseven.
(311) Interlined before Signed.   her
Witnesses.   Milly x Barker, (seal)
Sam'l Rosebrough.   mark
Franklin N. Moore.
Proved By Samuel Rosebrough at July Term 1847 and admitted to
Record.

State of Texas, Dallas County, July 23rd, 1846. I, J. A.
Simmons, considering the uncertainty of this life and being
weak in body, yet of Sound mind and memory, do make and pub-
lish this my last will and testament, to wit, that is to say,
I do give and bequeath to my Son Joseph, choice of my Horses,
Saddle and bridle, one bed.

Secondly, I do give and bequeath unto my beloved wife,
Hannah S. Simmons, all the rest of my property, Both real and
personal, and all money that I have on hand or may have Coming
to me in any way during her natural life, and at her death,it
(312) is my will that after giving to the younger children equal to
what I have given the 5 oldest, that the rest be equally divided between all my children.

(312)   Lastly, I do hereby appoint Hannah S. Simmons, my sole Executrix, to act without Giving Security in any way, and be at liberty to move property where she pleases. Witness my hand and seal.

                J. A. Simmons, (seal).

Acknowledged, sealed and delivered in the presence of,

Daniel Freeman.

John G. Gledewell.

Proved and admitted to record July Term of the Court 1847, by one of the witnesses, Daniel Freeman.

        In the name of God Amen. I, JACK N. LEFTWICH, of the County of Lincoln & State of Tennessee, being weak of body, but of sound mind and disposing memory, do make, ordain and publish this as my Last will and testament, hereby revoking and making void all other wills by me at any time made.

        First, I direct that my funeral expenses, and all my Just debts be paid as soon after my decease as possible, out of any money I may die possessed of or out of any that may first come into the hands of my executors.

        Secondly, I give & bequeath unto my beloved Wife Jane, during her natural life or widowhood, my negro George & John together with the following described tract of Land, to wit; beginning at the southeast corner of my original 209 acre tract purchased from William Pillow running thence Nobth 129 poles with the Section line, to a Syman Jacob Reeses Line thence west with my original line to the end of W. W. Gills Line thence north to W. W. Gills line, thence west to the top of the hill to A. G. Gills line, thence South to my original tract thence west to a beach at A. G. Gills gate on the branch thence down the branch with its meandering until a due South Course will throw the North & South fence near the Grave yard east of the line running to the Creek thence down the creek with L. B. Leftwich line to the peach tree Spring thence with the creek to opposite L. B. Leftwich house, thence to the cor-

(313) ner of R. N. Whitmans meadow, thence northly to a stake in my field, thence easterly to a rock corner near N. M. Whitmans gate, thence north to a rock corner thence west to the beginning. Also a tract Supposed to contain fifty acres beginning at a peach tree near A. G. Gills gate thence west with said Gills line for enough to run due South & Leave the Spout Spring on the west Side of the line thence with the meanderings of the branch to the creek, thence with the meandering of the creek to the South west Corner of the dower thence north with the Dowers line to the beginning, also 10 acres of Land for timber out of the South west corner of a 44 acre tract purchased from Samuel Garland & lÿing and adjoining the Land of Alexander Gill.

        Thirdly, I bequeath unto my said wife all my household & kitchen furniture, farming utensils, oxen wagon, two horses, 16 mothers, three cows and calves and a Sufficient quantity of corn, Pork, wheat, oats, hay & fodder for the next years provision, & all my stock hogs.

        Fourthly, my will and desire id that my son L. B. Leftwich live on the dower with his mother and take care of the farm

)313) and stock, and out of the profits of the same, she shall have
a sufficient and competent support, so as to enable her to enable her to live easy and comfortably. Any balance that may
accrue shall belong to my said Son and in case a separation
should take place between my wife and Son from any cause,my son
shall have all the Land lying east of the branch, east of the
house and an equal divisipn between them, of the stock on hand,
farming utensils and provisions, until the death of my wife,
and after her death, my said son shall have full possession of

(314) all the dower except the 50 acre tract and hold the Same for
him and his heirs and assigns forever, except about one acre &
a half around the meeting house, bounded by the tracks on the
east & west,on the south by the spring,on the north by my truck
patch fence, which I give to the church for their use as long
as they may continue to meet there for the purpose of worship,
and also that after the death of my wife, my said son L. B.
Leftwich shall have all the stock that may be on hand, all the
farming utensils and I further direct that all my lands not
named in the dower shall be sold about the first of November,
1848, in three Lots on a credit of one, two and three years,
in equal in stallments, the tract on which my son L. B. Leftwich
now lives in one lot, the Alexander Gill lot in another, with
20 acres added to it from the 44 acre Garland tract, the ridge
tract with a portion of my original tract added to it, and also the pork hogs, mules and the spare horses and the sheep that
may be on hand, on a credit of 12 months, and I also authorize
and direct my executors to sell my negro boy Samuel at the same
time on 12 months' credit, they shall first confine his sale to
the family, and if none of them will buy him, they may sell him
privately at what they may deem a fair price, taking a pledge
from the purchaser that he shall not be sold to a trader and
carried out of this section of County against his will, if he
conducts well, and I further direct that the proceeds of this
sale to be applied first to the payment of my just debts & the
balance to be divided amongst all my heirs, except my son L.B.

(315) Leftwich, so as to make each of my children an equal amount
counting to each the amount that I have heretofore advanced to
them, which is as follows: To my daughters, Fanny Bryant,
Rebecca S. Gill, Polly R. Reese, Catharine G. Stone, Sarah Jahe
Neese & Nancy Gill, three hundred dollars each, to Finetta Boon
Bryant, Eighty Dollars, to Martha Ann Leftwich twenty-four dollars, and I direct that my daughter Martha be Schooled,clothed
and focend according to what has been customary in my family,
free of charge to her, and at the expense of my estate, until
she comes of age or marries.

    Fifthly, I direct that after the decease of my wife, the
50 acre tract of Land attached to the dowery and remainder of
the 44 acre tract (Garland), added to it, and the negroes,boys,
George and John, household and kitchen furniture to be sold as
near upon the principal of the first sale as practicable, and
the proceeds equally divided amongst all my heirs, with the exception of my son L. B. Leftwich.

    Sixthly, whereas my son L. B. Leftwich has undertaken to
raise Patrick Purdon, and obligated himself to school him, and

(315) give him a horse, saddle and bridle, and a Suit of Clothes, my will is that my Estate shall be charged with the above articles and allowed to my said Son in the second division of my Estate, and I further direct that in case my negro boy George should die, then a hand shall be hired in his place until the year 1852, and paid for out of the amount arising from the second Division sale.

(316)   Seventhly, whereas I have raised my Grandson Wm. N. Bryant, my desire is that he shall remain with my wife until he comes of age, and if he should not so remain, then my will is that the amount of a years wages shall be deducted from his share of my estate.

     Eighthly, I hereby direct that my wife shall manage until the first sale, and the money arising from the Sale of Pork hogs or other property that may be sold, shall after paying the family expenses, be applied to the payment fo Reuben Bryants' claim, that is now due, and other neighborhood debts.

     And Lastly, I do nominate and appoint my wife Jane, executrix, and my son L. B. Leftwich and Lewis Newsom, and Joel Reese executors of this my Last will and testament, in witness whereof I have hereunto Set my hand and Seal this 5th day of June Eighteen hundred and forty-seven.

                         J. N. Leftwich, (seal).
Signed, Sealed and Published in presence of us.
Samuel Bone.
W. H. Bailey.
J N. Chilton x her mark.
Elizabeth Swan,x her mark, Proved by Samuel Bone and W. N. Bailey at July Term 1847, and admitted to Record.
                         Henry Kelso, Clk.

(317)   May 4th 1847. This being my Last will and Testament, first, I Commend my Soul to God, and my desire is that my wife Eunice B. Shull is to have all my property in the Town of Fayetteville, houses and parts of Lots, where I now live, and all other property in my possession, she is to have full control during her life or widowhood, if she marries my desire is when my youngest child comes of age, that all my property to be Sold on twelve months credit, and the money be equally divided amongst my wife and children, and my desire is that if she never marries she is to have full control her lifetime, and at her Death everything is to be sold on Twelve months credit, and equally divided among all my children.

     I appoint my wife and Daniel B. Shull my executors, to settle all my Business.
Test.   A. B. Shull.
William Temmins.
Joel Commins.
Proved and admitted to record at the August Term 1847.

     State of Tennessee, Lincoln County. The Last will and Testament of Henry Taylor, Senr., 6th of November 1845. I, HENRY TAYLOR,Senr, being in a perfect State of mind, and knowing the certainty of Death, do by this my Last will and Testament, after commuting my soul to God, an d a decent

(317) interment of my body, at the discretion of my friends. I
hereby bequeath So much of my personal property as will pay
all my Just Debts, and in the 2nd place, I will and bequeath
(318) to Henry Taylor, Junr, the farm whereon I live with all its
appertenances, upon the following condition, that if he, the
said Henry Taylor Jr. my youngest Son, do furnish me and my
beloved wife, Mary Taylor, during our natural life, provide for
us a comfortable living, with all my milling, firewood and
washing, with all the necessary attendance that should be reasonably expected.

3rd, I will my household and kitchen furniture to be e-
qually divided between my two daughters, Lucinda Keneday, and
Sarah English, also to Sarah Buckes, Dictionary, also to
Henry Taylor, my youngest son, constitution of the Asaite re-
formed church, the 2nd Vol. Brown Dictionary, my house Bible
and Psalm Books, I will to Hugh Taylor, the 1st Vol. of Brown
Dictionary, also my stock of cows and hogs to be sold and e-
qually divided among my children.

Witness.   Henry Taylor, Sen. (seal).
William Kidd.
Samuel N. Sloan.
Know all men by these presents, that I, Henry Taylor, Jr. do
bind myself and my heirs to the performance of the above ob-
ligations required by the Testator. Witness my hand and seal
this 6th Nov. 1845.

Henry Taylor, Jr. (seal).
Proved and admitted to record at August Term 1847.

(319)   I, AMBROSE TIMMINS, of the County of Lincoln, in the
State of Tennessee, do make and publish this as my last will
and testament.

First, I direct that my funeral expenses and all my Just
debts be paid as soon after my death as possible out of any
money that I may die possessed of or may first come into the
hands of my executors.

Second, I give and bequeath to my beloved wife Nancy the
Seven Small tracts of Land on which I now live, containing in
all two hundred and fifty acres, during her natural life. I
also give to my said wife in like manner, my two Slaves, Ned
and his wife, Sally, all my household & kitchen furniture, and
whatever Stock and farming tools she may think proper to select and retain, and also a Sufficiency of provision for their
Support for one year.

Third, I give and bequeath to my Son John, the Seven Small
tracts of Land bequeathed to my wife during her natural life, to
be taken possession of by him at my wife's death, which Land
lies about two miles west of Fayetteville, on both Sides of the
road Leading to Pulaski.

Fourth, I have heretofore given to my Son William, money
and other property which I designed shall be his portion of my
Estate.

Fifth, I have hereunto given to my daughter Mary Caldwell
a negro Girl named Polly, and a horse & saddle which I design
shall be her share of my Estate.

Sixth, I have given to my daughter Martha Ann Buchanan, a
Negro Girl named Celia, and a Horse & Saddle, a cow and calf,

(319) and feather Bed and furniture which I design shall be her portion of my Estate.

(320)   Seventh, I give and bequeath to my daughter Elizabeth, a negro Girl named Margaret, a horse to be worth not Less than fifty dollars.

Eighth, I have heretofore in various ways, and at divers times, Given and advanced to my daughter Abigail, wife of Isaac Tumey, what I designed shall be her portion of my Estate.

Ninth, I give and bequeath to my son Charles W. a negro boy named Mitten.

Tenth, I give and bequeath to my son Thomas, a negro Girl named Martha.

Eleventh, I direct that after my death, such effects as I may die possessed of and shall not particularly have been bequeathed, shall be sold at public Sale to the highest bidder, on a credit of Twelve months, and after the death of my wife, I direct that all the residue of my property be Sold in like manner by my Representatives.

Twelfth, Out of the proceeds of the Sales above directed, I give and bequeath to my three grandchildren, Ambrose T. Nancy & Rebecca Ann Tumey, the children of my daughter, Amanda Tumey and Jacob B. Tumey, the Sum of --- hundred Dollars, to be equally divided among them, should that Sum be derived from said Sales, if not then whatever Sum may be derived therefrom, unless the Same should amount to more than five hundred Dollars. Should Said Sales produce more than five hundred dollars, then I direct that the residue be equally divided among all my children or their heirs.

Lastly, I do hereby nominate and appoint my executors. In witness whereof I do to this my will set my hand and seal, this twenty Second day of January in the year of our Lord, one Thousand, Eight hundred & fifty-five, proved.

                                      Ambrose Timmins, (seal)

(321) Signed, Sealed & published in our presence and we have Subscribed our names hereunto as witnesses in the presence & at the request of the Testator, This 22nd day of January 1845.
B.W.D.Carty.
W. Bonner.
R.E.Neild.
J.Clarke Jr.

I, AMBROSE TIMMINS, have heretofore made and published my Last will and testament, as above, do make and declare this as a codicil thereto (to wit) my will and desire is that my wife Nancy retain possession of all my Slaves during her natural life, all my crop & Stock.

Secondly, I will and direct that part of the Land given to my Son, John , being 64 acres purchased of Alfred Smith, to
(321) my son Charles provided he pay Isaac Tumey & his wife Abigail, the Sum of Three hundred Dollars, and provided also that if he ever Sells the Same, be given the refusal of the Same to my sons John or William.

Thirdly, I give my son Thomas my Slaves, Ned & Sally, at my wife's death.

Fourthly, I give to my son William, twenty acres of Land, off the west end of the forty acres I purchased of John Greer,

(321) at my wife's death.

    Fifthly, If anything be left of the proceeds of the Sale in my will directed, after paying Jacob B. Tumey's children, the five hundred dollars I have given them, I direct that the Same be given to them and be divided among my daughter, Abigail Tumey and her children.

    Lastly, it is my desire that this Codicil be attached to and constitute a part of my will, to all intents and purposes.
(322) This 22nd day of August 1847.

    Attest.   Ambrose Timmons, (seal).

B. W. D. Carty.

W. Bonner.

J. V. McKinney.

    I, SALLY RHEA, of the County of Lincoln and State of Tennessee, knowing the uncertainty of this mortal life, and the Certainty of death, do make and declare the following to be my Last will and Testament, never having made any other or former will.

    First, it is my will that after my decease, that my body be buried in a plain & Christian like manner.

    Second, It is my will that my Just debts, if any, then be paid, and my funeral expenses be paid out of my estate, as soon after my decease as possible.

    Third, it is my will that after my death, my negro woman Kizzy and her two children, to wit, Tilda and Alfred, be sold upon a credit of Twelve months, taking good and Sufficient Security for the purchase money out of the proceeds of which sale I give to my Daughter Sally Ann Broyles and the heirs of her body, one Third, to my daughter Susan M. McLaughlin and the heirs of her body, one third, and to my Grand daughter, Frances, S. E. Smith, one Third. It is further my will that my negro boy John be sold at the same time, and upon the Same terms out of the proceeds of which I give and bequeath to my daughter Mary B. Smith & the heirs of her body, fifty dollars, To Attaman Isom & the heirs of her body, forty Dollars. To Rufus Smith, my Grand Son twenty*five dollars. I also give and bequeath to my Grand Daughter Frances S.E. Smith, my feather bed, with the Last bedstead I purchased with my two newest cov-
(323) erlets, my bed blankets with two Demity Counterpins, one broken with cords, three sheets and two new quilts. I also give to her one of my new corded Table cloths, also a Large white figured one that I purchased, I also give to her four Ewes of the best of my Stock, with their Lambs, if they should have them. I also give to my said Grand daughter Frances S.E. Smith my cow known as Motty Fan, also my Largest heifer, also my young horse. I also give to her ten of my best hogs, also the Sow that I purchased of Mrs. Guiden, with her eight pigs. I also Give to her a Small Table, also a Bureau that was her mothers, at her death, also a candle Stand. I give to my daughter Attamisa Isom, two of my Sheep Ewes, with their Lambs. I give to my son Brice M. G. Rhea four sheep, the balance of my sheep to be equally divided between my daughters Susan M. McLaughlin & Sally Ann Broyles. I give to my son Brice M. G. Rhea, a Bed, bedstead,

(323) and furniture, I give and bequeath unto my daughter Attamira Isom, my feather Bed, Bedstead & furniture, that I usually occupy, I also give her my dining table, I give and bequeath to my daughter Susan M. McLaughlin, one bed, bedstead and furniture. I give and bequeath unto my son Pleasant V. Rhea, a feather Bed, bedstead and furniture, or the proceeds, if he should prefer its being Sold. I give to Son-in-Law, Jacob Broyles and Susan M. Mc Laughlin, the Balance of my hogs, to be equally divided between them.. I also give to my Son-in-Law Jacob Broyles and Susan M. McLaughlin, my two work Oxen, also the Balance of my Cattle Except one unbroken Steer which I give to my Son, W.B. Rhea. I also Give to my son William B. Rhea, my largest kettle. I also give to my daughter-in-law, Nancy Rhea, thirty

(324) Dollars. I give and bequeath to my son-in-Law, Jacob Broyles, my Largest mule, I direct that my other two mules be sold & the proceeds to be equally divided between my daughters,Polly & Susan. I also give to my daughter Susan my Sideboard and p ress. I give to my daughter Sally Ann Broyles my Largest oven. I also give to my Daughters Sally Ann and Susan M. my Brass Kettle & tea kettle, to be divided between them as they may see proper. I give and bequeath to my daughter Sally Ann and my Grand daughter Frances S. E. Smith, my Stock of Geese and Ducks, to be equally divided between them. I desire that my clock, my writing desk, my farming tools,crop of wheat & Grainery crop shall be Sold and the proceeds applied first to incIose with a Substantial rock fence, the place where my husband and myself and others of my family may be buried, and the balance, if any, to be equally divided between my daughters, Susan, Sally Ann and my Grand Daughter Frances S. E. Smith.

I give and bequeath to my Son Pleasant V. Rhea, the amount of money arising from the Sale of the boy John, not herein before disposed of, Should my Grand daughter Frances S. E. Smith die without children living, at her death, it is my will that all the property herein before given to her, shall be equally divided between my daughters, Susan, Sally Ann and my Grandson, Rufus A. Smith. I give and bequeath the property of every description herein before Given, to my daughters,Susan, Sally Ann, Atemiraand Polly B. & to my Grand daughter Frances E. Smith, to my Son William B. Rhea upon Trust that he will

(325) Lend out the Same from time to time, and appropriate the interest to the use and support of my Said daughter and Granddaughter, respectfully, to whom Said Legacies are bequeathed and Should Said Trustee think the ease and comfort of my Said daughters and Grand-daughters would be promoted by having possession of any part of the propery bequeathed therein except the money, he is at Liberty to let them have possession of the Same, at the death of my Said daughters & GrandDaughter.

I desire that the legacies bequeathed to them respectfully, shall be equally divided among their children, respectfully. My Said Grand-daughter after She arrives at the age of twentyone years, and my said daughters are to be at liberty at any time they think proper to receive from Said Trustee, the whole or any part of their Said Legacies upon giving to Said Trustee receipts therefor,in the presence of, and attested by two

(325) witnesses. I do constitute and appoint my Son-in-Law,Jacob
Broyles executor of this my Last will and Testament, Witness
my hand & Seal this 13th day of June 1844. her
Attest.   Sarah x Rhea.
Corms. Norman.   mark
James Fuller. Proved by Fuller at Sept. Term 1847, and ad-
mitted to Record.

(326)   In the name of God Amen. I, JOSHUA EWING, of the County
of Lincoln and State of Tennessee, being of Sound mind and perfect memory, blessed be God, do this 29th June 1842, make and
publish this my last will and Testament, that is to say:
        1st, I give and bequeath my Soul to God who made it, and
my body to be buried in Christian like manner, without any
pomp or parade.
        2nd, I give unto my living wife,Mary Ewing, during her
natural life,one-fourth part of the Land that I now live on including all my present buildings, and after her death,to my son
Joshua Calvin.
        3rd, I give unto my sons, Samuel and William Donate, a
tract of Land that I purchased of Berry T. Parr, and an entry
joining it, exclusive of any minerals on Said tract of Land,
which if discovered, and any profits arise therefrom, I wish to
be equally divided between my sons Samuel & William Donate.
        4th, I give unto my Daughter Elinor, a tract of Land that
I bought of Asa Cross White, also another tract of Land that I
bought of Berry T. Parr,joining it both containing Eighty-two
acres.
        5th, I give unto my Son Robert, one-fourth part of the
Land that I am now living on, which is to be taken off at the
South Side, including the lieses that I give to Golightly and
Gibbs.
        6th, I give unto my sons, John and James Porter the other
half of the Land that I am now living on, to be equally divided
between them.
        7th, I give unto my daughter Eliza and Jane as much money
as the property was worth that I give to my daughter Eleanor,
which Sum of money to be made of the profits arising from the
(327)farm and land that I now have and in possession of,until my
heirs become of age, if there be any above family, Support and
discharge of debt, if not I want an equal part to be taken
from all the other Shares to make the above Sums of money for
my daughters Eliza and Jane.
        8th, I nominate and appoint my sons Samuel Ewing and
Robert Ewing, executors of this my Last will and testament,if
they can manage the Estate, agreeable to all the heirs, if not
I want them to choose three disinterested men to make the division consistantly, in witness whereof I have hereunto Set my
hand and Seal the day and date above mentioned.
Test   Joshua Ewing. (seal)
Zebulon Parr.
John M. Ewing. Proved Sept. Term 1847.

(327)   Lincoln County, State of Tennessee. In the name of God Amen. I, MOSES STONE, being in a low State of health and knowing that it is appointed for man to die, do make this my Last will and Testament, revoking all others made by me heretofore.

Item 1st, My wish and desire is that all of my just debts shall be paid out of my perishable property.

2nd, My wish and desire is that my wife Peggy Stone, shall keep all my estate, both real and personal, in quiet possession, during her natural life or widowhood, and to have the Sole management of the Same, and at her death or marriage, for it to be equally divided between all my children, namely John Stone, Peggy Stone, James A, Stone, Parthena Stone, Calvin Stone, Emily J. Stone, Marinda Stone, Moses F. Stone, and Emily J. Brown, daughter of Maltilda Brown, Deceased, and to her surviving husband Jesse Brown I bequeath one twenty-five cents. And to Isaac Williams who married my daughter Rebecca, now deceased, I also bequeath one twenty-five cents. As witness whereof I have hereunto Set my hand and Seal, this 29th June, one thousand Eight hundred and fifty one. A. D. her

Test.   Moses x Stone, (seal)

James Kyzer.   mark

James A. Stone. Recorded 14th Oct. 1847.

(328)   I, JOHN CRAWFORD, of the County of Lincoln, in the State of Tennessee, being in good health and of Sound mind and memory, do make & publish this my last will and testament, hereby revoking and making void all other wills by me at any time made (To wit):

First, I bequeath my Soul unto Almighty God who gave it.

Secondly, I direct that at my death that my farm and all that pertains to it, my dwelling house, and in general all my property, except Such as shall be otherwisw disposed of, shall pass unto the hands of my wife, Elizabeth, to be by her possessed and enjoyed during the time of her natural life, it is my will and desire that the farm and plantation shall be managed and directed by her, with the assistance of my two sons, John and Ezekial, who shall share in the crops and produce of the farm in proportion to their assistance they render in the same manner as they may have done during my lifetime. I further direct that in order to enable them to carry on the farm, there shall be retained for that purpose all my household and kitchen furniture, & cooking utensils of every description, all my farming tools, my wagon and two yoke of Oxen, four choice head of horses, four milch cows & calves, an average to of thirty head of hogs, an average Lot of Twenty head of sheep, one Set of Blacksmith Tools and one years Supply of every kind of provision, as meat, corn, fodder NC.

Item- I give and bequeath to my said wife Elizabeth, for and during the Term of her natural life, my three negro women, Hannah, Harriet and Peggy, with all their increase, my two men, Nelson and Jack, provided they can be managed on the farm, but if they become un-manageable I direct my executor to Sell them & apply the proceeds to the purchase of other farm hands to Supply the place of the Said Nelson & Jack.

Thirdly, I give and bequeath to my son Ezekial a horse, & to my daughters Emily & Martha Lucinda, a horse & Saddle each,

(328) provided they shall not have already received the Same from me before my death.

Fourthly, I direct the whole of my personal property, and effects remaining after the reservation and bequests Specified in the Second and Third Section above, shall be sold by my executors in the manner prescribed by Law, to the best bidder, on a credit of Twelve months, with good Security, and I direct them to collect all debts due me, as Speedily as possible, and out of the proceeds arising from Such Sales and collections, I direct them to pay my funeral expenses and all my Just debts, and Legal Liabilities, and after all these payments shall have been made, if any balance remain I direct such balance to be equally divided between my wife Elizabeth and the Seven children in Tennessee, viz, Nancy, John, Elizabeth, Margaret, Ezekial, Emily and Martha Lucinda.

(329) Fifthly, Should it so happen that my Sons John and Ezekial or either of them Should not think proper to Comply with the arrangement Stated above in regard to the management of the farm or should they not be able to keep it all in cultivation, in such case I direct my executors to rent to good tenants, Such portion as shall thus be rejected, so as to keep the Land in order & the Farm in repair proceeds, however my wife shall always retain during her natural life, one-third of all the Land and also the dwelling house, and all the other articles reserved to her use in the Sound Article Aforesaid.

Sixthly, At the death of wife Elizabeth, I give and bequeath to my sons John and Ezekial three hundred and two acres of Land on the North Side of my farm, being part of my Original purchase of three hundred and twelve acres, and also one hundred and forty acres of woodland on the North Side of a hilly Tract purchased of McCamels Estate, the whole to be divided into two equal shares, one for each, so that each shall have one-half of the available, and each one-half of the timber land, the remaining portion of all my lands together with the negroes above bequeathed to my Said wife during her lifetime and all o other property of every description remaining after her death,

(330) shall be sold in the manner prescribed by Law and the proceeds after paying the necessary expenses and lawful debts of the Estate shall be divided among the heirs to be hereafter named, in the manner following (viz) It is my desire to give to each of my children as nearly as may be an equal share, but as I have above devised to John & Ezekial to each, one-third of my Landed property I think they ought not to receive any more and I therefore direct them to be left out of receiving any share in this division, also some of my older children in Arkansas, & Some in Tennessee, have from time to time received various Sums as follows, viz, Hay, (or his heirs, $809. Wm. D. $927.00 James, $434.75 Naomi $367.00 Eleanor $403. Rachel $228. Nancy, $228. Andrew A. $317.50 Mary $270. Margaret $162. Elizabeth, $192. which amounts are charged to them.

Severally, in my book of acct. now in making the division aforesaid, I direct that the amount which each child has hitherto received or shall have received Before my death shall be rated & considered as part of his or her share of the proceeds of the Estate, and Share be so accounted for at the time of the

(330) division, so that each one of all my children, excepting only John and Ezekiel, for the reason above given, shall receive an equal share of the proceeds of the estate, but should it so happen that any one of the older children shall be found to have already received more than an equitable share, he shall not be required to refund or pay back anything, only he shall not receive any more on this principal. I direct the proceeds of my estate after the death of my wife, reserving to John and Ezekiel two thirds of the Land only, to be equally and equitably divided among my following named children, viz, Hays heirs, William D. James, Naomi, Elinor, Nancy, Andrew A. Mary Ann, Margaret, Elizabeth, Emily and Martha Lucinda and Rachel.

Lastly, I do hereby nominate and appoint the following persons to wit: Alexander McDonald, of Fayetteville, William

(331) F. Kercharal, Esquire, of Fayetteville and my son John Crawford, executors to carry out the intentions of this my Last will and Testament. In witness whereof I have hereunto Set my hand and Seal this Tenth day of January in the year of our Lord, Eighteen hundred and forty Six.

John Crawford, (seal).

Signed and Sealed in presence of the undersigned witnesses, the day and year above written.
Test.
R. C. Marcel.
A. S. Boone.   Admitted to Record at Oct. Term 1847.

John Armstrong's Last Will & Testament.   Lincoln County, Tennessee, Know all men by these presents, that I, JOHN ARMSTRONG, of the before named County and State, have this day bargained and conveyed to my Son Josiah R. Armstrong all of my Estate, real or personal that is to say, one hundred and forty acres of Land, it being the tract whereon I now live, together with all my Stock of Horses, Cattle, hogs, sheep, household and kitchen furniture, farming utensils, Blacksmith tools and wagon makers tools, and all notes and accounts that is coming to me for the consideration, that is to Say:

1st, About Eighty five dollars which I now owe him.

2nd, that he the Said Josiah R. Armstrong pay all my Just debts.

3rd, And that he provide for the Support and Comfort of his mother during her natural life, and also to Support and raise my four Grand children, that is to say; John Wesley Armstrong, Jasper Newton Armstrong, George Higgins and Sarah Jane Armstrong, this conveyance to have effect before and after my death, and to be recorded and Registered after my death, as witness my

(332) hand and Seal this 24th day of December 1846.

Witness.   John Armstrong, (seal).
Jas. D. Cole.
L. L. Cole.
J. L. Cole.   Proved and admitted to Record Nov. 1847.

I, JESSE NEES, of the County of Lincoln and State of Tennessee, do make, ordain and publish this as my Last will and Testament hereby revoking and making void all other wills by

(332) me at any time heretofore made.

And first, I direct that all my debts and funeral expenses be paid as soon after my decease as possible, out of any money that may come into the hands of my executors.

Secondly, I give and bequeath unto my beloved wife. Sarah Jane Nees, during her natural life or widowhood, all my estate, both real and personal, So that she may be enabled to raise and educate our children, and as each of our children may come of age, my desire is that She may at her option give to each Such portion as she may think right, and such portion to be charged by my executors to each.

Thirdly, I direct that after the death of my wife, all my estate both real and personal property be sold, the personal property on a credit of twelve months, and my lands on a credit of one, two and three years, and the amount of money arising from such sale, equally divided between all my children, taking into account what each may have had, and if my wife (333) should marry again, my will is that my property be sold as above directed, and all my Estate equally divided between my wife and all my children.

And fourthly, I request and direct that as soon after my decease as convenient, my Executors proceed to Sell such of my personal property on a credit of twelve months as they and my wife may consider un-necessary for her to keep on hand.

And Lastly, I do hereby nominate and appoint Joel Ness and Dempsey Sullivan, Executors of this my will. In witness whereof I do to this my will Set my hand and Seal this 30th day of October 1847.

Jesse Nees, (seal).

Signed, sealed and published in our presence, this 30th day of October 1847.
Attest.
W. G. Commans.
Samuel Brown.

I, SARAH SHAW, of the County of Lincoln and State of Tennessee, do make, ordain and publish this my last will and testament, being of sound mind and disposing memory.

Item 1st, It is my will that after my death that my body be interred in a plain or Christian manner.

2nd, It is my will that my Just debts and funeral Expenses be paid out of any money that I may die possessed of or may first come into the hands of my Executors.

3rd, I give and bequeath unto my Grand children Jesse B. John M. Sally Thomas, Hugh G. Robert F. Mary Ann, Margaret E. (334) and Hannah Shaws, heirs of my son John J. Shaws', heirs of my Son John J. Shaw, a certain tract of Land settled in the County of Lincoln, Tennessee, in the waters of Coldwater Creek the butt and bounds of which is minutely described in a deed Executed by Joab Heiflin, to me dated the 28th day of Nov.1846 & is of record in the Registers Office of Lincoln County, being the same tract of Land on which the said John J; Shaw now lives, to have and to hold the same to the above named heirs of John J. Shaw forever, against the Lawful claims of all persons, whatever. It is my will that my said son John J. Shaw Remain upon

(334) the above tract of Land with his Family without paying rent, and Support them thereon until his youngest child, to wit, Hannah Shaw, shall arrive at twenty-one years of age, at that time it is my will that my executors expose the said tract of Land to public Sale, on a credit of one & two years, & the proceeds be equally divided between my said Grand children, the heirs of John J. Shaw, in the event my said son John J. Shaw, should become dissatisfied with being on said Land & move off it before the said Hannah Shaw shall arrive at the age of twenty-one years, then it is my will that my executors proceed to sell the said Land on the credits above mentioned, and the proceeds to be applied to the Support & Education of said Grandchildren, heirs of John J. Shaw so far as they extend.

4th, I Bequeath to my Son Hugh Shaw above described tract (335) of Land in trust for my said Grand Children the heirs of John J. Shaw, who will according to the directions Laid down in this my will.

5th, I give to my son Hugh Shaw, my Blacksmith Tools and clock.

6th, I give to my son Hugh Shaw & Samuel Watson, Jointly, my clay bank mare called Tebb.

7th, I give my son Hugh Shaw one Feather Bed and furniture, also my Bee Stands & sheep.

8th, I give my cupboard to my daughter-in-law Dicy Shaw.

9th, I give to my Grand daughter Elizabeth Watson, my Bureau.

10th, I give to my Grand daughter Mary Jane Shaw my cupboard ware.

11th I give to Samuel Watson my dining table.

12th I Give to Samuel Watson one feather bed & furniture.

13th, I give to Mary Jane Shaw one feather Bed & furniture.

14th, I give to my son Hugh Shaw in trust for my Granddaughter Margaret E. Shaw my sorrel filly, now in the possession of John J. Shaw which my said trustee may let remain to aid in support of his family.

15th, I give to my Grand daughter Margaret L. Shaw my Loom.

16th, I give to my Grand daughter Mary Jane Shaw, choice of my milk cows & calf, also my saddle, also my oven & Hooks.

17th, I give to my daughter Peggy Watson, my Large Pot, also my Largest Pair of dog-irons, also my copper ware of every description.

18th, I give to my bound Girl, Mary Holman, one milk cow & calf, also my little Pot and skillet.

19th, I give to Hugh Shaw, my Largest wash Kettle, also my smallest dog Irons.

20th, I give to my son John J. Shaw, one Pot Rack.

(336) 21st, I give to Samuel Watson my steelyyard.

22nd, I give to my daughter-in-law Decy Shaw my spice moter.

23rd, I give to my daughter Peggy Watson my Large Jar.

24th, I give to Hugh Shaw my Potrack, also the remainder of my stock of cattle.

25th, I give to my Grand son William M. Shaw, the residue of my personal property of every description.

I hereby nominate my son Hugh M. Shaw my sole Executor, of

(336) this my last will and testament, & In testimony thereof I have set my hand this 20th day of October 1847.   her
Test.   Sarah x Shaw.
W. B. Rhea.   mark
Isaac J. Holman.
Proved and admitted to Record December, 1847.

In the name of God Amen. I, JAMES MARTIN, of Lincoln County, and State of Tennessee, do make and ordain this my will and testament. My will is that Nathan Pryors' wife, Elizabeth Pryor and her heirs shall have my home house Tract of land containing houses of all descriptions, with sixty-five acres attached, also fifty acres lying west of said tract afore mentioned, and also another tract of land lying North of Pryors land, called (Napes) tract, containing twenty-five acres. Also I give to Elizabeth Pryor & heirs two negroes by the name of Sam and Tom.

I will and request that my son John H. Martin shall have one hundred & thirty-three acres of land, lying south of this tract I now live on, and also twenty-five acres of land lying on the East side of Dukes Creek attached to this my home house place, and I further give to my son John H. Martin, a certain negro girl by the name of Liz. I also give to my son John H. Martin one road wagon, to him and his heirs forever.

(337)   I now give to my Daughter Susan Jane Robertson, one negro girl commonly called Babs. I also give her a fine bedstead with the bed & furniture, this my last will and Testament, made and attested the twenty third day of January in the year of our Lord, Eighteen hundred & forty-seven. In witness I have hereto set my hand.
Test.   James Martin.
Henry P. Womach.
James Cunningham.

I, ALANSON SHERRELL, do make and publish this as my last will and Testament.

First, I direct that my funeral expenses and all my debts be paid as soon after my death as possible out of any money that I may die possessed of or may come into the hands of my executors.

Secondly, I direct that my Beloved wife hold all the property belonging to my Estate during her widowhood, and if she shall marry, I further direct that she shall have one third of my Estate and I further direct that my two children shall be well educated.

Fourthly, and I do further direct that Joseph L. Sherrell, David S. Patterson, and my beloved wife be my executors, to this my last will and testament. In witness whereof I have hereunto set my hand and seal this 8th day of March 1848.
                                         A. A. Sherrell.(seal)
Acknowledged in the presence of us.
Joshua D. Brown.
John Maddox. Proved April Term 1848.

(338) I, JOHN MCKINNEY, do make and publish this as my last will and testament, hereby revoking all wills heretofore made by me.

First, I give to my son Ethelson McKinney, my horse, saddle, bridle, rifle, Gun and all the money that he now owes me, and I further direct that when my two younger sons shall become of the age of twenty-one years, that my said Elder Son Ethelson McKinney shall have one hundred and fifty Dollars more out of my estate, and I do further direct that the land now belonging to me, lying adjoining the Lands of Gannett Merrell and others, containing twenty-five acres, and also one other tract of Land Containing fifty acres adjoining the land of John Watkins and others, shall be sold to the highest bidder, when the said younger sons shall become of age, and out of the proceeds arising from the sale of said land, the said Ethelson McKinney is to have the said sum of one hundred and fifty dollars, and the balance of the proceeds of the land to be divided between the two youngest Sons, Reuben and Henry McKinney, and I do further direct also that my two younger sons shall have my bed and bedstead and furniture, and all my household and kitchen furniture, and all my working and farming utensils of every description. And I do further direct that shall either of my two younger sons, viz, Henry or Reuben McKinney die before they become of age, that his part of my estate shall be divided between Ethelson and the other younger son, and should it so happen that both the younger sons should die before they become of age that Ethelson McKinney shall have all that belong to my Estate. And I do further direct that my son Ethelson McKinney shall be the executor to this my Last will and testament. In witness whereof I have hereunto set my hand and seal this 21st day of April 1848.

Attest.
J. D. Brown
Joshua G.W. McDonell.

his
John x McKinney, (seal).
mark

(339) In the name of God Amen. I, WILLIAM BIRMINGHAM, being sound in mind, but Low in health, do hereby make this my last will and testament, hereby revoking all others. I do will and bequeath my property to my children, both Real and personal as follows (to wit):

1st, I desire all my Just debts paid. I Give and bequeath unto my son Berry Birmingham and his heirs, one negro boy Henry, and one bed and furniture, and no more.

I give and bequeath unto my daughter Amanda Jane Birmingham and her heirs forever, one negro boy, Frann, one bed and furniture and ten dollars worth of property, and one horse called Paddy, and no more to her.

It being my wish and desire for Berry Birmingham to furnish said Amanda Jane Birmingham with a negro Girl worth as much as said boy Frann, and he is hereby authorized to do so, and be her Guardian.

I give and bequeath to my three Sons Caswell Birmingham, Caleb Westley Birmingham and William Birmingham, one good horse, one bed and furniture and ten Dollars worth of property Each.

(339) To my son John Birmingham, Ten dollars worth of property.

I give unto my daughter Sarah Cox twenty dollars worth of property.

I do further give and bequeath unto my Seven children and their heirs forever, to wit: Curtis Birmingham, James M. Birmingham, John Birmingham, Sarah Cox, Caswell Birmingham, Caleb Wesley Birmingham and William Birmingham, to have each of them an Equal Share of all my land and the balance of my (340) personal property, and I do also appoint my two sons, Curtis Birmingham and Berry Birmingham, Executors to this my last will and testament, whereof I have hereunto Set my hand and seal this 22nd day of May, in the year of our Lord 1848. In the presence of God and these witnesses.   his
Test.   William x Birmingham, (seal).
A. J. Higgins.   mark
Thos. J. Anderson.
Ethelson McKinney.
Proved & admitted to Record August Term 1848.

I, JAMES FROST, do make and publish this as my last will and testament, hereby revoking and making void all former wills by me made.

First, I direct that all my Burial expenses, and all my J Just debts be paid as Soon after my death as possible, out of any money that I may die possessed of or may first come into the hands of my executors.

Second, I give and bequeath to my Sons William C. Frost, and John B. Frost, the tract of Land upon which I now live, containing about 150 acres, being all the Land I now own, to be equally divided between them.

Thirdly, I give to each of my granddaughters, Samantha and Sarah Cobble, twenty Dollars to be paid by my sons William C. and John B. Frost, out of the Land I give them, as the Girls above named become of age.

Fourth, I desire that the remainder of my property be Sold on the usual credits and the proceeds together with all the Balance of my Estate, I give to my daughter Lucinda Stephens.

Fifth, As a reason why I omit my daughter Barbara Jones (341) I consider that her Husband, Bell Jones has heretofore had an amount equal to what my daughter Lucinda Stephens will receive. In a certain lot off corn, and a parcel of whiskey, and my Interest in the season of a Slattun.

Lastly, I do hereby appoint William Tolly, my executor. In witness whereof I do to this my will Set my hand and seal, this 7th day of August 1847.
                                        James Frost, (seal)
Signed, Sealed and published in our presence, and we have Subscribed our names in the presence of the Testator, this 8th day of Sept. 1847.
Felix Davis.
James R. Wright.
Approved & Recorded at September Term 1848.

(341)   William William's Last Will. I, WILLIAM WILLIAMS, do
make & publish this as my last will and testament, hereby revoking all other wills by me made. And being desirous that
all my property should be disposed of according to my wishes.

First, it is my will and desire that all my just debts &
funeral expenses should be paid.

Secondly, I will & bequeath to my wife Louisa Williams,
should have during her lifetime or widowhood, the Smith tract
of land, containing Seventy-five acres, and the dwelling house
& lots where I now live, some five or six acres. It is my
will that my wife shall have one beast, two cows and choice
Heifers, one sow & shoats & pork hogs for one years provision
for her & children, corn & the wheat after paying Ann Isoms
what is owing, coffee & salt I wish allowed for one year for

(342) my wife and children, all the household & kitchen furniture I
wish to remain for the benefit of my wife & children, namely,
Margaret Ann, Mary Ann, Barton, Susan Delony, Peomelia Jonson,
William Edward, Thomas Stephenson, Samuel Jefferson, John
Clark. It is also my wish and desire that my Executors make
sale of all the balance of my property not disposed of as soon
after my death as practicable. It is my will that my executor
sell all my lands not named in my will as soon after my death
as will be convenient, on a credit of one & two years, taking
bond with two approved securities and a lien retained on the
land to secure the purchase money, after giving twenty days
notice of the time & place of sale. And after all my debts are
paid I wish the remainder to be divided equally between the a-
bove named children and my wife Louisa Williams.

Lastly, I do appoint Williams Stephens & Eli L. Hodge my
Executors to this my last will, this the second day of October
1848.   his
Test.   William x Williams,(seal)
A. M. Allred.   mark
James Smith.
Proven by the subscribing witnesses & ordered to be recorded
by Lincoln County Court at November term 1848.
Recorded 22nd, November 1848.

          William Griffis Last Will. I, WILLIAM GRIFFIS, of Lincoln
County in the State of Tennessee, being advanced in age & of
feeble & precarious health, but of Sound & disposing mind, do
make, publish and declare my last will & testament as follows:
(343)   First, It is my desire that as soon after my death as
practicable, my Executors pay all my debts and funeral expenses
out of the first money that shall come to their hands.

Second, I give and bequeath to my daughter Lucinda B.
Booker during her life, and at her death, to her children, then
living, and the children of such of her children as shall have
died leaving children, the child or children of such deceased
child, representing their deceased parent my four negro slaves
Mariah, Jack, George and Andrew, together with their increase.

Third, I give & bequeath to my son William A. Griffis, my
negro boy slave Hugh B. and one note for five hundred dollars
executed to me by Reuben A. McDonald and due the twenty fifth

(343) day of December 1848. Also one other note this day executed
to me by said Reuben A. McDonald for seven hundred and fifty
dollars due & payable on the twenty fifth day of December 1850,
to each of said notes, William McElroy is joint maker with
said Reuben A. McDonald as security.

Fourth, I give and bequeath to my grand-son John W. Wendell,
one note executed to me by Reuben A. McDonald & William McElroy
for five hundred dollars due & payable on the twenty fifth day
of December 1847.

Fifth, I give and bequeath to my grand-son Alfred James
Henderson Windell, one note executed to me by Reuben A.
McDonald & William McElroy for five hundred dollars due & pay-
able on the twenty fifth day of December 1849.

Sixth, I give and bequeath to my daughter-in-law Martha
Griffis, for and during her life, my negro girl slave Emily, now
in the possession of Said Martha Griffis, and at the death of
said Martha Griffis I give and bequeath the said girl Emily to
my son William A. Griffis together with her increase.

(344)   Seventh, It is my will and desire that my negro woman
slave Caroline at my death be emancipated and set free by my
Executors.

Eighth, & last, I hereby nominate and appoint Thomas R.
Griffis Executor of this my last will and testament.

In witness whereof I have hereunto subscribed my name and
affixed my seal this 11th day of November A.D. 1846.
                              Wm. Griffis, (seal).
The above named WILLIAM GRIFFIS, with whom we are personally
acquainted, did this day in our presence subscribe his name and
affix his seal to the foregoing, and also in our presence publish and declare the same to be his last will and testament, and
we have at his request, and in presence of each other subscribed
our names to the same as witnesses thereto, the day and date
above written.
G. W. Jones.
R. A. McDonald.
J. B. Clements.
Proved & admitted to Record at November term 1848 of Lincoln
County Court.

Samuel Tate's last Will. The last will and testament of
SAMUEL TATE, of Lincoln County & State of Tennessee. I, SAMUEL
TATE, considering the uncertainty of this mortal life and being
of Sound mind and memory do make and publish this my last will
and testament in manner and form following, (that is to say):

First, as soon as possible after my decease that all my
(345) just debts and funeral expenses be paid.

I give and bequeath unto my beloved wife Mary J. Tate all
my real and personal property for to be at her disposal for
the benefit of her and the children during her lifetime or
widowhood.

I give and bequeath unto my second son James L. Tate, one
bay mare.

I give and bequeath unto my third son Andrew B. Tate one
brown filly, and I will and bequeath that my youngest son
Robert J. Tate have a horse or fifty dollars.

(345)   And unto my five daughters, Lavina G. Tate, Tirza A.Tate, Agness J. Tate, Sarah M. Tate, Mary K. E. Tate, I will and bequeath each,one horse or fifty dollars.

My eldest son William V. Tate I will and bequeath that he have the money that his mare was sold for.

And lastly, I appoint my beloved wife Mary J. Tate and my oldest son William V. Tate as sole Executrix of this my last will and testament.

In witness whereof I have hereunto Set my hand and seal the twelfth day of October in the year of our Lord,one thousand Eight hundred and forty eight.   his
                        Samuel x Tate, (seal).
                        mark
Witnessed on the day signed & acknowledged his mark on the ---
J. V. McKinney.
John J. Tate.

(346)   The State of Tennessee, Lincoln County, Dec. 5th,1845. This my last will and testament. I bequeath to my wife,Sarah, all of my Loose property until her death which consists of, Horses, hogs, cattle, household and kitchen furniture and implements, and goods, unless they should leave by marriage, then She may help them to their proportionable part whenever such one of the seven children now living with us shall (viz) Polly, Catharine, Elizabeth, Darthueto, Samuel C. Matilda A. Daralee J. and at her death there shall be an equal Division of all my Goods and Chattles.

I also bequeath my land to my wife, her lifetime, then for it to be sold and the money to be equally divided and shared between Samuel C. and above named Six Girls, which my Executors will attend to in accordance to the above will and testament, and which I set my hand and seal, the day and date above named.
Test.   John x Strong, (seal).
Lemuel C. Mead.
John N. Sullinger. Admitted to Record, Dec. 4th, 1848.

(347)   I, ALEXANDER WILEY, being in a very low State of health, but of sound mind and perfect memory, and knowing that it is appointed unto all men once to die, do make and publish this my Last will and Testament, hereby revoking and making void all former wills by me at any time made.

First, I direct that my funeral Expenses and all my Just debts be paid as soon after my death as possible put of any money that I may die seized of or may first come into the hands of my executors.

Secondly, I give and bequeath to my beloved wife Margaret the plantation on which I now live, together with the tract of school Land lying west of where I now live, to be hers,during her natural life or widowhood. I also give to my said wife, four hundred dollars in money, and my Roan mare, together with all my household and kitchen furniture, plantation tools, and Stock of every kind, except such Items as may be hereafter disposed of to other heirs, to be hers during her natural life or widowhood, as specified in the first Item.

Thirdly, I give and bequeath to my daughter Jane, my childrens plantation of one hundred and Eighty-one acres, and four

(347) hundred dollars in money, also my bay Horse Coleman, with
saddle and bridle, and two good feather Beds and furniture.

Fourthly, I give and bequeath to my son Lewis B. Wiley,
one quarter Section of Land in Tishamingo County,Mississippi,
known as the Southeast Quarter of Section Seven in Township,
two of Range Eight East of the Bases Maredian according to the
plan of the survey of the Chickasaw Session,containing one hun-
(348)dred and sixty acres. Also Three hundred and fifty Dollars in
money, and further in the case of my son Lewis, whereas he is
charged in my Book with five hundred and seventy Dollars,which
I paid for his Tuition at College,I direct that he shall not be
required to pay the same or any part thereof to my Estate.

Fifthly, I give and bequeath to my son Milton H. Wiley,my
meek plantation containing fifty-two acres together with all
the Lands willed to my wife, to be his at her death or marriage,
also three hundred dollars in money, and my Sorrel horse,Peter,
saddle and Bridle. I also direct that so Long as my son Milton
lives with his mother, and cultivates the farm, after paying
all necessary expenses and what will be sufficient to support
the family, he shall have the benefit of the over-plus.

I also direct that so long as sister Nancy Wiley sees
proper to live with the family that she shall be treated with
respect and supported as firmly, and Lastly, I do nominate and
appoint my son Lewis B. Wiley, sole executor of this my last
will and Testament, in witness whereof I have hereunto set my
hand and affixed my seal, this fourth day of December 1848.

Alexander Wiley, (seal).
Signed, Sealed and published in our presence, and we have
signed our names in the presence, and at the request of the
Testator.
Wit.
Robert Drennon.
James Wiley. Admitted to Record,February Term 1849.

(349)   In the name of God Amen. I, JAMES ELLIS, of Lincoln
County, State of Tennessee, being of Sound mind and memory,
but calling to mind the uncertainty of human life,do make and
ordain this my last will and testament.

In the first place, I give and bequeath to my wife Dolly
Ellis, all my real and personal Estate during her lifetime,
after paying all my Just debts and funeral expenses &C, with
the exceptions of the fifty acre tract of Land now occupied by
my daughter-in-Law, Judy Ellis, and that fifty-acre tract of
Land I give and bequeath to my said daughter-in-Law,Judy Ellis,
during her lifetime or widowhood.

In the next place I give and bequeath to my Grand-daughter
Arena Ellis, after the death of my wife, my negro Girl,Peggy,
and my negro boy Thorn, after paying to her Sister Narcissa,and
Polly each, fifty dollars, to belong to her and her children
born of her body. I give and bequeath to my grand-daughter,
Narcissa Ellis and her children,born of her body, my negro
Girl Lucy, after the death of my wife. I give and bequeath to
my Grand-daughter Polly Ellis and her children, born of her
body, my negro Girl Chaney, after the death of my wife. I give
and bequeath to my daughter-in-Law Judy Ellis, during her

(349) lifetime or widowhood, my negro Girl Sookey, and at her death
or marriage. I give and bequeath to my Grand-son William Ellis,
the said negro Girl Sookey, and her off-spring, and I give and
bequeath to my said grand-son William Ellis, all my Land, after
the death of my wife, he paying to his sisters Narcissa and
Polly Ellis, one hundred dollars each.

(350)   After the death of my wife, I wish my negro woman Rachael
to be free, and have home in my land, during her lifetime, and
to have a cow and calf, and a hog or two, and I wish my grandson William Ellis, to have the care of her, and see that she
does not suffer. And the residue, if any, of my estate, after
defraying all necessary expenses, I direct that it be equally
divided amongst my said grand-children, except my rifle gun,
which I give to my Grand-son William Ellis.
     In witness whereof I have hereunto set my hand and seal.
this Sixteenth day of August, in the year of our Lord,
one thousand, Eight hundred and forty-five.   his
Test.   James x Ellis.
Andrew Buchanan.   mark
White Buchanan.

     I, JAMES ELLIS, make the following Codicil to the fore-
going will. I give and bequeath to my Grand-son William Ellis,
one bed, bedstead and furhiture, and one Trunk, and I also direct that after my death he shall have one years provision for
himself and mother, laid off out of such crop as may be in the
premises, by two disinterested persons. Witness my hand and
seal, this sixth day of August 1848.   his
Test.   James x Ellis, (seal).
Andrew Buchanan.   mark
Admitted to Record Feby, 1849.

(351)   I, THOMAS L. D. PARKES, of the County of Lincoln County,
and State of Tennessee, now living in District NO.1, being at
this time in good health and perfectly in my right mind, and
knowing I have once to die, do hereby make this my last will
and Testament.
     I wish my wife to remain on and have possession of the
whole of my two tracts of Land (J.E.) the tract known by the
name of the Hamilton tract, and the mill tract, also to have
Oney and Crener, Jeff & George, also Isaac, my smith, to do
with and manage so Long as She lives, also as much of the
household Stuff as she wants, then to be sold and Equally divided among my children.
     The balance of my lands, negroes & other property all
sold on a twelve months credit, and if the proceeds are not
Sufficient, I then wish the Mill tract to be sold and my debts
all paid, and if any then over paying all Expenses from the
first Sale, I wish it equally divided among my Lawful heirs,
and I wish the Same of the Mill tract should have to be sold,
as witness my hand and Seal this 25th day of Dec. 1845.
                                        Thos. L. D. Parkes.
N.B. My son Wm. hath had about two hundred Dollars which I
wish to come out of his part, also my Daughter Ann hath had
about two hundred Dollars, which I wish to come out of her part.

(351) Since the above was written, my daughter Ann. hath had about
Eighty Dollars more which is to come out of her part, now I
wish this matter distinctly understood. I acknowledged this
for the purpose within contained in presence of --
this 23rd day of January 1846.
Att.   Thos. L. D. Parkes.
G.W.S.Hart.
Zedaach Motlow

(352) (J.E.) On account of three letters written By A.M.Dean and directed to me, and the same being, as I consider as Insulting
as he the same A.M.Dean, was capable of writing, therefore my
Intention for writing these lines is to prevent him from ever
having the liberty of handling any more of my earnings, and for
this purpose I wish the Balance of Ann's equal part, if any there
be, to be placed in the Shelbyville Bank or some other Insti-
tution which may be considered safe, and to remain so during the
natural lifetime of the said A.M.Dean, and after his death to
be handed over to Ann, if living, to do as she pleases with, and
if she is not living, then to her children, if any living, and if
not, then to her Brothers and Sisters Equally. as many of them
as are still living, these matters I wish my Executor to attend
to without fail, January the 8th 1848, this my Codicil to my
will. I hereby give and bequeath my Boy Anderson to William A.
Parkes, my son, and I also give and bequeath to Eliza Parkes, my
wife, all the Balance of my Estate to have and to hold after
payment of all my debts, during her natural life or widowhood,
and to dispose of at her death as she thinks proper, and I
further appoint Martin L. Parkes, my son, Guardian for Ann
Dean, to hold and attend to her portion of my Estate, and I
further appoint Eliza Parkes, my wife, and William A. Parkes,
my son, my executors to the within.
Test.   Thos. L. D. Parkes.
Abbam Sittiff.
F. S. Mayfield. Proved, admitted to Record Feby, 1848.

(353)   State of Tennessee, Lincoln County, January the 26th, 1847.
In as much as it is appointed for all men once to die, I, JOHN
SMITH, of the County and State aforesaid, do make this my last
will and Testa, emt. In the name of Almighty God Amen, which
is as follows (viz):
          1st, No person shall administer on my little Estate.
          2nd, I bequeath to my wife Nancy Smith & my three young-
est sons, namely, Benjamin Chiles, Thomas Jefferson and
Napolean Polk Smith, to have and to hold in full possession,
One thirty acre tract of Land on which I now reside, and the
improvements thereof, also one other tract of Land, containing
forty-four acres more or less, entered by me and David Howell,
which Lands my three sons, above named, and my wife Nancy, to
have and to hold in full possession with all the appertances
thereunto, during her lifetime or widowhood, provided Nancy
Smith, my wife, should marry again, the above described Lands
and improvements are no Longer to remain in her possession, but
the above named three sons are to have and to hold in full
possession. the above described Land, with all the appertances

(353) thereto until the youngest one Napolean Polk Smith is twenty-one years of age.

3rd, The above named four Nancy, my wife, Benjamin C. Thomas J. and Napolean P. Smith are to have and to hold, my wagon and Oxen, Stock, hohs and my two mares, one cow and calf, and my stock of sheep.

Item 4- The Balance of my perishable property together with my working tools are to be sold on a credit of Twelve months to the highest Bidder, the farming tools.excepted.

5th, My daughter Elizabeth Delana is to have equal rights and privileges with my wife and three sons in above Land,property &C. during the time she remains single.

6th The tract of Land on which my son Joshua now resides, is for his benefit with all the improvements he may make in it, on the McColloch tract, on the fifty acre tract in barnes until my youngest son Napolean P. Smith becomes of age.

7th My three tracts of Land, viz, two in the state of Georgia, and one in Tennessee are subject to the improvements of any on all of my Lawful heirs to have and to hold until my youngest son bewcmes od age, at which time if my wife Nancy

(354) Smith is not Living, the whole of my Estate is to be equally divided among all my heirs, if they can make the division and agree, if not the whole of my Estate shall be sold and the proceeds arising therefrom to be equally divided between my Lawful heirs.

8th, The proceeds arising therefrom the sale of the perishable property and my tools shall go to defray the expenses of the execution of this will, and to pay my Just debts.

9th I do appoint my two sons John N. and William Smith. Lawful executors to execute the above written will.

In testimony whereof I have hereunto set my hand and seal, in presence of,
William W. Parkes.

    his   John Smith, (seal).
Allen x McColloch.
    mark

(355)   The State of Tennessee, Lincoln County. In the name of God Amen. Knowing that it is appoimted unto all men to die, a and being somewhat weak in body, but of sound mind and memory, I, LEWIS BLEDSOE, of said State and County, do make, publish, constitute and ordain this my last will and Testament,hereby revoking all others. When it pleases God to take me out of this life, I desire to be buried in a decent and Christian like manner, and recommend my soul to that God who gave it,and as to my worldly effects I dispose of as follows:

First, I desire the payments of all my Just debts.

Second, I give unto my Grand-son James Pinckney Bledsoe, when he arrives to the age of Twenty-one years, the Sum of fifty dollars.

Third, I give unto my great Grand-daughter and child of my Grand-daughter Mary Ann Burford, whose bame I do not know, the sum of Ten dollars, when she arrives at the age of Twenty-one years.

Fourth, I give unto my beloved wife Fanney Bledsoe, during her natural life, the entire tract of Land whereon I now

(355) reside, with the condition that my two daughters Drucillah J. Bledsoe and Sarah Ann Bledsoe, and my son James H. Bledsoe, live in the dwelling house with her, and have their support out of said tract of Land as long as they remain unmarried, free of any charge.

Fifth, I give unto my beloved Son Harvey M. Bledsoe, a young negro man by the name of George now in his possession.

Sixth, I give unto my beloved Son Stephen W·J.Bledsoe, a young negro man, now in his possession, by the name of Bob.

Seventh, I give unto my beloved Son James H.Bledsoe, a young negro man by the name of Terrel.

(356)   Eight, I give unto my beloved daughter Mary M. Bledsoe, a negro Girl now in her possession, by the name of Louisa.

Ninth, I give unto my beloved daughter Drucilla J. Bledsoe, a negro Girl by the name of Hannah, a good Cow and Calf, a horse to be worth Sixty Dollars, and a bed and furniture to be worth Thirty Dollars.

Tenth, I give unto my beloved daughter Sarah Ann Bledsoe, a negro Girl by the name of Lucy, a good Cow and Calf, a Horse to be worth Sixty Dollars, and a bed and furniture to be worth Thirty Dollars.

Eleventh, The remaining part of my negro property with such a selection of my Stock of Horses, Cattle, hogs and sheep, farming utensils, household & kitchen furniture, not herein-before devised. I give unto my beloved wife Fanny Bledsoe, during her natural life, and at her death or before, if she may think proper, the same by her to be divided out amongst my said Six children, namely, Harvey M. Bledsoe, Stephens W.J. Bledsoe, James H. Bledsoe, Mary M. Burford, Drusillah J. Bledsoe and Sarah Ann Bledsoe.

Twelfth, After the death of my said wife, Fanney Bledsoe, and after the marriage or death of my two Single daughters, namely, Drusillah J Bledsoe and Sarah Ann Bledsoe, I give unto my beloved Son James H. Bledsoe, the entire tract of Land whereupon I now reside, to have and to hold the same for his own proper use and behalf forever, and a bed and furniture worth Thirty Dollars.

Thirteenth, All of said property hereinbefore devised to my said three daughters, I give unto them and their lawful
(357) heirs of their Bodies, and not be subject to sale by their husbands when married, nor subject to the payment of any of their husbands' debts, but to be possessed by my said three daughters, and for their own proper use and behoof, and for the benefit of them and their families, if they have or may have any.

Lastly, I do hereby nominate and appoint my three sons, Harvey M. Bledsoe, Stephens W.J.Bledsoe and James H. Bledsoe, my executors, to this my Last will and Testament. In witness hereof I hereunto set my hand and seal this Tenth day of May, in the year of our Lord, one thousand Eight hundred& forty-Eight. Interlined on the second page of this will above the twenty-fifth line in the word proper= before the singing and sealing of the same.   her
                    Lewis x Bledsoe, (seal).
                        mark

(357) Signed, sealed, published and subscribed to in our presence, and that we subscribed our names hereto as witnesses in the presence of the Testator, and in the presence of each other. Tenth day of May 1848. Interlined the word May, in two places before signed.
Test.
Thos. J. Anderson.
W. E. Simms. Proved April Term 1849 & admitted to Record.

(358)   In the name of the Almighty God Amen. I, HENRY SNOW, Senr. of the County of Lincoln and State of Tennessee, being in a weak state of health, but of a sound and perfect mind and memory, and knowing that it is appointed once for all men to die, do make and ordain this my last will and testament.
     I, first and principally of all, do give and recommend my soul into the hand of the Almighty God that gave it, and my body I recommend to the earth to be buried in a decent Christian burial, at the descretion of my Executor or Executors and my friends.
     Secondly, I give and dispose of my temporal and worldy estate, in the following manner, viz: I first give and bequeath unto my beloved wife Anna Snow, all the land or parcel of land belonging to me, whereon I am now living on, being all the real estate that I am in possession of, during her natural life, and after her death to belong to my son Henry Snow, to be his, right and title free from any incumbrance of anyof my other children, or any other person or persons whatsoever &C. As my son Henry Snow has paid his two brothers viz, namely, William Snow and Daniel Snow, a full valuation for their part of the said land, now belonging to me during my lifetime, and his mothers also, and after our death the land or parcel of land to be the right and title of all the above named land to belong to my son Henry Snow. And also I have made a deed for the said land to him, that he might have a deed to show after I am dead and gone to eternity, as well as my last will and testament.
     Thirdly, I do also give and bequeath unto my beloved wife, Anna Snow all my household and kitchen furniture of every sort whatsoever, and after her death to be equally divided between my two daughters, Catharine Braden and Alchy Braden, and I also give and bequeath to my beloved Anna Snow three head of cattle and their increase, and after her death to be divided between my two daughters, namely Catharine Braden and Alchy Braden and to the heirs of their bodies, also it is my desire
(359) after my death to have all my stock of hogs and all my farming utensils and my mare, after leaving a reserved Colt, all to be sold and the proceeds equally divided between my six oldest daughters, namely, Rebecca, Honer, Nancy, Mary, Elizabeth and Margaret at my death, and to apply within three years after my death, the money if not applied for within three years time, then the money to be equally divided between my two youngest daughters aforesaid named, Catharine Graden & Alchy Braden, and to the heirs of their bodies, if there should be after my death any sort of grain, such as corn, wheat and oats &C, or any bacon than will support my wife Anna Snow, and it is my desire for it to be sold and the money to be divided between my two

(359) daughters, Catharine Braden & Alchy Braden, and the heirs of their bodies, and lastly, I ordain and constitute and appoint my son Henry Snow to be my Executor fo this my last will and testament, in witness whereof I have hereunto set my hand and seal this 26th day of April A.D. 1844.

Witnesses.   his
Jŏhnathan Tripp.   Henry x Snow, (seal).
J. Waggoner.   mark

Codicil. Whereas since the foregoing will was written I have become very frail and infirm in body, and a great measure unable to attend to my domestic concerns, and in consequence of the care and attention which my son Henry has paid to me in waiting and taking care of me, my will and desire is that the bequest made to my six daughters living in the State of North Carolina, namely, Rebecca, Honer, Nancy, Mary, Elizabeth & Margaret, descend and go to my son, Henry instead of them, which I think is little compensation enough for the attention he has paid me, in testimony I have hereunto set my hand and affixed my seal, this July 20th 1847. Signed and acknowledged in presence of us.   his

Witnesses.
James W. Holeman.   Henry x Snow, (seal)
W. B. Flack.   mark
James M. Spencer. Proved the 7th May 1849.

(360)   I, THOMAS GRANT, do make and publish this my last will and testament, hereby revoking and making void all other wills by me at any time made.

First, I direct that my funeral expenses, and all my debts be paid as soon after my death as possible, out of any money that I may die possessed of or may first come into the hands of my Executors.

Secondly, I give and bequeath to my beloved wife Frances Grant, my tract of Land that I now live on, and as much of my other property as my executor may think Sufficient to support her and her Children, to wit: Elizabeth Mary Jane Grant, George Harrison Grant, Charlotte Catherine Grant, & Virginia Frances Grant, during my said wife Frances' lifetime or widowhood, at which time it is my will that it should be equally divided between my above named Children.

Thirdly, I direct that all the rest of my property be sold under the direction of my Executor, and the proceeds applied to educating my above named Children.

Lastly, I do hereby nominate and appoint C. W. McGuire, my Executor, in witness whereof I do to this my will set my hand and seal, this 19th day of May 1843. his

                    Thomas x Grant, (seal).
                    mark

Signed, Sealed and published in our presence, and we have subscribed our names hereunto, in the presence of the testator, the date above written.
Josiah McCracken.
Joseph McCoy x his mark.

(361)   I, JANE BUCHANAN, do make and publish as my last will and
Testament, hereby revoking and making void all other wills by
me at any time made.
     First, I direct that my funeral expenses and all my debts
be paid as soon after my death as possible out of any money
that I may die possessed of or may first come into the hands
of my executors.
     Secondly, I give and bequeath all my undivided Interest
in my Father, Robert Buchanan, Dec'd, Estate, both real and
personal, consisting of Land, Negroes and money, also all manner of property that I may be in possession of, at the time of
my death, to my Brother Milton Buchanan. I do hereby nominate
and appoint Andrew Buchanan My Executor. In witness whereof
I do ti this my will set my hand and seal this April 27th 1849.
                         Mary Jane Buchanan, (seal).
Signed, sealed and published in our presence and we have subscribed our names hereto in the presence of the testator.
Howell Harris Jr.
Henry Clift.
Albert G. Gibson. June 4th 1849, Admitted to Record.

(362)   In the name of God Amen. I, JOHN BEATY, of Lincoln
County, Tennessee, being sick and weak of body, but of sound
mind and disposing memory, for which I praise and thank the
Almighty Dispensor of blessings, and being conscious of the
uncertainty of Human life and desirous of disposing of all
such worldly substance as it has pleased God to bless me with,
do make and publish this as my Last will and Testament,hereby
revoking and making void all other wills by me at any time
made.
     First I direct that my funeral expenses and all my debts
be paid as soon after my death as possible, out of any money
that I may die possessed of or that may first come into the
hands of my executor.
     Second, To my wife Joana Beaty, I give and bequeath in-
stead of Dower, Such portion of my Household and Kitchen furniture as she may think proper to take, in addition to one-
tenth part of all my other property and affects, as hereinafter Specified.
     Thirdly, I direct that all my remaining property of what-
ever description, including my Land on Cane Creek, Lincoln
County, Tennessee, and all money now on hand, now due or to
become due to me and not otherwise appropriated, as above, shall
be Subject to be divided into ten equal portions, whereof that
of my nine children, William B. Beaty, Martha who inter-married
with Thomas McClellen, Robert, David M.,John, Sarah, Andrew J.
Josiah and Jane, each shall have one of said portions for his
or her sole use and behoof forever.
     Fourthly, I direct that a majority of my Legatees may de-
termine the mode of dividing my thus devised Estate, whether
(363) by Sale or otherwise, but in the event that a majority of them
decide in a division of the Land by survey, then it is my will
and desire that my said wife shall have the portion of the Land
which shall include my dwelling and adjoining out-houses, if

(363) She so chooses.

Fifthly, Whereas some of my children have heretofore received from me either money or property, and it being my aim to do impartial Justice to all of them, I further direct that all of those who have received anything shall account for the same on a final settlement in such manner that no one of my children, except my oldest Son William B. Beaty shall receive or shall have received a greater portion than any one other of my children. And as regards my oldest son above named, taking into Consideration that he has at my request and desire remained with me during several years since his arrival at the age of Twenty-one, and that through that time he has managed my worldly concerns, It is my will and desire that he shall receive a full tenth part of all my clear estate independently of the Berry tract of Land, and of anything else which he has heretofore received.

Lastly, I do hereby nominate and appoint my son William B. Beaty and my son-in-Law, Thomas McClellen my executor. In witness whereof I do to this my Last will and Testament set my hand and seal this 9th day of August 1840.

John Beaty, (seal)

Signed, Sealed and published in our presence, and we do subscribe our names hereto in the presence of the testator, this 9th day of August 1840.
Isaac Southworth.
G. M. C. Edmondson.

(364)   Codicil. I, JOHN BEATY, the foregoing testator being in good health and of sound and disposing memory, for which I continue my thanks to God, am desirous in consequence of the death of my beloved wife Joana, and my dear daughter Sarah, to make this Codicil to the foregoing will.

Firstly, I declare that it is yet my intention to do impartial Justice to all of my children, and that it is my will that the principals of the above testament be carried out.

Secondly, To the end that this be done I direct that such of my children as survive me or Legal representatives shall divide all of my estate and effects among them equally, and that the distributor shall determine upon the method of so doing as heretofore provided in the above will.

Lastly, I hereby confirm all the other provisions of said will and still desire that Wm. B. Beaty and Thomas McClellen, will act as my executors. In witness whereof I do to this Codicil set my hand and seal, this 12th day of December 1841.

John Beaty, (seal).

Signed, sealed and published in our presence, and we do subscribe our names hereto in the presence of the Testator, this 12th day of December 1841.
Isaac Southworth.
Thomas B. Eastland.

(365)   I, JESSE STILES, do make and publish this as my last will and testament, hereby revoking and making void all other wills by me at any tome made.

First, I direct that my funeral expenses and all my debts

(365) be paid as soon after my death as possible, out of any money that I may die possessed of or may first come into the hands of my executor.

    Second, I give and bequeath to Samuel Stiles' children, now born, and those that may be born hereafter, legal heirs to said Samuel Stiles, the tract of land on which I have lived last before my death, and my negro girl Amanda.

    Thirdly, I direct that the balance of my effects should be equally divided amongst my lawful heirs-at-law.

    Fourthly, I direct that before Said division is made, my Father and Mother's grave should be nicely covered with a rock wall at my expense.

    Fifthly, I do hereby nominate and appoint W.M.Newman and Samuel Stiles, my executors. In witness whereof I do to this my will set my hand and seal,this 20th day of September 1849.

his
Jesse x Stiles.
mark

Signed, Sealed and published in our presence, and we the testator this the 20th September 1849.
W. H. McLaughlin.
Daniel McPhail.
James P. Lankerton. Proven at the County Court of Lincoln County, at October Term 1849, and ordered to be recorded.

(366)   I, John V. McKinney, of the County of Lincoln,State of Tennessee, do make and publish this my last will and Testament.

    It is my will that my son Rane McKinney take immediate charge of all my property of every description, real & personal, and money if there should happen to be any, and dispose of it to the best advantage, in payment of my debts & for the support of the family. And it is my wish that my son Rane McKinney, carry on and keep up the Drug Store that I now have in this place, in my name, and with my means for at least five years. The profits to be applied to the payment of my debts and the support of my wife, my daughters, Mary and Martha and John. And it is my will that my son Rane be compensated for his trouble, with any amount he thinks right- I know that he will do what is right and proper. If my negroes can be kept,they are to remain in possession of my wife during her life,for her use and support- and I earnestly hope that every honorable exertion will be used by Son Rane to pay my debts without the Sale of what few blacks I am in possession of: but if it cannot be done, choose kind, human masters for them. The two oldest children of Auch's, I want to be given to my daughter Mary and Martha- Mary to have Sally and Martha, Mary Jane- They are not to take them in possession during my wife's life,without her consent, and Rane concurring therein. If there is any property that Rane may think proper to sell after my death, I prefer that he sell it privately, I have but little, and do not want that little or any part thereof exposed for public Sale to the highest bidder, I repeat it, let that part of my property that my executor deem it necessary to sell, be sold by him privately, to the best advantage. And I hereby appoint my son Rane McKinney Executor to this my last will and Testament,

(366) and it is my will that he act as such without giving any Security. I have full confidence in him, consequently no one
else need require that he give security.

After the death of my wife and my family Circle is brok-
en, if there is anything in the hand of my son Rane belonging
to my estate, I want him to divide equal with my children or
their heirs, as the case may be. My Silver Watch I gave to
my Son John, & my double-barreled Shot gun & Rifle to my Son,
(367) Rane. My Children all are equally dear to me, I have but little,if any property to give them, but I leave them my love and
pray that they may all be brought to a knowledge of the truth
as it is Christ Jesus, and follow peace with all men, and Hol-
iness, without which no man shall see the Lord- Believe on the
Lord Jesus as our only Savior as the way, the truth and the life,
obey him in all things and we have the glorious promise of e-
ternal happiness in the world to come.

In testimony to the above will & Testament I have hereunto
set my hand and affixed my seal,the date above written.
Test.   J. V. McKinney.
Robert R. McKinney/
Charles McKinney.

I, JOHN V. MCKINNEY, do make this Codicil to my last will
and testament, and desire that the same may be taken as part
thereof.

I desire that the drugs, medicines &C, in my drug store
be Sold by my executors at private Sale,if practicable, for
payment of my debts, but that no more drugs be purchased by
them for the purpose of continuing the business, but that the
same be wound up as soon as practicable.

I also desire my executors, or such of them as may qualify
under this will, to sell the Store-house where my drugs are together with the ground attached thereto, for payments of my
debts,on a credit of one,or two years. If practicable I desire
the house & premises where I reside to be kept for the residence of my family, but if my debts cannot be otherwise paid,
I direct that such house & premises be sold by such of my executors as may qualify under this will, upon Such Credit as
they may think proper,and the proceeds applied to the payment
of my debts.

By my will I have given two slaves to my daughters,Mary &
Martha, I give and bequeath a small negro girl named Taylor,to
my daughter Tabehha, & the balance of my Slaves I desire shall
be equally divided between my three children Rane, Eliza &
John. Should the Slaves thus bequeathed to my three last named
(368) children, be of more value than those given to my three first
named daughters, as above Stated, my executors are directed to
cause Rane, Eliza & John to constitute the amount sufficient
to make the division of the Slaves equal.

If for the payments of my debts it becomes necessary to
dispose of any part of my slaves, I desire that those bequeathed
to my children Rane, Eliza & John, should be first sold by my
executors, and that then if necessary, the Slaves bequeathed to
my daughter Tabetha & Martha should be sold by my executors and
last of all & only should it be necessary to pay my debts,my

(368) executors will sell the Slaves bequeathed to my daughter Mary. It is my desire that all my other property should be exhausted for payment of my debts before my Slaves are sold.

I appoint my sons Rane & John, & my Relation, Robert R. McKinney, executors of my will, & desire such of them as may qualify under this will to sell all my land in the State of Mississippi, to pay my debts. In witness of all which I have hereunto set my hand & seal, this 1st of August 1849.

Test.   John V. McKinney, (seal)
Charles McKinney.
Rich White.
James Fulton.   Admitted to Recoed of the County Court of Lincoln County, at October Term 1849.

Henry Kelso. Clerk.

(369)   I, HARVEY ALLBRIGHT, being in a very low State of Health, but of Sound mind and Perfect memory, do make and publish this my last will and Testament, hereby Revoking all former wills by me at any time made.

First, I direct that my Funeral Expenses and all my Just Debts be paid as soon after my death as possible, out of any money that [1] may die Seized of, or may firstcome into the hands of my executors.

Second, I Give and bequeath unto my Mother Margaret All-bright all my Real and Personal Estate of Every description, both Land and other Property, to be at her Control and management during her natural Life.

And third, I do hereby nominate and appoint Robert Drennan sole Executor of this my last will and Testament. in witness whereof I have hereunto set my hand and seal this 1st day of October 1849.   his
                Harvey x Allbright, (seal).
                     mark
Signed, sealed and published in our Presence, and we have signed our names as witnesses in the presence. and at the Request of the Testator.
James E. English.
Simpson Abbot.

I, HARVEY ALLBRIGHT, having heretofore made and published my last will and Testament, do make and direct this as a Codicil thereto. I direct that in Case my personal property should fail to pay my debts, [1] do hereby Authorize and direct my Executors to sell such part or all my Real Estate for said purpose, and any over-plus of said sale to pay over to my mother Margaret Allbright, this 2nd day of Oct. 1849.
                          Harvey Allbright, (seal).
The above Codicil signed, sealed in our presence, and we Subscribed our names in the presence, and at the Request of the Testator.
Simpson Abbot.
Alexander Allbright.

(370)   The last will and Testament of MOSES HARDIN Sr. of the State of Tennessee, Lincoln County. I, MOSES HARDIN, considering the uncertainty of this mortal life, and being of sound mind and memory, do make and publish this my last will and Testament in manner and form following:

1st, I give and bequeath unto my beloved wife Orpah Hardin, my Plantation and four Negroes vix; Eady, Sarah, Mandy and Harry, her natural lifetime.

2nd, At the death of my wife, I order that my land shall be sold and the proceeds equally divided Between Salina I. Carrigan, Wiley K. Hardin, Moses L. Hardin Jr. & Benjamin W.D. Hardin.

3rd, After my death I give and Bequeath to my son Moses L. Hardin, one negro Boy, Andy.

4th, After my death aforesaid, I bequeath to my son Benjamin W. D. Hardin, one negro Boy Tom.

5th, At the death of my wife I give and bequeath to my son Moses L. Hardin, one negro woman and child,Sarah & Mandy, and their increase, if any.

6th, At the death of my wife, I give and bequeath to my Son Benjamin W.D. Hardin, one negro woman Eady and her increase if any.

7th, I give and bequeath to Alfred W; Hardin heirs, one hundred Dollars, to be equally divided at the death of my wife.

8th, I give and bequeath to Stanford H. Hardin heirs, One hundred Dollars, to be divided equally at the death of my wife.

9th, After the death of my wife, all the goods and Chattles of every description to be sold and two hundred Dollars to be appropriated to the heirs of Alfred W. Hardin and Stanford H. Hardin, and the balance, if any, to be equally divided between Salina I. Carrigan and her heirs, Wiley K. Hardin, Moses L. Hardin and Benjamin W.D. Hardin.

10th, At the death of my wife, I give and bequeath to Saline I. Carrigan and her heirs one negro man named Harry. In witness whereof, I have hereunto set my hand and seal, this 12th of May 1849.

Test.   Moses Hardin, (seal).
Woodruff Parks.
Thomas M. Wilson.

(371)   April the 3rd day 1833. I set down knowing that it is appointed for man to die, to state my wish respecting of my worldly affairs, and to state my wish in respect of what the Lord has blessed me with.

Item the first, it is my wish that all my Just Debts to be paid, and as all my children is all of age, and left me, but my Daughter Nancy, it is my desire that they should be satisfied with what I have given them, and if my wife dies without a will it is my desire that my Daughter Nancy should have one hundred Dollars out of my Estate before it should be divided, and then have an equal share of the rest, but if my wife chooses to make a will, it is my desire that she shall give it as she chooses, for it is my desire that she shall have all of my Estate,after paying off my Debts, to do as she sees fitting, and I do appoint

(371) her as administrator of my Estate, and hope that the Court on-
to hold her to security, same giving under my hand and seal,
this 3rd day of April 1833.

Witnesses.   Thomas Dance, (seal).

Stephen M. Dance.

Louis Garner.

Thomas Dance.

Richard E. Bennett. At Court held for Halifax County, the
25th day of November 1833.

    The within written Last will and testament of THOMAS DANCE,
dec'd, was exhibited in Court, and proved by the oath of one
of witnesses hereto subscribed and ordered to be Certified, and
at Another Court held for the said County the 23rd day of Dec.
in the year aforesaid, the said will was further proved by the
Oath of one other of the witnesses thereto subscribed, and ordered to be Recorded.

Test.

Samuel Williams, Clk.

(372)   And at another Court held for the xaid County the
25th day of August 1834. On the motion of Sarah Dance, the executrix therein named, in the last will and Testament of
THOMAS DANCE, Deceased, who made Oath thereto according to Law
and entered into bond in the Penalty of $1000. Conditioned as
the law directs, Certified is Granted here for obtaining probate of said will in Due form.

Test.

William Holt. A copy Test, Wm. Holt, Clk.

    I, PHILIP PHAGAN, of the County of Lincoln and State of
Tennessee, do make and publish this my last will and testament,
revoking all former wills and testaments heretofore made by me.

    1st, It is my request that my Executor and Executrix, here-
inafter named, shall pay all of my Just debts as soon as may be.

    2nd, I give and bequeath to my beloved wife Jane, fifty dol-
lars in Cash, my black mare and one cow and Calf, and all of my
corn and fodder.

    3rd, I give and bequeath to my Daughter Martha, the sum of
three dollars, added to the previously given to her for which
I hold a Receipt.

    4th I give and bequeath to my son John the sum of three
dollars, added to the Amount previously Given to him, for which
I hold his Receipt.

    5th, I give and bequeath to my Daughter Sarah, the sum of
three dollars, added to the Amount previously given for which
I hold her Receipt.

    6th, I give and bequeath to my Daughter Mary Dale, the
fifty acres tract of Land on which she now lives, Absolutely,
her paying to the Executor and Executrix, One hundred and fifty
dollars.

    7th, I give and bequeath to my Daughter Margaret, the sum
of three hundred and fifty dollars.

    8th, I give and bequeath to my Daughter Elizabeth, the sum
of One hundred and fifty dollars.

(373)   9th, I give and bequeath to my son Philip T. Phagan, the tract of land on which I now live, absolutely, his Paying to the above named Margaret and Elizabeth two hundred & fifty dollars, to be equally divided between them as a part of the above sums named, and bequeathed them in three years after this will is recorded, and two hundred, fifty dollars to the said Margaret and Elizabeth to be equally divided between them, also as part of the above sums named and bequeathed them to be paid within six years after the recording of this my will. Also I give to said Philip T. my Sorrel mare, my wagon, wheat Fan and all of my farming utensils. I also give and bequeath to loving wife, all of the balance of my stock of horses, cows. hogs, sheep, and household, kitchen furniture and all debts or money that maybe due me at my death, after paying off my Just debts, and the balance to Margaret and Elizabeth that I have named, and bequeathed over and above the sum of five hundred dollars, that my son Philip T. is to pay them and no security to be required of her, said Jane, my wife, for refunding of said property and money.

      I do hereby nominate and appoint my beloved wife Jane, and my son Philip T. Phagan, my Executors to this my last will and testament. Witness my hand and seal this 19th day of Nov' 1849.

Test.

Wm. Stephens/.

William D. Bright.

William Lay.

                                      his

                               Philip x Phagan, (seal)

                                  mark

(374)   I, MARTHA C. MCCONNELL, do hereby make and declare this to be my last will and testament, hereby revoking all other wills or parts of wills.

      Item the first, It is my will and desire that my son, Robert K. McConnell and my daughter Mary E. have the house and lot in which I now live, and do hereby give to the said Robert and Mary E. the said House and lot, each to have an equal share.

      It is my will and desire that all my household and kitchen furniture be divided between the said Robert and Mary, in equal Shares, with the exception of the bed on which I am now lying, & this one I desire to be given to my Servant Girl, Caroline, for kind attention to me in this my last Sickness. In the division of my household and kitchen furniture as aforesaid, it is my desire that the said Robert have my my hand Irons, and that the said Mary have my Largest Looking Glass.

      Item 2nd, I give unto my said son Robert, my Pony Horse.

      Item 3rd, It is my will and desire that the house and Lot in which John A. Waddle and my son-in-law H. C. Holaman now lives be sold to pay all my Just debts.

      Item fourth, I hereby nominate and appoint my son Robert K. McConnell and W. F. Kircharal my executors to this my Last will and Testament. In Testimony whereof I have hereunto set my hand this October 3rd, 1849.

                                 Martha C. McConnell.

Signed & published in our presence, 3rd Oct. 1849.

Joe Commans.

S. M. McElroy. Admitted to Record Dec. 1849.

(375)   I, RACHEL GRAY, of Lincoln County, Tennessee, being of sound mind, do make and order this my last will and testament.

First, I desire all my Just debts be paid.

2nd, I give and bequeath to my Daughter Frances Smith, wife of Francis Smith, the following property, One Bed and furniture & Bedstead. I want what money I may have after paying my Just debts & funeral expenses, to be equally divided amongst my Children. I appoint my friend John Goodrich, Executor to this my last will and Testament. Witness my hand and seal this 13th day of July A.D. 1846.

                            her

Test.   Rachel x Gray, (seal).

James Fulton.   mark

John T. Morgan.

We, Moses H. Bonner and Tunstall Gregory, do state that the nuncupative will of FENTON GREGORY, was made by him on the 5th day of August 1849, in our presence, to which we are specially required to bear witness by the Testator himself, in the presence of each other, that it was made in his last sickness in the house of his father, Tunstall Gregory, which was his own habitation or dwelling place, he never having been married and the same is as follows: to wit, It was his will and desire that his effects should be disposed of, after his decease in the following manner, that his brother and pardner, Brown Gregory, should retain possession of all and singular, his estate, real and personal of every kind whatsoever, until he shall have paid all the debts and liabilities of him, the said FENTON GREGORY, and after all his debts should be paid, It was his will and desire that the right and title to all the lands he owned in Lincoln County, Tennessee, be vested in his brother Brown Gregory and his heirs and assigns forever, in fee simple, the remainder of his effects or estate of every kind and de-

(376) scription whatever, he Decreed should be equally divided between all his other brothers and sisters, to wit: Sarah Eslick, Emily Gregory, Mary Parkes, Elizabeth McCartney, John F. Gregory, Ruth A. Gregory and Martha T. Gregory, said FENTON GREGORY died on the 14th day of August 1849. Made out by us, and signed this 23rd day of August 1849.

T. Gregory.

M. H. Bonner.

I, KATHERINE CARRIGER, do make and publish this as my last will and Testament, hereby revoking all other wills by me at any time made.

First, I direct that my funeral expenses and all my Just debts, if I should owe any, be paid as soon after my death as possible, out of any money I may die possessed of or that my Executor may have first come into his hands.

Secondly, I give and bequeath unto my daughter Elizabeth Martin, One dollar.

Thirdly, I give and bequeath to my Grandson Ido Carriger, one Feather Bed and furniture, which I have set apart for him.

Fourthly, I direct that my stock and other property be sold on a twelve months credit, except such as is hereby specially bequeathed, and the proceeds of such sale together with

(376) all money I may have on hand at the time of my death, or that may be due or owing to me in any way, to be equally divided between my said Grand-son Ido Carriger, and my Seven following named Children, (to wit), Margaret, Mardis, Leonard Carriger, Sarah Ingle, Mary Eaton, Cynthia Boone, Thomas J. Carriger and Christian Carriger, and lastly, I hereby nominate and appoint (377) Samuel Boone, my Executor. In witness whereof I do to this my will, set my hand and seal this 26th day of June 1849.

```
Test.                                               her
W. H. Bailey.                         Katharine x Carriger.
Joel Rees.                                          mark
```

    In the name of God Amen. I, HENRY BECK, of the County of Lincoln, and State of Tennessee, considering the uncertainty of this mortal life, and being of sound mind and memory, blessed be God for the same, do make and publish this my last will and Testament in manner and form following:

    First, I give and bequeath my Immortal Soul to God who gave it.

    Second, I direct my funeral expenses and just debts to be paid as soon, by my Executor as possible after my decease.

    Third, I give my Brother, Adam Beck, one hundred dollars, and to my Bro. Devault Beck, one hundred dollars.

    Fourth, I give to Abraham Barnes, Cherry, the negro girl he has living with him.

    Fifth, I give to Dr. John Wood, my negro boy named Lewis.

    Sixth, and lastly, as to all the rest, residue and remainder of my real and personal estate, lands, negroes, goods and chattles of what kind and nature soever, I give and bequeath the same to my beloved wife Louisa C. Beck forever, and I hereby appoint Abraham Barnes my executor of this my last will and Testa,emt, hereby revoking all former wills by me made. In witness whereof I have hereunto set my hand and seal this 17th day of April A. D. 1850.

                      Henry Beck. (seal).

Signed, sealed and delivered in presence of us.
William Wyatt.
Joshua Highes.

(378)   I, GEORGE GEE, a FREE Man of Colour, do make and publish this as my last will and Testament, hereby revoking and making void all other wills by me at any time made.

    First, I direct my funeral expenses and all my debts be paid as soon after my death as possible, out of any money that I may die possessed of or may first come into the hands of my Executor.

    Secondly, it is my wish and desire that my Executor, out of any money that may come into his hands, buy my two children Esther and Cynthia, provided they can be bought at anything like a fair price, my said two children Esther & Cynthia is now owned by Doctor William Bonner, if my Executor should buy my two children, then I want the balance of the money, if any on hand, to be equally divided amongst my other children. If my Executor should not be able to buy my two children as above, then and in that case I want all my money to be equally divided

(378) amongst all of my children, except my daughter Mary, who is
the youngest child by my first wife, I want her to have twenty-
five dollars more than the rest of my children, and if my two
children should be purchased by my Executor, I want in the
dividsion amongst the other children for my daughter Mary to
have twenty-five dollars more than the rest.

Thirdly, I want the Lot I owned in Fayetteville, and now
occupied as a Bake Shop, to be rented out by my Executor until
he can sell the same for Eight hundred dollars, whenever my
said Executor can do that I wish him to sell it and when the
money is collected for said lot, as above, I want it equally
divided amongst all of my children, except my two children,
Esther & Cynthia, as I consider that they will have an equal
share by the purshase of them, should however, my Executor not
be able to buy my two children as before mentioned, then, and
(379) in that case, I want them to have an equal share with the rest
of my children.

Lastly, I do hereby nominate and appoint John Goodrich,
My Executor. In witness whereof I do to this my will set my
hand and seal this 5th day of December 1845.   his

George x Gee,(seal).
mark

Signed, Sealed and published in our presence and we have sub-
scribed our names hereto in the presence of the Testator this
5th day of December 1845.
Thomas C. Goodrich.
D. W. Russell.
(There is a will on this Book at Later date proven at
July Term 1830, making this here void.)

Whereas, to wit: I, GEORGE GEE, a Freeman of colour,
made and published my will and Testament some months ago,which
will is now in the possession of one Elijah M. Ringo and cannot be readily got at or had, and whereas to wit, since the
making of said will I have purchased my son Wiley from James
Fulton, Robert Farguharson & R. A. McDonald at the price of
twelve hundred dollars, and have paid to said Fulton,Farguhar-
son & McDonald, seven hundred dollars, leaving a balance yet
unpaid of five hundred due the 25th Dec. 1849. Now my desire
and request is the following disposition may be made of my
property.

First, that my Real Estate in the Town of Fayetteville,be
sold by my Executor on such credit as they may think best.

Second, I want my Executors to pay the five hundred dollars yet unpaid for Wiley, wherein it becomes due.

Third, I want my Executors to purchase from Doct William
Bonner, my two youngest children Esther & Cynthia, provided
they can purchase them at a reasonable price.

Fourth, I want my executors to keep possession, and under
their care and control, my son Wiley until he makes and pays
back to my said Executors the sum of Eight hundred dollars,at
(380) which time the said Wiley is to be free. My desire and request
is that said Wiley and my two youngest children Esther &
Cynthia remain in the state of Tennessee, provided the Laws of
said State will allow and permit them to do so, if the Laws of

(380) Tennessee will not allow them to remain here. Then and in that case, I want them to be emancipated and move to Liberia.

Fourth, I want the balance of my property to be equally divided between the balance of my children named in the will now in possession of Elijah M. Ringo, as aforesaid, witness my hand and seal this 1st day of November 1848.

If Cynthia & Esther are not purchased, I want them to have an equal Interest with the rest of my children.

                          his
                  George x Gee, (seal).
                        mark

Signed, sealed and delivered in the presence of,
W. Bonner.
C. P. Beavers.

In the name of God Amen. I, JOHN MOORE, Senr. of Lincoln County & State of Tennessee, Calling to mind the mortality of the body that men must die, & being weak of Body, but of sound memory & Judgment, do make and constitute this my last will and Testament.

First of all, I give my soul to God, who gave it, in Hopes, of its Eternal well being through merits of a Crucified Savior, and my Body to be buried in decent manner, without pomp or unnecessary expense, and my worldly property I dispose of in the following manner, viz:

First of all I give & Bequeath unto my well Beloved wife Martha, her two beds & the furniture, to be hers & at her disposal at her death. Also I give and bequeath unto my son James McC. Moore, one bureau & Clock, also one Cupboard & furniture, also all my stock, sheep & likewise the tract or planta-

(381) tion of Land whereon I now Live, and bounded as follows: viz: Beginning at a hickory in the North boundary line of an original Tract, held Jointly Between myself and Brown Parkison, but now Divided. Running thence East 65 poles to a hickory, thence north twenty & a half poles to a stake, the south West Corner of A. M. Galloways land, thence east with his line sixty-Seven poles to a post Oak, then South forty-Eight & half poles, to a Black oak, thence west sixty-seven poles to a white oak, thence South eighteen poles to a stake, the North-west corner of said entry thence east sixty-seven poles to a Chestnut & Hickory, thence south twenty-three and half poles to a stake, thence West sixty-seven poles to a stake on the original line, thence South with said line twenty-three & one fourth poles, to three hickories, thence west sixty poles to a stake, thence North, ninety-two & half to the beginning, I likewise nominate & appoint my son James Mc. Moore, my executor of this my last will and Testament. All the balance of my property not mentioned in this my last will & Testament, I leave and bequeath unto my wife Martha, to be at her disposal as she pleaseth.

In witness whereunto I have set my hand & affixed my seal, this 15th day of March 1849.
In presence of us.   John Moore, (seal).
John M. McFerrin.
William G. Moore.

(382)   I, MARTHA LEATHERMAN, being of advanced age, though of
sound mind and memory, I do make and publish this as my last
will and Testament, hereby revoking and making void all other
wills by me at any time made.
          First, I direct that my funeral expenses, and all my debts
be paid as soon after my death as possible out of any money
that I may die possessed of or may first come into the hands of
my executor.
          Secondly, I give and bequeath unto my son George Reed,
Nancy Ann Wilson, wife of Andrew Wilson, and Mary Kennedy, wife
of John Kennedy, all of my property, real and personal, to be
equally Divided Among them three, with the exception of my
large Bible, and likeness, then I desire George to have extra,
also I give and bequeath Jonas Leatherman's likeness to Nancy
Wilson, wife of Boone.
          Last of all, I do hereby nominate and appoint George Reed
and Andrew Wilson my executors to this my last will, in witness
whereof I do to this my last will set my hand and seal this
5th day of August 1843.
                    Martha Leatherman, (seal).
Signed, sealed & published in our presence, and we have subscribed our names in presence of the Testator.
Test.
Boone Wilson.
David J. Hobbs.

(383)   Being weak in Body, but sound in mind. I make this my
last will and Testament, revoking all others.
          First, after paying all my Just Debts, I give and bequeath
unto my Beloved wife Sarah C. and Daughter Sarah E. L. Dismeeks,
the whole of my Estate, both real and personal, provided there
be no other Heir in a given time, say nine months. Should
Sarah C. my wife marry my desire is that the property shall remain as though it was in my possession, and Should Sarah E.L.
my Daughter live to be old enough to marry, and does marry, then
I wish an equal division of property of every description between them, and Sarah, my wife to have a guarantee of her proportion through her agent so long as she may live, and after
her death she can dispose of it as she may think proper, this
the 23rd of May 1846.
Test.   E. E. Dismeeks. (seal).
James D. Grisard.
Hiram Reese.
          I appoint my Trusty friend A. J. Carlass and William Lay,
Senr. my Executors, to the above will as written.
                              E.E.D.

          State of Tennessee, Lincoln County. In the name of God
Amen. I, ARCHER BEASLEY, being of sound mind and disposing
memory, for which I thank Almighty God, and Calling to mind
the uncertainty of human life and knowing that it is appointed
for all men once to die, and being desirous to dispose of all
such worldly substance as it has pleased God to bless me with,
do make and ordain this my last will and Testament in manner
and form following: that is to say principally and first of all

(383) I give and bequeath my soul into the hands of Almighty God,
who gave it, and my body I recommend to the earth to be buried
(384) in decent Christian Burial, at the discretion of my Executors.

Secondly, I give and bequeath to my beloved wife Nancy,
all my real and perishable property of every description, during
her natural life, and at her death I give and bequeath to my
beloved son Liberty, all my land and my perishable property at
the death of my beloved wife, to be sold and the money arising
from the sale to be equally divided betwixt Ethelbart E. Davis
and the lawful heirs of Elizabeth Hobbs, that is share and share
alike, equally.

And lastly, I do hereby constitute and appoint my beloved
son Liberty Beasley. Executor of this my last will and testament, hereby revoking all other former wills or testaments by
me heretofore made. In witness whereof I have hereunto set my
hand and seal, this twenty-second day of February, one thousand
eight hundred and thirty-three.

Archer Beasley. (seal).

Signed, sealed and delivered to be the last will and testament
of the above named ARCHER BEASLEY, in presence of us, who at his
request and in his presence have hereunto subscribed our names
as witnesses to the same.
Abraham Summers.
William G. Summers. 26th March 1839.
John Trantham.
A. G. Downing.

(385)   For the love and affection I entertain for Caty Roberson,
I do hereby give, transfer and convey to her my tract of land
in the State of Tennessee, district No. 19. and bounded as
follows: to wit, beginning at a post oak north of tract of land
that Clas. R. M. Daniel now lives on and running thence North
one hundred and thirty-eight poles to small red oak, and two
red and chestnut pointers in the South boundaries line of tract
of land in the name of Smith Scoggins, thence east with Scoggins
line passing his South East Corner at 52 poles Crossing a creek
bearing a south east in all 58 poles to sweet gum and dogwood,
thence south at 9 poles crossing a creek bearing South east in
all one hundred and thirty-eight poles to white oak in McDaniel
north boundary line, thence west with the same 58 poles to the
beginning for the said Caty Roberson to have and hold the same
During her widowhood and after she should die or marry again
I covenant and agree myself for Stephen Sawyer to have and hold
the same which is my last written testament. May the 7th 1850.
Test. N. B. I give and bequeath to my wife Caty Roberson all the
perishable property I have. for her to put it to the use of her
maintenance, to the best advantage the said Caty, my wife sees
proper, which is my last will and testament.   his
Test   Starkey x Roberson, (seal).
Thomas George.   mark
John Spencer.

      I, GEORGE GEE, a free man of Colour, do make and publish
this as my last will and Testament, hereby revoking and making

(385) void all other wills by me at any time made.

First, I direct my funeral expenses and all my debts be paid as soon after my death as possible, out of any money I may die possessed of or may first come into the hands of my Executors.

Secondly, I desire that my House and lot in Fayetteville
(386) Tennessee be sold by my executors on a credit of one, two and three years.

Thirdly, I desire that all the money I may have on hand at my death ot that may come into the hands of my Executors be loaned out by them at lawful interest, and the Interest arising out of the loan of said money to be annually divided amongst my Children (to wit) Ruth, Philip, Simeon, Nelson, Wiley, Jenny Mary, Esther and Cynthia and my wife each of them to share and share alike, but in the event of the marriage of my wife my desire and request is that she Ceases to draw any more of my Estate either in money, property or otherwise, and after such marriage takes place, my desire is that my Executors then divide the interest arising from the loan of said money by my Executors equally and annually betwwen my nine children before mentioned.

Fourthly, My desire is that when my youngest child becomes to the age of twenty-one years, that all my estate, whether in money or otherwise be equally divided amongst my Children and wife, provided always and upon the express condition that my w wife has not married before my youngest child comes of age. In the event my wife should marry before my youngest child becomes of age, then and in that case, it is my wish and desire that all of my property be equally divided between my children.

Lastly, I do hereby nominate and appoint Henry Kelso and John Goodrich My Executors, in witness whereof I do th this my last will and Testament set my hand and seal this the 22nd day of July 1848.   his
                              George x Gee, (seal)
                                      mark
Signed, sealed and published in our presence, and we have subscribed our names hereto in the presence of the testator, this 22nd day of July 1848.
Constant P. Beevers.
Samuel J. Isaacs.
W. D. Blake.

(388)   Whereas, to wit, I, GEORGE GEE, a FREEMAN of Colour, made published my will and Testament some months ago, which will is now in the possession of one Elijah M. Ringo, and cannot be readily got at or had, and whereas, to wit, since the making of said will I have purchased my son Wiley from James Fulton, Robert Farguharson & R.A. McDonald, at the price of twelve hundred dollars, having paid to said Fulton, Faragharson and McDonald, seven hundred dollars, having a balance yet unpaid of five hundred due the 25th Dec. 1849. Now my desire and request is the following disposition may be made of my property.

First, that my real Estate in the Town of Fayetteville be sold by my Executors on such credit as they may think best.

Second, I want my Executors to pay the Five hundred dollars yet unpaid for Wiley, when it becomes due.

(387)   Third, I want my Executors to purchase from Doct William
Bonner, my two youngest children Esther & Cynthia, provided
they can purchase them at a Reasonable price.

     Fourth I want my Executors to keep possession and under
their care and control my son Wiley until he makes and pays
back to my said Executors the sum of Eight hundred dollars at
which time the said Wiley is to be free, My desire and request
is that said Wiley and my two youngest children Esther &
Cynthia remain in the State of Tennessee, provided the laws of
said State will allow and permit them to do so, if the Laws of
Tennessee will not allow them to remain here, then and in that
case I want them to be emancipated and moved to Liberia.

(388)   Fifth, I want the balance of my property to be equally divided between the balance of my Children named in the will, now
in the possession of Elijah M. Ringo aforesaid, Witness my
hand and seal this 1st day of November 1848. If the said
Cynthia and Esther are not purchased I want them to have an
equal interest with the rest.   his
                         George x Gee.)seal).
                              mark
Signed, sealed and delivered in the presence of,
W. Bonner.
C. P. Beevers.

     I, JAMES TOOLE, do make and publish this as my last will
and Testament hereby Revoking and making void all other wills
by me at any time made.

     First, I direct that my funeral expenses and all my debts
be paid as soon after my death as possible out of any money
that I may die possessed of or may first come into the hands
of my executors.

     Secondly, I give and bequeath to my dearly beloved wife
Catharine Toole, all the property (both Real and Personal) of
which I may be possessed at the time of my death (should she
survive me) for and during her natural life.

     Thirdly, it is my will and desire that the land on which
I now live shall become the property of my son William P.Toole,
in manner following, that is to say, he shall choose and appoint one man of reputed honesty and sound Judgment, and my
Executor shall choose another man, also of reputed honesty and
Sound Judgment, to appraise the value of said Land, exclusively
of any and all improvements, the said William P. Toole may
have put upon or made to it, at his own expense, whether of
money or labor, and should the Appraisers so chosen and appointed disagree as to the true value of said land, then they
(389)the said appraisers shall choose a third man of reputed honesty
and sound Judgment, to decide upon its true value and should
neither two of said appraisers agree in their Judgement as to
the true value of said land, then the two that are nearest agreed
shall split or divide the difference and their decision shall
be conclusive, and binding upon the parties, and the price so
decided upon shall be paid by the said William P. Toole to the
executor of this my last will and Testament, in three ahnual
instalments, of one-third in one year from the date of said decision, another third in two years, and the remaining third in

(389) three years from the said date and should my wife Catharine
Tool survive me)(to whom I have given a life estate in said
land) then, said appraisers only to appraise and my executor
only to sell the remainder of said land to the said William
P. Toole, in manner aforesaid, but should the said William P.
Toole not survive me or not wish to become owner of said land
then my Executor after giving due nothice to sell said Land or
the remainder, if my wife survives me, to the highest bidder,
on a credit of One, two & thre years' retaining a lien on the
Land until the purchase money is paid. It is also my will &
desire, and I hereby direct that my Executor, as shortly after
my death as is convenient, if I survive my wife (or if my wife
survives me) then as shortly after her death as is convenient
tó sell all my personal property on a twelve months credit,
taking bond and good security.

Fourthly, I give and bequeath to my daughter Ruth Ann Toole,
two hundred dollars, out of any money that may first come into
his (my Execubors) hands, not otherwise provided for.

(390) Fifthly, I give and bequeath to my Grand-daughter Lucinda
C. Dewoody a riding horse of the value of twenty-five dollars,
and a womans saddle of the value of twenty-five dollars,provided
the said Lucinda be living at the time the said Executor shall
come into the possession of the means to pay for them, and if
she be not then living, he the said executor shall furnish my
grand-son Sylvester Dewoody and brother of Lucinda, a Horse
and a mans' saddle, of the above named values. It is my will
and desire that the two hundred dollars given to my Daughter Ruth
Ann Toole, if she be not living at the time contemplated, but
having lawful heirs of her Body living, then the said two hundred dollars to be equally divided amongst or between them.

It is also my will and desire that after the bequests of
two hundred and seventy five dollars are provided foe (If practicable) that the residue of my Estate that is to say the remainder of the proceeds of the State of my Lands together with
the proceeds of the sale of my personal property as will as of
all debts and dues whatsoever that may be owing to me shall be
equally divided between the said Ruth Ann Toole and my other
children their Representatives.

Lastly, I do hereby nominate and appoint Howell Harris,Jr.
My Executor. In witness whereof I do to thid my will set my
hand and seal this 2nd day of June 1849.

James R. Toole,(seal).

Signed, sealed and published in our presence and we have subscribed our names hereto in the presence of the Testator, this
2nd day of June 1849.
Joel M. Harris.
Nathaniel Millard.

(391) The last will and Testament of Andrew Gleghorn. I,ANDREW
GLEGHORN, being of sound mind and memory, and considering the
uncertainty of this life, do make and publish this my last will
and Testament, and hereby revoke all former wills made by me,or
purposely to have been made by me.

First, I will and bequeath that John W. Gleghorn have

(391) sixty-four acres, two thirds of his share to be laid out in the south East Corner of Fathers old tract, the other third to be in the Hills.

Secondly, I will and bequeath that the balance of the Land be equally divided between the balance of my children, Betsey Jane, Hugh, Mary Elenda, Martha, Minerva, Sarah, Susan, Rebecca Urshala Elgiva.

Thirdly, I will that Elgiva's Share be laid off so as to include the dwelling and spring, also I will that the residence be occupied by the family as a residence until she becomes of age.

Fourthly, I will and direct that if the Executors think proper at any time, with the consent of all the children, they may sell the Lands Belonging to Betsey Jane, Hugh, Mary Elenda Martha, Minerva, Sarah, Susan, Rebecca, Uershula Elgiva.

Fifthly, I will and direct that if the Lands be sold, a guardian or guardians be chosen or appointed as the age of the child may be, to take care of the proceeds, said Guardian bound as the Court may direct.

Fifthly, I will that if the Lands belonging to Betsey Jane, Hugh, Mary Elenda, Martha, Minerva, Sarah, Rebecca, Uershula, Elgiva, be not sold, that they be plotted and divided, and that Each child draw its share as it comes of age.

Sixthly, I will and direct that the open Lands be rented until sold or the children becomes of age, and that the rent be appropriated to the support and educating the children by the Executors.

Seventhly, I will John W. Gleghorn, have his horse and saddle, and Betsey Jane, have the new side saddle, and Hugh my saddle.

Eighthly, I will that John W. and Betsey Jane have a Bed-stead for each and bed and clothing, and the balance of the (392) household furniture to the balance of the family, the present crop and stock to be appropriated to the use and benefit of the family, and after my Just debts are paid, John W. have fif-ty dollars, if there be that much, and if there be any more, it be applied to the support of the family.

Lastly, I ordain and appoint John Watt and William A. Gault, Executors, to this my last will and testament, in Test-imony whereof I have set my hand and seal this August the 17th, year of our Lord, One thousand and Eight hundred and fifty.

Andrew Gleghorn, (seal).

We, the undersigned, do hereby certify that ANDREW GLEGHORN, was of sound mind and memory, on the day that he made the above will and Testimony, and we signed as witnesses at his request, and he signed this in presence of each of us.

Robert Gleghorn.

Joel C. Pigg.

I, JAMES McCREE, do make and publish this as my last will and Testament, hereby revoking and making void all other wills by me at any time made.

First, I direct that my funeral expenses, and all my just debts be paid as soon after my death as possible, out of any money I may die possessed of or may first come into the hands

(392) of my executors.

Secondly, I give and bequeath to my beloved Mother, Elizabeth McCree, an equal share of all the property and money that I may die possessed of.

Third, I give and bequeath to the heirs of my beloved sister Eliza McAfee, consort of Jesse McAfee, an equal share of all my effects.

Fourthly, I give and bequeath to my beloved sister Cintha Reed, consort of George Reed, an rqual share of all the property, money or other effects that I may die possessed of.

(393)   Fifthly, I give and bequeath to my beloved Brother, Carroll McRee an equal share of all the property, money and effects that I may die possessed of.

Sixthly, I give and bequeath to my beloved sister Adalin Paysinger, consort of Thomas A. Paysinger, an equal share of all of the property, money and effects that I may die possessed of.

Seventhly, I give and bequeath to my beloved Brother David W. McRee, an equal share of all the property, money and effects that I may die possessed with.

Eighthly, I give and bequeath to Gallon McRee, an equal share of all the property, money and effects that I may die possessed of.

Ninethly, I give and bequeath to my little sister Elizabeth McRee, an equal share of all the property, money and effects, that I may die possessed of.

Tenthly, I give and bequeath to my sister Delina McRee, an equal share of all my property, money and effects that I may die possessed of.

Eleventhly, I give and bequeath to my sister Sarah E. McCree, an equal share of all the property, money and effects that I may die possessed of.

Twelfthly, I give and bequeath to my Brother John McRee, an equal share of all my property, money and effects that I may die poswessed of, taking out of John's share a thirty-four dollar note, (with Interest) which I hold against him, with Mother's security, to said note, as wish his not to be disturbed on said note of hand.

Lastly, I do hereby nominate and appoint P. W. Harper and John W. Watt my Executors, in witness whereof I do to this my will set my hand and seal, this 21st day of August, 1850.

James McRee, (seal).

Signed, sealed and published, and we have subscribed our names hereto in the presence of the Testator, this 21st August 1850.
P. W. Walton.
H. C. Roberts.

(394)   I, ROBERT MCCLELLAN, make and publish this as my last will and testament, hereby revoking and making void all other wills by me at any time made.

First, I direct that my funeral Expenses, and all debts be paid as soon after my death as possible, out of any money that I may die possessed of or may first come into the hands of my Executors.

Secondly, I give and bequeath to Sarah McClellan, my negro man Jacob, and at her death to become the property of Mrs. Sarah McClelan's three oldest children, (viz): Robert J., Margaret B.

(394) and Susan J. all three to be Equally interested in Said negro man at the death of their mother Sarah McClelan.

Thirdly, I give and bequeath to the heirs of my daughter, Jane Davis, the former wife of Absolam Davis, Six hundred Dollars, to be Equally divided between her Six children. It is my wish and I also make it a part of this my last will that Henry Davis' heirs are to be Entitled to one hundred dollars, which is their father's interest in the above six hundred dollars, and that William Davis's heirs to receive one hundred dollars, their father's interest in the before mentioned Six hundred dollars.

Fourthly, I give and bequeath to the heirs of my daughter Sarah Wilson (who was the wife of James Wilson) Six hundred dollars, to be Equally divided between the heirs of her body.

Fifthly, I give and bequrath to the heirs of my daughter Nancy McNite, Six hundred dollars, to be divided Equally between her two children, Robert McNite and Samuel McNite.

Sixthly, I give and bequeath to the heirs of Eliza McClelan, Mary Gregory and her heirs, William McClelan and Joseph McClelan, my Negro man Bill which is at this time in Williamson County, and all the money that may be due me after (395) paying my funeral Expenses, my debts and Eighteen hundred dollars as directed in this my last will, the balance together with the negro man Bill as before mentioned , to be Equally divided between Eliza McClelan heirs, Mary Gregory and her heirs William McClelan and Joseph McClelan. It is my will and my wish that the negro man Bill be sold on a credit of twelve months to the highest bidder. I want Eliza McClelan's heirs to have one fourth. Mary Gregory and her heirs one fourth. William McClelan one fourth, by him accounting for One hundred and fifty dollars, which I paid him and Joseph McClelan one fourth.

Seventhly, I give and bequeath to Mrs. Sarah McClelan two youngest daughters Maria Thompson McClelan and Sarah Elizabeth Wilson McClelan, my negro man Granville at this time hired to Henry Kelso to be equally interested in said negro man. I also give and bequeath to them my two beds and furniture, and my chest.

Lastly, I do hereby nominate and appoint John G. McClelan and John Clark Jr. my Executors. In witness whereof I do to this my will Set my hand and seal this the 20th July 1850.

Test.   his
Robt. R. McKinney.   Robert x McClelan, (seal).
Jefferson Kelso.   mark

(396)   State of Tennessee, Lincoln County. In the name of God Amen, the Holy Trinity, Father, Son and Holy Spirit Amen. Whereas I, ANDREW W. WALKER, Being in my proper and reasonable mind, have thought proper to make, constitute and ordain this my last will and Testament.

To wit: Item the first, My will and desire is that all my Just Debts be paid in the first place.

Item the Second, My desire and wish is that my wife, Elizabeth Walker, Hold and possess all my lands, Estate (To wit) the tract of land I now live on, containing One hundred and

(396) nineteen acres,more or less. Also the present Crop of Corn
belonging to the same, also two other small tracts of land
Situated and lying over the creek on the ridge, One containing twenty-four acres, the other contains twenty acres,more
or less, and lies Joining together, Bounded on the North By
the widow Roundtree's land, on the East by Joseph Longs, on
the South by William Brown's land, and on the West by L. H.
Shaws', and David Roughton's land Together with all the improvements or in any wise appertaining to the same, and all
the household and kitchen furniture,also the farming tools,
and all the Stock of every description what ever thereunto belonging or in any wise thereunto appertaining, also my two
negro Boys, Berry and Emuery, this property my wife Elizabeth,
is to Hold and possess during her natural life or she remains
my widow. But in case or provided she should marry, she thereby forfeits all her Right Title and claims to said Dowry whatever except one feather Bed and furniture, and Five dollars in
money.
     Item the third, I give and bequeath to my son John F.
Walker, Five dollars, Two daughters America Jean Walker Five
dollars, Columbia Walker Five dollars to be paid to each of
them when they become of proper age to Receive the same.
     Item the Fourth, I give and bequeath to my daughters'
Polly Anthony, Five children (To wit) To Caroline Anthony,Five
dollars, Andrew W. Anthony Five dollars. To Jacob Anthony, Five
dollars, To George W. A. Anthony Five dollars. To Elizabeth
W. Anthoney, Five dollars, to be paid over to them as they ar-
(397) rive at a proper age to receive it. I give and bequeath to all
the rest of children (To wit) Cincinatha Edens,Maria Walker,
Peggy Ann, Margaret Sullivant, Laureat Walker, Jane M. Walker,
Thompson Walker and Nancy Walker, Each an Equal share of my Estate, also Harriet Walker to have an Equal Share with the rest
of my children. In case my wife Elizabeth should decease before Nancy Walker, my youngest child becomes of age, I desire
that all my children that is not left home or married and left
and gone to themselves, Should Continal and live together until
She should Become of age. If it should So happen that you do
not wish to continue to live together in the way I have prescribed, In such an event I want my Executors to sell every
Species of property belonging to my Estate and divided agreeably to this my last will and Testament.
     Lastly, I appoint and constitute Elizabeth & Jas. W.
Walker my Executrix & Executor, June 18th,1840.
                                   Andrew W. Walker.
(398) Witnesses.
B. H. Berry.
W. P. Edde.
T. H. Shaw.

     A Codicil to the before Testament or will which this is
intended to be a part (To wit), I give and bequeath to my wife
Elizabeth, a negro Girl named Mary about twelve years old, I
also give to my wife Elizabeth, my negro man named Sampson,
about --- years old, which negro man Sampson, I Bought of
Elisha Wommack, and give him the opportunity of redeeming,and

(398) in case said Wommack does redeem him I give the money to my
wife Elizabeth, to purchase her another negro, together with
all the before mentioned property of all sorts and description
whatever. I give to my wife Elizabeth Walker during her natural life or as long as She remains my widow as before mentioned. I also give to my wife Elizabeth One negro Boy named
Arch, nine or ten years old, also one negro Boy named Rufus,
Five years old, this and all other property which I may have
in possession at my decease or death, and the money I have in
hand or in any way due me by note or account whatever. I also
give to my wife Elizabeth one negro woman named Winney, about
Twenty-three or four years old, and one Boy child named William

(399) Silas, about Seven months old. I do also give to my wife Elizabeth one negro boy child about Five months old, by the name
of Sampson, it is my desire that this Codicil be attached to and
Constitute a part of my will to all intents and purposes.
        And I do hereby constitute and appoint my wife Elizabeth
Walker, Executrix, and Ambrose L. Parker, Executor to this my
last will and Testament, this the 3rd day of August 1850.
                         Andrew W. Walker, (seal).
Signed, Sealed and published in our presence and we have Sub-
scribed our names hereto in the presence of the Testator, this
day & year above written.
J. A. Saintclair.
F. Motlow.
Jane H. Show.

(400)   I, JAMES A. BUCHANAN, of the County of Lincoln & State of
Tennessee, Being weak of body, but of sound mind and disposing
memory, Do make and publish this my last will and Testament.
        First, I bequeath my Soul to God who gave it.
        Second, I direct that all my Just debts & funeral expenses
be paid out of my money that I may die possessed of.
        3rd, I give to my brother David S. Buchanan, all of my
wearing apparel & Sword, and one half of my Books and the other
half of my books I give to my Cousin John M. Smith, they to
divide them equally between them as they may see proper.
        4th, I give to my well loved Aunt Patsey (wife of Alfred
Smith) for her kind and motherly attention to me in my Sickness, my Buggy & Harness.
        5th, I give to my Uncle Alfred Smith my Saddle.
        6th, I give to my two beloved Sisters Amanda H. M. and
Minerva A. Buchanan to be equally divided between them the balance of my estate of every description, consisting in the principal part, of one note on my Uncle Alfred Smith, for nine
hundred & fifty-two dollars, and I also give to them (my said
two sisters) all that portion of my Father, Moses Buchanan,
Estate, both real and personal, which I might have been entitled, to be equally divided between them as first related.
        7th, I nominate and appoint my Uncle Alfred Smith, my exe-
cutor to this my last will and Testament, believing that he
will have the Same honestly executed. Given under my hand &
Seal this the 3rd day of August 1850.
                         James A. Buchanan, (Seal)

(400) Signed, & Acknowledged in our presence the day & date above written.
St. George Martin.
John M. Smith.

(401)   I, Allice R. Sharp, of the County of Lincoln and State of Tennessee, being in an ordinary State of health, but knowing the uncertainty of life, and the certainty of death, and being of sound mind and disposing memeory, do make, ordain and publish the following as my last will and testament, hereby revoking and making void all other & former wills by me made.

First, it is my will and desire that after my death I be buried in a plain, decent and Christian like manner and that all my just debts & funeral expenses be paid by my executors, hereinafter named, as Speedily as possible after my death, out of any money on hand or from the proceeds of any property here-inafter directed to be sold by my said Executors.

Secondly, I give and bequeath to my Son Benjamin F. Sharp, my yoke of oxen, one cow & calf of his choosing, my big sorrel mule I also give and bequeath to my said Son Benjamin two of my best feather beds, bedstead & furniture, my china press & furniture, that belongs to it, my clock, also two of my best plows, two best hoes, chopping ax, also all my tools & farming utensils of every description, together with all The residue of my household & kitchen furniture, which are of little value, the most of the tools now on hand having been purchased by my said son with his own money, since his arrival of age.

Third, I give and bequeath to my daughter Nancy Gray, one cow & calf next choice after Benjamin, my mare & Buggy.

Fourth, I will and direct that all the residue of my stock
(402) of every description be sold by my Executor as soon after my death as he may think best, and upon Such time & terms as may Seem applied by my Said Executor as herein after directed.

Fifth, I give and desired to my son Benjamin, my tract of land I purchased of John Branson, containing about ninety-Six acres, I also give & bequeath to him my negro boy Anthony John Westly & Girl named Martha. I also give to him all notes, ac-counts & their claims I may have at the time of my death, out of which together with the proceeds of the Stock herein before directed to be Sold with any money I may have on hand at my decease he is to set apart for the use and benefit of my grand-daughter Allice Ann Reed Sherrell, three hundred dollars, which said amount is my will and desire, Shall remain in the hand of my Said Son Benjamin, and loaned out at interest for her sole use & benefit, until she shall arrive to the age of twenty-one years, at which time he shall pay over to her the Said Three hundred dollars with all the interest he may have received on the Same, But if the Said Allice Ann, Should die before She Shall arrive at the age of twenty-one years, then the same to be equally divided between my daughter Nancy Grays & my Said Son Benjamin F. Sharp.

Sixth, I give and bequeath to Said grand-daughter, Allice Ann R. Sherrell one feather bed & furniture.

(402)   Seventh, I give to my daughter Nancy Gray one feather bed & furniture, also my Sugar chest & small Square Table, I also give to my daughter Nancy my negro woman Nelly, my negro boy named Fortune, to her & her heirs.

(403)   Eighth, I give and bequeath to my grand-daughter Bathea Gracey, my negro girl Eliza, I also give to her one feather bed & furniture.

Lastly, I hereby nominate, constitute and appoint my Said Son Benjamin F. Sharp, Executor of this my last will & testament. In witness whereof I have hereunto Set my hand & Seal this nineteenth day of February in the year of our Lord, One thousand, Eight hundred & forty-nine. Signed, Sealed and acknowledged in the presence of us.

E. M. Ringo.   Allice Sharp, (seal).
Jno. M. Bright.

Whereas I, ALLICE A. SHARP, having made the foregoing, as my last will & testament, but before the Signing and publishing thereof, I have thought proper to make the following alteration in the 5th item, my executor is directed to set apart out of the fund directed in Said 5th item, the sum of three hundred dollars, and One feather bed & furniture, to my grand-daughter Allice Ann Reed Sherrell, when She Shall arrive at the age of twenty-one years or Sooner, if my executor Should think proper, and in the event of her death before arriving at age or before payment, the said bequeath to be divided as before directed in the 5th item of the foregoing. Signed, Sealed and acknowledged in the presence of us.

E. M. Ringo.   Allice Sharp. (seal).
Jno. M. Bright.

(404)   I, WILLIAM KENNEN, of Lincoln County, State of Tennessee, do make & declare this to be my last will and Testament.

I will and bequeath my property both real and personal to my first & Last children which I had by my two wives, Amelia & Polly.

I will that my property remain unsold fot the Term of Five years from my decease and remain in possession of Samuel D. Buchanan, provided he lives on my farm and works the same and takes care of the family for which he is to reveive a proper compensation for his Trouble, to be agreed upon between him and my executors if at any period of the time of above mentioned, my executors Should deem it proper to have my property taken from the possession of S. Buchanan and Sold, they have the power to do so. I give to my two Grand children William A. Short and Francis E. Short, one hundred dollars each, provided at my decease, I hold the Amt. I am in Possession of at this time and if my property diminishes in value they are to suffer a Consequence or equal dimintion in the above Legacy to be determined by my executors to be paid to them when they become of age, without interest. I have given to my son Mosaweather L. Kennen, a horse and saddle, to be worth one hundred dollars, the same to my son Ellsworth R. Kennen a horse and saddle, worth one hundred Dollars, to Samuel D. Buchanan, a horse and saddle worth seventy Dollars, a cow & calf, Bed & furniture, worth forty dollars, at the division of my Estate the above amounts to

(404) be taken from their respective shares. I hereby appoint
Charles McKinney and John V. McKinney. Executors to this will,
signed, sealed and delivered in the presence of us this
15th day of August 1839.
Test.   William Kennen. (seal).
Peter G. McMullin.
W. C. Riggin.

It is further my request that my executors whom I have appointed shall not be obliged to give Security and it is further my request that my children (15)Ezabella Redearce I.
Kennon. Sarah, Rebecca Louiza and Amanda Christiana, shall receive six months Schooling, at a Common neighborhood school,
this 15th day of August 1839.
Test.   William Kennen. (seal).
Peter G. McMullin.
Wm. C. Riggin.

(405)

State of Tennessee, Lincoln County. I, JAMES WEST, do
make and publish this my Last will and Testament, hereby revoking and making void all other wills by me at any time made.

First, I give to the heirs of my son William West, five
dollars.

Second, I give to my son Rhodes West, five dollars.

Third, I give to my son James S. West five dollars.

Fourth, I give to my son Alfred West, five dollars.

Fifth, I give to my daughter,Margaret Divin,five dollars.

Sixth, I give to my daughter Elizabeth's Heirs five
Dollars.

Seventh, I give to my daughter Sarah Luster,five dollars.

Eighth, I give to my wife,Margretta, my sons Josephus and
Andrew Jackson, my tract of Land that I now live upon,to have
and possess equally during the life or widowhood of my wife,
and should she marry I give to be equally divided between my
sons Josephus West and Andrew Jackson West. I also give to my
wife Margret, my son Josephus and my son Andrew Jackson each,
one bed, bedstead and furniture, and also the remaining part
of my household and kitchen furniture.

I also give to them my stock, horses, Cows, hogs and sheep,
including my oxen, my cart and all my farming utensils. I give
to my two sons,Josephus and Andrew Jackson, my Gun and all my
Books to be equally divided between the two. I also have Two
notes on Pleasant Holbert, not yet due, which I want to be collected, and out of them to pay all my Just debts and funeral
expenses, and the remainder,if any, to be eavally divided between my wife and my two sons,Josephus and Andrew Jackson.

Lastly, I do hereby nominate and appoint Pleasant Holbert,
my executor. In witness whereof I do to this my will set my
hand and seal this 6th day of May,1850.
                              James West,(seal).
Signed,sealed and published in our presence, and we have subscribed our names hereunto in the presence of the Testator,this
the 6th day of May 1850.
Test.
Matthew Wilson.
John Wood. Wm. McMillan.

www.ingramcontent.com/pod-product-compliance
Lightning Source LLC
Chambersburg PA
CBHW082353270326
41935CB00013B/1610